Pro Football Digest

Edited By
Robert Billings
in cooperation with
Football Digest Magazine

Follett Publishing Company / Chicago

T-0426

PRO FOOTBALL DIGEST STAFF

EDITOR
Robert Billings

CONTRIBUTING EDITORS
Tim Weigel
James Kloss
Don DeBat

ARTIST
John Downs

PRODUCTION ASSISTANT
Deborah James

ASSOCIATE PUBLISHER
Sheldon L. Factor

This book was prepared in cooperation with Century Publishing Company and their Century Sports Network Magazines including: *Auto Racing Digest, Baseball Digest, Basketball Digest, Football Digest* and *Hockey Digest*.

Statistics and records appearing in this book are through the courtesy of Elias Sports Bureau, Inc. and the National Football League.

ISBN 0-695-80426-X   Library of Congress Catalog #73-83468

Table of Contents

The History

A Brief History of Pro Football

Once upon a time (that's the way most fairy tales and rags-to-riches stories begin), before television and tight ends, football was a simple game. College boys played it on Saturday afternoons, and there was nothing fancy about it.

Football had been imported from England, so it was played the way they played it in the English colleges. The ball — sometimes leather, sometimes rubber-covered — was large and round. The "game" was often no more than an excuse for a free-for-all between the freshmen and sophomore classes at the big Eastern schools. Only after a convention of schools in 1876 were the rules of rugby generally adopted: 15 men would make up a team, and touchdowns would count. A few years later, when blocking was finally approved, true American football was born.

At the turn of the century, no one dreamed of making a living playing the game. If he liked it well enough, he could pick up a few extra dollars ($50 if he was star caliber, $5 more likely) playing on Sunday; the rest of the week he held down a regular job — or played college football (which was why he couldn't play on Saturday). There was no such thing as a contract, so players moved around. In 1915, for example, Knute Rockne played against the Columbus Panhandles six times — on six different teams.

This brand of pro football grew up largely in Pennsylvania. Within 50 miles of Pittsburgh, men from the mines played the game on Sundays. The first contest between teams made up entirely of professionals was played in 1895 in Latrobe, Pennsylvania. The Latrobe YMCA beat Jeanette 12-0, and the players took home $10 apiece. Before long the game spread to New York and west into Ohio. It couldn't match the tradition of college football, nor the devotion that college players brought to the game; but crowds of 5,000 and more at the professional games were not unusual, and teams began to develop followings.

In Philadelphia, Connie Mack organized the Athletics as a professional football team to match his baseball champions, even using the big pitcher Rube Waddell in his lineup. The Athletics were one of the first attractions. They had the distinction of playing in the first night game in 1902 in Elmira, New York (where lights were placed along the sideline), and in a round-robin indoor tournament at Madison Square Garden in 1903, with teams from Franklin, Pennsylvania; Watertown, New York; and Orange, New Jersey. No football would be played indoors again until 1932, when the Chicago Bears moved into Chicago Stadium to avoid a blizzard and beat Portsmouth 9-0 for the league championship.

In its earliest years the pro game was played roughly but cleanly. Most players wore ribbed shin guards and pants padded at the knee. Few wore helmets. Amidst the blood and bruises, the game had all the finesse of a bare-knuckled fight. Still, there were few serious injuries. Sheer strength, sound wind, and stamina were key attributes.

The most popular offense was the old-fashioned T formation. The quarterback squatted low behind the center, bending deeply at his knees and waist until he was closer to the ground than the center. The fullback lined up a step behind the two halfbacks. Deception consisted of the quarterback seeming to pitch the ball back to one man, but instead flipping it over his head to another; or the halfbacks would cross and reverse the ball on their way into the line. Running plays brought an enormous pileup, with both lines crashing and the offensive backs shoving hard to push their man through.

The forerunner of the forward pass was the quarterback kick. Many quarterbacks learned to kick the ball short distances with great accuracy so that an eligible back could run downfield and recover it—as the rules permitted. When the forward pass was legalized in 1906, the impact was slight because so few players had mastered throwing the large ball.

Not running or passing but kicking was the most important element of early football. A goal from the field scored more than a touchdown. Originally five points, it crept downward and became less valued over the years. A touchdown only gave the offense the right to try for a goal kick—as teams do today in the point after touchdown. With only three downs instead of four, it was also important to have a good punter to move the opponents back. The demands of the game thus assured that the great players would be great kickers.

No player in the early 1900's was greater than Jim Thorpe. Already the most famous athlete of his day, and fresh from his Olympic victories, Thorpe was decidedly a great football player for his or any other time. A Sac and Fox Indian from Oklahoma, he stood about 6'1" and weighed about 190. He could run from goal line to goal line in full uniform in just over ten seconds; on offense or defense he hit like a piledriver; and he could consistently kick a football 80 yards — and drop-kick a field goal 50 yards. George Halas, owner of the Chicago Bears, played against Thorpe several years. "He blocked with his shoulder and it felt like he hit you with a four-by-four," Halas remembers. "On defense, he never tackled with his arms and shoulders. He'd leg-whip the ball carrier. If he hit you from behind, he'd throw that big body across your back and damn near break you in two."

When Thorpe joined the Canton Bulldogs in 1915, he rejuvenated professional football in Ohio. It had languished in ill repute since 1906 when the fierce rivalry between Canton and neighboring Massillon had been torn by scandal. Now Thorpe's drawing power brought fans back to the ball parks — as many as 8,000 for a Canton-Massillon game. For the first time, pro football seemed like a game America might take to. It was ready to become a business.

Jim Thorpe

The Formation of the National Football League

Joe Carr

The birth of what is now the National Football League took place on September 17, 1920, in Canton, Ohio. On a warm evening, inside the automobile agency of Ralph Hay, owner of the Canton Bulldogs, representatives of 11 teams met to form the American Professional Football Association. These clubs paid the $100 membership fee: Canton, Cleveland, Dayton, Akron, and Massillon, Ohio; Rochester, New York; Hammond and Muncie, Indiana; and Chicago, Rock Island, and Decatur, Illinois. (The Decatur Staleys moved to Chicago after a year and became the Bears.) Appropriately, Jim Thorpe was elected president of the new league.

Not for ten years was a regular playing schedule drawn up. Meanwhile, each team made its own arrangements. One consequence was that the champion in any one year might win the title simply by playing more games. In 1925, Pottsville beat the Chicago Cardinals in the last game of the season and thought it had won the championship. But Chris O'Brien, the Cardinals' owner, quickly scheduled two more games against rag-tag opposition. Instead of 9-2-1, the Cardinals finished the year 11-2-1, as against Pottsville's 10-2-0, and claimed the title. Hopping mad, Pottsville scheduled another game for itself, but the league disallowed the victory.

By 1922 the National Football League (as it was now called) had 18 teams and a new president, Joe Carr of Columbus, Ohio. Carr saw the young league through its most haphazard years — disputes over championships and player eligibility, and the constant shifting of franchises from city to city. How primitive the game still was is typified in a story about George Trafton, the Bears' great center. In a game against Rock Island in 1920, Trafton made himself an object of hatred by helping dismember five Rock Island players, including one specially hired to do the same thing to Trafton. Rock Island fans hated Trafton as much as their team did. When the final gun sounded, Trafton's sprint for the exit did not go unnoticed by George Halas, the Bears' playing owner. At the next game in Rock Island, Halas handed the day's take — $7,000 in cash — to Trafton at the final gun. "I knew I'd be running only for the $7,000," Halas explained, "whereas Trafton would be running for his life."

It was part of the flavor of the times — tiring rides in sooty trains, with the dressing room in the baggage

The Chicago Bears of 1922: (front row l. to r.) Laurie Walquist, Joe Sternaman, Walt Pearce, Andy Lotshaw (trainer), Ed Sternaman, George Bolan and Ralph Lanum. (Back row) George Halas, Hugh Blacklock, Joe LaFleur, Fred Larson, "Hunk" Anderson, "Hec" Garvey and Harry Englund.

car; half the backfield late for the game; some crowds pathetically small; roughhousing and all-night card games; and riotous celebrations of unexpected victories. Players rarely earned more than $250 a game, but they loved playing as much as those who today earn 20 times as much.

The game itself was changing. It was, by the 1920's already vastly different from what old-timers remembered. For one thing, a neutral zone now separated the opposing linemen, and both sides crouched low, ready to drive a shoulder hard into their opponent's body or cuff him with an open hand.

The quarterback no longer squatted low to the ground. He called the entire play out loud at the line of scrimmage, using numbered signals. Only occasionally, as on a time out, would the play be called in a huddle.

Seven offensive men had to be on the line of scrimmage, making it more difficult to attack with concentrated speed and power. So ends and tackles were used more frequently as ball carriers, pulling out of the line and swinging into the backfield to take a handoff. This was the early forerunner of the wingback formation which ultimately would modify the old-fashioned T.

The forward pass, though still not the revolutionary weapon it would become in time, was now a standard part of the offense. It could be thrown as far as the passer dared. It was no longer a free ball if it fell to the ground, and the defense could not hit the potential receiver before he had his hands on the ball. Trick plays involving the forward pass became a part of most offensive strategies — a fake pass and an end-around, or a lateral to an end who then threw long downfield. But a pass on first or second down was almost unheard of; so was a pass thrown on the run, or to a halfback coming out of the backfield. The ball was still large and difficult to handle. Many quarterbacks flung it sidearm, though swiftly and accurately.

The drop-kick became the popular way of kicking field goals. Great kickers like Paddy Driscoll, Thorpe, and Charlie Brickley could score from the 50-yard line. A kick that ended up in the stands or outside the park had to be recovered, even while the teams waited around: no one thought to play a game with more than one ball. It was expensive. On a rainy, sloppy day, the ball became a sodden leather mass, almost impossible to handle—and the game became as difficult to watch as to play.

The Coming of Red Grange

Red Grange

Professional football was an interesting but small affair until November 22, 1925. On that day Harold "Red" Grange signed to play with the Chicago Bears, and the face of the game changed overnight. To understand why is to appreciate just what Grange represented to Americans in 1925. He was not only the most exciting football player of the 1920's "Golden Age" of sports, he was at the time probably the most spectacular player ever.

For three years at the University of Illinois, Grange had dazzled Big Ten teams. He had gone east and destroyed Penn. In three seasons he rushed for 3,637 yards. In 1924 against Michigan he ran for touchdowns of 90, 65, 45, and 55 yards *in the first ten minutes*. Sportswriters couldn't coin superlatives quickly enough. The Galloping Ghost, they called him, or the Wheaton Iceman (because he supposedly lugged ice during the summers in his home town of Wheaton, Illinois — a glamorous touch).

As Grange neared his last collegiate game against Ohio State, speculation about his turning professional reached a fever pitch. Even those school leaders who invoked his duty to stay at Illinois knew that Grange was talking with the Chicago Bears. He had been doing it through his "business manager," a Champaign, Illinois, theater man named C. C. Pyle ("Cash and Carry," the papers soon dubbed him). After undercover negotiations in Chicago, Grange signed. The Bears guaranteed him $3,000 a game against a percentage of the gate receipts.

Red sat on the bench in a raccoon coat as his new teammates beat the Green Bay Packers in Wrigley Field the following Sunday. On Thanksgiving Day, 1925, in a snowstorm, Grange made his debut against the crosstown rival Cardinals. It began one of the most incredible schedules in the history of professional sports: ten games in 16 days, as Grange and the Bears crisscrossed the East and Midwest.

If Grange did not always play up to his press clippings on the tour, financially he was a smash. And he brought enormous publicity and respect to pro football. Thirty-six thousand people came to Wrigley Field to see him in his first game against the Cardinals. Grange earned $12,000 as his share of the gate. (Ordinarily the Bears and Cardinals would have drawn about $14,000 *total*.) On the field, Paddy Driscoll, the Cardinals' great kicker, punted away from Red all afternoon. "One of us was going to look bad," Driscoll said, "and I decided it wouldn't be Driscoll." The game ended in a scoreless tie.

Over the next two weeks, Grange was infrequently sensational, but the fans seemed satisfied. Most of the crowds were astonishing: 28,000 against Columbus in Chicago; 35,000 against the Frankford Yellowjackets in Philadelphia; a stupendous 65,000 in the Polo Grounds for a game with the New York Giants (in which Grange scored a touchdown); 25,000 in Boston against the Providence Steam Rollers.

Ten games from November 29 to December 13 — a grueling, bone-bending pace. It told on all the Bears, not only Grange. Hardly a man on the team escaped injury. In Pittsburgh, Red was kicked on the arm and suffered a severe hemorrhage. By the end of the tour he was dog weary. The Bears lost their last four games of the tour, but Grange could feel good about the $50,000 he pocketed, even if he had not given the fans as many touchdowns and long runs as he would have liked.

But Pyle and the Bears were not through milking the Grange appeal. In January and February 1926 the Bears toured the South and West, playing nine more games in 30 days. When it was over, Pyle and Grange each made another $50,000.

There is little doubt that pro football needed a star of Grange's stature to establish itself as a major spectator sport. He revolutionized public interest in the game, as Babe Ruth was doing in baseball at about the same time. (In New York, during Grange's first grinding tour, the great Ruth had visited Red in his hotel room and had told him, "Keep your head up. Get the dough while the getting is good, but don't break your heart trying to get it.") Suddenly college football players everywhere began to talk of professional careers. The great Four Horsemen of Notre Dame hurried east to sign with the Hartford Blues. It was a new era: Grange's first year was Jim Thorpe's last.

Grange and Pyle had a dispute with the Bears the next year and launched their own league with a team in New York. Ironically, Grange injured his right knee in a game against the Bears in Wrigley Field in 1927. He was out of football a whole year, then rejoined the Bears in 1929. "That injury ruined my career," he says. "I never could run or cut again. I was just another halfback." Not quite: he became an outstanding defensive back and saved a championship for the Bears in 1933.

Chicago led New York 23-21 in the final seconds of the first championship playoff, when the Giants' Harry Newman passed over the middle to Dale Burnett. Only Grange was between Burnett and the goal line, and New York's Mel Hein was running alongside Burnett in position for a lateral. But Grange reacted in a flash, tackling Burnett high and wrapping his arms around him. The lateral was never thrown, the gun sounded, the Bears were champions.

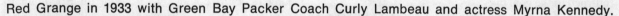

Red Grange in 1933 with Green Bay Packer Coach Curly Lambeau and actress Myrna Kennedy.

Growing to Maturity

The late twenties and thirties were years of consolidation for the National Football League. Weaker franchises were sorted out, several strong ones were built. In 1926, a year after Grange turned pro, the league had 22 teams. Many of them played scatter-shot schedules. By 1928 only ten teams remained, and only six of these would still be around in 1973 — the Chicago Bears, Chicago (now St. Louis) Cardinals, Detroit Lions, Green Bay Packers, New York Giants, and Philadelphia Eagles. The Washington Redskins did not appear until 1937, when George Preston Marshall transferred his Boston franchise to the nation's capital.

Marshall, a colorful and cantankerous man, was an innovator almost from the day he came into the league in 1932. The next year he convinced his fellow owners to form two divisions of teams, standardize the schedule, and play a world championship game between the division winners. The same year he and George Halas pushed through two important rule changes: the forward pass was made legal from any spot behind the line of scrimmage, and the goal posts were returned to the goal line.

The first College All-Star game was played in Chicago in 1934. The collegians held the Bears scoreless. In 1935, Bert Bell, a part-owner of the Eagles, proposed what has turned out to be the single most important rule in pro football — the player draft. Bell knew that the Eagles had little chance of luring the best college players away from the big three — the Bears, Giants, and Packers — who could afford to pay better salaries and who commanded greater prestige. Under the new draft system, those teams that finished lowest were given first crack at the best college talent.

This radical innovation in professional sports did not have a real impact for several years, until the top teams had used up their accumulated wealth of talent. But in time the draft served to equalize the strength of teams throughout the league, making it difficult for any team to dominate the game for more than three years at a time.

On the field the pros were as ready to experiment as they were in the front office. Seeing the kinds of crowds that would turn out for a real attraction, and the greater salaries to be made, coaches and players began to spend more time at practice. The Chicago Cardinals were first to use an out-of-town training camp when they went to Coldwater, Michigan, in 1929.

Practices often concentrated on complicated pass plays and spinners out of wingback formations. The fullback, five yards behind center, took a direct snap, pivoted, handed off to a circling halfback, or kept the ball, spinning in a complete circle and plunging into the line — or any of scores of variations. Occasionally a pro team spread its offense from sideline to sideline. Such razzle-dazzle was usually intended to entertain the spectators, but clearly the passing game was on the rise. The ball was slimmer and easier to throw, and the rules now favored the pass.

The teams that dominated pro football in the late twenties and thirties were the first stable franchises. Hard work, not a little luck, and, most of all, great players made them. Despite the nation's tattered economy, pro football survived and grew.

In New York, Benny Friedman helped keep the game alive. A brilliant and imaginative quarterback from Michigan, he played for the Giants from 1929 to 1931 and closed out his career with the Brooklyn Dodgers. Fans could always count on Friedman to

Earl (Curly) Lambeau

put on a show regardless of the score, and so they came to watch. The Giants also had Ken Strong, a hard-driving back from N.Y.U. who joined the club in 1933, and Mel Hein, one of the great centers of all time, who had come from Washington State in 1931.

The Giants won championships in 1927, 1934 (when they changed to sneakers at halftime to rally and beat the Bears on a frozen field in the title game), and 1938. They were runners-up five times between 1929 and 1939.

The Green Bay Packers were often beating the Giants out of the championship. Green Bay is the great anomaly in big-time professional sports: a small-town success. In 1919, when Curly Lambeau formed the Packers with the help of the Indian Packing Company, Green Bay was a town of about 30,000. Besides being the longest continuous franchise in football history, Green Bay has been a great one. Nowhere else did the game evoke such early frenzy as in Green Bay; no rivalry has been more grudging than the Packers and the Bears. It was sweet for Green Bay to beat the big-city boys — and that included most of the league.

The Packers won their first championship in 1929, repeated in 1930 and 1931, and again in 1936 and 1939. Big Cal Hubbard, a giant tackle, and Johnny "Blood" McNally, a slashing, deceptive halfback, both joined Green Bay in 1929 and anchored the team till the mid-thirties. Clarke Hinkle, a powerful fullback, came in 1934, and great passing quarterbacks, too — Arnie Herber in 1930 and Cecil Isbell in 1937. But for spectacular grace, no one could match the Packers' Don Hutson, the tall, skinny end from Alabama who joined the team in 1935. He became the greatest pass receiver of all time.

Hutson had wonderful speed and could catch a football no matter what his position. No defensive back in the league could stay with him. In 11 years he caught 101 touchdown passes, far more than anyone who has ever played the game. With Herber and later Isbell throwing to Hutson, and Lambeau fashioning an attack that took maximum advantage of the forward pass, the Packers were a mighty force in the National Football League throughout the thirties.

In Chicago, Red Grange only began a parade of talent that culminated in a championship for the Bears in 1932. In 1930, George Halas hired Ralph Jones to coach the team and to revitalize the T formation (with the help of Halas and Clark Shaughnessy). In his first season as head coach, Jones found a rookie fullback from Minnesota named Bronko Nagurski and a rookie quarterback named Carl Brumbaugh. Nagurski became one of the most feared ball carriers of all time; Brumbaugh became a model for T quarterbacks.

Although the Bears won a championship only once more in the thirties (1933), they added outstanding players: Beattie Feathers, the first halfback to rush for more than 1,000 yards in a single season (he had Nagurski blocking for him); Bill Hewitt, a fine all-round end; "Automatic Jack" Manders, first of the great place-kickers; and Joe Stydahar and Danny Fortmann, two exceptional linemen. At the end of the decade came fullback Bill Osmanski, center Bulldog Turner, end Ken Kavanaugh, halfback George McAfee, and a quarterback from Columbia named Sid Luckman. This gathering of talent set the stage for an explosion in 1940 that rocked the football world.

Luckman was the key. As the first great T-Formation quarterback, he showed what potential the new attack had. A clever ball handler, a superb passer, a good runner, and, above all, a strategist on the field, Luckman made the man-in-motion T go. He led the Bears to a division title in 1940. They went to Washington to play the Redskins for the championship on December 8.

Don Hutson

Perhaps no team was ever more perfect than the Bears were that day. It was the most incredible performance by any team in the history of the game. Ten different Bears scored touchdowns during the long afternoon. At the end of the game the Bears were passing for conversions in order to save footballs. "I think we deserved to win," Halas said afterward. The final score was 73-0.

Repercussions of the Bears' victory were felt throughout football, in the colleges as well as among other pro teams. The new T formation had everyone talking and studying. A new era was at hand.

Beattie Feathers (l.) and Bronko Nagurski of the Chicago Bears.

The War Years and After

Hardly had coaches begun to understand the new striking power of the T formation as refined by Jones, Shaughnessy, and Halas, than World War II intervened. Playing ranks were decimated. The Bears lost the heart of their great 1941-42 team, though they won the title again in 1943 after losing to the Washington Redskins in 1942.

The Redskins were a power in the league throughout the war years, mostly because Sammy Baugh was still around to throw passes. This tall, lean Texan had come to Washington in 1937. He wasted no time turning the league on its ear. Working from tailback in the single wing, Baugh showed that it was possible to win football games with the forward pass alone. He was deadly accurate from any position and had uncanny timing. He led the Redskins into the championship game four times between 1940 and 1945, winning the title in 1942.

Despite the heroics of Baugh and a few others, pro football marked time during the war years. The Cleveland Rams dropped out of the league altogether for a year; Pittsburgh merged with Philadelphia in 1943, and the next year with the Chicago Cardinals.

With the end of the war, the National Football League looked forward to a new era of growth and prosperity. Instead, it was confronted with a new league, the most serious challenge it had faced since the 1920's. The All-America Conference was the brainchild of Arch Ward, sports editor of the *Chicago Tribune*. He first proposed the idea in 1944, when many of the NFL's players were in service, and when the best college talent was going directly into the armed forces instead of signing with NFL clubs. It was a propitious time to assemble the playing nucleus for a new league.

The All-America Conference began play in 1946 with franchises in Los Angeles, San Francisco, Buffalo, Baltimore, Chicago, New York, Cleveland, and Miami. The war of attrition between the two leagues lasted for four years and cost the AAC owners some $11 million. Some teams discovered quickly how difficult it was to buck the established competition: the Rockets could not sway Chicago fans from the Bears and Cardinals, and the Yankees had their troubles against the Giants in New York. Miami could not make a go of it even without competition.

Still, the new league signed some impressive players

Sammy Baugh

and produced some interesting teams. In Cleveland, Paul Brown put together in the Browns some of the finest teams of all time. (The NFL Cleveland Rams, after winning the championship in 1945, had moved to Los Angeles. There, with the help of players like Bob Waterfield, Norm Van Brocklin, Tom Fears, and Elroy Hirsch, the Rams beat off the furious competition of the Los Angeles Dons of the All-America Conference.)

The struggle between the two leagues ended after the 1949 season. In a "merger," the NFL absorbed the AAC's three best teams — the Browns, the San Francisco 49ers, and the Baltimore Colts. NFL Commissioner Bert Bell arbitrarily settled the matter of distributing talent from the dissolved teams. The NFL headed into the 1950's with 13 teams in two divisions.

On the field, the rise of the quarterback and the passing game continued. In a brief reversal, Greasy Neale, coaching the Philadelphia Eagles, devised a simple defense to handle the spread-end offense and won two championships with it (1948-49). But the device was soon solved by splits in the offensive line and by the three-end offense (wide receiver, tight end, and flanker). This three-end version of the T, with variations (such as the slot formation), is still the basic offense in pro football.

A Golden Era

By the end of the 1950's professional football was the most popular spectator sport in America. Most parks in the league were filled for every home game. For eight years beginning in 1952, the NFL broke its attendance record each year — from 2,052,126 in 1952 to 3,140,409 in 1959. It was almost impossible to buy a season ticket in New York, Baltimore, Detroit, Chicago, Los Angeles, and San Francisco.

There were two reasons, mainly. First, the advent of television made fans of millions who had never bothered to see a game in person. Second, the style of the game was exciting — more so than baseball, anyway. Action — even violence — characterized every play. (Football also seemed better suited to coverage by television than any other sport.)

Television's role was decided on early. Baseball teams had handled TV rights individually, and in most cases televised home games as well as those away. But NFL experiments (such as in Los Angeles) indicated that such a policy might cripple attendance. Commissioner Bell urged the plan of televising away games and blacking out home games. It still exists. No one can prove that this policy preserves sellout crowds; from time to time fans have risen up in protest against it. But clearly it has reaped riches for the owners—and thus for the players, too. Later the league would negotiate a single television contract, with the proceeds divided equally among all the teams. This approach only fattened the calf.

It was in the fifties that pro football became the specialized game it is today. When the free-substitution rule was readopted in 1950, coaches began to cultivate separate offensive and defensive teams. Players appeared who could only punt or place-kick —or, in some instances, do no more than hold the ball for the kicker. (Even in the late forties it had not been unusual for great players to "go both ways." Johnny Lujack, when he came to the Bears in 1948, played as a defensive back while he was learning to play pro quarterback. And Chuck Bednarik, the outstanding center of the Philadelphia Eagles, played defensive linebacker as well as offensive center for several years. Today such "risks" are unheard of.) The result of specialization was to make the game rougher (because players were better rested and could go harder while they were in the game) and more sophisticated (because players could pay more atten-

tion to the area of the game that involved them).

Probably the most interesting—if not also the dominant — figure in pro football in the fifties was Paul Brown, the coach and part-owner of the Cleveland Browns. He had been weaned in one of the nation's football hotbeds, as coach at Massillon High School in Ohio. Then he moved on to Ohio State and to Great Lakes Naval Station. Brown was a shrewd judge of talent, and the first Browns team he assembled in the All-America Conference proved it. From Ohio State he plucked kicker Lou Groza, end Dante Lavelli, and Bill Willis, a granite-like guard. In service football, Brown noticed three players whom he now brought to the Browns: Marion Motley, a 240-pound bull of a fullback; Mac Speedie, an end who could catch the long pass; and Otto Graham, a thinking quarterback who passed with daring and ran with aplomb, and who was to become the mainstay of the Browns through the mid-fifties. These men were the nucleus of Paul Brown's team. He knew how to mold them.

Brown's attention to detail and quest for perfection were perfectly attuned to pro football's new age of specialization. His iron discipline frequently provoked ridicule from other teams in the league, but his players did the job and rarely complained. They learned to keep in shape the year round and to take written notes at skull sessions—in short, to make football a full-time job as Brown himself did.

Strategically, Brown's contribution to the game was to open up the use of the forward pass still further. Otto Graham did not hesitate to throw the ball in situations that horrified most coaches. He made Paul Brown's intricate pass patterns work. The Cleveland passing attack, with its variety of potential receivers on every play, became a model for the league. The Browns won three championships in the fifties—in 1950, 1954, and 1955 (after having won four consecutive titles in the All-America Conference) — and made believers of those who thought they were just another team from a mediocre league.

At the other end of the spectrum from Brown's methodical approach during the fifties was the devil-may-care style of Bobby Layne. With the Detroit Lions, Layne gave the Browns fits more than any other team. A blond Texan, he had signed with the Chicago Bears in 1948, only to find himself a poor third behind quarterbacks Sid Luckman and Johnny Lujack. After a year on the bench he was traded to the New York Bulldogs and then to Detroit, where he found himself and became one of the most glamorous quarterbacks in the game. Layne, it seemed, was always winning the big one with a last-second touchdown pass. His targets were Doak Walker, the small halfback from S.M.U. who became one of the high scorers in pro football history; or Leon Hart, the giant end from Notre Dame; or other talented receivers like Jim Doran, Dorne Dibble, and Cloyce Box. The Lions' ground game was led by Pat Harder, acquired from the Cardinals, and Bob Hoernschemeyer. Joe Schmidt, a tough middle linebacker, led an aggressive defense. The Lions won championships in 1952, 1953, and 1957, each time beating the Browns in the playoff.

When Otto Graham retired in 1955, fullback Jim Brown became the Browns' featured attraction. He was surely one of the two or three greatest runners of all time. Bobby Layne spent his waning years with the Pittsburgh Steelers. But still another great quarterback appeared in 1956: Johnny Unitas. He inaugurated a dynasty for the Baltimore Colts and went on to enjoy perhaps the greatest career of any quarterback in the history of the game.

Unitas had not been able to make it with the Steelers, so he played sandlot football and begged the Colts for a tryout. Made the team and halfway through the season was sent in to replace the injured George Shaw. Unitas proved to be a mar-velous passer and play-caller, but above all a leader, a man without fear. His confidence ignited his team. In countless last-ditch situations he took the Colts calmly to victory.

To go with Unitas the Colts had a fleet halfback and receiver named Lenny Moore, a big fullback named Alan Ameche, the incomparable end Raymond Berry, and a defense featuring Gino Marchetti and Big Daddy Lipscomb.

Baltimore won its first championship in 1958 in a sudden-death title game with the New York Giants that is often spoken of as the greatest football game ever played. At the half the Colts led 14-3. The Giants rallied with a stout defense, and late in the fourth quarter finally took a three-point lead before the screaming New York fans. With less than two minutes to play, the Colts took the ball on their own 14-yard line. Conserving his time (no one was ever better at using the final two minutes of a game), Unitas completed three passes to Berry, then held the ball for a tying field goal with seven seconds to play. It was 17-17 and sudden-death overtime, the first in pro football history.

The Giants won the toss and received in the fifth period, but the Colts held them and took the ball on their own 21 after the punt. From there Unitas took the Colts methodically downfield (disdaining a field goal) until Ameche plunged into the end zone from the 1-yard line. It was a modern classic. Later, most observers agreed that Unitas' cool had made the difference in this best of all championship games.

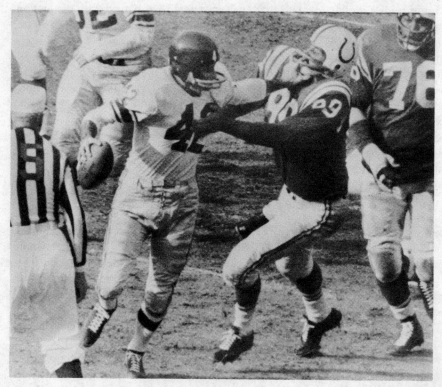

Baltimore Colts' defense men Gino Marchetti and Gene (Big Daddy) Lipscomb.

The 1960s

As the sixties began, the clamor for season tickets in NFL cities and the lucrative television receipts of the owners, together with the new prosperity and leisure of the American people, attracted those with money to invest in sports. Lamar Hunt, a young Texas businessman, was the moving force in organizing the American Football League, the fourth to use this name since 1926. The AFL began play in 1960 with teams in eight cities—Boston, Buffalo, Denver, Dallas, Houston, Los Angeles, New York, and Oakland.

The fierce competition for college talent between the two leagues produced skyrocketing player salaries. A high point was reached in 1964 when the New York Jets of the AFL gave Joe Namath a $400,000 contract. Namath had been a star quarterback at Alabama. The Jets hoped to lure New York fans away from the Giants and give the new league some glamour. Namath did the trick. With the help of the New York press he became an overnight celebrity, as much for his colorful social life as for his play.

Television was crucial to the success of the AFL. Unlike other attempts at new leagues, the AFL could bargain with the networks for a multi-million-dollar contract for television rights to its games. This boodle, when divided among the teams, made the difference between profit and loss for most of them and enabled the AFL to continue its war with the NFL.

It lasted till 1966 when the two leagues agreed to combine. They would play a championship game (soon dubbed the Super Bowl) beginning in January 1967. Inter-league play would begin in 1970 under two realigned conferences of three divisions each. Despite the merger, AFL teams still suffered charges of mediocrity until Joe Namath led the Jets to a Super Bowl victory over the Baltimore Colts in 1969, the first win for an AFL team.

The first two Super Bowls were won by the Green Bay Packers whose coach, Vince Lombardi, was easily football's most impressive personality in the sixties. As a lineman at Fordham in the thirties, Lombardi had been one of the famous "Seven Blocks of Granite." Later he was an assistant coach for the New York Giants.

When he came to the Packers as head coach in 1959, this once-legendary team was in last place. In three years he made them champions and eventually won five world championships in nine years. His sharp eye for talent helped, but mainly Lombardi counted on drive and discipline to make his teams great. His game plan was rarely complex: Lombardi thought the best way to break an opponent was to attack his strength, not his weakness. His plays were simple, but executed with perfect efficiency. The "Green Bay Sweep," an orthodox cutback run, became the most feared maneuver in pro football.

Lombardi's players worshiped him, and in turn he urged them to greatness—Bart Starr, Paul Hornung, and Jim Taylor in the backfield; Forrest Gregg, Fuzzy Thurston, and Jerry Kramer in the line; and a tough, mobile defense led by middle linebacker Ray Nitschke. It was strange to hear huge athletes like Kramer talk about "love" being important to the Packers' success. Others thought Lombardi a martinet, or worse. He was so intolerant of injuries that players feared to ask for rest short of a broken leg. Yet it was hard to argue with a man who demanded the best from everyone. "He treated us all the same," said Henry Jordan, a Packer lineman, "like dogs."

The Packers' élan and professional integrity were such that even in defeat they played with distinction. But mostly they won. No game showed why better than the 1967 championship, played in subzero weather in Green Bay. The Dallas Cowboys led 17-14. With only seconds to go the Packers had the ball, fourth down on the Dallas 1-yard line. The safe thing was to kick a field goal and send the game into sudden-death overtime. Instead Green Bay went for the touchdown, the players knowing that if they failed they would lose about $2,700 apiece and the Super Bowl game. They made the touchdown.

The sixties produced many great players. The Bears had two of them in Gale Sayers, a halfback with phenomenal moves who rewrote several records before his career was cruelly cut short by knee injuries, and Dick Butkus, a savage middle linebacker whom some coaches have called the greatest all-round football player ever. Merlin Olsen of the Rams and Bob Lilly of Dallas were outstanding defensive linemen, and at Cleveland Leroy Kelly picked up where Jim Brown left off. Still, the 1960's belonged to the Packers and most of all to Vince Lombardi. When he died of cancer in 1970, after having gone to the Washington Redskins as coach and part-owner, he was eulogized not only by fans and players. His invincible belief in hard work and the will to victory were old-fashioned standards; in an age marked by fakery, hedonism, and contempt for work, Lombardi's approach touched many Americans.

The Future and Its Problems

In the 1970's professional football's future seems well assured. No one would argue that the demand for tickets is drying up, or that television's interest in the sport as a viewing attraction is waning. Still, pro football has its problems. Not the least of them concerns what over the last two decades has been the game's strong point: excitement.

The fact is that pro football games are duller than they used to be. It is no coincidence that the sport enjoyed its greatest ascendancy when the forward pass (and especially the long "bomb") became the chief offensive weapon. Anything might happen on any play. For the past several years the game has become more routinized. Watching a game on television any Sunday, one may think he has seen every play, every situation the preceding week.

There are a few reasons for this turn of events. First, specialization has bred standardization—one cornerback plays like another cornerback; one team's "two-minute offense" is pretty much like another team's. Individual differences are subordinated to systems.

Second, defense now dominates the game. There has not been a significant offensive innovation in 20 years. Instead, the emphasis now (thanks to the influence of Vince Lombardi) is on *executing* basic plays and controlling the ball.

Third, the zone defense has made the successful long pass a rarity, thus removing one of the game's more exciting plays. (The National Basketball Association has outlawed the zone defense in its sport in order to give the individual player a better chance to strut his stuff.)

League officials are aware of this tendency of the game toward stagnation. They tried to do something about it in 1972, moving the in-bounds markers farther toward the center of the field. This maneuver was thought to be a potential boon for the passing game: it would allow receivers to utilize more of the field. In fact, it encouraged a resurgence of the running game. More backs gained over 1,000 yards than in any other year in history. The ground game has a certain hard-nosed fascination about it, but it does not usually produce the kind of excitement the fans like.

One has the feeling that fans are itching for a revolutionary new offense that would give the game back to the attacking units. No such animal is on the horizon, despite experiments with the I formation and the triple-option.

Far more crucial than the style of the game is the role of television. Sad to say, the major TV networks now virtually control professional football because of the money reaped by the owners from telecasting rights. The networks not only consult on the scheduling of games, they also influence the pace of play on the field—all at the expense of the fan who pays his way into the park. It is no longer a surprise (though no less tolerable) to see an official time out called after each punt has been fielded, so that television can squeeze the necessary number of one-minute commercials into the game. Artificial playing surfaces insure that television will be able to bring its viewers a clean, mudless (antiseptic, almost) contest, with those names on the backs of the jerseys (put there to satisfy TV) perfectly readable. No player prefers artificial turf—but who's helping to pay his big salary?

It does not seem likely that the game will be able to break its dependence upon the networks. Television's influence over it will grow rather than diminish, with unpredictable consequences.

Expansion of the league, so much a feature of the 1960's, has slowed to a point where the caliber of play has finally begun to recoup its losses. And the persistent fear of "overexposure" (*too much* pro football on television through too long a season) has not really materialized. No, the big problem for pro football today is whether it can overcome its slick, big-business motivations. It is surely not the same game as it was when George Trafton ran from the field at Rock Island with the gate receipts under his arm. The players are bigger and faster now. So is the buck.

EVOLUTION OF THE BALL

See page 26 for the rules affecting the ball.

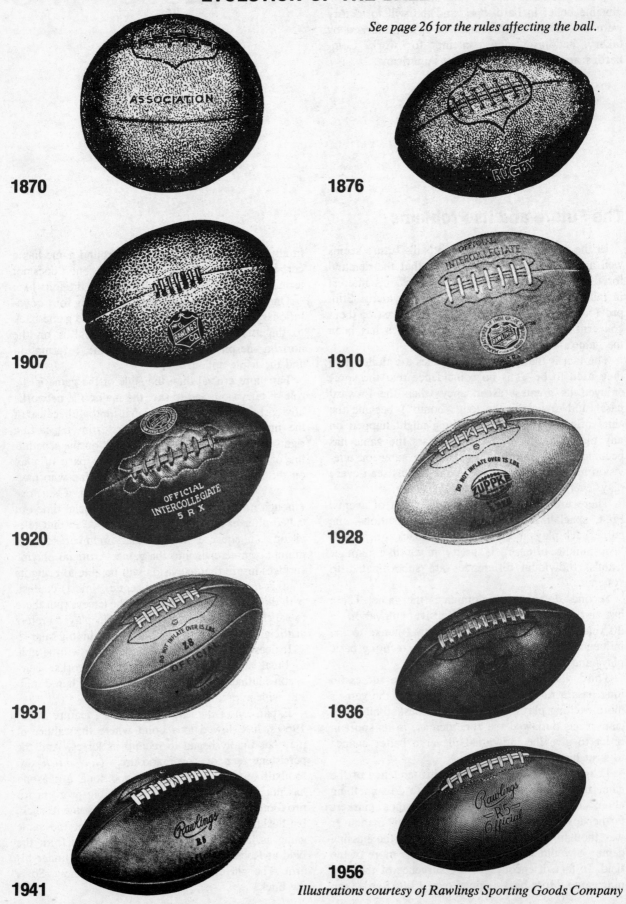

1870

1876

1907

1910

1920

1928

1931

1936

1941

1956

Illustrations courtesy of Rawlings Sporting Goods Company

The Rules

Rules and How They've Changed the Game

Pro football is the most complicated, yet the most brutally fundamental game man has played. Despite all its hidden strategy and tactical decisions, in the end the contest is decided by hand-to-hand combat for the possession of a few yards of land.

Just as the tactics of warfare have been adjusted to meet political and technological change over the years, so have the rules of football become more scientific and refined.

Football has always allowed men to use mental quickness and bodily grace to combat an elemental physical brutality. But today the game is becoming more intensely violent. Bigger, stronger, faster men in lighter, more effective equipment crash together with steadily mounting force.

During the game's first 50 years, many skirmishes over the rules involved proponents of the forward pass versus those of the run. Many men felt that throwing the ball was cheap, even cowardly, and that no real football team would rely on the pass.

Pop Warner, one of football's great coaches in the early days of pro football, had some clear thoughts on the subject: "I think passing should be illegal," he said. "Something should be done to curtail the wild, promiscuous, glorified football that some teams now indulge in. They throw long forward passes and figure on the percentage basis that if one of these connects they will fluke a touchdown and win the game. That's what I'm against. I think a game of

football should be (won) strictly on a merit basis."

This question of running or passing, as Pop reminds us, pervades the entire field of football strategy. Looking back on the 1972 pro football season, we can almost hear the old coach breathing a sigh of relief. The pendulum seems to be swinging Warner's way again.

A 1912 Carlisle College play by Pop Warner.

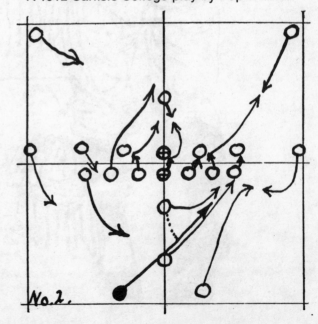

The Year of the Hashmark

Early in 1972 the National Football League owners approved a rule change of seemingly mild importance. The rule states: "The in-bounds markers for an NFL playing field will be moved 23 yards, 1 foot, 9 inches from each sideline, leaving 18 feet, 6 inches (the width of a goal post crossbar) in the middle."

When the hashmarks—those small vertical lines— were moved tighter, closer to the middle of the field, pro football's running game exploded. The "outside" opened up for the running backs; defenses loosened and became vulnerable for tackle-to-tackle shots.

As every armchair quarterback knows, the football is placed on a hashmark at the start of each play if the preceding play ended wide of the hashmark. In past seasons hashmarks were 20 yards from each sideline. This distance was increased by ten feet, 9 inches on each side, giving offensive units a total of more than seven yards additional operating room for wide plays.

Changing the hashmarks, along with an unusually talented bunch of runners, made the 1,000-Yard Club less than exclusive in 1972. A record ten runners joined up in the "Year of the Hashmark." Three others came within striking distance of the magic number. The previous high for 1,000-Yard Club membership was six in 1962.

How did the hashmark change spur the running game? For one thing, it greatly increased the so-called "weak side" area of the zone pass defense. The zone defense has always regarded the sideline on the weak side as an extra defensive player—in effect, a twelfth man. Because of the protection offered by the sideline, the weak side safety was able to play looser, play the ball, or provide double coverage against super pass-catching threats such as Dallas's Bob Hayes.

Fran Tarkenton, quarterback of the Minnesota Vikings, noted how the new, three-yards wider corridor on the weak side made the safety's job much more difficult. "If you consider that 15 yards down-field from scrimmage now means an additional 45 square yards of territory to cover, you can grasp how this rule change might alter the balance of power in favor of the offense," he said.

A Wider Battlefield and the Wishbone

In football, the ultimate triumph belongs to the offense, at least as far as most fans are concerned. In order to win, a team must put points on the score-board—and that's where the excitement lies. But pro football in recent years has seen fewer and fewer long bombs, thanks to the perfected zone defense.

The long punt return is a rarity, too. More often than not, a field goal is the difference between winning and losing.

What rule changes may help inject more offensive power and excitement into the game? After the Year of the Hashmark, just about anything could happen. Take the zone defense, for example. Johnny Unitas has a simple solution: "A lot of people have suggested outlawing the zone defense. It makes sense. Fans come out to see exciting play; an offense trying to beat the zone has to be methodical. It is forced to take short yardage and forget about the long pass."

Other experts believe the answer may be as simple as widening the field to dilute the zone. What would happen if the field were not 53 but 65 yards wide, as in Canadian football? With the wider field all kinds of interesting options appear. A team without a good T-formation passer—the Chicago Bears, for instance—probably could improve its attack by relying on a running quarterback operating off the Wishbone formation. The Bears' weak passer, Bobby Douglass, who used the option and the broken pass play in 1972 to rush for nearly 1,000 yards in only

Moving of the hashmark has greatly increased the weak-side area of the zone pass defense and has made it more difficult to provide double coverage against super pass-catching threats such as Dallas's Bob Hayes.

141 carries (a 6.9 yard average), might turn the corner even more frequently on a wider field.

If the Wishbone were operated successfully, teams might have to abandon the zone defense. And, the beefy front fours—which now anchor a successful NFL defense—would become almost obsolete against a combination of the Wishbone and the wider field. The Wishbone formation spreads a defense from one sideline to the other, forcing it to rely on lateral speed and pursuit rather than pass rushing, size, and power. Nor is there a practical way to cover a Wishbone receiver except man-for-man. Against a Wishbone team, double coverage is as difficult and unlikely as zone coverage.

"In the pros, we are geared to stop the pass," says Hank Stram, coach of the Kansas City Chiefs. "If we use the Wishbone option to make the defenses worry about the run, it will put more pressure on the defense to contend with the pass. It will give the pro offense a new dimension."

The option maneuver is the key to the Wishbone: the quarterback either hands off or carries himself. If the play is executed properly, not until the last split second—when the quarterback makes his decision to run or to pitch the ball to another back—does the defense know where the ball will go.

The Wishbone offense, by making the defense run-conscious, might even pave the way for a re-opening of the pass routes. It might even force defenses to abandon the zone on the wider field and resort to man-to-man coverage on wide receivers. The Wishbone on the wider field would be particularly effective for the pros inside the 20-yard line, where defenses now clog all avenues leading to the goal line.

"It would be easy," says football coach John McKay of the University of Southern California, "for a pro team to put in three Wishbone plays and a pass against the type of defense the pros use on the goal line. It's the standard 6-5 defense everybody uses. The quarterback could just walk into the end zone."

Stram and McKay aren't the only coaches who feel that a change to the Wishbone might enliven pro offenses. Chuck Fairbanks, whose Oklahoma Sooners operated the triple-option Wishbone T to perfection, says he may introduce the offense to his New England Patriots for the 1973 season.

Fairbanks would have to change the style of Jim Plunkett, who's strictly a passer—or run the Wishbone under another quarterback. The Patriots also have Brian Dowling who did plenty of running as a Yale quarterback, and Alan Lowry of Texas, who used the triple-option in defeating Alabama 17-14 in the Cotton Bowl.

Let's borrow another feature from Canadian football—the 25-foot-deep endzone. Together with a wider field and the Wishbone formation, more new scoring possibilities appear. No longer would the offense be congested when the football is moved inside the 20-yard line. Speedy flankers would be able to run deep pass patterns and defenses couldn't key on the run by the Wishbone quarterback.

Some added offensive leverage might result from a rule change allowing a pass receiver to catch the ball with only one foot in bounds, instead of both feet as now required. Like the Wishbone offense, this adoption of a college rule could give the defense something else to worry about along the sidelines and in the end zone.

Interference and the Judgment Call

If you are an offense-minded fan—and who isn't? —you'll turn purple at some proposals now being considered to emasculate pass interference penalties.

Some students of the game have argued that too many games are being decided frivolously on interference judgment calls. A rule change was suggested recently to reduce the penalty for pass interference to 15 yards, rather than placing the ball where the infraction occurs as referees now do.

Advocates of the offense counter by suggesting that if interference occurs within two minutes of the end of the half or the game, the offense should have the option of stopping the clock for the succeeding play. Some offense fanatics have even insisted that basketball-type rule be adopted whereby a player may foul out if he commits two inerference infractions in the same game.

The Four-Point Play

Kicking specialists almost always lead the NFL in scoring. Many are so proficient—especially from inside the 40-yard line—that fans often yawn through this phase of the game. As a result, one of the real possibilities in future years is a rule change that would involve some sort of a graduated point scoring system for field goals. We might, for instance, see the awarding of additional points for especially long kicks and fewer points for the "chip-shot" field goal. Imagine the effect on the game if four points were given for a field goal of 45 or more yards, three points for a kick from between the 30 and 45 yard lines, and only two points inside the 30?

The fewer points awarded in close would encourage many teams that normally would be satisfied with a "sure" three points to drive in for the touchdown instead. Teams with kicking specialists who can bomb the ball through the goal posts from 45-plus yards out could score those few extra points to break up a tie game. The end result would be a great deal of added drama in the kicking game, and probably even more of an upsurge in immigration to the U.S.A. of more stoop-shouldered soccer-style kickers. Others argue that a field goal's worth should be based on the distance the offensive team moved the ball themselves.

Some experts would like to see the return of the two-point conversion. The American Football League first adopted it in 1960, awarding two points for a successful run or pass (but just one for a place kick) from the two-yard line. The rule was dropped when the AFL merged with the NFL, but restoring it might add offensive drama.

Other phases of the kicking game may come under close scrutiny to enhance the offensive opportunities. Imagine what a good runback man could do if kickoffs were made from the 30-yard line instead of the 40.

Rules on Violence and the Inevitable Ouch!

With all the rules changes that have been worked since football began to make the game more satisfying to watch and less lethal to play, no solution has been found to a problem that grows more pressing every season—how to protect the human knee from crippling injury.

The best young quarterback in the game, Joe Namath, now stumps about on legs with knee joints that grind together like a couple of unlubricated cam shafts. It's so painful there's a question if he will play another season.

The jagged scar on the inside of the leg, from lower thigh to tibia, has become almost as famous a badge of the modern pro football player as missing teeth were to his gridiron fore-fathers.

Knee injuries usually happen when a blocker or tackler hits a leg that is solidly planted in sod.

Not only the ball carriers suffer knee injuries. Even the granite monsters who play in the trenches on the line of scrimmage have proved to be breakable when too much pressure is suddenly applied to this vulnerable joint.

How much can rule changes do to minimize the violence and injury in pro football? The answer is not much, unless the fans will accept a much daintier game that may not be fun to watch or worth paying to see.

Can the rules of battle be changed to protect the quarterback? It is hard to imagine fans sitting still while the NFL prevents the feeding of the Christians to the Detroit Lions. Perhaps the knees of future quarterbacks will be saved by a change in the offensive formations—abandoning the pocket passer in favor of the multiple offense and occasional sprint-out passes with a "moving pocket." The "power I," from which any back can carry the ball in any direction with equal effectiveness, can make it more difficult for the defense to read the play and key on a single man, thus reducing the effectiveness of the wholesale charge on the quarterback.

Yet Johnny Unitas, who admits that it hurts to be sacked, considers his life safer in a passing pocket: "The referee protects you when you're back to pass," Unitas says. "He keeps warning defensive linemen to play it clean. But once the passer starts to run, he's a runner, not a quarterback. The referee no longer gives him any special protection. The defense can go after him, and does. It's a big difference." The problem has no sure answer.

Rules in the Early Years

Through the years, rule changes have played a large role in shaping football into the game we know today. Power was the main feature of the game before the turn of the century, when any number of players might play behind the line. A guards-back or tackles-back play belonged in every professional team's repertoire.

At the start of the game, most teams formed into a V-shaped wedge with the ball carrier protected inside. There was no real kickoff in old-time American football; the game began when the ball was put in play by being kicked by a member of the team that won the privilege. The rules did not specify how far the ball was to be kicked or who was to touch it.

So the kicking team would start on the dead run for the enemy lines and on the way one player would lean over and touch the ball with his toe, thus "kicking" it within the meaning of the rule. Promptly the wedge would form around the ball carrier, and the entire team would try to smash its way through the enemy ranks, with the ball carrier holding fast to the belt of the man in front.

The forward pass was supposed to have been "invented" in the 1900s, but there was plenty of passing in the early days, too. Most of it was lateral, in from out-of-bounds; but the ball also was flipped from hand to hand in the field of play. Because the ball was big, fat, and shaped like a stunted watermelon, it didn't lend itself to the spiral pass, so it was thrown like a baseball or discus. A pass belonged to anyone who could recover it: a man awaiting the catch could be knocked down before he received the ball, and an incomplete pass was a free ball.

Pushing the ball carrier or hauling him by means of a harness was an accepted way of advancing the ball. "Blocking" in this early version of the game did not mean taking potential tacklers out of the play or protecting the passer or kicker; it meant stopping the enemy's advance, which usually was done by setting every shoulder against the massed rush line of the attacking team and holding fast.

The ball carrier was not "down" until he admitted

it, so he might lie buried beneath a pile of bodies for some time, with the breath nearly pressed out of his lungs, before he gave up and cried: "Down!" Occasionally his surrender was hurried with a well-placed fist.

In the early 1900s the game became more sophisticated and opened up so that the ball could be seen more easily by spectators. Slugging had long been done away with, and team managers generally agreed it was better to use neutral officials who would not hesitate to eject men who used feet or fists to injure an opponent.

Several changes in the rules were made in the early years dealing with the size and shape of the football itself. The first mention of the football in the rules book came in 1894, but the rule simply stated: "The ball must be made of leather and hold air."

By 1899, specific mention was made that the ball used should be made in the shape of a "prolate spheroid." By 1911 official weights (14 to 15 ounces) and measures for the football were intro-

RULES AND THE SHAPE OF THE BALL

IF THERE HAD BEEN such a thing as a "Super Bowl" way back in the 11th century in England, where the first semblance of football had its beginnings, chances are that the rival teams might have insisted on the alternate use of a Dane's skull and an inflated animal bladder.

Early history is sketchy, but it is certain that sometime after 1042, when a 28-year Danish occupation of England terminated, workers, after digging up the skull of a Danish soldier, devised a game out of "kicking the Dane's head." Games were between teams of neighboring villages and the "field" was the area between the competing villages. The first team to reach the other's village won.

Probably because kicking hard skulls hurt their toes, "futballe" players soon were using as their ball an inflated animal bladder, probably that of a cow or a pig.

Futballe was banned in England for about four centuries, but when the ban was rescinded early in the 16th century, the soccer-type sport was immediately very popular. Rugby, a new game in which running was permitted, was introduced in England in the mid-1800s and both soccer and rugby made their way to America at about the same time.

The first intercollegiate "football" game between Princeton and Rutgers in 1869 was strictly a soccer game and several other Eastern colleges quickly took up the sport. Harvard students, however, favored what they called the "Boston Game," a version of soccer where running was allowed. Soon Harvard was playing rugby and other colleges found they also preferred that sport.

Out of this union of soccer-playing and rugby-playing colleges, American football evolved. By 1880, an original attempt was made to set up some American football rules and almost annual rules changes since that time have brought the game into its present focus.

As the game changed, so did the ball. From the start, American football teams played with an egg-shaped ball, similar to the rugby ball. As late as 1887, however, a noted sports historian reported that "neither in Rugby or American Football is any mention made of the size of the ball or of the materials of which it should be made."

Research into the archives of the Professional Football Hall of Fame in Canton, Ohio, shows that the first mention of the football in the rules book came

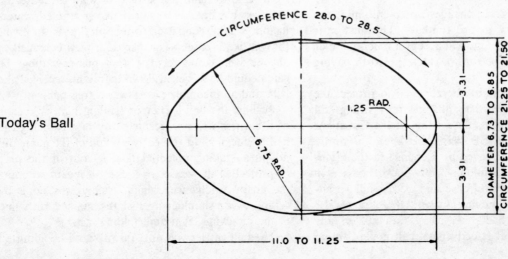

Today's Ball

CIRCUMFERENCE 28.0 TO 28.5

6.75 RAD.

1.25 RAD.

3.31

3.31

DIAMETER 6.73 TO 6.85
CIRCUMFERENCE 21.25 TO 21.50

11.0 TO 11.25

duced. Other measurement changes, all tending to slim the ball, were made in 1929 and 1933, and in 1934 specifications were adopted that are still standard today.

Manufacturing improvements in lacing, selection of leather, lining, tanning, and sewing all have tended to make a better football and one that is also easier to pass. The evolution of the football closely parallels the rise of the forward pass and thus has influenced a basic aspect of the game and its popularity. Only the drop kick suffered: the slimmer football, while more easily punted, made drop kicking an obsolete art.

The drop kick, which had originally been a mere evasion of the spirit of the rule for putting a ball in play, became a key feature of the game in the early 1900s. The big, blunt-nosed ball bounced fairly true if it was not dropped from too great a height, and men discovered that a strong leg could drive the ball over the crossbar as far away as the middle of the field.

in 1894, but the rule simply stated: "The ball must be made of leather and hold air!"

By 1899, specific mention was made that the ball used should be made in the shape of a "prolate spheroid." By 1911, some standard weights and measures for the official football were introduced for the first time. Other measurement changes, all tending toward the slimming of the ball, were made in 1929 and 1933 and then, in 1934, the specifications that are still standard today were adopted.

Manufacturing improvements in such areas as the lacing, the air intake, the selection of leather, the lining of the football, tanning and sewing all have tended to make not only a better product, but a football that is easier to pass.

The "fat to slim" evolution of the football parallels closely the increasing use of the forward pass and has played its obvious effect on the basic aspect of the game and its popularity. On the other hand, the slimmer football, while more easily punted, has made dropkicking an obsolete art. Most of the game's great dropkickers had passed from the scene by the start of World War II.

From the Dane's skull and an inflated animal bladder—which, incidentally, is probably about the only time a football was ever really a "pigskin"—to the sleek and modern, high-quality job of today. The football has indeed come a long way!

Evolution of Rules Concerning the Football

1887 "It is a simple fact that neither in the Rugby code or in that of the American College Code is any mention made of the size of the ball or of the materials of which it should be made . . ."

Henry Chadwick, sports historian

1894 *Official Football Rules*—"The ball shall be made of leather and hold air."

1899 *Official Football Rules*—Rule 1, Sec. d . . . "The football used shall be of leather, enclosing an inflated rubber bladder. The ball shall have the shape of a prolate spheroid."

1911 *Rule 2* . . . "The ball shall be made of leather, enclosing a rubber bladder. It shall be tightly inflated and shall have the shape of a prolate spheroid—Circumference, long axis, from 28 to 28½ inches; short axis, from 22½ inches to 23 inches. Weight, from 14 ounces to 15 ounces."

1929 *Rule 2* . . . "The ball shall be made of leather (natural tanned color) enclosing a rubber bladder. It shall be tightly inflated with a pressure of not less than 13 pounds nor more than 15 pounds and shall have the shape of a prolate spheroid—the entire surface to be convex.

"The circumference, long axis, shall measure not less than 28 inches, nor more than 28½ inches; short axis, not less than 22 inches nor more than 22½ inches; the length of the long axis shall measure not less than 11 inches, nor more than 11¼ inches. The weight of the ball shall be from 14 ounces to 15 ounces."

1933 *Rule 2 . . . Only change from 1929 rule:* ". . . It shall be inflated with a pressure of not less than 12½ pounds nor more than 13½ pounds . . ."

1934 *Rule 2 . . . Changes from 1933 rule:* "The ball shall be made of pebble-grained leather (natural tanned color) without corrugation of any kind, enclosing a rubber bladder."

". . . short axis, not less than 21¼ inches, nor more than 21½ inches . . ."

1942 *Rule 2 was rewritten in 1942 to the basic general language that is in effect today. Except for change in terminology, however, the specifications, as defined in the 1934 rule, were not changed.*

The Present *Quoting Rule 2—Ball.* ". . . Ball shall be made up of an inflated (12½ to 13½ pounds) rubber bladder enclosed in a pebble-grained, leather case (natural tan color) without corrugation of any kind. It shall have the form of a prolate spheroid and the size and the weight shall be: long axis—11 to 11¼ inches; long circumference—28 to 28½ inches; short circumference—21¼ to 21½ inches; weight—14 to 15 ounces."

Rules and the National Football League

When the National Football League began in 1920, the game was thought to have reached a state of "perfection." The rule that kept seven men on the scrimmage line had wiped out the last vestige of the old flying-wedge attack. The forward pass could be thrown more freely, and the pros used it far more often than the collegians dared. The dropped pass was no longer a free ball, nor did it go over to the enemy if it sailed out of bounds. The potential re-receiver was protected by the rules so that he could not be assaulted before he touched the ball. The neutral zone kept the scrimmage lines rigidly separated. Today's fan, if transported back to that golden era, would at least recognize that the clubs were playing football.

One oddity of the game—the punt out—was changed in 1920. Before the rule revision, the point from which a goal after touchdown was to be tried was determined by having the scoring team punt the ball out from the goal line. Another player on the scoring team was out in the field to catch the ball and wherever he caught it was the point from which the extra point was to be kicked.

Even after this change, the conversion attempt was not made from scrimmage. Instead the kicker stood in front of the goal posts while the opposing team lined up along the goal line. At a signal the enemy would rush with hands upraised to try to block the kick.

The kicker, who had no blockers in front of him, still had plenty of time to get the ball away, and was much more likely to be thrown off by the vision of this army of attackers bearing down on him than he was to have the kick blocked.

One of the first major rule changes in the 1920's made college players ineligible for NFL competition until their classes had graduated. The rule was designed to prevent college stars such as Red Grange from competing in the pros the day after their last college game (as Grange did with the Chicago Bears in 1925).

Aerial Warfare in the 1930s

Most of the excitement in the early 1930's originated in Chicago where George Halas was experimenting with new formations while his Bears were winning league championships. The greatest player in Chicago at the time was Bronko Nagurski, the one-man team who could play every position on the field and was the most destructive blocker and runner since Jim Thorpe.

Bronko's effectiveness was doubled by a rule change that the professionals adopted in 1933. It permitted a back to pass the football forward from *anywhere* behind the line of scrimmage. (Previously he had had to be five years behind the line.)

This rule allowed the Bronk to come charging at the line—where the defense would mass to meet him—then stop, jump, and flip a pass over the line to a receiver just a few yards beyond.

Another rule change in 1933, the year the pros finally declared their independence from the intercollegiate rules committee, moved the goal posts back to the goal line. (The college rules committees had pushed them to the rear of the end zone to cut down on injury and prevent the use of the goal posts as extra linemen on defense.) This prompted a revival of field goal kicking and, along with the rule change in passing, assured spectators an exciting pro game that cut down on the number of scoreless or low-scoring ties.

By the mid-1930's rule changes eliminated the old wasteful way of "running the ball out" on the sideline play. Hashmarks appeared, and the ball was brought far enough in bounds to provide room to run the next play.

The real strategic advances in pro football in this era came through the forward pass and the new T formation. Sammy Baugh and Don Hutson challenged the traditional pattern of the game, while the Bears' refurbished T burst upon the scene in 1940, when they beat Washington 73-0 for the championship.

The T designed by the Bears spread the ends and halfbacks a couple of yards to loosen the defense, and often one of the halfbacks would trot out to the side of the formation just before the play started. This "man-in-motion" idea had been used by single-wing teams before, but never with the T. The halfback in motion could run downfield for a pass, or crack back on the defensive end if the play was a run around end.

In the new T, the quarterback kept his hands in contact with the center's pants, and the center snapped the ball into the quarterback's hands without looking. The center, therefore, was able to look straight ahead and be more useful for blocking in the front line. A rule change eventually enabled the center to hold the ball in one hand, if he wished, with just the front end of it in contact with the ground. Then he had a forearm free to block charging defenders.

The same year the Bears destroyed Washington, other subtle rule changes were adopted. Clipping penalties were reduced from 25 to 15 yards, and all distance penalties were limited to half the distance to the goal if the penalty would place the ball closer than that.

A rule change in 1946 came as a result of a freak play in the 1945 title playoff game between the Cleveland Rams and the Washington Redskins. Sammy Baugh and his Redskin mates had been pushed back to their own goal line in the early moments of the game. Here the poised passer calmly took the snap from center, stepped into his own end zone, and waited for his receivers to get into the clear. But when he passed, the ball bounced against one of the uprights and fell to the ground in the end zone.

It was an automatic safety and gave Cleveland two critical points which helped to win the game 15-14. A month later the rules were changed to make a forward pass incomplete upon striking either team's goal post.

In 1949 the NFL catered to the trend toward specialized talent—unlimited free substitution.

Under this rule, adopted permanently in 1950, players could enter and leave the game at any time, instead of playing for most of the 60 minutes. The consequence of this new rule was startling—and depressing to those who defined football in terms of man-to-man power struggles.

Sammy Baugh of the Washington Redskins helped make the forward pass a major strategic advance.

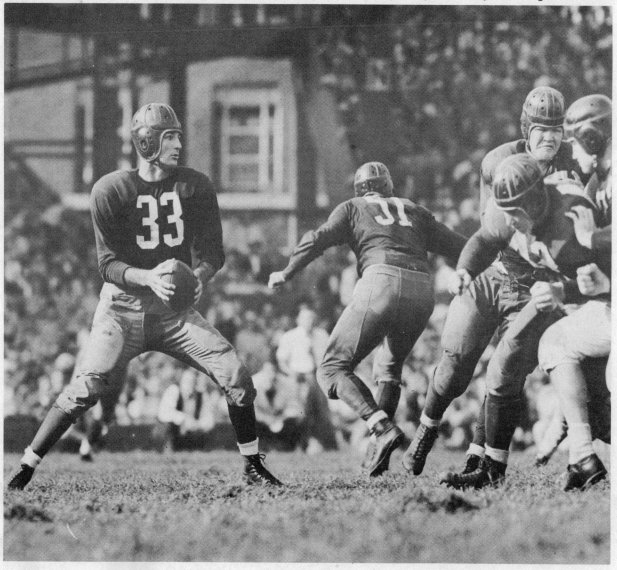

A Period of Sudden Death

When the Baltimore Colts played the New York Giants for the 1958 NFL championship on a frosty Dec. 28 in Yankee Stadium, the outcome of the game really was decided by a rule change made more than a decade earlier.

Use of "sudden death" overtime to break ties in championship games was adopted in 1947. However, the rule's importance to pro football didn't come into focus until a Colt field goal by Steve Myhra knotted the score of the 1958 title game at 17-17 with only seven seconds remaining on the clock. After 8 minutes and 15 seconds of the first sudden death play in history Alan (The Horse) Ameche blasted through the Giant line from one-yard out for the decisive touchdown. Baltimore didn't even try for the extra point.

As pro football moved into the 1960s, the sudden death rule was used to break ties in other divisional playoff and championship games.

The Dallas Texans (now the Kansas City Chiefs) beat the Houston Oilers 20-17 in sudden death to settle the 1962 American Football League championship.

In 1965 the Green Bay Packers nipped Baltimore 13-10 on Don Chandler's field goal in a Western Conference playoff game after 13 minutes of sudden-death overtime.

A 1971 divisional playoff and pro football's longest game—ended after 82 minutes and 40 seconds when Garo Yepremian, the left-footed Cypriot, kicked a 37-yard field goal in the second sudden death overtime period for a 27-24 Miami Dolphin victory over Kansas City.

Sudden death has proven to be such a key part of the game that NFL owners now are considering a rule change that would allow using it to break ties in league games. Dallas Cowboy's owner Tex Schram, chairman of the committee in charge of the proposal, is pushing for sudden-death and detects growing support: "I feel we have a realistic chance of getting it," he said.

Other rules had to be revised in the 1960s to accommodate changes in equipment and for sheer safety of the players involved in America's most violent spectator sport. In 1962 the NFL made it illegal to grab the face mask of any player. Previously, the grabbing of face masks of all players, except the ball-carrier, was legal.

The Pros and the Tube

As pro football became more television oriented, and team owners began to realize the fat paychecks their franchises could receive from network TV, changes were grooved to fit the tube.

In 1960 lettering of player's names on the backs of their jerseys was adopted by the American Football League so the TV viewers of the wild and wooly "junior" circuit could get to know the players in the new league.

The AFL also voted to make the scoreboard clock the official timing device to keep arm-chair quarterbacks and the fans in the stands aware of the crucial seconds as they tick away. After the NFL and AFL merged, both followed the clock ruling.

In 1965 the color of NFL official's penalty flags was changed from white to bright gold. The reason for the change was to make the flags easy to see against the green grass and on color TV.

The same reasoning prevailed with the switch of the color of goal posts to bright gold the following year. In 1967 the owners voted for a single-standard goal post and required the playing field to be lined with a six-foot wide white restraining strip. The band of white made it easy for all the easy-chair referees viewing the instant replays at home to decide if a runner stepped out of bounds.

If TV brought all these changes for the fans, it also gave the players something too. Many a weary football player gave thanks for the extra time out or two in the final quarter, while those rich television sponsors got in their final commercial messages.

In the late 1960s and early 1970s some players became so adept at stopping the clock in the final minutes, that a rule change was brought in to help speed up the game. Owners observed some quarterbacks, such as Ram Roman Gabriel, intentionally heaved the ball to the ground toward a receiver in the nearest vacant zone, over the back of the endzone, over the sideline, or even into the stands.

This stalling tactic, used in tight situations when quarterbacks had trouble reading confusing defenses or when all receivers were covered, was restricted sharply by a rule change in 1971.

The NFL owners approved a change that judged on one criteria: whether the passer was making a deliberate attempt to prevent loss of yardage.

Enforcement had previously been sloppy and quarterbacks were avoiding losses by dumping the ball off in the general direction of anyone who looked like a teammate and getting away with it.

As the game expands in the seventies one thing is clear about future rule changes. They will be geared for safety, but above all to increase the excitement of the television viewer, the new and most important consideration in the game.

The Greatest Games

Chicago Bears vs. New York Giants December 17, 1933

The game was a milestone in National Football League history because it was the first championship playoff ever. The previous spring, the club owners agreed to try an idea proposed by George Preston Marshall, owner of the Redskin team. Marshall suggested splitting the league into two divisions. That promoted interest in the race for division titles and set up a natural championship match between the two winners.

This playoff game also symbolized an "opening up" of football that three important rule changes had brought about in the 1933 season. All three rules helped the offense.

First, the ball was brought in at least ten yards from the sidelines after each play, giving the offense more room to operate.

A second change moved the goal posts from the rear of the end zone up to the goal line, giving field goal kickers a closer shot.

The third innovation, one that played an important role in this championship contest, permitted passing from any point back of the line of scrimmage. Previously, the passer had to be at least five yards behind the line.

On a nice day for football, 25,000 fans showed up at Wrigley Field. It was one of the largest crowds in Chicago since Red Grange, the "Galloping Ghost" at the University of Illinois, joined the Bears in 1925 and gave the infant pro football scene a drawing card.

In addition to Grange, the Bears had Bronko Nagurski, a fear inspiring fullback. Coach George Halas built this 1933 team around Nagurski.

Halas was already experimenting with a form of man-in-motion style T-formation. Nagurski would charge towards the line from his deep fullback position and take a handoff.

Defenders would grit their teeth and hurl their bodies at the line to stop Nagurski. Sometimes they did, often they didn't. Occasionally it would be a fake with a pitch or pass to unprotected spots in the defense.

The Giants had a well balanced, diversified offense and solid defense. Both were anchored by Hall-of-Famer Mel Hein, playing center and linebacker.

The Giants also had a slick passer and ball handler in tailback Harry Newman. Newman was to have a fine day in this game, passing for 201 yards and two touchdowns. His percentage was an eyebrow lifting 13 out of 19.

The first half ended with the score Giants 7, Bears 6. A Newman pass play and successful point after touchdown more than matched two field goals by Jack "Automatic" Manders. One kick was a 40-yarder aided by those closer goal posts.

Manders kicked another field goal later in the game. The season record up to this time was only ten and Manders had kicked three in one game.

There were a couple of strange plays in the game, both by the Giants.

In the first quarter the Giants tried to sneak by with a bizzare center eligible "pass." The team even quietly alerted the officials to the play so there could be no question about its legality.

It worked, or was supposed to work this way: Hein the center, had all the linemen on his right except the left end who shifted back a yard before the snap, making Hein an end after a wingback moved up to the line on the far right.

Newman came right up under Hein like a T-formation quarterback instead of in the usual tailback formation the Giants used. Hein snapped the ball back between his legs and Newman put a "pass" right back in Hein's hands, then dropped back, faking that he still had the ball.

Hein was also supposed to fake a block then amble downfield unnoticed. But like any linemen who find their hands on the ball, Hein got flustered and immediately started to run. A Bear safety man spotted the lumbering lineman and knocked him down, 15 yards short of the goal line. The Giants failed to score on that drive.

In the second half, the Giants pulled an unintentional razzle-dazzle play that did work.

Newman handed off to the Giant's power runner Ken Strong on a reverse to the left. But Strong saw that there was no hole in the line. So he looked around, saw Newman standing idly by and flipped the ball back to him.

Newman was a bit shocked but began scrambling around to his right. Strong meanwhile had wandered into the end zone, unnoticed by the Bears. Finally Newman saw him waving madly behind the goal line and hit him with a pass. At the time it brought the score to 21-16, Giants. The Giants liked that play so

Bill Hewitt (without helmet) of the Chicago Bears laterals to Bill Karr for the winning touchdown in the 1933 National Football League championship game.

much they tried it in later games, but it never worked again.

Newman was hot in the second half. He moved the Giants 73 yards to a score with his strong passing arm.

The Bears, meanwhile, were not without a trick or two of their own. They worked a fake punt for a 67 yard pass. Then they scored on a bit of deception involving the awesome Nagurski.

The Bears snapped the ball and Nagurski got it and started on what looked like a typical Bronko charge into the line. Suddenly he braked to a stop. Then, more like a moose than a gazelle, Nagurski executed a little jump pass to right end Bill Karr who waltzed untouched into the end zone behind the amazed Giant defenders.

Late in the fourth quarter, with the score 21-16 in favor of the Giants, the Bears tried the same number from the New York 33. Nagurski faked, did his little ballet, and this time left end Bill Hewitt took the jump pass.

But Giant halfback Dale Burnett was ready this time and ran over to stop Hewitt. At the last second Hewitt lateralled to Karr who got a block and ran for a score. The Bears led 23-21.

The Giants made one more try and almost matched the Bears pass-lateral play for a score. Newman threw to Burnett who turned and headed for the Bear goal line. And he had a teammate trailing him, ready for the pitch.

The only Bear defender left was Grange, one of the best defensive backs in the game.

Grange could see the lateral shaping up so he instinctively grabbed Burnett high around the shoulders. Burnett's arms were pinned and Grange brought him down.

The game thus ended with a Bear hug that was anything but affectionate. And the Bears became the first champions of the two-division NFL.

Chicago Bears vs. Washington Redskins December 12, 1937

IN THE rugged world of professional football, sportsmanship often fails to extend beyond the players benches into the stands. Fans want victory by the good guys, their team, and violence, destruction and defeat for the villains, the visitors.

So it was the ultimate tribute, when 15,878 shivering miserable Chicago fans—disappointed by the imminent defeat of their beloved Bears—stood as one in icy Wrigley Field and applauded Slingin' Sammy Baugh as he left the field late in the game.

Baugh, one of the greatest passers in the history of the game, had led his Washington Redskin team to a 28-21 lead that proved to be the final score. Baugh had put on a spectacular performance, a memorable performance, and the Chicago fans appreciated it.

And this was Baugh's rookie year, the first in a distinguished, 16-year career that stretched from the game's adolescence to maturity.

In his rookie season, Baugh completed 99 of 304 passes for 1,463 yards in 12 games. He was intercepted only 15 times. And this was when the old wing formation was still to be replaced by the modern T-formation, drop-back passing style. It was also a time when football players still played both ways, and Baugh was outstanding on defense, and was the finest punter in the game.

Baugh had been brought to the Redskins by the flamboyant showman of the professional football world, George Preston Marshall.

Marshall, had taken his team from Boston to Washington. Even with a good team, the Redskins had not drawn well in Boston. After Marshall saw 30,000 fans show up for a playoff game with the Packers on neutral ground in New York, he decided to move the team and picked Washington.

The Redskins had a solid team in 1936. With the acquisition of Baugh, they were a great one in 1937.

Marshall did not exactly pluck Baugh directly from the Texas Christian campus where young All-American Sammy had already earned his "Slinging" nickname.

Baugh, however, had signed a pro-contract with the St. Louis Cardinal baseball team. But there was a player named Marty Marion ahead of him at the shortstop position that Baugh played. So Marshall was able to convince Baugh that he would be better off flinging a football from the deep tailback spot than hoping to get in a major league baseball game to fling a baseball from the deep hole at short.

At the time of his signing with the Skins, Baugh was reported to be the highest paid pro football player in history. Estimates ranged from $7,000 up to $20,000.

And on the day of the championship game with the Bears, the winning team stood to pocket an extra $225 per man. The losers' share would be $127.

Baugh had appeared in Chicago earlier in the year, leading the College All Stars to a 6-0 victory over the Green Bay Packers in Soldier Field.

The day of the playoff game was wretched. The temperature was 15 degrees but the wind that whipped through Wrigley Field dropped it much lower.

The frozen field would have been better suited for hockey except for the jagged, frozen chunks of turf that treacherously littered the playing surface.

Some fans lit fires under the stands to keep warm as they waited for the opening kickoff.

But Baugh was to overcome the playing conditions and the "Monsters of the Midway"—the charging Bear line that sent him hobbling off the field in the second quarter.

On the first play, standing in his own endzone in his typical wide-stance, Baugh threw a 43-yard pass from the tailback spot to Cliff Battles. Later he hit three straight passes, giving steam to a Skin drive that lead to a score.

The Bears matched that drive, however, with Bernie Masterson flipping up the middle to Jack Manders, good for 51 yards to the Skin 11. Two plays later, Manders was in the endzone to tie the game.

Soon the Bears were marching again, and with a good mix of the ground and air games made it 14-7. But the Redskins had even more to worry about than the score at this point: Baugh had to be helped off the field after a jarring clash with the Bear players.

But Baugh came back to toss a strike to Wayne Millner who maneuvered across the Bear secondary, took the ball at midfield and went all the way. The game was tied.

Then the Bears used their awesome power to run the ball right over the Skins. Lead by the bruising fullback Bronko Nagurski and Manders again, they

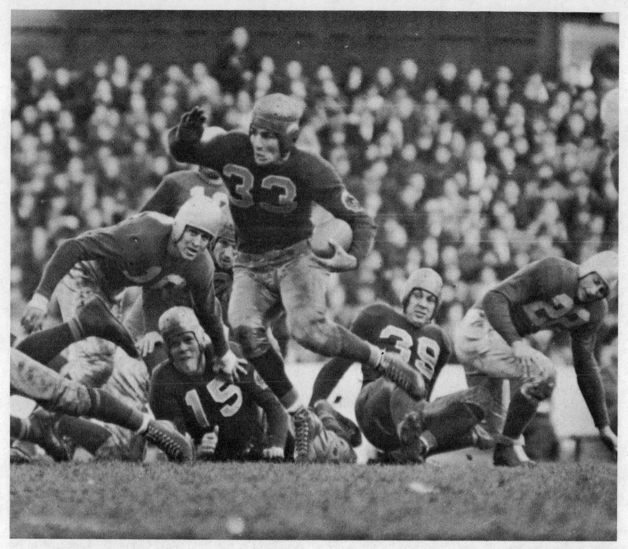

1937 was Sammy Baugh's rookie year, the first in a distinguished 16-year career. Pictured here against the Brooklyn Dodgers, Sammy shone on both offense and defense.

went to the Skins three, where the Redskin line held and almost forced a turn-over on a bobbled lateral.

But when the Skins put up an eight-man line, the Bears' Masterson just lobbed the ball over center for a TD. Score: 21-14 Bears.

But Baugh bombed back. He sent his right end, Millner down deep, hit him at midfield and again Millner outran the Bear defenders for a 78-yard score. The game was tied again.

It was in this third quarter that Baugh broke the game open. Mixing short strikes with runs the Skins moved downfield. A pass to Ed Justice from the 35 gave the Skins the lead 28-21.

The third quarter was the one that convinced the Chicago fans they were seeing a master at work. Baugh completed seven of nine passes for 220 yards and three touchdowns.

But there were still 15 minutes of playing time on the clock, and the shivering Bear fans expected their

team to warm their souls with more scores. But the fans and the Bears were disappointed.

The Bears did threaten twice, moving first to the Skins 24. But four passes all fell incomplete and the drive ended. Later the Bears moved 70 yards in five plays. A fight broke out in front of the Redskin bench when Baugh was jostled out of bounds. Time was running out.

The Bears made it to the Redskin seven-yard line. But the icy field betrayed the home-town team. Masterson slipped for a seven-yard loss.

Then a pass into the end zone went incomplete. It was virtually over.

Baugh soon left the field to the plaudits of the fans. He had beaten a good Bear team which had devised a special defense using five linemen and six-defenders, radical for that time.

Baugh had written the opening chapter on one of the greatest individual stories in pro football, his own.

Chicago Bears vs. Washington Redskins December 8, 1940

IT WAS the most devastating, complete rout in the history of pro football.

With the championship of the National Football League at stake, the Chicago Bears rolled to a shattering 73-0 victory over a bewildered Washington Redskin team.

And only a few weeks earlier the Redskins had defeated the Bears 7-3 at the end of the regular season, holding the Bears to only a field goal!

But in the championship game the Bears scored 11 touchdowns. The fledgling T-formation came of age in this game. The Bear offense, with an awesome mix of passes and "counter play" runs, moved with impunity towards the Redskin goal line.

The defense was overwhelming, invincible, intercepting eight Redskin passes.

On this cold December day, the Chicago Bears played virtually flawless football. The team approached perfection.

The Bear players were, of course, jubilant. They had their revenge against a team that had called them "crybabies" and "quitters" after the 7-3 game.

The Redskin players? Some cursed, some were silent and a few actually wept in shame as the score mounted before a crowd of subdued, embarassed Redskin fans in Griffith Stadium.

Aside from the astonishing score, the game was a milestone in football history because it established the T-formation as the standard offensive line-up in football, from the sandlots to the pros.

Soon after this game, the old wing back formations faded into a historical curiosity. The 1940 Redskins used a double wing formation propelled by their incomparable passer, Sammy Baugh.

From the double wing, Baugh would send out four fast receivers in an offensive blitz that often burned the standard three-man defensive backfields of the era.

The Redskins were a solid team. They had Baugh, the slinger, whom some still insist was the greatest quarterback the game has seen. They had other stars, including backs such as Max Krause, Ed Justice and Jimmy Johnston and end Charley Malone.

All in all the Redskins of 1940 were considered a better team than their 1937 championship squad.

The Bears had some of the greatest talent ever assembled on the 1940 team. They had linemen like center Bulldog Turner and Joe Stydahar and Danny Fortmann. In the backfield they had George McAfee, the Gale Sayers of his day, and right halfback Ray Nolting and fullback Bill Osmanski.

And at quarterback, Coach George Halas had picked Sid Luckman from Columbia University. Luckman was a skilled all-around athlete with the brainpower Halas wanted in a quarterback to run the multitude of plays off the new T-formation.

And the Bears had great depth, a fact illustrated in the championship game when Halas emptied the bench and the Bear "scrubs" continued to pile up the points.

Nevertheless, the Bears had had a disappointing season. They lost three games, including the final one to the Skins.

The Bears were convinced, however, that they had been "robbed" in that final contest by a bad call. With 40 seconds left in the game and the Redskins leading 7-3, the Bears completed a pass from midfield to McAfee who made it to the one.

McAfee faked an injury and the officials stopped the clock for the Bears, but gave them a five-yard penalty. On the final play, Osmanski appeared to be open for a pass. But the ball bounced off his chest and time ran out.

The Bears roared at the officials, claiming Osmanski's arms had been held. But the referees were not about to listen and the game was over.

The Redskins began jeering the Bear players as they left the field. They called them "crybabies" among other things. The Washington press picked up the theme and orchestrated it into a concert of catcalls.

And to top it off, the flamboyant Redskin owner, George Preston Marshall, popped off in public about the pouting Bears.

"The Bears are not a second half team. They're front runners—quitters. They're just a bunch of crybabies," he said.

The crafty Halas took those words, and like a master chef, concocted a bitter, but potent psychological nostrum for his team.

Halas clipped the news stories and pinned them to the Bears locker room bulletin board. He rubbed the salt of the Redskin taunts in the wounded spirits of his players at every opportunity.

"They got so worked up I was afraid they would

kill the Redskins, not just beat them," Halas chuckled later.

Halas, however, made further preparations for the Bear revenge. He called his friend and advisor Clark Shaughnessy, coach of the Stanford football team. Shaughnessy, one of the most ingenious football minds in the game, had worked with Halas on the invention of the T-formation.

Although the formation had been around for some time, and Halas's teams had used it, the system had not yet reached its potential.

Shaughnessy, whose Stanford team was awaiting a Rose Bowl game with Nebraska, flew from the West Coast to confer with Halas on strategy for the Redskin championship game.

After intensive study of Redskin game films, he noticed a flaw in the Redskin defense. The Bears had used a man in motion series in the earlier match-up and everytime a back moved laterally in motion a Redskin linebacker followed him.

Shaughnessy reasoned that counter plays to the opposite side would be an effective offensive weapon. So he devised a series of such counter plays and sharpened up the Bear offense.

The Bears were ready.

The weather on game day was crisp but sunny. "There was a feeling of tension in the air," Luckman recalled, "as though something tremendous was about to happen."

It did. The Bears got the opening kickoff and immediately tested Shaughnessy's theory. Nolting went in motion to the right. A Redskin linebacker moved with him. Luckman handed off to McAfee who went up the middle for seven. The Bears grinned.

Legend has it that the next play was the first of the counter plays. Films show it wasn't, however. It was an off-tackle slant by Osmanski to the same right side.

It was a spectacular play, nonetheless. Bullet Bill saw a hole at tackle close so he dipped to the outside and ran down the sidelines. At the Redskin 30 it appeared that two defenders had the angle and would close in and stop the play.

Suddenly, a vicious block by end George Wilson wiped out both defensemen and Osmanski ran on across the goal line. It went for 68 yards.

It was a sweet score for Osmanski, the man who couldn't make that winning catch in the earlier match.

That play set the pattern for the day. The Redskins had a chance, perhaps, to break that pattern early in the game. When they got the ball on the kickoff the Redskins started a drive on the ground at first.

Then Baugh sent his receivers out of the wing on the wing and threw a strike to Charley Malone who was open at the Bear 4-yard line. Malone looked back for the ball and was blinded by the sun. The pass slipped away from him and the drive stalled.

It was the last opportunity for the Redskins.

The Bears counter-marched 80 yards on 17 plays, with Luckman sneaking over from the two. When they got the ball again, second string fullback Joe Maniaci ran 42 yards to make it 21-0.

Baugh was soon taken out of the game and played little in the second half. The Redskin coaches saw no reason to let their star's reputation suffer by association with the debacle.

In the second quarter, the Bear's showed they were mortal, fumbling away a drive at the Skins 16. Baugh threw ten straight passes, taking his team 63 yards to the Bear 18. But that threat ended with an interception.

Before the half, Luckman hit end Ken Kavanaugh who made a leaping catch, evaded two defenders and made a 30-yard score.

It was 28-0 at halftime. The Bears came growling out of the locker room, however, remembering the "quitters label" the Skins has pasted on them.

The Bears scored seven more times in the second half. With a smiling Luckman on the bench, the Bears scored quickly after a desperate Washington series gave them good field position.

It was Nolting for ten yards followed by another Nolting run, for 23 yards up the middle. Baugh was badly faked out at the goal line.

Not much later, McAfee intercepted a Roy Zimmerman pass and zig-zagged up field for a 34-yard scoring play. By this time the score was 48-0.

Later Turner returned another interception for a score, and going into the fourth quarter the Bears lead was 54 to 0.

A double-reverse and 44 yard run by Harry Clark, a quick opener from the two after a recovered Redskin fumble; and finally a 50-yard drive with Clark going in from the one ended the blur of Bear TDs.

It was over except for the extra point attempt. At this point the Bears were passing for the conversion rather than kicking.

Why? After the tenth touchdown an embarrassed Washington management had to inform the officials on the field that the Bears extra point kicks had depleted the supply of footballs. There was only one left.

Halas, sensitive to the pecuniary plight of the Skins management, perhaps, and in a position to be magnanimous, agreed to pass for the point. The Bears made the point after the tenth TD and missed the try after the 11th.

In all the Bears gained 382 yards rushing and completed seven of ten passes for 119 yards. The Redskins got only 22 yards on the ground and in their desperation completed 20 out of 50 passing attempts for 223 yards, with eight interceptions.

The score by quarters went 21-0, 28-0, 54-0, 73-0.

The T-formation, as executed by the revenge-seeking Bears, matured under the attention the game focused on it.

Cleveland Browns vs. Los Angeles Rams December 24, 1950

FOOTBALLS and snowflakes seemed to float through the air in equal numbers in this Christmas Eve aerial extravaganza which ended with the Cleveland Browns on top, 30-28.

The Browns, with Otto Graham at quarterback, and the Rams, with Bob Waterfield doing the throwing, pushed the passing game to limits rarely achieved before in a National League Football championship game.

The approach to the game was epitomized by the Ram's pre-game strategy. In a reversal of the old chestnut about the need for a running game in order to establish a passing attack, the Ram's coach's figured it just the opposite.

"Our passing set up the runs," said offensive coach Hamp Pool. And the runs were not just your ordinary run-of-the-mill runs.

The Rams had designed a variation of the Statue of Liberty play in which the quarterback would drop back, fake a pass, and hand off to a halfback on a reverse.

The game started fast, with scores by both teams within three minutes. It ended with an exciting, desperation drive by the Browns that succeeded, and an attempt by the Rams that didn't. In between, the scoreboard kept rattling as the teams scampered across each other's goal lines.

There was an added interest in this contest, which in a sense was a kind of forerunner of the first Super Bowl between the NFL and the American Football League.

Cleveland had just joined the National Football League in 1950, moving over from the All-American Football Conference. The Browns had dominated their old league where they won the title from 1946 through 1949.

NFL fans had scoffed at the Browns before the start of the 1950 season. The rap was that now the Browns were in the "big leagues" and would fold under true professional competition.

The Browns didn't, however, live down to the reputation they were being saddled with. Cleveland lost only two games during the regular season, both to the New York Giants.

But the Browns managed to squeak by New York in a playoff game and found themselves facing the formidable Rams before a crowd of home-town fans in Cleveland's Municipal Stadium.

Both teams had great quarterbacks and receivers. The Browns included Mac Speedie, Dante Lavelli and Dub Jones. Waterfield could throw to Tom Fears, Elroy Hirsch and Glenn Davis. And he did.

On the first play of the game, Waterfield cranked up and connected on an 82-yard pass play to Davis, setting a record for the longest pass play and longest reception in a playoff.

The Browns had set up a new, modernized 5-3-3 defense designed to stop the pass. Davis had faked a block then beat the secondary to send the Browns coaches back to the drawing board.

The Browns, meanwhile, got the ball and within minutes Graham threw to Jones for a 31-yard scoring play.

The rest of the game had a see-saw flavor, although the Browns actually led only once until the final winning drive.

The scoring by quarters went 14-7 Rams; 14-13 Rams; 28-20 Rams; and finally 30-28 Browns.

The Browns led early in the third quarter, 20-14, only to see the Rams score 14 points in 21 seconds.

Those points were tallied first on a 71-yard drive. Then on the first play from scrimmage by the Browns following the kickoff, Marion Motley fumbled and the Rams Larry Brink ran it into the end zone for a Ram score.

The Browns found themselves behind early in the fourth quarter by eight points. They got seven of those points on a drive capped by a 14-yard pass play. Lou Groza kicked the extra point to make it 28-27.

The Cleveland coach Paul Brown, the Svengali of the sidelines, sent in the plays that made the drive work. The Rams had to lay back guarding against the long pass.

Brown had Graham go to the short stuff. He also decided to give Graham the go-ahead to run, already anathema in the age of the passing game and the invaluable quarterback. Graham did run and made some key yardage in the Brown's fourth quarter comeback.

With 1:50 left on the clock, the Browns got the ball on their own 32, still one point behind. On the first play Graham couldn't find an open receiver so he ran for 14, out of bounds to stop the clock.

Next, he hit Rex Baumgardner for 15. After miss-

The running of Cleveland's quarterback, Otto Graham, brought the Browns some key yardage.

ing a pass, Graham connected with Jones to the Rams 22. Another pass to Baumgardner took the ball to the 11. There were 40 seconds left. Graham ran with the ball to the center of the field. He got a yard and perfect position for the field goal attempt.

A chant went through the stands. "Groza. Groza!"

The big, burly tackle moved into kicking position. He was the Santa Claus that would deliver a big Christmas gift—the NFL title—to the Brown followers

During the regular season, "The Toe,'" had kicked 13 field goals, a regular season record. And Groza had kicked two in an 8-3 play-off squeaker over the Giants.

The Rams had little hope, although earlier in the game an extra point conversion had failed when the snap got away and Groza stood watching helplessly.

This time it all went according to the book. Groza put it through to give Cleveland the lead 30-28.

There was still time for the Rams to try a desperation play. After the kickoff, Waterfield was replaced by the strong-armed Dutchman, Norm Van Brocklin. Van Brocklin wound up and heaved the ball upfield. But it was intercepted on the five and the game was over.

This game produced six playoff records and tied three more. Graham hit 22 of 32 attempts for 298 yards and four TDs. Waterfield made 18 of 31 for 312 yards and one TD. It was classic offensive football and it sure wasn't dull.

Baltimore Colts vs. New York Giants December 28, 1958

WHEN football fans argue about the best games, this is the one that many—maybe most—insist was the greatest ever played.

For the first time a National Football League championship game went into "sudden death" overtime. But it had even more than that.

It had two fine teams, a magnificent goal line stand by the Giants, and come-from-behind rallies by both teams, including the Colt's final drive in the closing seconds to tie the contest at 17-17 and send the game into thrilling overtime.

And this game had 25-year-old Johnny Unitas, who led the Colts to a 23-17 victory and the title. Unitas gave a fantastic performance, perhaps one that epitomized all that was great in the long career of this all-time, all star quarterback.

When fans remember Unitas they are likely to remember him as he was in this game, with his cagey play calls, precision execution to match his precision football mind his ability to keep cool under the constant pressure of the Giants front four.

In the final two minutes of this game, Unitas earned his reputation as a quarterback who could "milk the clock" when it counted most and come up with the big plays when a big play had to be made to stave off defeat.

The 1958 Colts also had Ray Berry, the man who formed the other end of the classic Colt passing combination for so many years: Unitas to Berry. The Colts had strengthened the team with running back Lenny Moore, tackle Jim Parker and Big Daddy Lipscomb. Baltimore had breezed through the regular season to the divisional title. The only concern the team had was an injury to Unitas. But Unitas had recovered and was ready for the big one.

The Giants, meanwhile, had struggled through the season in the early going. After a poor start, the team got a divisional tie, winning the final four games, including the last one against the Cleveland Browns for the tie. Pat Summerall won that one by booting a field goal home from somewhere close to mid-field in a blinding snowstorm. The Giants met the Browns again in a playoff and beat them 10-0.

Throughout the season, the New York team depended primarily on the defense, which had a front four of ends Andy Robustelli and Jim Katcavage, and tackles Roosevelt Grier and Dick Modzelewski. Sam Huff anchored the defense from his middle linebacker spot.

The Colts came on strong in the first half and the Giant defense had to put out a super effort to keep the game close. Unitas was on target, with his calls, passes and handoffs. Once, even though the Giants secondary was playing in perfect position, Unitas beat it with a 60-yard bomb to Lenny Moore. At the half the score was 14-3 Colts.

In the third quarter, Baltimore threatened to break the game open. Unitas moved his club on a drive down to the Giant's three yard line and a first down. The Giants dug in.

Three times New York stopped the Colts from crossing that goal line. Allan "The Horse" Ameche tried twice and Unitas once on a sneak. On fourth down, Cliff Livingston threw Ameche for a loss back to the five. The Giants held.

For the Colts, who had disdained a field goal which would have given them a full, two-touchdown lead, the goal-line stand seemed to sap some of the team's confidence and drive.

But it gave the Giants the lift they needed. New York started to move now. Charley Conerly hit Kyle Rote who took the ball to the Colt 25, where he was hit and coughed up the ball. But his teammate Alex Webster scooped it up and took it all the way to the one yard line. Mel Triplett went in for the score.

Then, with the score 14-10 in favor of the Colts, the Giants shocked the Colts with a quick score the next time they got the ball. Conerly hit Bob Schnelker for 46 yards. Then Frank Gifford took a 16 yard swing pass and ran for the TD. Suddenly the Giants had the lead, 17-14.

The Colts were put in desperate bind as the fourth quarter moved on, but they were unable to get anything together. The Giant line was storming in on Unitas for big losses. Late in the quarter the Colts had to punt. The Giants had the ball with the clock running towards the two minute mark. A first down for the Giants would give them a chance to all but kill the clock and the Colts' chances.

The Giants almost did it. With third and four yards to go for the first down, Gifford broke to his right and shot forward. A wave of Baltimore players washed over him and brought him down. When the officials untangled the pile of flesh, they found the Colt's 6-4,

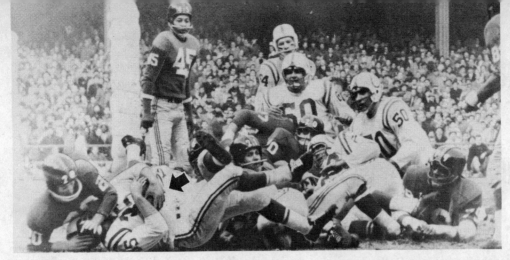

Alan (The Horse) Ameche, at left, goes in to score the Colts' first touchdown in the second period.

245-pound lineman Gino Marchetti on the bottom with Gifford. Marchetti broke an ankle making the play. But the official measurement showed the Giants were just inches short of that vital first down. The Giants decided to punt, and Don Chandler made it a good one, down to the Colts 14.

With 1:56 left, the Colts were down by three points and were 86 yards away from the Giants' goal line. Unitas went to work.

He missed his first pass, but a toss aimed at Lenny Moore was good for 11. Unitas knew the Giants would be laying back, guarding against the long bomb with time so short. So he kept to the shorter stuff in spite of the extreme pressure. He went to Berry and hit him three times. For a clutch catch for 25 yards. Then twice more, Berry grabbed the ball, milking the plays for 16 and 21 yards. With only seven seconds left, the ball was on the New York 13 yard line.

All that remained to cap one of the most memorable drives in football history was for Steve Myhra to kick the field goal and tie the game. The Colts' regular center, Leo Sanford, had been injured early in the game. So Buzz Nutter was called in to make the snap. An earlier Baltimore field goal attempt had been blocked. But everything went right for the Colts this time. The kick was good, the score tied, and sudden death began.

Baltimore coach Weeb Ewbank was convinced that the muddy turf had helped the Giants great goal line stand in the third quarter. So after losing the coin flip before the start of the overtime period, the Colts took the goal at the opposite end of the field.

In the overtime, every play was critical. Every play was a potential game winner or loser. New York had the first chance, but had to punt the ball away.

Baltimore got the ball on its own 20. The final and winning drive began with the Colts moving confidently, almost as though victory were ordained by some greater force beyond the playing field. The Colts and Unitas could not be denied on this final effort.

Unitas started cautiously, staying on the ground for the most part. A long pass to Lenny Moore almost clicked, but Lindon Crow was just able to tip the ball.

A key play came after big Modzelewski got through to dump Unitas for an eight yard loss. It was third down and 15 to go to keep the drive alive. With running back Moore in a slot formation, Unitas dropped back. He saw Moore was covered so looked for Berry. Berry was not only open but his defender had slipped. Unitas waved Berry farther upfield then hit him for a 20-yard gain.

Unitas' football savvy paid off in one of the biggest plays of the game. Unitas had been dumped repeatedly throughout the game. Now he had his revenge.

Unitas figured it was time for a play to take advantage of the hard charging Giant linemen.

"Modzelewski had been blowing in there pretty good," Unitas explained after the game. "When I came up to the line, I saw that Huff was going to back up to try to take away the passes to Berry."

So Unitas gave the ball to Ameche on a trap. Modzelewski was taken out by a devastating block by guard George Preas and Ameche ran for 23 yards down to the 20. The Giants had been caught in a pass prevent formation. And it was Unitas who caught them.

The ball was moved to the Giant 9 yard line, well within field goal range. But Unitas and the Colts wanted to fulfill their destiny by going all the way.

Forsaking conservatism completely, Unitas threw the ball, a risky pass right to the goal line. Jim Mutscheller grabbed it and went out of bounds on the one.

It all ended at 8 minutes and 15 seconds of overtime, with Ameche flying through a huge hole opened by Alex Sandusky, George Preas, Moore and Mutscheller.

The Baltimore fans exploded into a wacky frenzy of joy. They flooded the field and cavorted in impromptu victory celebrations long after their heroes had managed to escape to the locker room.

And throughout the country, millions of fans who had watched the contest on television were reluctant to shut off the tube and return to the hum-drum of everyday life. They continued to talk about the game and continue to do so to this day.

Some observers feel that this game so captured the imagination of sports fans in America, that it established professional football on a par with that other sport which called itself the national pastime.

Dallas Texans vs. Houston Oilers
December 23, 1962

AFTER 77 minutes and 54 official seconds of battle spread over six quarters of football, the Dallas Texans out-survived the defending champion Houston Oilers to take the American Football League title.

This was only the second "sudden death" overtime game in pro football, but the end hardly seemed sudden. Both teams seemed to be suffering more from a lingering illness that proved fatal to Houston first. Some strange malady prevented both teams from grasping victory when it was close at hand.

A rookie named Tom Brooker finally put an end to the affair with a field goal that gave Dallas the victory by a 20-17 score.

Sometimes a game can be memorable not only for the things that go right, but for the things that go spectacularly wrong, like a wrong-way run. This game had one of the game's "greatest goofs", an incredible blunder that could have cost Dallas the championship.

The blunder occurred at the start of the sudden death overtime period when the team captains walked out on the field for a crucial coin toss.

A light drizzle had turned the Jeppesen Stadium playing field into a mud hole. There was also a tricky 14-mile-per hour wind. Both the condition of the field and the wind were critical factors dictating strategy on the coin toss.

Dallas coach Hank Stram knew that his team had been struggling on offense all through the second half. Although Houston had managed to tie it 17-17, Stram thought his defense and punting game were still strong.

"We'd be in better position if we kicked off and tried to hold them deep in their own territory," Stram recalled.

"So we wanted to kick off and we wanted to take the wind," Stram said.

Stram knew that if Houston got the chance to kick off, George Blanda would kick the ball out of the end zone with the help of the following wind at his back.

That would put Dallas at its own 20, and the way things had been going, the Texans would probably have to punt—against the wind—giving the Oilers good field position. And Blanda, with his great toe, wouldn't need much to get into field goal range.

"So we wanted to kick off and we wanted to take the wind," Stram said.

He gave Dallas offensive captain Abner Haynes careful instructions: pick the north goal and the following wind if Dallas won the toss. Houston of course, also was well aware of the playing conditions and had figured out the same strategy. It too would pick the north goal if the coin came up its way.

Both teams watched anxiously as the coin was flipped. Haynes called it right. Dallas won the toss. Stram sighed with relief.

But then Haynes' mind fogged and went blank. He forgot the detailed discussion and decision on strategy. Haynes blurted out the wrong choice. He said Dallas wanted to kick-off!

The announcement stunned all parties to the contest. The Houston fans were stunned. The Houston players were stunned. The Dallas players were stunned. Stram was stunned.

Amazement gave way to fury and agonized frustration on the Dallas bench. Shock gave way to joy on the Houston side.

"We thought we were crazy," Blanda said later. "We thought they were crazy."

As it turned out Haynes was saved from total humiliation and perhaps from "sudden death" at the hands of his own teammates and coach by the events of the game.

The game was scoreless throughout the fifth quarter and the teams switched goals at the start of the sixth.

With the wind at his back, Brooker kicked his winning field goal three minutes into the sixth quarter.

But when the teams lined up for the kickoff to start the sudden death period, it looked bleak for Dallas.

Dallas had to kick off into the wind and Houston started on its 25 yard line. But Houston had to punt. They ran two plays that had the second-guessers babbling.

Blanda had started the series by hitting Willard Dewveall for nine yards. It was second and one, and Houston seemed to have a drive going.

Then instead of the short plunge for the first down, Blanda made two unorthodox calls. He tried two short flips to running back Billy Cannon. Both tosses were poorly thrown and Cannon was unable to get them.

"If there was any turning point, it was my dropping those two passes," Cannon later said. "If I catch the ball he (Blanda) is a hero." Blanda was not to be a

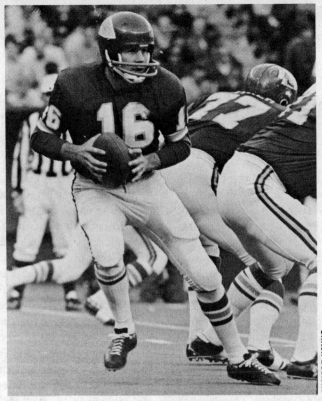

Lenny Dawson

hero on this day.

Dallas got the ball but could do nothing. And a feeble punt into the wind netted only 27 yards, giving Houston the ball on its own 45—great field position.

But Blanda was intercepted on this drive and Dallas brought the ball to the Houston 47—great field position. The Texans couldn't do a thing and punted to the Oilers 12. Bad field position for Houston.

But Blanda roared back. He hit three passes for 12, eight and 15 yards, mixed in some rushing plays and brought his team all the way to the Dallas 35, well within his kicking range, especially with the wind at his back.

But Houston was not ready to kick at that point, and tried to move closer to the goal posts. A running play lost a yard. Then Blanda tried a pass. It was intercepted by a defensive end, Bill Hull, who ran it back to midfield.

Ironically, Hull admitted later that he was confused on the play. He had dropped off the line to act as a fourth linebacker. The ball came right at him and he held on.

The game went into the second overtime. The stars for Dallas in the winning drive were crafty Lenny Dawson, the quarterback, and a running back named Jack Spikes, who had been injured much of the season and played behind flashy rookie Curtis McClinton.

Spikes grabbed a Dawson pass and took it to the Houston 38, the Texans' deepest penetration since the first half. Dawson sensed an Oiler blitz and sent Spikes through the line for 19 yards. A couple more plays set up the ball in the middle of the field at the 17 yard line.

Brooker, the rookie kicker, came out on this field. His teammates were afraid to say anything that could upset or unnerve him. But he came through, sending the ball through the uprights to end the long struggle.

It was a frustrating day for Houston, which seemed to dominate most of the play following an early 17-0 Dallas lead.

Blanda completed 23 of 46 passes for 261 yards, but also threw five interceptions.

A typical irony of the game occurred when Houston and Blanda had a chance to win the game with time running out near the end of the second half.

Blanda lined up at the 35 for his field goal attempt. In his long career he had made many from that distance.

Sherrill Headrick, a Dallas linebacker, who rarely rushed on kicking situations, said he wasn't going to on this occasion either.

"But I took a step and saw a hole in the middle, so I decided to blast in there," he recalled.

The kick hit Headrick's outstretched hand and fell to the ground.

Green Bay Packers vs. Baltimore Colts December 26, 1965

THIS WAS A battering, bruising brawl of a NFL Western Conference play-off game—three hours of battle which ended in a 13-10 sudden death overtime victory for the Green Bay Packers on a chilly, darkened Lambeau Field.

It was an unusual contest in which both teams were without their starting quarterbacks. For the Packers, the position was filled by well-traveled quarterback Zeke Bratkowski. For the Colts it was the unlikely halfback Tom Matte who almost pulled off an upset with a gutsy performance at a position he hadn't played since college.

When the game was over, many of the starting players were on the bench. They had been knocked out of action by the punishing contact. The Packer's Paul Hornung had been turned from a Golden Boy into a black and blue mass of aching bones and muscles. As he sat on the bench, Hornung could scarcely draw a breath without pain.

Others like Boyd Dowler, Ron Kostelnik and Henry Jordan joined the wounded list. Herb Adderley, the Packer defensive back, and not exactly a pussycat, called it the roughest game he'd ever played in.

Both teams had identical 10-3-1 records going into the contest. But Baltimore had lost starting quarterback Johnny Unitas and his backup Gary Cuozzo. Both were injured and completely unavailable.

So the vital quarterbacking job fell on Matte a hard playing, rugged, running back who had been a roll-out quarterback at Ohio State. But he had been primarily a runner even then, rarely throwing a pass.

Matte went into the championship game with plenty of determination, little experience at the position, and the plays taped to his wrist.

The Packers, meanwhile, had their outstanding quarterback Bart Starr ready to go. But he didn't last long. The match got off to a disastrous start for the Packers and the crowd of 50,484 fans who came to watch them.

On the very first play, Starr threw a pass to tight end Bill Anderson, who held it—long enough for a completion but then bobbled it after a hard shot from the Colts' Lenny Lyles. Don Shinnick picked up the loose ball and ran 25 yards into the Packer end zone.

In addition to the shock of the sudden score, the Packers fans were horrified to see Starr being picked up from the ground and helped off to the sidelines.

Starr had tried to knock out some of the Colt interference on Shinnick's runback. Instead he got knocked out of the game himself with a rib injury. Starr was able to come back to hold on extra point and field goal attempts. But that was it. His job went over to the 34-year-old Bratkowski.

Only 21 seconds had elapsed on the clock.

Bratkowski was able to move his team but mistakes stopped all the early Packer scoring thrusts.

Baltimore moved in the second quarter on the ground from its own 25 to the Green Bay 7 yard line. Matte, Lenny Moore and Jerry Hill supplied most of the yardage in the drive. Lou Michaels kicked a three-pointer after the Pack defense stiffened. It was 10-0 and seemed to be shaping up into an upset.

Then a break for the Packers. A pass interference call gave them the ball and a first down on the Colt 9 yard line. Goal to go.

The Packers had their great backfield duo of Hornung and the vicious Jim Taylor. And there were only two yards between them and pay dirt. But there were also a few sizeable obstacles like Ordell Braase and the other Baltimore linemen.

The obstacles proved insurmountable this time. In a determined goal line stand, the Colts held. Taylor was thrown back, then Hornung was stopped for a loss of a few feet. On fourth down Taylor was stopped inches from the goal line.

In the second half, with the score still 10-0, the Packers got another break. A bad snap from center forced the Baltimore punter Tom Gilburg to jump high in the air for the ball. He got it, but wasn't able to get a kick off before Packers swarmed over him.

The Pack had the ball on the Colt 35. Bratkowski threw the ball at Carrol Dale, who made an amazing catch even after being tripped. This time the Colts couldn't stop the Packers, and Hornung smashed into the end zone from the one to make the score 10-7.

The Packers seemed to be in control from this point, but, again, interceptions stopped them from going all the way for the lead or even tying points.

Finally, with 9:03 left in the game, the Packers started from their own 28. Dowler took a pass for 11. Then a few plays later, it appeared that the Colts had thwarted the drive and perhaps the Packers hopes of winning.

Bratkowski was nailed back on his own 42 for a

Tom Matte

loss. But the officials charged Billy Ray Smith of the Colts with unnecessary roughness. Green Bay got the ball on the Colt 43 along with a first down.

"A lousy call," Smith fumed.

The Packers went down to the 20. A touchdown would have given them the lead and an apparent victory. But the drive sputtered and Green Bay had to try for the tie.

With 2:02 left, Don Chandler made it look easy to the relieved Packer fans in the stands. It was sudden death.

The Packers won the toss but could make only two yards on its first series. The Colts got good position on their 41 after the punt. But they had to punt too. Green Bay soon punted again. This time Matte almost made it.

Matte began rolling. He ripped off 22 yards in three straight carries. At this point, the Packer defense made a change in alignment. Willie Davis explained later that he moved to play head-on against the Colt tackle and let linebacker Ray Nitschke take the outside. It worked.

After the switch, Matte was stopped for losses of one and two yards. With the line of scrimmage the Packer 37, Michaels had a chance to end it. The snap was low. His kick was short.

Now the Packers began to move, largely on the combination of Bratkowski to Bill Anderson. That combo may not be remembered as readily as Starr-Dale or Starr-Dowler, but in this game it was everything.

Anderson was a castoff who had come out of retirement. A former Washington Redskin tight end, he had eight catches for 78 yards in the game.

Even though he was a bit foggy from a hard shot he took in the game, Anderson "beat our zone defenses" with hook patterns, Colt coach Don Shula conceded later.

The Brat hit Anderson on the final drive for 18 yards to the 42 yard line. Later Dale made a tip toeing, dancing catch at the sidelines for 18 yards, taking the ball to the 26. Green Bay ran three plays into the center of the line, gaining eight yards and keeping field position for a kick.

This was it, finally. The old pro Chandler kicking, with the hurting Starr holding and center Bill Curry making the snap. It rose in the twilight, heading towards the goal posts so far away. It was good. The victory stirred enough adrenalin in the Packers to enable them to jump and cheer a bit. The Colts stamped and screamed and argued and swore it was wide. To no avail. The Colts stormed off the field, the losers, but not defeated.

Green Bay coach Vince Lombardi praised his team for overcoming that first play disaster. Bratkowski ended up with 22 of 39 passes for 248 yards.

Lombardi did give credit to the Colts and Matte. And Matte deserved something. He threw only 12 times, completing five for 40 yards. But he carried the ball 17 times for 57. And if not for that defensive shift, the quarterback who wasn't might have done it all anyway

Green Bay Packers vs. Dallas Cowboys December 31, 1967

"THIS WAS IT. This was our greatest game," Vince Lombardi said after the dramatic ending to this National Football League championship contest that many remember as the "Ice Bowl."

For millions of fans who watched in the warmth of their living rooms or for the 50,000 who suffered in the stands of Lambeau Field, this game produced one of the most memorable images in football:

With only 13 seconds left, Green Bay quarterback Bart Starr, number 15, squirmed into the Dallas Cowboy end zone behind jarring blocks by guard Jerry Kramer and center Ken Bowman.

That do-or-die play gave the indomitable snowmen of the north, the Packers, a 21-17 victory and their third straight NFL title and the right to go on to the Super Bowl.

And for the Cowboys, the defeat marked the second year in a row that the Packers had kept them from reaching the top. The defeat also wiped out a courageous effort by the Cowboy's heralded "Doomsday Defense."

The game was played under miserable conditions. It was 13 degrees below zero. The playing field was an icy tundra.

The shivering fans, had, in spite of reason, filled the stadium, and huddled under blankets and sleeping bags. They warmed their bodies and spirits by cheering their beloved Pack on to victory.

When the game began the fans were glowing. The Packers scored the first time they got the ball, moving 82 yards in 16 plays. A Starr to Boyd Dowler pass up the middle finished the drive.

Then, early in the second quarter, the Packers went down to the Dallas 43 where Starr called for one of his favorite gambits. With third and one, he pitched the long bomb to Dowler, who beat Mel Renfro and scored. It was 14-0 Packers and looked like a laugher.

But as the two and one-half hour game crept to within five minutes of the end, the Packer fans' hopes had dropped along with the temperature. The Cowboys, spurred by their defense, were leading 17-14.

The Dallas defense dumped Starr eight times during the game for 76 yards in losses. On one of those dumps, with the ball at the Pack 26, Willie Townes smashed into Starr and jarred the ball loose. George Andrie picked it up and ran into the end zone. It was only a 14-7 Packer lead now.

With less than two minutes left in the first half, Packer receiver Willie Wood fumbled a punt. The Cowboys got the ball and cashed in with a field goal, making the score 14-10. Dallas dominated the third quarter, but missed on two scoring opportunities. Finally, in the fourth quarter the Cowboy offense came up with something.

Halfback Dan Reeves threw an option pass to Lance Rentzel and with Bob Jeter out of position, Rentzel went 50 yards to score. Dallas led 17-14, for the first time in the game.

With less than five minutes left, the Packers got the ball on their own 32 yard line. Across the frozen turf, the goal line stood a distant 68 yards away. It was the Pack's last chance.

"Maybe this is the year we don't make it, that it all ends," guard Jerry Kramer thought as his team huddled before the start of the final drive. "But I knew every guy made up his mind that if we were going down, we were going down trying."

The Packers could do no less than a do-or-die effort, because they had Lombardi on the sidelines, pacing in his longcoat and Russian cap, like a commissar whose quota called for victory and victory alone. Lombardi had forged his men into champions. This would be the test of their mettle.

The test began. Starr threw a play-option pass to running back Donny Anderson. It picked up six yards. Then Chuck Mercein—a running back the Packers picked up from the Washington Redskin taxi squad—went off tackle on a slant for a first down to the Packers 45.

A pass to Boyd Bowler gave the Packers another first down to the Dallas 42.

Then a near-disaster for Green Bay. Anderson moved to the outside and tried to throw an option pass. But he was nailed by the 6'4", 265-pound Townes, who crashed through the blocking to bring Anderson down for a nine-yard loss.

The cold crept into the Packer fans' bones. The Cowboys were fired up. But Starr and the Packers kept their cool.

Everyone knew Starr would throw and he did, twice. Both were complete and both went to Anderson for ten and nine yards and a critical first down.

The ball was on the 30 yard line now. The clock showed 1:35 left.

Packer Boyd Dowler (86) on the receiving end of a Bart Starr pass. Pursuer is Mel Renfro.

Starr had noticed that Mercein was not being covered closely when he left the backfield on passing plays. So Starr floated a pass out to Mercein in the flat. With a great individual effort, Mercein eluded Cowboy linebacker Chuck Howley. Mercein, who seemed trapped for no gain, made 19 yards.

"There was no traction. The advantage had gone to the offense," Howley said later.

Now, with first and ten on the Dallas 11, Starr "suckered" no less than Dallas All-Pro tackle Bob Lilly.

Guard Gale Gillingham pulled to the right. It looked like a Packer sweep. Lilly followed Gillingham leaving a big hole at the line. Mercein shot through the gap for eight yards down to the 3 yard line.

Now there were 54 seconds left. The Packers called time.

When play began, Anderson got the ball and the big back got two yards and a first down. With 30 seconds left, Anderson got the call again. The footing was bad and Anderson was stopped for no gain. Ten precious seconds had been spent for nothing.

But Starr went to Anderson a third time. This time the ice cut his feet out from under him before he reached the line. Anderson was able to stumble back to the one—but no farther. The play cost another four seconds and the Packer's last time-out.

The clock showed 16 seconds. Starr went to confer with Lombardi. The Packers had two more plays but it was doubtful whether they could run off more than one. A field goal would tie it 17-17, sending the game into overtime.

Starr said the thought of a field goal never entered his mind. Lombardi said:

"I just got stubborn. I told them that if they couldn't put the ball in the end zone, they didn't deserve to be NFL champions."

So Lombardi asked about the footing. It was bad.

The linemen and backs could not dig in. Lombardi finally sent Starr back to the huddle. Ask the lineman about a play call, he said.

Starr and his linemen decided that a wedge would be best, rather than one-on-one blocking. They looked over the Dallas line and ruled out Bob Lilly as the man to run at. Lilly comes in low and hard.

They settled on Jethro Pugh, 6'6", 260-pounds and an outstanding left tackle. But he had only two years of pro experience and charged higher than Lilly.

There is some dispute whether the decision to have Starr keep the ball or hand off was made in the huddle. Kramer recalled that it was. Starr, however, says the decision was made as the teams lined up for the snap.

He said that as he bent over center Bowman, the icy footing and Anderson's slip on the previous play "flashed through my mind." And in a similar spot a year ago in game against San Francisco, Starr had kept the ball.

The teams squared off, great clouds of steam pouring from their nostrils.

"I dug my cleats in, got a firm hold with my right foot, and we got down in position," Kramer said.

Starr barked "hut."

Kramer bolted off the line and slammed into Pugh almost before Pugh had moved. With Bowman's help they pushed the massive lineman aside. Townes, the Dallas end on Pugh's side, tried but couldn't quite close the gap.

Starr chugged and squirted through the hole, stretched out and landed over the goal line.

There was a kickoff with 13 seconds left. The ball sailed out of the end zone. No runback. Two Dallas passes by quarterback Don Meredith, who was more dud than dandy in much of the game, fell incomplete and the Packers once again proved their greatness.

New York Jets vs. Baltimore Colts
January 12, 1969

JOE NAMATH and his Jets took a giant step forward for that portion of mankind that played in the American Football League. The Baltimore Colts, on the other hand, and the National Football League, had a great fall. And so the Jets shocking 16-7 victory in this Super Bowl III, established the two leagues on an equal basis. David beat Goliath. The upstart American Football League slingshoted down the supposedly invincible champions of the venerable NFL.

Before the game in Miami's Orange Bowl, the Jets were considered—if at all—with condescension, if not contempt—by the seers and sages of the press and by NFL fans throughout the country. Even AFL fans outside of Fun City must have quietly conceded a mismatch.

Twice before in the newly-created Super Bowl contest, the Green Bay Packers had clearly established that the game was super only because it had one super team in it—the NFL representative. The Super Bowl was devised after the merger of the NFL and AFL and in games I and II, the Packers easily beat the Kansas City Chiefs, 35-10 and the Oakland Raiders, 33-14.

And there was little reason, so most thought, to believe that the Colts would not carry on that tradition. They had won 15 regular season games, even without Johnny Unitas, who was out with a sore elbow. In the NFL playoff game, the Colts trounced the Cleveland Browns, 34-0, the fourth shutout of the year for the Baltimore defense.

One of the major weapons in the Colt's defensive arsenal was the strong front line and constant threat of the blitz. Few quarterbacks had been cool enough to withstand the pressure and pick the holes left by the shifting zone defenses of the Colts.

On offense, Coach Don Shula had been content to devise a conservative attack, based on a steady, punishing ground game. With Unitas out, the Colt's passing attack was usually limited to short strikes thrown by old veteran Earl Morrall. Morrall made up in experience and determination what he lacked in chraisma. As Unitas's sub, Morrall was good enough to lead his team to the Super Bowl and win the Most Valuable Player Award that year in the process.

And the Jets? What did they have to disprove the oddsmakers, who had generously tabbed them only three touchdown underdogs? Well the Jets had Joe Namath, "Super Joe," "Broadway Joe."

Namath was a man who had it and didn't mind flaunting it, whether it was his playing talent as a quarterback, or his other talents off the field. Away from the game, Namath lived the swinging life. He liked girls and he liked something stronger than milk, and to hell with the two-dimensional, bubble gum card image of the football player as a saint.

Namath never tried to hide his life-style and he said whatever was on his mind. Before the Super Bowl Namath said:

"We're going to win."

"He said we were going to win for sure. We won. He didn't lie. He never does," said Jet tackle Dave Herman.

The Jet's coach, Weeb Ewbank, also thought his team could win if they could keep to the strategy he had prepared. Winning a Super Bowl is incentive enough for any coach, but Ewbank had additional reason for wanting a victory. Six years earlier he had been fired as coach of the Colts, after nine years and NFL titles in 1958 & 1959. Ewbank had collected some Colt castoffs to buttress the Jet team. He wanted this game badly.

To achieve his dream, Ewbank devised a deceptively simple game plan. During the season, the Jets had often capitalized on Namath's strong arm and went all out through the air. Usually the aerial blitz worked, with a couple of notable exceptions when Namath was intercepted ten times in two games.

Ewbank knew that to beat the Colts, however, the Jets would have to play near-errorless ball. That meant no fumbles and no interceptions. Instead of a flashy, go-for-broke approach, he worked out a game plan of straight power running plays mixed in with short hook and flare passes. The Jets worked on execution rather than eccentricity as the big game approached.

One other matter of strategy: Ewbank not only prepared his men for the fearsome Colt blitz, he felt he could use it to his team's advantage. Ewbank was hoping the Colts would blitz and often.

The game itself was a curious mix of tortoise-like cautious football by the Jets coupled with the confident hare-like attack of the Colts, who were, nevertheless, frustrated throughout the day.

The Colts often seemed ready to blow the game open, especially in the first half. But a combination of bad luck and ineptness in key situations, prevented the Colts from crossing the Jet goal line. The Jets' hang-tough defense also had something to do with it.

On the Colts first drive, they marched downfield with authority. Four first downs in eight plays. But then three Morrall passes sputtered, Lou Michaels missed a field goal from the 27. No points.

Later, the Colts' Lenny Lyles forced George Sauer of the Jets to fumble, giving Baltimore that ball on the New York 12. But three plays later, a Morrall pass bounced high off of the intended receiver, Tom Mitchell. Jet cornerback, Randy Beverly, who was out of position on the play, snatched the football for an interception. No points for the Colts.

And after a fine 58 yard run by halfback Tom Matte, the Colts failed again. The Jets bad boy defensive back Johnny Sample made an interception on the 2 yard line. Still no points for the Colts.

The Jets meanwhile, launched their game plan and soon found that fullback Mat Snell could run the ball right through the highly regarded Colt line. Snell following consistent blocking by guard Bob Talamini, tackle Winston Hill and halfback Emerson Boozer was to pound out 121 yards on the ground this day.

Later Hill admitted that the Colts' great defensive end, Bubba Smith was not up to par. "He must have been hurting," a still surprised Hill explained.

Snell carried the ball four times to spur an 80-yard Jet drive in the first half. Snell himself went over from the 4 yard line. Seven points for the Jets. Still none for Baltimore.

When Namath had to throw, he kept it simple and short to left end George Sauer. Namath said later he didn't feel he was throwing particularly well.

"But he (Sauer) was making some great catches," Namath said.

The Sauer-Namath rapport, worked to beat the Colt blitz. They had agreed that when the Colt safety moved up to blitz, Sauer would fake inside then fly outside. It worked.

Throughout the game, it seemed that the Colts could not believe the Jets would send Snell right at them on weakside slants. The Colts also kept waiting for a Namath bomb. Instead he stuck to his peashooter.

Near the end of the first half, with the Jets leading 7-0, the Colts tried some flim-flam. Matte took a handoff then flipped it back to Morrall. Jimmy Orr was wide open 42 yards downfield in the Jet end zone. But Morrall never saw him, some say because of the crowd that had already gathered behind the end zone.

Morrall threw down the middle into a crowd and was intercepted again.

The Jets went into the locker room feeling that maybe Namath was right when he said they would

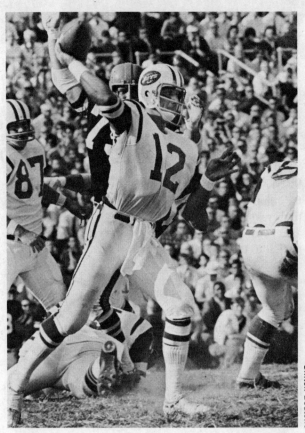

Joe Namath

win. They began to believe in themselves. The Colts, however, didn't believe it—not yet anyway.

Baltimore came out for the second half ready to fight. But the fight was taken right out of them when Matte fumbled on the first play from scrimmage.

Jets linebacker Ralph Baker fell on the ball on the Colt 33. Five plays later the Jets' Jim Turner kicked a field goal from the 11. The Jets lead now 10-0. Ewbank said later that Matte's fumble was a turning point.

Turner added two more field goals in the second half, while Baltimore became more and more bogged down, unable to do anything right.

Shula finally made a desperation move. He sent the ailing Unitas into the game to see if some of the old magic was still there. The stoop-shouldered supersandlotter trotted in with those high-topped shoes and pigeon toed gait.

The stage was set for a movie script ending. The old crew cut injured pro comes off the bench to vanquish the pesky upstarts with their cocky, long-haired man-about-town quarterback.

It didn't happen that way. Unitas did lead the Colts to a token touchdown. But his timing was off. His aching elbow bothered him and he just could not save face for the Colts or the NFL. The era of parity between the leagues and the ascendency of the "new breed" of the independent long mained player had arrived.

Miami Dolphins vs. Kansas City Chiefs
December 25, 1971

IT WAS THE longest game in pro football history, 82 minutes and 40 seconds. Some say it was also the greatest game in football.

It was a game in which the players literally appealed to their gods for victory as the match stretched on into a sixth quarter.

"By the end people on both sides—grown men—were praying on the sidelines for victory," recalled KC quarterback Len Dawson. "I've never been in a game where the players, unashamedly and openly prayed on the sidelines before."

Perhaps the Dolphins prayed harder. Before a stadium packed with Kansas City fans, the Miami kicker, Garo Yepremian, sent the ball through the uprights. It was truly sudden death for KC by a score of 27-24.

Miami was the new American Football Conference champion.

In the last four years the Chiefs had lost only three home games. Only weeks earlier the Chiefs had defeated their arch rivals, the Oakland Raiders, in this same stadium.

And at several points in this playoff game, the Chiefs appeared to be on their way to victory, only to have the stubborn Dolphins fight back successfully.

And with less than two minutes left in regulation time, the Chiefs were on the Miami 31 yard line with the man called the best kicker in football waiting to do his thing and give the crowd a Christmas day they would long remember.

That man was Jan Stenerud. Somehow he missed that field goal. To put it simply, he blew it. As his coach Hank Stram told reporters later, "It all came down to one indisputable factor. They made their kicks and we missed ours."

When Stenerud's soccer-style kick failed to hook through the goal posts and sailed straight past the right upright, his teammates were stunned. The champagne taste of victory they had begun to anticipate turned into the vinegar of disappointment.

"We were shocked. For a few minutes we didn't believe it had happened," Dawson said. "But we didn't give up. We never did give up."

When the game began it appeared that everything would go exactly according to the Chiefs' game plan, except perhaps for the weather. Instead of biting cold, which Kansas City reasoned would bother the warm-

weather Floridians, it was an unseasonably warm 63 degrees.

The Chiefs had known they would have to play a patient game against the zone defenses that Miami coach Don Shula had brought with him from the Baltimore Colts. The Chiefs plan called for ball control, and this they did the first time they got the football. The Chiefs took seven minutes to move down to the Miami 24 where Stenerud kicked a field goal.

The KC defense, meanwhile, was stifling the Dolphin's offense. Later, Dawson flipped a swing pass to running back Ed Podolak who took it in for a score. It was 10-0 Chiefs and looking good for the two-time AFL champs.

"But for some unknown reason we let it slip away," Dawson recalled.

That mysterious essence that the sages call "momentum" deserted the Chiefs and infused the Miami team instead.

Miami quarterback Bob Griese orchestrated a stirring mach that concluded with a booming crash into the end zone by Larry Csonka from the 1 yard line.

Yepremian booted a 14-yard field goal to tie the score at 10-10 as time was running out in the first half.

In the second half, KC pulled ahead twice but could not prevent Miami from knotting the score each time. First Jim Otis got the final yard of a Chief drive. Miami marched back with Jim Kiick going over from the one.

Going into the fourth quarter, the Chiefs stuck to their plan of controlled football. Podolak scored his second TD on an off-tackle run. It was 24-17 Chiefs. But with about two minutes left, Griese hit tight end Marv Fleming with a short hook pass from the five and tied it again.

As the teams lined up for the kickoff, Dawson said he felt his team was going to win it right then. It almost did.

Podolak took the kickoff and, instead of following the usual KC runback pattern to the sidelines, he started up the middle of the field. At his own 30 he cut to the outside and was in the clear. Little Yepremian, the only man between Podolak and the goal line, made a token move towards the thundering KC running back. Podolak veered away slightly. It was enough to give a Miami defender the angle and he was able to catch Podolak at the Dolphin's 22. But

Miami's Lloyd Mumphord blocks a field goal attempt by Kansas City's Jan Stenerud.

it was a stunning 78-yard kickoff return.

The Chiefs lost some ground in the next three plays, back to the 31. With only 35 seconds left Stenerud trotted out on the field, missed the field goal, lost his unofficial claim to the title "best kicker in football," and lost a chance for victory for the Chiefs.

In the first quarter of sudden death overtime, the Chiefs and Stenerud got another chance. KC worked the ball to the Miami 35. But this time the field goal attempt was blocked.

Then the game turned into a grueling battle of defenses and the punting teams. Time ticked on and Christmas Day meals grew cold and conversation stopped in the nation's homes as 60 million football fans followed the contest.

Finally the play that set up the coup de grace. It was a "roll right, trap left" which suckered the KC linemen completely. The ball was snapped and Miami flowed right. Csonka got the ball cut back across the flow behind guard Larry Little who was shocked to find no one in front of him to block. Csonka grabbed on to Little's rear and the Odd Couple rambled downfield for 29 yards.

Now it was Yepremian's turn. The little Cypriot tie maker, a Detroit Lion reject, had been by-passed in the selection of AFC Pro Bowl kicker, Stenerud was picked instead, even though statistically he had had his worst season.

As the teams lined up for the 37-yard field goal attempt, 50,374 partisan KC fans stood up along with players on both benches. The stadium was quiet as the ball was snapped, bodies clashed, and Yepremian's foot met the ball.

The ball soared towards the goal posts and eyes switched from it to back judge Adrian Burke. They waited, like Romans at the Coliseum waiting to see whether their favorite gladiators would get the thumbs up signal that meant life, or thumbs down that meant death. The official shot his arms up into the air. The kick was good. It was death.

The silent gloom in the vast stadium was broken only by the faint sounds of joy and elation from the Miami players as they carried Shula off the field.

"The Dolphins jumped and cheered in that stunned, silent stadium," Dawson said later. "A few Chiefs cried, but no one said a word. It was a game we'd all remember forever."

THE GAME I'LL NEVER FORGET

By Don Maynard, New York Jets

There's no question in my mind as to the game I'll never forget. To me it was the biggest game I've ever been in. It was the New York Jets against the Oakland Raiders in Shea Stadium for the American Football League championship on a cold windy day, Dec. 29, 1968, before over 62,000 win-starved New York fans.

Some of my teammates might pick our next game, our Super Bowl game against the Baltimore Colts as their most memorable game. We went into that game about 17 to 20 points underdogs and came out the winners. But to me the one against Oakland was bigger. If we hadn't of won that one there would have been no Super Bowl game for us. To me there just wasn't as much pressure riding on the Baltimore game as there was with the Oakland game. The way I figured it just getting into that game we already had $7,500 won. That took a lot of the pressure off.

So everything was riding on that game with Oakland. They were the defending AFL champions. They had the experience under their belts. They had already played in the pressure of championship games and the Super Bowls. That kind of experience is awfully important in championship games. It can keep you on an even keel when you get hit by a bad break or two.

For the Jets this was our first championship game of any kind. For our first few years in the league we were a pretty weak team. Now we were rebuilt, but we were still young in a lot of spots.

The Jets-Raider games were always pretty much of a knockdown and dragout affair. We always seemed to go at each other pretty good, and we weren't in the best of health. The last time we played the Raiders back in the middle of November I had a real big day, catching about ten for over 225 yards, but they scored twice in something like the last nine seconds to beat us 43 to 32 after it looked like we had it wrapped up.

Joe Namath got hit late in that game by Ben Davidson, their big defensive end, and got a fractured jaw on the play. After that game one of the writers asked Joe how he hurt his jaw and he told him, "I must have done it eating breakfast this morning."

So Joe was hurt, and George Sauer, our split end missed the last three games with an injury and missed out on the reception leadership by a couple of catches. I missed the last three games with a pulled hamstring

and lost the receiving yardage title by 15 yards, but when you're winning those things aren't that important.

We figured we could move the ball on them, but we knew we were going to have to play good defense to beat them because with Daryl Lamonica throwing to receivers like Fred Biletnikoff and Warren Wells and with runners like Hewritt Dixon and Pete Banaszak they could put a lot of points on the board in a hurry.

The wind is a fierce thing in Shea Stadium and we figured that at times it would be like a twelfth man on the field for us. We knew the wind, knew how tricky it could be and there was no way the Raiders could know it the way we did.

It was at our back in the first quarter. The Raiders won the toss and elected to receive giving us the wind. Our defense stopped them and Joe put us right to work.

I had a big day against their cornerback, George Atkinson, the first time against them. They were primarily a man-to-man team then with a lot of bump and run. So Joe decided to go to work on him. We started with the quick outs and sideline passes. He threw four times in that opening drive and three of them were to me. On the last one I ran a sideline pattern in the end zone and Joe hit me for about 14 yards and a touchdown.

Our defense stopped them without a score again and we moved the ball upfield again to the Oakland 26 before we stalled out. From there Jim Turner kicked a 33-yard field goal to make it 10-0 and it started to look easy. But after you've been in the game for a while you know that the good teams come clawing back just when they have to.

Oakland did. Now they had the wind and Lamonica drove them in. He hit Biletnikoff for 29 yards and the touchdown. Biletnikoff had a great day. He caught something like ten passes for 190 yards against us. But we stopped him when we really had to.

It was our turn again. We worked the ball down to the Oakland 29 and on fourth down Turner backed up and kicked a field goal into the swirling crosswind from 36 yards out. Blanda hit one for them just before the half from 26 yards out and we went into the locker room ahead 13 to 10.

We took the second half kickoff but couldn't get

a score and then Lamonica drove them deep into our territory. One of the keys to the game I think, is when our defense stopped them on our two and made them settle for a tying field goal by Blanda from the nine.

That goal line stand was a big tonic to the offense and Namath rolled us in for a score to take the lead again, hitting our tight end Pete Lammons for the touchdown from about 20 yards out.

It was comforting going into the fourth quarter when we had the wind at back again with that touchdown lead, but Oakland narrowed the gap when they drove down inside our 15, but once again our defense held. They were magnificent all day. Lamonica ended up with 401 yards passing but produced only one touchdown out of all that yardage. They were forced to settle for another field goal by Blanda.

Then things took a big turn. We were nursing the ball upfield, running with Matt Snell and Emerson Boozer and throwing the short, control passes, but I guess we went to the well once too often.

The call was a short out. I ran straight down about nine yards and made a sharp cut to the sideline, but Atkinson was ready this time. He stepped in front of me, picked off the pass on about our 37 and ran it back to the five before Joe knocked him out of bounds. One play later Pete Banaszak banged over for the touchdown.

There was a big letdown on our bench when we came off the field after that interception, but I knew we could come back. While we were waiting for the kickoff I went over to Joe and told him I thought I could beat Atkinson deep. He said, "OK, as soon as we get back in." One thing about Joe, he's got confidence. Nothing will ever shake it either.

Earl Christy gave us a good return out to our 32 and on the first play Joe hit George Sauer for a first down on the 42. We got back in the huddle and he looked at me as much as to say, "now?" I shook my head, "now!"

For most of the game Atkinson was playing right up on the line bumping me at the snap of the ball. Now he was laying off about five yards figuring he'd give us a couple of short ones if he had to but he didn't want to get beat deep.

At the snap I took off. I gave a fast feint to the sideline, but mostly I just tried to fly right past him. We were shoulder to shoulder, Atkinson and me and Joe let it fly.

When I looked up the ball was coming right on target to my inside shoulder, but just as I started to make my move to catch it a sudden gust of wind hit it and blew it to the other side. My mind went blank except for that ball. Somehow I shifted my hands and my head reached for it and felt my hands close around it. I was concentrating so hard on that ball I could feel the pebbley grain under my fingers. I was knocked out of bounds on the Oakland 4 yard line, but we were sure in good shape.

On the very next play Joe ran a play action, looked for Lammons who was covered, looked for Sauer who was covered, looked for Mathis who was covered. I ran about a four-second delayed hook into the middle as the fourth receiver and before I knew it I saw the ball coming right into my belly. That proved to be the winning touchdown.

Our defense made three more great stands to keep the Raiders out of the end zone, Verlon Biggs tackling Lamonica on our 26; Ralph Baker recovering a fumbled lateral at our 30, and stopping them in the closing minutes.

It wasn't the touchdown catch I remember so much it was that first one for 50 yards to set it up. As far as I'm concerned it was a million dollar catch, and I know it was the greatest catch I've ever made. One writer called it "the most memorable pass play in the history of the Jets." That's good enough for me. You can't improve on that.

THE GAME I'LL NEVER FORGET

By Larry Wilson, St. Louis Cardinals

THE DALLAS COWBOYS, for some reason, and the Cards had formed one of those natural rivalries since the day they came into football. I can't really explain it. I don't suppose anybody could. But its been a bruiser, every game we've played since they've come into the division with us.

Every game has been tough. Some have been great defensive battles with scores like 12-10, 10-10, 16-6,

and there have been some one-sided routs. We've beaten them by scores like 52 to 20 and 34 to 7, and they've whipped us 46 to 21 and 31 to 13, so you never know what's going to happen when these two teams meet.

Now take the game we played on a Monday night in the middle of November in 1970 in Dallas. It was our ninth game of the season and a big one for both teams. We had played earlier in the year and had beaten the Cowboys 20 to 7 in St. Louis. We were leading the division with a six and two record and they were one game behind at five and three. A win would put them in a tie and in position for a stretch run. A win would put us in great position for the division title.

Dallas had to win, but we were hot, coming into the game off two straight shutouts, 44 to 0 over Houston and 31 to 0 over New England.

Both teams were hitting real good and about the middle of the first quarter Ron Widby got off a long punt to Johnny Roland. He took the ball on about our 26, made a couple of great moves to get by the initial coverage, picked up a couple of blocks and made a great return, 74 yards for a touchdown. Johnny isn't known for having all the speed in the world, but it seemed like everyone on Dallas either had a shot at him or laid a hand on him, but he kept it moving and breaking tackles, right up the middle all the way, and put us on top.

That score held up through the first quarter and into the second and then we ran one of their own plays on them and completely fooled them. We had the ball on their 48, and if I remember right it was third and short. We were running the ball well and running it to our left. Our quarterback, Jim Hart, called a flanker reverse. Roland and MacArthur Lane started to the left and that drew the tight Cowboy defense over and then Hart slipped the ball to John Gilliam.

The Dallas defense had shifted to stop the line smash and Gilliam turned the corner clean, and with his kind of speed there was no one going to catch him. That and a field goal by Jim Bakken gave us a 17 to 0 halftime lead.

Dallas was moving the ball at times, but they couldn't move it when they had to. Our defense seemed to have them confused. We were running a lot of safety blitzes on them and mixing in some zones, and I guess they weren't really looking for the zones because we hadn't shown too much of it up to then.

I suppose I ought to say a little something about the safety blitz about here. A lot of people like to say I invented it or originated it or something like that. I've seen things printed to that effect and I've heard announcers refer to it. It's very flattering, but it isn't quite true.

The man who is responsible for it was our defensive coach, Chuck Drulis, and the man who was the inspiration for it was our other safety, Jerry Norton. Norton was always very quick getting up to the line and even into the backfield making tackles. During practice and in summer camp he used to run it and every time he did it he broke up the play. It was this success that caused Drulis to put it into our regular defensive game plan.

Actually the safety blitz is the safest kind of blitz you can run. When you put something like that in your defensive game plan, the other fellow has to prepare for it and he has to make certain adjustments for it. When you run a safety blitz you are either outmanning them at a certain spot or you are forcing them into a tight formation that takes away a lot of the threat of their passing game. So just the threat of the safety blitz is often as potent a defensive weapon as the blitz itself.

We did something else that game that surprised the Cowboys. Roger Wehrli took Bob Haynes man-to-man. That's something that very few teams and few players would ever try. He took Haynes alone right across the middle and had absolutely no deep help at all. He not only did the job, but he made two interceptions on passes to Hayes to stop Dallas drives. I don't think any deep back ever played a better game than Roger did that night.

We also did a job on their other wide receiver, their flanker Lance Rentzel. I don't think he caught a ball in the two games we played them that year.

The third quarter was scoreless, but we broke it wide open in the fourth. Roland got two more touchdowns, one on a ten-yard run and the other on a three yard plunge, and Roy Shivers finished it off with a 29-yard run right up the middle.

They got nothing. They changed quarterbacks from Craig Morton to Roger Staubach but that didn't do them any good. They made a couple of drives and had first downs on our six and then on our five, but we stopped them both times. You have to be lucky to get a shutout because a team can get three points just by getting it to your 40 or so, but by the time they got it down deep they needed touchdowns desperately, not field goals.

Towards the end of the game the fans started chanting, "we want Meredith—we want Meredith—we want Meredith," calling for their former quarterback, Don Meredith who had retired and was the color man on the TV broadcast.

That must have made Meredith feel pretty good because from time to time the Dallas fans had voiced a little of their displeasure in his direction when he was playing.

So we shut them out. Really gave them a whipping, 38 to 0. That was the first time since 1935 that a team had registered three straight shutouts, when the New York Giants did it, and it was the first time Dallas had ever been shutout.

They were a big play team and we never let them make the big play. It was a good feeling and in the locker room everyone was feeling good. With five games to go we had a good grip on the division.

There's a sad sequel though. In our next five games we tied Kansas City 6-6, beat Philadelphia, and then lost our last three. Dallas, apparently thoroughly demoralized, went on to win their last five to win the division, beat San Francisco for the conference championship and went into the Super Bowl against the Baltimore Colts.

It could have been different. It should have been different, but, until something else happens, the night we beat Dallas 38 to 0 will have to stand as the game I'll never forget.

THE GAME I'LL NEVER FORGET

By Ed O'Bradovich, Chicago Bears

THAT'S ONE I don't have to think about. The Game I'll Never Forget—I think it was the greatest game ever played. It was the Chicago Bears versus the New York Giants, the number one city versus the second city for the championship of professional football.

It was the offensive team against the defensive team. It was the best pitcher against the best hitter. It was David versus Goliath.

The Giants, with Y. A. Tittle and Frank Gifford and Del Shofner, were the most explosive team in football. They were far and away the highest scoring team. That year, 1963, they scored almost 450 points, almost 100 points more than the next most potent team.

The Bears, well we were just the opposite. We weren't flashy. We were just tough and dogged. That year we led the league in defense, allowing opponents only 144 points, a record, and established 14 NFL defensive records along the way. We were so stingy that three of our opponents couldn't get a touchdown, and no one scored more than 21 points against us. We used to tell the quarterback Bill Wade and the offense to just get us 11 points and we'd do the rest.

These are the kind of games that give the fans something to talk about for a couple of weeks while the teams are getting ready to go after one another. Could we stop that Giant attack? That was the question.

They were favored by a couple of points. I don't remember how many, but it could have been 20 and it wouldn't have mattered to us. We knew what we had to do and we felt that no one could beat us. We really felt that, and we believed it.

George Allen was our defensive coach then. Everyone knows by now what a positive thinker Allen is and beyond that he's also an innovative thinker. Allen was one of the first coaches to systematically chart the other team's tendencies, what they do in a given down and distance situation from a given part of the field.

The Giants, he told us all week, were a very stereotyped team. They used a basic running game with Joe Morrison and Phil King, and Tittle ran a lot of play action passes to freeze the rush, draws and screens. That's no knock on him, because he was a master at it. But Allen got us ready for him and we knew what to look for.

We had something else going for us on the field. In our linebackers, Joe Fortunato, Bill George and Larry Morris we had three of the greatest instinctive, intuitive players who ever walked out on a field. They always knew where the ball was going, and time after time I can remember them hollering over to someone to get ready because it was coming right at him. Sure enough it almost always did.

The Bears also had a little incentive going too. It was the Giants who humiliated us 47 to 7 in the 1956 championship game and that wasn't so long ago that we still didn't have a couple of fellows around who remembered that embarrassment, fellows like George and Fred Williams.

Sunday, December 29, 1963 was cold, about 10 above zero at game time with a good sharp north wind to clear the lungs. The field had been soft, but now it froze, and clumps of frozen turf stood up like sharp stakes.

The Giants were a finesse team, a lot like the Cowboys are today. They'll show you a lot of different looks and waltz you to death if you let them, but we didn't intend to let them. We went out there to really lay it to them. Play rough rock and sock football, make them think they were in an alley fight. That was our game anyway. That's always been the Bears' game.

Things don't always work out the way you want though. They took the opening kickoff and went right to work. From an objective point of view I suppose you'd say Tittle was beautiful. He went through his repertoire, keeping us off balance and ended up by throwing a pass to Gifford in the end zone.

The Giants had given up a lot more points than we had, but they had a good defense, with fellows like Dick Modzelewski, Andy Robustelli, Sam Huff and Jim Patton. Those are Hall of Fame guys, and they had plenty of playoff experience. They had been in five championship games in the previous six years.

What I'm trying to tell you is that we couldn't move the ball against them.

Back they came. They worked it back inside our 40 and we started to stiffen. They were in a second or third and long. I don't remember the down too well, but it was one of Tittle's screen pass situations. That's what he did. Only Larry Morris was waiting for it out in the flat.

Morris picked it off and set sail, a clear field in front of him. He ran it back about 61 yards and then just ran out of gas, completely out of gas, and stumbled and fell at the Giant five. Bill Wade smashed it at them a couple of plays and then sneaked it in himself from the two to tie the score.

They weren't through by any means. We fumbled one to them in our own territory but managed to keep them out of the end zone. They settled for a Don Chandler field goal from 13 yards out. We figured they had their 10 points for the day.

As the game wore on we got tougher and tougher. Our defense was really coming on and we could feel it. I just knew we were going to do something, make some big play. I could feel it.

We had them backed up deep in their own territory. It was second and long and in the defense huddle Fortunato called the play and before he gave us the signal to break he said, "this is a perfect situation for the screen. Watch for the screen."

Fortunato was going on a blitz, and when I saw the Giant tackle in front of me, Jack Stroud, taking an extra deep drop to block I knew it was a screen and went to the flat.

Tittle threw it my way. It was a little in front of me and over my head. From somewhere I reached back and put on a burst. I got to the ball, went up

reaching and came down with it. I started to go for the goal line, but Stroud and it seemed like the entire Giant team caught me from behind and tried like hell to get the ball away from me. But there was no way they were going to get it.

The thing to do these days, of course, is to jump up and down and slam the ball into the ground. But I didn't. There was a different kind of emotion for me. I just let it lay there on about the Giant 14 and as I was moving towards our sideline it just kept running through my head, "my God, please, get a touchdown."

Wade threw a quickie over the line to our tight end, Mike Ditka, and he fought his way to the one for a first down. Wade took it in from there.

The lead was ours. We knew we had the game now, but apparently Tittle didn't. He drove them down from his own 20 after Roger LeClerc missed a field goal, but we stopped them when Bennie McRae intercepted in the end zone.

Wade gave the ball to Ronnie Bull. He hammered out a first down in two tries, but in another three tries Bull came up about a half-yard short. We had to punt.

From their own 16 yard line they started to work against a clock that showed only 1:34 to go. They ate up 30 yards in three quick completions, missed a couple, and then threw to Gifford for a first down on our 39 yard line.

Once more Y. A. cranked it up. This time he was aiming for the end zone. Richie Petitbon, our safetyman went up and came down with the ball.

I'll always remember Tittle slamming his helmet into the ground. Once, twice, three times he slammed it, and then walked dejectedly to the bench. But then again there's a lot I'll always remember about that game.

THE GAME I'LL NEVER FORGET

By Sonny Jurgensen, Washington Redskins

NOT ALL philosophers would make good quarterbacks, but every good quarterback I ever met somehow developed a pretty wide philosophical streak.

You have to learn to live with those fumbles and interceptions, your own mistakes and everyone else's. You have to learn to take victory in stride and defeat without losing your optimism.

Speaking personally, I suppose that I, in a way, have the reputation of being maybe a little more philosophical than most quarterbacks. Well, chalk that up to the hard, adventurous football life I've led, and maybe that's why it's kind of hard to pin me down

on that *one* game I'll never forget.

If pressed real close maybe I'd pick two games, two games that we won in the last couple of seconds.

The first game was a game we played way back in 1961, Oct. 29, 1961, to be exact. I was with the Philadelphia Eagles then and we were playing the Washington Redskins.

This may surprise some of the younger fans but that was back in the days when the Eagles were one great football team.

We were the defending world champions of professional football. The season before we defeated the

Green Bay Packers, 17-13, to win the crown. Norm Van Brocklin was our quarterback that year, but he retired and I took over.

We had a 5-1 record going into that game and had great ambitions of winning our second straight championship. It was also a game that started to make a philosopher out of me.

We seemed to be coming from behind all day. They scored then we scored. Then we fumbled on our own 24 to hand them an easy touchdown, and they added a field goal before Pete Retzlaff got free for his second touchdown catch.

As I remember that game now, we had almost no ground game. I think we wound up with minus rushing yardage. That's something that does things to a quarterback's philosophy, too. So I wound up, if you'll pardon the pun, and just kept throwing most of the time.

Bobby Walston kicked a couple of field goals in the second half and his second one gave us our first lead, 20-17 late in the fourth quarter. I was praying for the defense to hold, but with less than a minute to play Norm Snead threw a touchdown pass.

When you're down with only seconds to play you have to hope beyond hope for a long kickoff return. But the Skins kicked it almost out of the end zone, so there we were with 80 yards to go and about 50 seconds to do it in.

But like I said you have to have confidence and optimism. I went into that huddle with the attitude that we had all the time in the world. The rest of the team must have believed me because we went right to work.

I hit Walston with two straight to move the ball down to the Redskins' 41, bang, bang, just like that. I missed the next one and now we were down to just about 20 seconds to play. I knew I needed one more completion for a good shot at a tying field goal, but figured I had enough time to still go for the win.

Tommy McDonald, a fiery little competitor out of Oklahoma, thought we could still do it too. So with that kind of positive thinking we did it.

Tommy said they were playing him tight to the outside so he ran a slant towards the post to draw the cornerback and safety man over and then broke quickly back towards the flag. I just laid it up there and let him run under it. He caught it around the 10 and would have run through a wall to get it into the end zone, and there were only something like 13 seconds remaining on the clock when the referee threw up his hands.

That was one big game because it was an important game and anytime you pull one out in the closing seconds it's a big thrill. That's what we did to Dallas one year too.

This time I was playing with the Washington Redskins. It was the second to last game of the 1966 season. It was a crazy season for us. We played some outstanding games and we played some pretty bad ones too. The week before we beat the New York Giants, 72-41, to set all kinds of records for scoring. But the previous game we could score only three points against the Cleveland Browns.

But just a couple of weeks before that the Cowboys beat us, 31-30, when they drove from their own three yard line to our 13 after all their time-outs had been used up and then kicked a field goal to beat us. So we had some evening up to do.

Another thing you learn about football sooner or later, if you play it long enough, is that games are won and lost in the second half. And even more than that they are won or lost in the fourth quarter and even beyond that in the last few minutes of play. So you don't get too excited no matter what happens in the early going.

We went into the fourth quarter all tied up at 17 apiece. Then it all broke loose.

Dan Reeves broke loose on a run of almost 70 yards to put them on top. We came right back and I hit Jerry Smith with a pass for the tying touchdown.

Dallas brought it right back and took the lead on a short run by Don Perkins. Again confidence and optimism paid off and I hit Charley Taylor with a bomb of about 65 yards to tie the score again.

Taylor had switched from running back to split end just a couple of games before and it sure was a comfort to me to see him out there on the wing. He really opened up our passing game.

Our defense came through and stopped the Cowboys and they had to punt with just a couple of minutes left to play. I spread everybody out and gave the ball to A. D. Whitfield a couple of times.

Whitfield was a former Cowboy and all that stuff you hear about how guys like to show up the team that traded them—well you can believe it.

A few runs by Whitfield, a couple of passes and we had good field position. Running the ball had forced the Cowboys to use up all three of their time outs and now we had it down close to their 20.

I just took my time standing there watching that clock down second by second and talking to the referee, telling him what a terrible position I'd be in if he was giving me bad information on the time remaining.

I remember our coaches were running all over the sidelines trying to find me to give me some instructions, or something. Anyway when it got down to eight seconds I called time out and in came Charlie Gogolak and kicked it right through.

That, I figured would give the Cowboys something to philosophize over.

THE GAME I'LL NEVER FORGET

By Alex Karras, Detroit Lions

WHEN YOU'VE played defensive tackle for 13 years for the Detroit Lions like I did, you really have to do some thinking to come up with a game you'd like to remember.

The "Game I'd Like To Forget" would be more like it, or maybe the season. How about "the Career I'd Like to Forget?"

It's especially hard for a defensive lineman, a tackle, to remember anything. You're always getting hit in the head and that tends to have a disturbing effect on the memory.

And you know how coaches are; when you lose nobody played a good game. You can lose by one point or 3-0 and to hear them tell you when you watch the films they walked right over you every play.

Of course, that's not true. That's just what the coaches say, and everybody knows what kind of people coaches are. Besides, once you get conditioned to losing you expect everybody to tell you you were lousy.

I remember once we won a game, but the coaches were so used to losing that they chewed everybody out anyway just from force of habit. That's how things went in Motor City.

But I suppose if I was going to pick a game to talk about, a game I'd want my wife, my children and my mother to be proud of, it'd be the game we lost to the Philadelphia Eagles on Thanksgiving Day, November 18, 1968.

The game was played in an actual quagmire. I had never seen a quagmire before and for that reason alone I was anxious to play that day, and that's part of what I remember.

For those of you who have never seen one, a quagmire is something that happens when one fellow plays out his option and is signed by another team. Pete Rozelle, the commissioner, declares a quagmire and awards the other team the other team.

Anyway it is necessary to rain for two days and nights to produce quagmirical conditions. So we lost, 12-0, as Sam Baker, remember good old Sam Baker with those high shoes, kicked four field goals. I remember reading later that that put him in second place in all-time scoring, only about 1,000 points behind Lou Groza. For that reason alone I was proud to be part of that game. It gave me a feeling of participating in history.

But even though we lost, I felt I personally played a great game. I really did. By that I mean I didn't do anything wrong all day. When they tried to run my hole I was there and I made the tackle. I made something like 19 or 20 personal tackles that day. That's an unheard of number for a defensive tackle. But now you've heard of it.

Now I think that was really something. After all I was only a defensive tackle. I didn't pass the ball, or catch the ball or run with the ball. My natural talents were undeveloped. But that's not unusual at Detroit either.

Maybe I ought to tell you a little about playing defensive tackle. On one side of you is their center, usually a quick sneaky guy. On the other side of you is their tackle, a big, hairy guy whose knuckles drag when he walks. In front of you is their guard, usually a dirty-talking guy with bad breath, except Jerry Kramer, who wouldn't talk at all because he was taking notes for his next book.

These are all big guys and I'm just a little fellow. So when we were out on the field I'd say, "Hi fellas," and try showing around some pictures of the wife and kids. I can't remember if that ever worked or not.

Another handicap was that I can't see. I need glasses to talk on the telephone. I wear them to bed at night so I can see my dreams. Oh, you've heard that one.

So, all in all, I consider it a remarkable achievement just staying alive after playing in Detroit all those years.

Now about that game I'll never forget; another thing I'll never forget about it is that we saved Joe Kuharich's job. We got off to a good start that year and won our first three games. Then we learned Joe Schmidt was the coach and lost the next 22 or so.

But the Eagles weren't even that lucky. They knew right away that Kuharich was their coach so they lost all their games. They came into that epic, quagmirical encounter with a sparkling 0 and 11 record.

Those Philadelphia fans were howling for Joe's scalp. They were in a slight dilemma though. They knew that if the Eagles didn't win any games they'd get first pick in the college draft, and everybody knew that the first pick that year was going to be O. J. Simpson.

But some fans were afraid that if the Eagles got first

pick they wouldn't be smart enough to take O. J., or worse, they wouldn't want to pay him anything. (You know, I played five years before I found out that they were supposed to be paying *me*.)

Then some other fans thought that Kuharich would go out and win a game or two just so he wouldn't have to get the number one pick, and just to spite them. Some of those fans have nasty, nasty minds. They don't appreciate the unselfish nobility of the owners and coaches in this great game of ours.

But in a way, we made history that day. Never let it be said that the Lions couldn't rise to an occasion. We rose up and bowed down to the Eagles. We saved Joe Kuharich's job. At least for that day we did.

We did that a lot at Detroit. We saved a lot of coaches' jobs. The opposing coaches though, never our own.

That's the game I want to always remember. I know I played well, no matter what the coaches say, and we made Joe Kuharich happy, even if it was just for a day or so. That's what this great game of ours is all about anyway—sportsmanship. Isn't it?

THE GAME I'LL NEVER FORGET

By Carl Eller, Minnesota Vikings

THE MINNESOTA VIKINGS matured as a team and I think I matured as a player on a cold, blustery day in Metropolitan Stadium Nov. 10, 1968.

That was the day we beat the Green Bay Packers, 14-10. It was our second victory that year over the Packers, the defending world champions, and the first time the Vikings ever beat the Pack twice in one season. It was also the first time we had been able to beat them in Metropolitan Stadium ever.

It was a big game, a tough game, and as I tell you about it, I think you'll learn why.

When games are talked about it's usually in terms of the scoring—who scored; how many touchdown passes were thrown; who gained the yardage and who made the catches. But I think any knowledgeable football man will tell you it's your defense that makes you a winner or a loser.

I didn't score any points that day, but I did play what I think was a big part in stopping the Packers from scoring, and that's just as important.

We were playing a Green Bay team that had just come off two straight Super Bowl wins and were still in there trying to make it three in a row.

We were still a young team under a new coach, Bud Grant. I hadn't been around too many years. Alan Page, our great tackle, was just starting to come on strong, and we looked at Jim Marshall and Greg Larson as the greybeards.

Our secondary was young and most of our key offensive players, like Joe Kapp and Gene Washington and Dave Osborn had just a couple of years experience.

The Packers had all those great old veterans like Bart Starr, Forrest Gregg, Ray Nitschke, Jerry Kramer, Boyd Dowler, Willie Wood, Herb Adderly, Bob Skoronski, Carroll Dale. Their names were house-hold words. They were well coached, well disciplined and had the confidence that only years of winning can give to men and to a team.

We beat them the first game, fairly easily, 26-13 the second game of the season. We were in control of that game all the way and until very late were leading, 26-6.

But in this game they were fighting to stay alive for a shot at the division title and another trip to the Super Bowl. We went into the game tied with the Chicago Bears for the lead, and as we went along the scoreboard told us that they were beating the San Francisco 49ers.

This was almost two games in one. In character the two halves didn't even seem like it was the same game. In the first half our offense played almost flawless football, and then in the second half the burden fell on the defense.

Green Bay scored first with a field goal, but then Joe Kapp took the team down the field for two long scoring marches.

The first one covered close to 70 yards. We crunched it out in about 14 plays. The longest gain was a 14-yard run by Bill Brown, and Kapp mixed in a couple of short passes to Tom Hall and Washington.

Our offense kept the ball most of the second quarter. Green Bay, I think, had the ball for only eight plays that quarter as Kapp and the boys moved the ball almost 90 yards, mostly on the ground, with Brown scoring his second touchdown of the game on a short plunge.

But in the second half it was the Packers controlling the ball and our defense on the field. If I recall right we were only able to make two first downs the entire second half and one of those came by penalty.

The Packers took the second half kick-off and drove down for a touchdown with Donny Anderson going over on a short plunge to cut our lead to 14-10.

Now it was really a game, a game that any mistake or big play could win or lose.

The Packers took the ball again and drove it deep into our territory. On second down Starr dropped back to pass. I managed to fight my way past Gregg's block and was going full speed when I hit Starr just as he cocked his arm. He went down for a 10-yard loss, but, I'm sorry to say, was shaken up by that tackle. When he was hit running with the ball a little later he was forced to leave the game.

I was sorry to see that happen because while we play and hit as hard as we can we never want to see anyone get injured.

They tried to fool us with the old Packer sweep and we stopped that. On fourth down they tried a field goal. I shot the gap, cut to my right across the kicker's angle, moving to where the ball was going to be, jumped as high as I could and managed to get my hand on the ball.

Zeke Bratkowski, another Packer old pro, replaced Starr and late in the fourth quarter had his team deep into our territory again.

It wasn't anything I saw. The Packers were just too smart to tip a play off; it was just something I sensed. I just knew they were going to try to run the sweep my way.

I got off the ball as fast as I ever have in my life, and hit Anderson before he had a chance to do anything. He fumbled, and Paul Krause recovered for us on our own 18 with just a little over two minutes left in the game.

That just about wrapped it up for us. And as far as I'm concerned that was the making of the Minnesota Vikings.

That win gave us the confidence we needed. We went on to win our division and in the years since then we have always been in championship contention.

That game really brought our defensive unit together. We had a really great day. We sacked Green Bay quarterbacks, Starr and Bratkowski five times; forced three Green Bay fumbles and recovered each one, and blocked their field goal try in the fourth quarter when a successful kick would have put them in position to win with another field goal.

Personally it was a big game for me. For me I think it was the game that started it all. It was my first good day against Forrest Gregg, one of the greatest offensive tackles of football.

It was a game in which I was able to make a lot of big plays, and it proved to me and all of us that we could do it when we had to.

THE GAME I'LL NEVER FORGET

By Leroy Kelly, Cleveland Browns

THE GAMES you remember, well, it's funny, sometimes you remember them for the strangest reasons. Most of the time you go along and play the games as they come, one by one, one after another, and they tend to blend together sometimes as if it was the same game all over again every time you take the field.

You do the same things every time. You play the same teams over and over, mostly, until pretty soon everyone looks like everyone else and every game is like every other.

Maybe I'm just unusual. I know some fellows can remember just about every play of every game, but not me. I don't remember too many of them, not really remember them I mean. But the ones I do remember, well, I guess you'd call those the games I'll never forget.

There are two of them really, and they are as different as it's possible for two games to be. In one of them I played very little, and in the other I had about as great a day as I've ever had as an individual.

That game was a few years ago in San Francisco. November 3, 1968 was the date, but I wasn't sure of that. I had to look it up to make certain. But what happened out there on that field I'll remember, I guess, for the rest of my life.

I like to think of it as the game that got us into the NFL championship game against the Baltimore Colts, although we played it exactly in the middle of the season, if you can say there is a middle to a 14-game schedule.

Going into that game we were staggering. We had won only three of our first seven games and it looked like the St. Louis Cardinals were going to be the first champions of the newly aligned Century division. Nothing was going right for us and we went into Kezar Stadium in Frisco to play the 49ers who were always tough at home.

The team was pretty down. We just couldn't pull ourselves together. We knew we had to have something or someone wake us up. I had the feeling it could be me. I felt good, I felt strong, and it looked like it was going to be what I call a Leroy Field. That's what I call it when the track is wet, slow and slippery. Other fellows may hate to play under those conditions, but I love them. For some reason or other I've always been able to go on a wet, muddy field.

Frisco and Brodie didn't seem to mind the field either though. We scored first on a field goal, but then the 49ers came back with Brodie whipping touchdown passes to John David Crow and Clifton McNeil to put us down, 14-3, and for a minute it looked like the season was going to come to a fast end right out there on the west coast just a few days after Halloween.

It was now or never, or at the earliest next season. But I'll say one thing about my team, we weren't used to losing, and we didn't like the idea of losing. So we pulled our chin straps a little tighter and went at them.

We didn't try and play catch-up. We started to grind them. The ball was inside our 30 and our quarterback, Bill Nelson, gave the ball to me. Then he gave it to me again, and again and again. It felt real good, and when we got the ball down to the Frisco 32 yard line he threw it to Milt Morin, our tight end running a post, for the touchdown.

From then on it was our game. I like to think that those 40 yards I gained to start that drive really got us going and kept us going for the rest of the season.

I was hot and Nelson knew it. The fellows up front who do the blocking knew it too and they really put their shoulders in to it. I carried it again and again on that sloppy field, my kind of field, and I ended up with 174 yards in 27 carries, the best day rushing I've ever had. We did it the hard way too. It wasn't any one long run to set up the big average. My longest run was 32 yards right up the middle on a trap, and my only touchdown was a two-yarder.

We ended up winning eight straight that year to get into the playoffs. We beat the Dallas Cowboys, who were at least two touchdown favorites, and went on to play the Baltimore Colts for the NFL title.

I'd like to forget that one, but the first time we played the Colts for the championship, that one I'll savor.

I was a rookie then playing behind Jim Brown and Ernie Green. We had a good team, but not a great one. Baltimore was supposed to have the great team with Unitas, Ray Berry, Jim Parker, Gino Marchetti, Lenny Moore and all those guys.

It's not the game itself I remember so much because I didn't play all that much. I was on the specialty teams—running back kickoffs and punts and getting down under them to try and make the tackle when we were doing the kicking.

But it was a great thrill for me as a first year player to be in a championship game and be associated with great players. I used to just love to watch Jim Brown run.

The Colts with Unitas and Moore and all those guys, heck I was in high school when they won their first championship and it was really a great feeling, almost unreal, to be getting ready to play them. And getting ready to play them was just about the whole game.

The Colts were big favorites, a couple of touchdowns I think. The papers were full of stories about how they were going to run over us. We wouldn't be able to stop Unitas, Moore, Berry and Mackey on offense and wouldn't be able to move the ball against Marchetti and Miller and Logan and Lenny Lyles and Pellington and Shinnick. "The Browns Who?" Or "The Browns What?" the papers seemed to be saying.

Someone on our team was smart enough to clip those stories and pin them up on the locker room bulletin board. We couldn't help seeing them. They were right there in front of us, hanging up for two weeks, the headlines jumping out at us every time we walked by.

That really got us up. We were practicing every day out at Case Western Reserve University to save the field for the game and on the bus ride out there the guys were hollering back and forth — "The Browns Who?"—"Hey, Ryan, you're a nobody."— "Jim who? Jim Brown?" and all kinds of stuff like that.

The day of the game that wind came whipping in to Municipal Stadium off Lake Erie at about 20 miles an hour. The temperature was down to about 30, and the sky was kind of sloppy. The Colts weren't prepared for that, and I don't think they were prepared for us either. Truthfully, I think they were a little complacent. They thought they had us in the bag.

The first half was scoreless. Right after the kickoff we got the wind behind us and we got rolling. Lou Groza kicked a 43-yard field goal. Our defense held again and the Baltimore kicker couldn't do any better than about 25 yards. I called for a fair catch and we were in position again.

Frank Ryan didn't waste any time. Gary Collins faked an outside cut and then broke it off to the post. Ryan hit him perfectly for 18 yards and a score. Again their punter got off a poor kick and on an identical play Ryan hit Collins with a 42-yard scoring pass. We scored another 10 points in the fourth quarter including another bomb to Collins and that was the ball game.

The referee shot off his gun with 27 seconds still on the clock as our fans were pouring all over the field. I fought my way to the dressing room just happy that I was part of a victory. It may seem funny for a running back to say, but I'll always remember those tackles I made in that game running down under kickoffs and punts.

By Gale Sayers, Chicago Bears

THE TOUGHEST thing about being a pro rookie is that you're scared. You're scared all the time.

And you worry. You worry about whether or not you can make it. You think about those great stars you've read about all your life. You think about those giant linemen you have to run through. Those vicious linebackers and those swift, hard-hitting defensive backs.

You worry about whether you're good enough. You worry that maybe the skills you've worked on ever since you were a boy won't be able to carry you through against stiffer competition.

On the outside I might have shown confidence, but inside there was that question mark. It was there especially after some supposedly smart football men said I'd never make it as a running back in the National Football League.

Real confidence comes with doing it and even when we arrived at Bloomington, Minnesota that sunny Sunday morning of Oct. 17, 1965, I still didn't feel that I had done it yet, at least not to my satisfaction.

Coach George Halas broke me in slowly during the exhibition season, running back punts and kick-offs for starters and he was nursing me along slowly into the regular line-up.

The Bears, as we often do, got off to a slow start. We had a lot of rookies that year and we opened with two games on the West Coast. The San Francisco 49ers really drubbed us and the Los Angeles Rams beat us out of a game we should have won. Then the Green Bay Packers gave us a lesson in fundamentals.

In the second half of that Packer game we started to come together and the following week we got back at the Rams. We beat them pretty good. I scored on a 80-yard pass from Rudy Bukich and I threw a touchdown pass myself, a 26-yard option pass to Dick Gordon.

We knew we'd be in for a tough afternoon with the Vikings because Fran Tarkenton always gave us a lot of trouble with his scrambling and passing, and there was Bill Brown, an ex-Bear who always did great things against his old team.

Right from the start, it looked like it was going to be our day. Ronnie Bull broke one up the middle and went 34 yards for a touchdown. Within 36 seconds, we had another. The Vikings' Tom Hall fumbled the kick-off and we recovered on the Minnesota 14. On the very first play Bukich shot a pass to Johnny Morris for the score. Bears-14, Vikings-0.

We must have relaxed a little though because the Vikings came back with a field goal and touchdown to close the gap and then we traded field goals to walk off the field with a 17-13 halftime lead.

Coming back on the field I started to feel real good. It was like a wave of confidence coming over me. I felt like I could do anything I had to do.

I even felt that way after Cox kicked another field goal and Brown broke a 40-yard touchdown run to put them in the lead for the first time, 23-17. I just felt that no matter what they did we could come right back.

We took the kick-off and drove upfield. Bukich mixed up the runs and passes, and when we got to the Vikings' 18-yard line Rudy called a pass. The play put me one-on-one with a linebacker. I made a move to the inside and then veered quickly. The ball was right there and we had six more points, and the lead, 24-23.

A scrambling quarterback like Tarkenton can break down all your defensive keys and he was in rare form. He drove our guys crazy and marched the Vikings in for another score. They were on top again.

Back we came, and when we marched it down to the Minnesota 25, Bukich called a play similar to the one we had just scored on. It isolated me on a linebacker. When you get in that situation no linebacker in football should be able to keep up with any running back if there is enough field to run in. Rudy laid it right in there and once again the Bears were back on top, 31-30.

After that second touchdown I was standing on the sidelines near coach Halas and Chuck Mather, our backfield coach, walked over to him and said, "George, whatever you're paying Gale Sayers, it isn't enough."

That really made me feel good, and the adrenalin was really flowing as I was standing there on the sidelines yelling at our defense to stop Tarkenton and get that ball back.

That Tarkenton was really masterful. He took his team the length of the field, mixing his runs and passes and scrambles and using as much of the clock as he could until finally he slipped the ball to Tommy Mason who drove the final four yards into our end zone. That put them six points up on us, 37-31, the fifth time the lead had changed hands that half.

I looked up at that clock as I trotted out to line up for the kick-off and saw there were only two minutes and 18 seconds left to go. I knew we could do it though. I felt so good I felt like I was gliding, not even touching the ground.

I was just praying that they wouldn't squib it, that they'd kick it deep so I could get my hands on it.

Our blocking wedge was all formed there on the 20-yard line—Dick Butkus and George Seals and Dick Evey and those fellows. We had the return on to go to the left.

Fred Cox hit the ball and I was so anxious to get it that it seemed to be drifting so slowly down to me. I kept telling myself not to get anxious, to wait for it, and don't start to run before I had it in my hands.

I caught it on the four. I started to move straight up the field and then Butkus and Seals blasted the Vikings aside. I cut to my left through a big hole and there was daylight.

I was running free. There were only two men with a chance to stop me, both angling over from the opposite side of the field. When they got close enough I gave them a head and shoulder fake to the inside.

They were forced to break stride just slightly and I just turned it on down the sideline.

Touchdown! And the Bears were back on top.

The only thing wrong was that Tarkenton still had enough time, about two minutes, to move his team into position for a field goal. We only led by a point.

Dick Butkus took care of that. He intercepted a Tarkenton pass on the Minnesota 45 and returned it down to the 10. On the first play they gave me the ball straight ahead and those linemen, Mike Pyle, Jim Cadile, Mike Rabold really blew the Vikings out of there. I could have almost walked it in.

That was really great. I went on to have a bigger afternoon than those four second half touchdowns. Later that year I tied the pro record with six touchdowns in our second game with the 49ers. But it was a bigger thrill getting them against Minnesota because we really needed them.

After the game I heard coach Halas say to the reporters something about "Red Grange, George McAfee and Gayle Sayers, and not necessarily in that order gentlemen."

That's when I really knew I belonged, and that's why I'll never forget that game.

THE GAME I'LL NEVER FORGET

By George Blanda, Oakland Raiders

PLAYING THIS game of football for some 30 odd years, man and boy, can leave a fellow with an awful lot of memories. Last season alone, coming off the bench in all those games, I had enough thrills to last a lifetime.

But the game I'll really never forget, the prototype of all those storybook last-minute finishes, was a game we played against the Kansas City Chiefs Oct. 24, 1965.

I was still with the Houston Oilers then, but I knew it wouldn't be for too long. We weren't doing too well that year after years as one of the reigning powers of the American Football League.

The fans were getting down on everyone, and they were especially down on me. I've noticed that the quarterback is always the first to get booed. They thought I was getting too long in the tooth and thought it was time to bring in a new pitcher.

And that's exactly what they did for this game against Kansas City. The youth movement was on and Don Trull was given the start against the Chiefs.

Well, it seemed that even youth was on the side of the Chiefs. They started Pete Beathard and by halftime they had an easy 17-0 lead. The only consolation I had sitting there on the bench was that Lennie Dawson was sitting this one out in favor of the youngsters too.

Apparently they soon got tired of youth because during halftime the coaches told me to get loosened up, that I was starting at quarterback.

When I trotted out onto the field into the huddle I heard one long chorus of boos. So the first time I laid my hands on the ball I dropped back and let it fly. I wanted to throw it right down some of those big mouths. Charlie Frazier was off and flying, too, and we connected for a 66-yard touchdown play.

Our defense held. We got the ball back in real good field position. I tried one smash at that big Kansas City line and then I dropped back again and this time it was Ode Burrell in the clear and I hit him for six points, the play covering 49 yards overall.

We got the ball right back again and this time, just to change the pattern, we took the field in shorter bites. On the last one I hit our tight end Willie Frazier for 17 yards and a touchdown. Bang, bang, bang, three touchdowns in four minutes!

With still 11 minutes left to play in the third quarter, we had rallied to take the lead 21-17. And still we weren't through. Our defense was just as hot as the offense and once again they stopped the explosive Chiefs. And once more we took the ball and marched it in. This time the pay-off was a nine-yarder from me to Willie Frazier, our fourth touchdown of the quarter!

That widened the lead now to 28 to 17 and looked like we might just run away with the game, except that the Kansas City coaches must have felt they had seen as much of youth as they wanted to see that day and sent Lennie Dawson into the game.

Like the cool veteran that he is, Dawson didn't get excited. Instead he brought the team back together, marched them upfield and narrowed the score a little with a 29-yard field goal.

The tide was still high for the Oilers though. We took the ball and brought it right back up the field. For the final nine yards, I found Bob McLeod for the touchdown. That made the score, 35-20, and things were looking mighty cozy in Houston. Even my pals in the stands were cheering.

Dawson got a quick one right back though. He hit his fullback, Curtis McClinton with a little swing pass and McClinton was unstoppable as he ran the ball into the end zone, a 40-yard TD play.

Trailing by 15, the Chiefs decided to go for a two-point conversion. Dawson rolled out, got outside the linebacker and then threw for the score when the cornerback had to come up to prevent him from running it in.

With a seven-point lead and just a few minutes left to play, we probably tried to play it a little too conservative. Jerry May, Bobby Bell, Buck Buchanan and that gang are a mighty tough outfit to run on, especially when they know you're coming.

We couldn't get the first down and had to give up the ball. The Chiefs came down against the clock and with about a minute and a half to go Dawson hit Otis Taylor with a eight-yarder for the score.

We still had the lead 35-34 and the Kansas City coaches were forced to make a decision—to go for an almost certain one-point kick and a tie, or to gamble for two points and the lead.

I'm glad they went for the two-point play. If they had played for the tie we might have been content to take the tie, too, and sit on the ball the remaining minute and some seconds. They went for the two and made it. Now they had the lead 36-35 and with just under a minute and a half to go.

To tell you the truth, I couldn't wait to get my hands on that ball. I just knew I had another good shot left and I wanted to show some of those folks a thing or two who had been screaming for my scalp.

We got a pretty good run back and got the ball out-of-bounds to kill the clock, but when I huddled the boys up, that Kansas City goal looked a long ways off, only 60 yards, but it looked like a couple of miles.

Now, in a situation like this every six-year-old kid in America with his nose in front of a TV set knows that the defense is going to maybe give you the short stuff and play to stop you deep. Those Kansas City safetymen were playing so deep they were almost offside for next Sunday's game.

So I figured if they were going to give us the short stuff, we might as well take it. The main thing is not to get over-anxious yourself, because a team quickly reflects a quarterback's moods. That kind of stuff rubs off real easy.

And so does poise. So I acted like we had all the time in the world. I swung one out to Charlie Tolar, our fullback, and he rambled for 17 yards.

Next I hit Burrell with a shortie for six yards. I figured that wasn't as good as the first one, so I went back to Tolar again and this time we worked it for 12 yards, and that gave us a first-down on the Kansas City 27-yard line.

From that position it would have meant a field goal try of about 35 yards but we wanted to work it in a little closer, if we could, for as much of a sure thing as it's possible to get.

We had them out of the prevent now, but I figured they'd still be looking for the little swings, so I got cute and hit tight end Willie Frazier on a curl pattern down to the 9 yard line.

The clock was down to 17 seconds now and Jack Spikes trotted out and booted one home to put us on top 38-36, a winner. I wasn't doing any kicking because I injured my knee the week before.

When I walked off that field, a thousand thoughts were racing through my head. One of them was that I could hang up right there and never have a more satisfying moment or a greater day on which to do it.

On one half of a football game I had thrown for over 300 yards and five touchdowns and nursed over 400 yards total offense out of a team that barely made a first down in the first half.

I thought it was ironical that two old pros like Lennie Dawson, and myself, who had both been benched in favor of youth, should come off the bench and treat the fans to one of the most gritty, exciting games ever played.

I also got a lot of satisfaction for serving up a big helping of crow to almost 35,000 fans who had been yelling for my scalp and made them enjoy eating every exciting morsel. They booed me when I came out, but now they were screaming their heads off.

Like I said, there's been a lot of games, but that's the one Old George will never forget.

By Ray Nitschke, Green Bay Packers

THERE HAVE BEEN a lot of big games for me since I've been with the Green Bay Packers. It seemed that from the moment Vince Lombardi took over as head coach every game became a big one.

In his second year—1960—he took us right into the Championship game. I'll never forget the sight of Jimmy Taylor fighting and grinding in frustration as Chuck Bednarik tried to hold him down as time ran out with us trailing the Philadelphia Eagles, 17-13.

That was the first big game. Then there was the thrill of our first World's Championship, 1961, when we defeated the New York Giants, 37-0, in the first title game ever held in Green Bay.

There was the tremendous satisfaction of winning three consecutive world championships and the first two Super Bowl titles.

Just to be Green Bay Packers meant something special to us, and we went into that first Super Bowl game against the Kansas City Chiefs knowing that we were carrying not only our own pride, but the reputation of the entire National Football League.

Beating Oakland in the Super Bowl the following year was quite a kick too, but not quite as big as that first game against the Chiefs.

But the game I'll never forget, the game that means something *extra* special to me was the 1962 World's Championship game against the New York Giants.

It not only meant something special to me, it meant something special to the Giants too, something very special.

They had something to prove. After we beat them, 37-0, in the championship game in Green Bay, the New York writers and fans got down on the Giants. They said they were "humiliated." That's not my word, understand, that's the word used by the fans and newspaper men.

I knew the Giants had an excellent team, a team with outstanding personnel. Their quarterback was Y. A. Tittle, and for receivers he had Del Shofner, Frank Gifford and Joe Walton. Their running backs were big, strong and tough, Phil King and Alex Webster.

They had an experienced offensive line anchored by center Ray Wietecha and tackle Roosevelt Brown.

The Giants had a tough defensive unit with Sam Huff, Andy Robustelli, Rosey Grier and Dick Modzelewski up front and Dick Lynch, Erich Barnes and

Jim Patton in the secondary. This would be their fourth title game in five years.

The Packers had something to play for, too. We were defending champions and we meant to put up an honorable defense. And this was a sort of homecoming for coach Lombardi.

Lombardi had been an assistant coach with the Giants before coming to Green Bay. There was always some talk that he really wanted the job with the Giants and had been passed over in favor of Allie Sherman. Whether that was true or not didn't matter because Vince Lombardi wanted to win every game he was ever in.

It seemed that both teams played through the season just to get it over with and get back at one another again. We sort of coasted to the Western division championship, winning 13 games and losing only one. The Giants eased in with a 12-2 record.

The title game was scheduled for the home of the Eastern division leader and it seemed that the fans started thinking of nothing but that game from the middle of November on.

And finally, on Dec. 30 we got there. New York was wild with excitement. Everywhere we looked there were signs; *"Beat Green Bay—Bushville U.S.A."* For a week the crowds in Madison Square Garden, going there for the fights, the hockey games and the basketball games would break out in a chant, *"Beat Green Bay."*

When we took the field for our pre-game warmup there were more fans in the stands, an official count of 64,892, than lived in Green Bay. They let out a great chorus of boos.

They booed us for a solid hour. They hooted us as a team and they booed us individually when the starting lineups were introduced.

It was less than a perfect day for football. The frozen field forced us to change our cleated shoes for ripple soles. A howling wind of 40 to 50 miles an hour swept through Yankee Stadium raising great brown clouds of dust. The temperature was down to about 15 degrees by kickoff time and the wind was numbing.

Those were the worst conditions I've ever played under, and I'm including that 13-below game we played in Green Bay when we beat the Dallas Cowboys.

The frozen ground didn't give us much traction. It was hard to change directions and we had to take short, choppy steps to keep from slipping. But our guys up front, Forrest Gregg, Jerry Kramer, Fuzzy Thurston, Jim Ringo and Norm Masters kept digging and Jimmy Taylor kept churning and about halfway through the first quarter we got it close enough for Jerry Kramer to kick a 26-yard field goal.

The Giants put the ball in play and started coming upfield. The feeling and probing was over. Tittle couldn't throw long in the wind, but he was deadly with the short stuff and kept mixing in the runs with Webster and King.

They got it down to our 15-yard line and then I got lucky. I knew Tittle liked to use his tight end, Walton, and I figured this might be the spot for one of his over the line quickies. So before the snap of the ball I cheated a little to my left and when he threw for Walton I made a desperation lunge for the ball.

I tipped it, and it landed right in the hands of our outside linebacker Dan Currie, who was a real tower of strength for us. That got us out of the hole and both teams exchanged a few punts until with about four minutes left in the half Currie hit King real hard and knocked the ball loose and I fell on it on the Giants' 34.

Paul Hornung hadn't played much for us that year. He injured a knee in October and was used sparingly. That's why Kramer took over the place kicking duties. But Paul was in the backfield when Starr crouched down behind Ringo.

He got the ball and handed off to Hornung running to his right. It looked like the old Packer sweep, but suddenly Paul slowed down, straightened up and hit Boyd Dowler for a 25-yard gain down to the Giant seven.

On the next play, Taylor, who carried 31 times

that frigid day, and was bruised for a month afterwards, rammed right through big Grier and Sam Huff for the touchdown.

We went into the locker room leading 10-0, and for the only time in my football life I was so miserable, numb and cold I didn't feel like coming out to play the second half. But what a half it was.

The Giants weren't dead and their backs were to the wall. Halfway through the third period they stopped us dead way down deep in our own territory. Max McGee had to punt from our end zone, but he never got it away. It was blocked, and Jim Collier fell on the ball for a touchdown.

The Giants must have smelled blood or revenge because they stopped us dead again. Then another break came our way. McGee punted to Sam Horner, but with the crazy wind and frozen fingers he couldn't hold the ball. I got a good start, and the ball took a Green Bay bounce. I fell on it at the Giants' 42. A few plays later Kramer kicked a 29-yard field goal and we had a little breathing room.

He kicked one about the same distance near the end of the game to make the final score, 16-7.

It was a great win for us, defending our championship, and our defensive team was unscored on in eight consecutive quarters of championship play.

I was lucky enough to be chosen Most Valuable Player. It could have been any one of a number of players, and I looked upon the honor as being a tribute to our entire defensive team.

But, anyway, nobody ever called us *"Bushville U.S.A."* anymore. From then on it was *"Titletown U.S.A."* And let's face it, it's got to give you a little extra kick for the smallest town in major league sports to knock off the biggest city in the nation. That's the game I'll never forget.

THE GAME I'LL NEVER FORGET

By Len Dawson, Kansas City Chiefs

SOME PEOPLE have called it "the greatest game ever played." Others have called it the most exciting. It was the longest game ever played, and it held the nation spellbound on a Christmas day when it should have been nothing more than a diversion. It was also the game I'll never forget.

And that's saying a lot, because I've been around a long time, college and pro about 20 years. I've been fortunate to always play with good teams and there have been a lot of big games. When I was at Purdue all

of our Big 10 opponents were big games and there was always Notre Dame. Before the Chiefs came to Kansas City we were the Dallas Texans and there was that overtime game with the Houston Oilers for the American Football League championship.

Then there were the two Super Bowls. The first was the first Super Bowl ever played. It was against the Green Bay Packers. The second was against the Minnesota Vikings. Those games gave me enough memories to last a lifetime. Surely these were the most important games I have ever played in.

But the game that has burned itself the deepest into my memory was the now famous sudden-death, six-quarter Christmas Day game against the Miami Dolphins.

There was something about this game right from the beginning that set it apart from any other game I've ever been in. For one thing it was an extremely emotional game, more emotional than either of the Super Bowl games the Chiefs had played. By the end the people on both sides, grown men, were praying on the sidelines for victory. I've never been in a game where the players unashamedly and openly prayed on the sidelines before.

It was the most exciting game I've ever been involved in. The Chiefs seemed to take control at times but the Dolphins always came back. At one point, with only seconds left, and Jan Stenerud, the best place kicker in football lining up a straight on 31-yard field goal they seemed to have conceded defeat.

Somehow he missed. Earlier he seemed to be hooking his kicks to the left with his side-footed soccer style. This time he seemed to allow for it, but the ball just hung out to the right and sailed wide of the right upright.

There was a terrific cheer from the Miami bench in the otherwise quiet stadium. A moment ago they had conceded the victory to us and now they were given new life. It was a tremendous emotional lift for them. We were shocked. For a few minutes we didn't believe it had happened, but we didn't give up. We never did give up.

Going into the game we were ready. The players' concern is usually with their individual matchups, but as the quarterback my concerns were more general. Would the weather affect the game. We all thought that cold weather would hurt the Miami team more than us, but the game time temperature was an unseasonal 63 degrees.

My concerns were whether or not we could move the ball against the Miami defense. I thought of our game plan and of the things I was sure we could do against the Dolphins and what we couldn't do. I knew, for instance, that they would try and double cover Otis Taylor in almost all situations, and especially on third down situations. We knew that Don Shula had installed a replica of the Baltimore Colts zone when he took over and that ball control and patience were necessary to beat it.

We started very strong and broke on top. The first time we got the ball we held it for seven minutes. A screen pass to Ed Podolak, a 16-yard shot up the middle by Wendell Hayes, Podolak again up the middle, an incomplete pass to Otis Taylor, two more running plays and then Stenerud kicked a 24-yard field goal.

Again our defense smothered the Dolphins and again we marched the ball. This time we held it for four minutes, and on the eighth play of the drive I threw a little swing screen to Podolak and we led 10-0.

We had the game under control. Everything we did we did right. On offense our execution was exact and stunning. On defense we were aggressive and determined. But for some unknown reason we let it slip away.

Just as we had dominated the first part of the first half now the Dolphin offense dominated the second half. Until now there offense had been standing on the sideline watching us work almost to perfection. Now it was their turn. Bob Griese engineered a great drive and Larry Csonka crashed into the end zone from the one to put them right back in the game.

They got the ball right back and raced the clock down the field. With time running out Garo Yepremian kicked a 14-yard field goal to tie the score.

Once again we took control and marched the ball in for a touchdown, with Jim Otis, our tough, short yardage, back getting the final yard. But this time Miami seemed determined not to let us pull away.

Back they came with almost a duplicate of our drive with Jim Kiick going over from the one. Now we were entering the final quarter, the time when mistakes magnify, and one break can mean the game.

We still stuck to our game plan, control the ball and don't force it. It paid off again when Podolak scored his second touchdown of the game with a short burst over tackle. With time grinding down we now led 24-17. But Miami hadn't given up yet. With about two minutes to go Griese hit Marv Fleming, his tight end, with a five-yard hook in the end zone and we had a tie ball game.

There was no doubt in my mind that something was going to happen, that we were going to pull it out. I just sensed it as I watched the teams line up for the kick off.

The ball went to Podolak, a tremendous workhorse for us all day. He started up the middle. Our blocking wedge cleared out the first men down and he cut to the outside at about the 30. Near the 50 he cut away from the kicker, Yepremian. He was in the clear now and it was a footrace between Ed and a Dolphin defensive back who had the angle.

With a burst of desperate speed Curtiss Johnson caught up to Ed and made a saving tackle, but not before he reached the Dolphins' 22-yard line, a dazzling clutch kickoff return of 78 yards.

We ran the ball for three plays and got the time down to only 35 remaining seconds. We could feel victory. But somehow it didn't come. Stenerud missed. Miami ran off what was left of the clock and punted. For a while we debated the possibility of a 62-yard free kick off a fair catch, but at that distance we didn't want Mercury Morris to get his hands on the ball.

The Chiefs won the toss to receive the kickoff to start the sudden death. We caught a second break when the Dolphins were offside after kicking the first one into the end zone. Podolak ran the second one out to our 46. We worked the ball carefully down to the Dolphins 35 and Stenerud came in to try a 42-yard field goal, well within his effective range. But it was blocked and the ball rolled dead on the Miami 24.

Now what had been a game of grinding offense became a battle of pit-slugging defenses. Neither team had punted for four quarters but now it became a punting duel. The first 15 minutes went by and the teams changed goals. Almost half the sixth quarter went by. The players on the field were still struggling, bone tired but determined.

Then the nightmare. The play flowed to the right, but Csonka blasted back on the trap to the left. Our defense was completely fooled. He ran for 29 yards deep into our territory. It was the break the Dolphins had been praying for. Yepremian came in and kicked a 37-yard field goal to end the longest game in pro football history at 82 minutes and 40 seconds.

The Dolphins jumped and cheered in that stunned, silent, stadium. A few Chiefs cried, but no one said a word. It was a game we'd all remember forever.

THE GAME I'LL NEVER FORGET

By Dick Butkus, Chicago Bears

SATURDAY I could barely walk. I tried to jog a little at practice, but it almust crumpled up on me. The knee was swollen and it hurt like —. All that night I just dozed and kept waking up. I lay there flat on my back, afraid to get up, afraid to try and put any kind of weight on it.

I didn't know what was going to happen and I was scared. Our team doctor Dr. Ted Fox operated on the knee in January, but there were some complications. I hadn't done a thing all through camp. The exhibition season came and went and I got in just a couple of quarters, two in the second to last game and about three in the last preseason game. Fox told me the knee was bothering me because I was pushing it too hard, trying to do too much, but you just can't stand around while everyone else is working. You don't even feel like part of the team.

Game day came and it felt a little better. Dr. Fox told me to go out and warm up and see how it felt then we'd decide what to do. I went out there thinking, 'if it works, fine. If it doesn't, well, I'll just have to sit one out.'

That's what I was telling myself, but inside I was nervous and worried and I was so sensitive in that direction that I thought every nerve in my body was running right down to my right knee.

The weather at least was on my side. It was a misty, rainy day. That made the Astroturf in Soldier Field a little slipperier. That made me feel good. That Astroturf is miserable stuff.

It's great for the fans who sit up there and see this neat, almost immaculate field. But the next time you're watching a game remember that under that thin green rug is a skinny sheet of sponge rubber and then rock-hard asphalt. Worst of all there's no give or slide as there is on real turf. You plant your foot to make a cut or make a block or tackle and your foot stops—bang—just like that on these fake fields.

There's no skid and it sends a shock right up to your knee. But with the mist and dampness putting a thin coating on the field we could get a little slide instead of those knee-shuddering stops.

The early birds took the field. We're the guys who shag the balls for the kickers, Bobby Joe Green our punter, and Mac Percival, our place kicker. On the Bears we like to keep it a defensive players prerogative. It brings us a little closer together.

So I was out there with Doug Buffone and Ross Brupbacher and Joe Taylor and Jerry Moore and some of the other fellows throwing the ball around and shagging kicks and fooling around, but mostly worrying about my knee.

It felt pretty good running forward, and even running backwards it felt all right. It got so that I didn't know if I was feeling my knee because there was actually some pain or because I was just thinking about it so hard.

I went back in the locker room before anyone else and Fox asked me how the knee felt. I told him it was feeling much better. It felt fairly strong and the pain seemed to go away once I got warm and loose. We just taped it up and with just five quarters of exhibition play I went out to play the Pittsburgh Steelers in the opening game of the 1971 season.

Everyone wants to get that first game. It sets you up in a positive mental attitude right away and gets you looking forward to the next game instead of looking backward and asking yourself why? and what you should have done differently. You worked hard just to get this far and if you blow it you feel like all that work was wasted and you have to start all over again.

Pittsburgh had a good team, a young team, an improving team. They certainly weren't going to be the push-overs they were when we played them a couple of years ago and really mauled them, nailing them for a couple of safeties.

Now they had good young quarterbacks in Terry Bradshaw and Terry Hanratty, some good running backs in John Fuqua and Preston Pearson and Warren Bankston and a real tough defense. It was probably on defense that they had improved most of all.

It was a slugfest from the opening kickoff. The Steelers thought they were contenders for the division title and they acted like it. The Bears, well we were the Bears, playing a very physical game, our kind of game.

Our defense was really up. I don't see how we could have really played much better. We made a few mistakes, but nothing really major. And, most important, we were forcing, getting the turnovers, taking the ball away from the Steelers and giving it to our offense in good field position.

We were hitting, we were aggressive and we were dictating the game to them instead of just sitting back and waiting for them to come at us.

I intercepted one pass on a screen play but it was nullified because we were offside. On the very next play Bradshaw threw one over the middle and I guess he wasn't reading the defense right because I grabbed that one too. I grabbed off another one later in the game and just missed a fourth when I slipped.

We seemed to have Bradshaw confused all day. We kept showing him different formations and different alignments and every series we'd do something different. One series we'd play man-to-man. The next we'd go zone. Then we'd go combination zone and man-to-man and then we'd blitz every play. We tried to keep him guessing, keep him off balance and not give him a chance to pick up any tendencies.

But going into the fourth quarter we were still behind 14-3. The offense just couldn't get anything going. We never gave up, but the clock kept ticking off the seconds. It was getting awfully fine now. We punted again and knew they were going to try and eat as much of that clock as possible.

They ran an end sweep with Fuqua. Big Ed O'Bradovich, our defensive end, hit him high and hard and knocked the ball loose. Bru scooped it up and ran about 30 yards for the score. That made it 14-10. But now we had to give them the ball.

That score really set the defense on fire. Now we really smelled blood, but there were only about two minutes left. As we were standing along the sidelines for the kickoff our coach, Abe Gibron, told me they'd probably try to kill the clock with some trap plays. He told me if I could see it coming to go ahead and blitz. We might force another fumble.

We kept them inside their own 30 yard line on the kick-off return and I knew Bradshaw wasn't going to throw the ball if he could help it.

I had one of my intuitive visions. While they were still in the huddle I could see the play.

They tried to run a trap. Their center, Ray Mansfield, moved to his left to block our tackle, Bill Staley, and I shot right up the hole. For a split second I thought I could get the hand-off. I hit Bankston just as hard as I could, trying to drive right through him, the instant he touched the ball.

It popped loose and we got it. Kent Nix came off the bench and threw it in for the winning touchdown.

That was so satisfying I can't begin to express it. The day before the game I couldn't walk—then to have it come out like that.

THE GAME I'LL NEVER FORGET

By John Unitas, Baltimore Colts

I'LL NEVER FORGET the sight of Lennie Moore's flashing white spats verring and cutting and flying over the frozen turf in Baltimore's Memorial Stadium.

That was the run that made the Baltimore Colts. It gave us our first Western division title and set us up for our first world championship a couple of games later—the sudden death overtime game against the New York Giants.

To be honest, I suppose most people would expect me to pick that world championship game, which some have called "the greatest game ever played." But my own favorite came a couple of weeks earlier, on Nov. 30, 1958.

We went into that game a hot team, eight and one, with our only defeat at the hands of the Giants a couple of weeks earlier 24 to 21. We were up against the San Francisco 49ers, a great team with some of the most outstanding players in the game. A Colt victory assured us at least a tie for the division championship.

They had Y. A. Tittle at quarterback, Joe Perry and Hugh McElhenny at running back, Leo Nomellini, Bob Toneff, Gordy Soltau and Bob St. Clair up front.

The first half was a Baltimore nightmare. Almost 60,000 fans were there to cheer us to our first title and we stunk the joint out.

Tittle drove his team 80 yards for a score after the opening kickoff. They ate it up in 11 plays with Y. A. sneaking in for the score.

We couldn't move the ball, and back came the 49ers. Milt Davis broke up their drive with an interception, and then we got fired up enough to move in for the tying touchdown.

But that was all we could do. Bert Rechichar missed a field goal from the Frisco 38 and they came storming back. Tittle, Perry, and McElhenney gobbled up that yardage and it was 13-7 so fast I was back on the field before I could catch my breath.

They had us bottled up deep and on third down I dropped back to pass, but big Toneff hit me into the nickel seats and the ball was rolling free. Alex Sandusky fell on it for us on the one, but then Ray Brown punted it out only to the 27.

Tittle made the most of his chance. He hit Clyde Conners with a pass to the three and McElhenny took it over from there. Now we were down, 20-7.

There was at least some hope because Ordell Braase had blocked Soltau's try for the extra point after the second 49er touchdown. That at least gave us something to shoot for.

We only fell deeper into the hole. Usually sure-handed, Lennie Lyles fumbled the kick-off and had to fall on it on our 6-yard line. I dropped back to pass and Nomellini broke through, came in high, and deflected the ball.

It sailed right into the hands of the 49ers line-backer, Matt Hazeltine, and he walked in for the score as I lay buried under a ton of Nomellini.

Mercifully, the gun sounded for the half. It was a dismal offensive performance. I completed only five of 17 passes for something like 25 yards, and we managed about another 60 or so rushing.

I can talk about it now and not make it sound like an alibi, but I was playing with some fractured ribs and the aluminum and rubber harness they had me in was causing me some problems. But there is no excuse for the kind of performance we put on. When you're out there you either do it or you don't. You don't look for alibis.

We got the second half kick-off and started moving. On the 49er side of mid-field, we started to bog down a little and then came one of those plays everybody likes to call turning points. We had a fourth and one on the 49er 41.

We had no choice. We had to go for it. I handed the ball to Alan Ameche and the "Horse" got us that big yard.

That wound us up again and a couple of plays later I hit Moore with a pass down on the three and Ameche took it over.

Our defense was really coming on now. You can talk about great defense and great front fours just about forever, but I'll still go with ours—Gino Marchetti, Art Donovan, Big Daddy Lipscomb, Don Joyce up front; Bill Pellington, Leo Sanford and Don Shinnick behind them and Carl Taseff, Johnny Sample, Milt Davis and Andy Nelson in the secondary.

We should have sliced up that ball and gave each of those guys a piece of it.

They earned it. They made the plays. After they stopped the 49ers again, good old John Unitas fumbled the ball to Jerry Tubbs on the Colts 23. But once again the defense stepped in and Ray Brown intercepted a Tittle pass in the end zone.

We got out of the hole when Jim Mutscheller made a great catch and run for a 59-yard gain. On third down I found Ray Berry, good old third down Ray Berry, on the 49er 16. A couple of plays later Ameche took it over and we had the score down to 27-21.

Then came another of those great, turning point, key, defensive plays. That's what sportswriters always call them, but to me they're just football.

The 49ers had it third and one on their own 40. They gave the ball to McElhenny and it looked like he got mobbed by 11 Colts. They had to punt and the ball rolled dead on our 27.

The clock showed a little over 11 minutes left but I wasn't worried about time. I knew our defense had the momentum. I just wanted to make sure I didn't get too anxious.

So I lined Moore up at halfback and called a sweep to the left. Nothing fancy, just a straight power sweep. Lennie took the hand-off and bellied back a little to let the blocking form.

The left guard and tackle, Art Spinney and Jim Parker, collapsed the 49er line. Ameche threw a block. Moore turned the corner and started upfield. Then Berry threw a block.

Lennie twisted away from the cornerback and with the pursuit coming heavy, cut back sharply toward the middle of the field. I was just another spectator now, cheering him on.

Looming up ahead of him was our big right tackle, George Preas. Together they went all the way, 73 yards for a touchdown.

The place was bedlam when Steve Myhra booted home the extra point to put us in the lead, 28 to 27.

I remember afterwards in the locker room Lennie telling reporters that he didn't know what he was doing, he just cut everytime he saw a Frisco jersey and followed Preas in for the touchdown.

Don't you believe that. Lennie Moore was one of the cleverest fellows who ever stepped out on a football field. He always knew what he was doing. You can argue about your game-breakers all you want, but me, I'll take Lennie Moore.

After that it was anti-climactic. We drove in for another touchdown. I threw an eight-yarder to Berry that tied me with Cecil Isbell's record of having thrown at least one touchdown pass in 23 consecutive games.

To tell you the truth I didn't even care. I knew we had the title. The first championship any Baltimore team had won since John McGraw played in town.

The fans boiled down out of the stands and went hysterical. They carried every player off the field right to the locker room.

I sure was happy for the defense. It was the only rest they had that day. And as for me, well, I'll never forget it.

THE GAME I'LL NEVER FORGET

By John Brodie, San Francisco 49ers

THERE WAS a riot before the game and for all I know there might have been one after, too.

We were going to play Baltimore. The lead in the Western division was at stake and this was the second to the last day of the season. There wasn't any more time to be jockeying for position.

Baltimore was in first place and we were tied with Detroit, just a breath, one deep breath, behind. What started the riot was that about 10,000 more fans showed up at Kezar Stadium then they had seats for. They started to carry booths, cops and gates with them into the stands. I guess they felt that it was time for the 49ers to win something and they wanted to be there when it happened.

Now I can be very objective about this game, most of it anyway, because I played in so little of it. Let's see, it was Dec. 8, 1957, and I was a rookie out of Stanford and all my boyhood heroes were now my teammates, fellows like Y. A. Tittle, Hugh McElhenny, Leo Nomellini, Billy Wilson. I could read you the program, but I won't.

The Colts had some pretty good guys themselves, like John Unitas, Lenny Moore, Alan Ameche, Ray Berry, Gino Marchetti, Big Daddy Lipscomb. In fact in a year they were going to make a little history, but that's peeking.

They beat us in Baltimore a couple of weeks before 27 to 21 in the last couple of minutes and everyone was looking for the same kind of game.

That's just what it turned out to be too, the same kind of game, rough, tough with neither side giving an inch. I was on the phones along the sidelines all day, and although the score didn't get up quite as high as most people thought it would I can tell you those spotters upstairs were plenty excited.

The Colts were nursing a lead, 13-10, and Y.A. got the boys moving. I was doing a lot of cheering. He got it down to the Baltimore 10-yard line for a first and goal with about a minute left and it looked like the old pro was going to pull it off.

On first down he went back to pass. His feet and the wet turf got a little mixed up. He righted himself, started to move but that big Baltimore front four got to him for a loss of two. He was slow getting up. Then he asked for time and started coming towards the sidelines.

At first I thought he was just coming over to talk to our coach, Frankie Albert. The next thing I knew Albert was telling me to get my helmet. 'Hey' I said, 'You got to be kidding.' I swear Tittle looked all right to me.

Besides, this was no time for him to be getting hurt. This was no movie. Hollywood's a ways down the road, down south. Things like this just don't happen in the big game. A least I didn't think so.

But the next thing I knew there I was getting shoved out onto the field and as I was trotting to our huddle I was thinking to myself, 'now ain't this a dilly. We got to score a touchdown and we got it second and 12 with only about 50 seconds to play.'

Now I'll admit that it certainly wasn't the spot for it. I know I was supposed to be tense and nervous, but the outlandishness of the whole situation gave me the giggles. 'Now ain't this some kind of state to be in?' I kept asking myself.

I hadn't played a play all year, not thrown a single pass or made a single handoff and here I was going in with 50 seconds to go and the game in my hands. That'd make any sane person giggle.

I sure hoped those fellows in the huddle weren't looking for any leadership. They were going to have to supply it, not receive it. Got there, knelt down, looked at all those grimy faces and issued my first orders in a clear, crisp voice.

'Well, anyone got any bright ideas?'

We decided, the huddle had suddenly changed from a monarchy under Tittle to a democracy under Brodie, we decided that I should roll out to the right. If I was too scared to pass I could always run.

The situation was too ludicrous for fright. So I rolled right and threw to Billy Wilson in the end zone. The ball got to him all right, but he almost got annihilated. He just got buried. It looked like everyone on the Colts got a piece of poor Billy on that play. He must have felt like a couple of 49ers were whacking him too.

All right, so now we had it third and goal on the 12 and now the time was down to about 44 seconds. The time didn't really matter now, not unless I could scramble for half a minute or so. We were just down to two more plays. The next one, and then probably let Gordy Soltau try a field goal for the tie.

We huddled up again and I guess the boys had had enough of my leadership. In one play we had gone from a Tittle monarchy to a Brodie democracy to a McElhenny monarchy.

"Just put it in the left corner," McElhenny said.

He didn't say to who, but I wasn't arguing. I was just priming myself for my second pass of the season.

I dropped back the customary seven-eight yards and threw it. Never did see what happened after that. I was just smiling up into the scowling face of big Art Donovan. I was about to ask him what day this was when I heard a tremendous roar. Then I remembered that we were playing at home.

That meant that somebody on my team must have caught that ball. It turned out to be McElhenny after all. The stadium went absolutely goofy, and Donovan swore.

Now who could forget that?

THE GAME I'LL NEVER FORGET

By Bubba Smith, Baltimore Colts

REDEMPTION is such a soul satisfying thing. There is a deep down pleasure and satisfaction in proving to yourself and the world that if a mistake wasn't corrected at least you didn't let it happen again.

That's why we walked off that field with our heads up after beating the Dallas Cowboys in Super Bowl V. We had proved to ourselves that we could win the big pressure games, and that's why it'll be the game I'll never forget.

We waited two years to get back in there, two years since the New York Jets embarassed us 16 to 7 in Super Bowl III. We were supposed to be a cinch to win that one, but we were flat, made mistakes and never really got going.

Going down to Miami this time to get ready for the game we knew what to expect. We knew what to do. It's a funny thing, but if you don't know exactly what you have to do you have a tendency to slough off, to have fun, go through all sorts of publicity stunts and never really get your mind on what you're down there to do—get ready for a tough game of football.

That's one of the things that hurt us against the Jets. That's no alibi though, because they hadn't been there before either and they played well. But we weren't going to make the same mistake against the Cowboys.

In my own mind I kept telling myself to get ready to go all out the whole game. To play well I've got to be prepared to put the pressure on the offense the

whole game. I've found that that's the only way to approach the game, and the only way to play once you're on the field. Once you relax, the momentum can swing so fast you can go from 14 points ahead to 14 points behind in a matter of minutes and never get going to catch up again.

You've got to go all out every play of the game, and that's what I was getting ready to do.

We knew the Dallas team pretty well. In all the times we played them we lost to them only once and that was the year after the Jets beat us. We were out of it by then and the game didn't mean very much to us so we really weren't too ready to play. But this was different. This Super Bowl was for all the prestige of being the champion plus all that money, $15,000 a man to the winners.

Games don't always play the way you imagine them in your mind though. We put ourselves in the hole right away, deep in the hole as we were to do so many times that afternoon. Ron Gardin, in the deep safety position, fumbled the Cowboys' punt in the first quarter and Cliff Harris recovered for Dallas on our nine.

On first down Duane Thomas got four to put them in pretty good shape, but on second down Mike Curtis shot the gap and threw him for a two-yard loss. Craig Morton overthrew his receiver in the end zone on third down. I didn't see who he was trying to throw to. I was too busy with Ralph Neely to worry about getting his name or number. Fourth and seven and they kicked a field goal to go ahead 3-0.

Our offense couldn't get going and we were back out there right away. Walt Garrison ripped off some good yardage, and there is a very underrated running back. He can get that tough yardage. Then we made a bad mistake. Bob Hayes got between and behind Jerry Logan and Charley Stukes and caught a bomb. We also got called for roughing Morton after the pass was thrown and the Cowboys had a first down on our six.

Somehow we sucked it up and dug in and held them again. Twice they had first downs inside our ten and twice we held them to field goals. In the long run those plays were as important as any in the game. We had to feel good coming off the field after our second goal line stand.

When things are going bad you just reach back and keep scrapping, and clawing and just hang in there until you catch a break. The main thing is not to give up.

We didn't, and we got that break. John Unitas threw for Eddie Hinton. It bounced off Hinton's hands and went right to the Dallas cornerback, Mel Renfro. But it must have caught Renfro by surprise because it went through him too. Our tight end, John Mackey, hustling all the way was in the right spot, caught the deflection off Renfro and ran for the touchdown. The play covered 75 yards.

Some people have called that a lucky play. I don't think it was lucky. I think it was great play on the part of John Mackey. He could have quit anywhere along the line, when Unitas threw to Hinton, or when Renfro deflected the ball. But he didn't. He just kept hustling and turned a busted play into a score. Actually we could say Dallas was lucky because they blocked the extra point try. But that was a great play on their part.

Another mistake set Dallas up again though. Unitas was back to pass, couldn't find anyone and then started to run. Lee Roy Jordan and Chuck Howley both hit him. He fumbled, and Jethro Pugh recovered

at our 28. This time we couldn't stop them. Thomas got a couple. Morton passed to Dan Reeves on a swing pass down to our seven and then he repeated the play to Thomas for the score.

That gave them the lead, 13-6, but I wasn't worried. Our offense was starting to move the ball. But we also kept making those killing mistakes.

We drove it down deep but Renfro intercepted on about the 15. Then with two minutes to play in the first half we had a first down on their two. We couldn't get it in. Their defense made a great stand. On fourth down we said the heck with the field goal. But they held.

What happened right after the second half kickoff probably decided the game. Our Jim Duncan was back to receive and fumbled. The Cowboys recovered deep in our territory. They worked it down to a first down on our 2 yard line. The handoff went to Thomas. We were in a goal line gap defense with everyone pinching in towards the center. Thomas got hit hard and fumbled. Duncan and Billy Ray Smith pounced on the ball.

That was probably the key to the game. If they had scored it would have made it 20 to 6 and that would have been a steep hill for us to climb. But after that the breaks started going our way. Some of them at least. One that didn't was Cornell Green punching the ball out of Hinton's arms as he was running free for a touchdown.

But Rich Volk intercepted a pass and ran it back from the Dallas 34 to the three. Tom Nowatzke battered his way in from there and that tied the score.

Then with the score tied and just over a minute left to play deep in his own territory Morton threw for Reeves along the sideline. The ball bounced out of Reeves' hands and right to Curtis. He ran it back to the Dallas 28. There would be no sudden death overtime today.

Three plays to run out the clock and Jim O'Brien came in and kicked the winning field goal. And that was redemption, man.

It was a game that I truly will never forget.

THE GAME I'LL NEVER FORGET

By Herb Adderley, Dallas Cowboys

THERE ARE few times when a man can look back and say truthfully, "I won that game. Without me we would have lost." I'm talking about team games now, especially the game of football where each man depends so much upon the other ten, and where the

offense and defense are so dependent on each other.

But I can look back to one murky, muddy Sunday in Green Bay, Wisconsin and truthfully feel that on that day a young fellow named Herb Adderley made the big difference in the ball game.

To set the stage for you, all I have to tell you is that it was Oct. 7, 1962. The Green Bay Packers were the defending champions of professional football. We thought we were going to repeat. The Detroit Lions didn't think we should. We both thought this game would settle it.

They thought they could beat us. We were the champions and they figured they could knock us off and use us as a stepping stone to a championship of their own. There was no love lost between the Packers and the Lions. Every time we played in those days, it was with a little extra of that complete abandon that Vince Lombardi liked to talk about.

Our game plan was very simple, smother them on defense and ram it down their throats on offense.

It started that way when our offense marched the ball over 70 yards right from the opening kick-off. Jimmy Taylor was going great and he got well over half of that yardage by himself. We were playing our game, keeping the ball and eating up the clock. But when we got down close, the Lions' defense really tightened up and Paul Hornung had to kick a 15-yard field goal.

We went back in and made them give up the ball, but then the Lions got the break that turned the game around. Bart Starr went back to pass, but our blocking broke down. Starr was hit, fumbled, and Karras recovered the ball on our 34 yard line. That gave the Lions a tremendous lift and Dan Lewis scored from just outside our 5 yard line six plays later. They went into the lead 7 to 3.

From then on we were like two beasts locked at each others throats. Our offense was able to move the ball, but twice we turned it over on mistakes. We thought we could fool the Lions by having Tom Moore throw the option pass, a Hornung specialty, but he underthrew Boyd Dowler and Yale Lary intercepted. Then later, after another long drive, Hornung threw one intended for our tight end, Ron Kramer, but he underthrew him and the ball sailed right into the arms of their outside linebacker, Carl Brettschneider.

In the third quarter our offense started another drive from deep in our own territory. Looking back now, that was one of the keys to the game. We held their offense in check, but we couldn't make them turn the ball over, we couldn't force them into mistakes so we were always starting drives from deep in our territory.

Do that, especially playing the basic kind of ball control game we played, and any little mistake along the way can stop you. This time we got down to about the Lion's 7 yard line, but again we were stopped, so on the last play of the third quarter Hornung kicked another 15-yard field goal to close the gap to 7 to 6.

Now the game intensified. It was for blood. We kicked off, and for once we couldn't stop the Lions. They knew they needed some points. Even a field goal now would put us in a deep hole. They drove the ball down to our 34 yard line, but we tightened up and with nine minutes to go Wayne Walker missed a field goal from the 41.

We came off the field cheering for our offense: "Go! Go! Go! Get some points!" The whole bench was up. Starr threw one to Dowler for a first down. Then he hit Max McGee for another. We ran a couple and then he hit Ron Kramer for another first down. We had the ball down on the Lions' 40-yard line, but again we stalled. Hornung came in and tried one from the 47 yard line, but the ball was wide to the left. It had the distance, but from the right hashmark it went wide.

With six minutes left to play the Lions took the ball on their own 20. They had to move the ball to kill the clock. We had to stop them. They ran on first down for a couple of yards. They ran it again on second down, but got very little. On third and long, Plum completed a pass to his tight end Gibbons for a first down.

The clock was moving and again they started the pattern all over again. Run for a short gain. Run again, and again Plum gambled and put the ball in the air, and again he completed it to Gibbons for the first down.

Time was really getting short now. We were going to have to use our time outs now just to save whatever time we could. The drizzle, which had been steady throughout the game seemed to be getting heavier. They ran and ran again, and for the third time on third down Plum went back to pass. He must have thought we'd be looking for him to go to Gibbons again so this time he changed the pattern.

Barr came straight out at me, and about ten yards off the line of scrimmage he cut to go to the sidelines. But he tried to cut it a little too sharp. His foot slipped on the wet field. He went down and there was that ball just hanging in the air in front of me. I didn't think. I just reacted. I took two steps up, caught it and started down the sidelines. I don't remember who caught me, but by the time they did it didn't matter. I was able to run it back about 40 yards to the Detroit 18 yard line. With only 33 seconds left Hornung came in and kicked his third field goal of the game. We won, 9 to 7.

We went on to a great season, finishing 13 and 1 in the regular season and beat the New York Giants for our second straight world's championship. Later on Vince Lombardi told me that if it hadn't of been for my interception he would have never been able to write his book, *Run To Daylight*.

Building a Team

The Golden Draft

That vital winter ritual known as the player draft has been held by the National Football League since 1936. This complex ceremony, conducted by small enclaves of football brain trusts in smoke-filled hotel rooms, was originally designed with the avowed purpose of helping the weaker teams in the league. These teams would be given the privilege of picking first, enabling them to skim off the cream of the college crop of seniors.

Not incidentally, however, the draft prevented a lot of costly, cut-throat financial competition and inter-club squabbles over the rights to some particularly desirable gridiron specimen.

That's how it worked most of the time, with the most notable exception the era of the early 1960's when the American Football League and the NFL waged their pre-merger battle of dollar bills over some highly-rated and not-so-highly rated college players.

Football owners and commissioners have argued— often before Congressional committees—that the draft is vital to the survival of quality professional football. And it is, at least to the clubs involved.

Mistakes that a team makes in the draft can be much more costly and much harder to correct than those made on the playing field. A poor draft can sentence a club to also-ran status, or worse, for years.

And so today, as it has been in the past, a great deal of the man-hours and dollars in football administration go into the selection of the rookie batch.

Player drafts are something like vintages and wine. Some years the ivy-covered campuses produce plentiful crops of young players with the potential for greatness, near-greatness and for good, serviceable if not super careers.

In other years, the harvest is thin, the product lacks character, potential and depth. Only a few players will be salvaged and found palatable to the computerized brain-trusts of the clubs. The rest will be tried quickly, and used occasionally, if at all.

In many years there are one or two individual products who stand out above the rest and who go on to achieve distinction in the pro football wars.

A few drafts have produced some of the game's greatest players, including some that were tabbed for stardom from the beginning and some who blossomed and matured in the actual competition of professional football.

Like connoisseurs of wine, football fans argue over the merits of some of the greatest drafts in history and the players that qualify those years for that distinction.

Over the past decade, during that turbulent time of the AFL-NFL war, one year stands out as the nominee for "Greatest Draft" of the modern era: 1965.

The 1965 draft produced one of the most remarkable 1-2 picks for an individual team in pro football history.

The Chicago Bears, using two first round picks,

selected linebacker Dick Butkus out of the University of Illinois and running back Gale Sayers from Kansas.

The Bears, incidentally, might even challenge that dual selection with the one they made in the very first draft in 1936. They picked Joe Stydahar and Danny Fortmann, who both eventually got into the Football Hall of Fame.

George Halas, however, did lose the number one pick of all the teams in 1936, halfback Jay Berwanger, the Heisman trophy winner from the University of Chicago. The Bears bought the rights to Berwanger from the Eagles.

But Berwanger demanded a no-cut, two-year contract at $12,500 a year. Halas thought this was outrageous, not entirely for monetary reasons, he said.

Berwanger took a job in a rubber company for $25 a week and never did perform again before the cheering multitudes.

In 1965, Papa Bear loosened his purse strings somewhat to get Butkus and Sayers. And they were well worth it. Though the Bears were never champions, Sayers and Butkus provided a powerful drawing card that kept the seats filled through some awfully lean years for the club.

Both Butkus and Sayers toyed with the AFL representatives who were so eager to secure their services. But, both admitted that they wanted badly to play in the NFL with its prestige, history and future security.

"At that time I thought, and it was the accepted thinking, that the American League was the inferior

(Above) Papa Bear George Halas. (Below) Dick Butkus (51).

Ronald Mrowiec

league. Whether it was or not was immaterial," Butkus said.

As it turned out, Butkus, Sayers and another young potential superstar of the 1965 draft—Joe Namath—were all involved in some fast behind the scenes manipulations by the AFL powers.

Denver had been hot for Butkus. Kansas City wanted Sayers, the "Kansas Comet," a home-state product that would be a sure box-office draw.

Butkus and his agent-attorney, Arthur Morse, talked to Denver, but not seriously. Morse, however, knew that some of the real money in the fledgling AFL was in New York, where Sonny Werblin was trying to buy some quality players to boost the league. If Denver, which drafted Butkus, would trade the rights to New York, Morse might do some serious talking.

Werblin did make some tentative feelers towards Butkus, but meanwhile, the Bears drafted him and offered a deal over $400,000.

"Later I found out that Werblin was playing a waiting game," Butkus said. "He was trying to get the biggest name he could to commit to the Jets. Everyone knew that a strong New York franchise would make the league that much stronger. It paid off for him. He got Denver to give him their number one pick and he took Joe Namath."

About the same time, another big AFL money man, Lamar Hunt, owner of the Kansas City Chiefs, contacted Butkus and, apparently under the mistaken impression that Butkus was sewed up for the AFL, Hunt asked Butkus to convince Sayers to sign with the Chiefs.

"I found out later what the deal was supposed to be," Butkus said. The league was fighting for prestige. They hadn't done too well in signing name players in the past, so this year they were supposed to sign a player for any team and straighten things out later," Butkus said.

Sayers recalled the time when he was drafted as one of confusion for him. The Chiefs had picked him as their number one choice. The San Francisco 49ers seemed to show the most pre-draft interest in the quiet young halfback, and Sayers thought that's where he would be going.

Sayers learned just before the draft was held that the teams with the first three picks, the Giants, the Bears and the 49ers wanted running backs. The three at the top of the list were Sayers, Tucker Frederickson of Auburn and Ken Willard out of North Carolina.

"Something happened. San Francisco took Willard instead," Sayers recalled. The 49ers regretted the choice ever after. Because although Willard gave them good service, he was not in the super star category with Sayers.

Hunt did make an 11th hour pitch to get Sayers into the KC fold. He had one of his men almost literally pull Sayers from the stage where Ed Sullivan was presenting the All-American team. Hunt offered Sayers a $27,500 three-year contract with a $50,000 bonus. Sayers turned it down.

Butkus, of course, went on to become the premier middle linebacker in football, a perennial All-Pro who epitomizes the brutal determination of a man totally committed to pitting his considerable talents against the enemy on the playing field.

Sayers, although his career was cut all-too short by knee injuries, wrote new chapters in the record books and forged unforgettable memories for football fans with his often unbelievable open field running ability.

It didn't take long for Sayers to show his greatness. In his rookie year he scored the still-standing record of 22 touchdowns—six in one game against that San Francisco club—he also piled up 2,272 yards in that year as well. In 1966 his total yardage of 2,440 set the NFL record.

Sayers was the NFL's Rookie of the Year. In the AFC, the rookie honors went to Namath, who was also chosen player of the year in 1968.

Namath the sleepy-eyed super star, helped put the AFL on firm footing. Eventually he and his Jets boosted the AFL to parity with the NFL after the two-league merger, when they upset the Baltimore Colts in Super Bowl III in 1969.

Namath had been the number one pick of the St. Louis Cardinals in the NFL.

Frederickson was the number one pick of the entire 1965 draft. But like many of the top picks in football history, he never was able to achieve the greatness expected of him, because of injuries in his case.

The AFL did get some other bona fide stars in that draft, in addition to Namath. Oakland picked and signed Fred Biletnikoff of Florida State, an outstanding receiver who led the AFC in 1971 with 61 catches for 929 yards.

Biletnikoff was the Detroit Lion's third round draft pick. They had chosen Tom Nowatzke, the Indiana fullback, on the first round.

Otis Taylor succumbed to Lamar Hunt's siren call and checkbook and went on to become one of the best receivers in the business. It should be noted that the Philadelphia Eagles selected Taylor, on the 15th round!

In any draft, the top choices are important and more often than not these picks will perform somewhere near expectations. But the thing that scouts and directors of player personnel and coaches dream about is the "sleeper". The guy who comes out of a tiny college somewhere, like Taylor did out of Prairie View, and blossoms into a star.

Another outstanding player who wound up in the AFL was Jim Nance, who went to the Boston Patriots. Nance led the league in rushing in 1966 with 1,458 yards and in 1967 with 1,216 yards.

The Bears, who had three first round picks, lost

their third man, defensive end Steve Delong, to San Diego.

Tackle Mike Tilleman out of Syracuse was drafted by the Minnesota Vikings and eventually wound up with the Houston Oilers.

For the NFL, the 1965 player vintage included some players who became All-Pro standouts at their positions, ranking near the top of their profession if not, perhaps quite at the all-time, super status level.

There was middle linebacker Mike Curtis, of Duke, who has rewarded the Baltimore Colts for their first round selection of him by anchoring the defense for the team for many years.

The Colts also picked Oklahoma offensive lineman Ralph Neely on the second round, but Neely quickly went to Dallas Cowboys, where he has excelled ever since.

The Minnesota Vikings used their first two picks to get receivers and got two of the best: Jack Snow of Notre Dame, followed by Lance Rentzel of Oklahoma. Unfortunately for the Vikings, they gave Snow to Los Angeles and Rentzel went on to Dallas.

And there were other good men in that '65 bunch. The Bears signed Dick Gordon, of Michigan, who led the league in pass receiving in 1970. Ed Flanagan, the center from Purdue, was picked on the fifth round by the Lions.

The Eagles got Gary Garrison, a wide receiver from San Diego State, on the sixth round. Although, you recall, the 15th round pick, Otis Taylor, got away.

The Steelers signed Roy Jefferson out of Utah on the second round, and the Washington Redskins picked defensive back Kent McCloughan of Nebraska on the third round. Chris Hanburger, the "aging" linebacker who helped the Skins to a championship in 1972, was selected on the 18th round!

To round things off, other players who were in the '65 player heap, were Craig Morton, the California quarterback, who was the Cowboys' first choice; Jethro Pugh, the massive Dallas tackle, from Elizabeth City Teachers College, an 11th round choice; Roy Hilton, of the Colts; Donny Anderson, of the Packers; Dave Osborn, the Vikings hard working running back; and Don Croftcheck went to the Redskins. There were many more who proved to be solid, journeymen football players.

Today, when all but a handful of teams have joined a computerized player evaluation system, a crop like the 1965 one would probably blow the transistors right out of the BLESTO-V, CEPO or TROICA data bank.

Rarely could so many players get top marks on such characteristics as height, weight and speed, competiveness, character, mental alertness, body control, quickness, agility, and strength.

There have been some outstanding number one picks and rookies over the past decade, men like Dave

Parks, of San Francisco, number one in 1964; John Brockington of Green Bay, rookie of the year in 1971; Calvin Hill, a star for Dallas in his rookie year of 1969.

But for quality and depth, 1965 ranks tops.

One of the closest contenders for "greatest drafts," some will argue, was 1962.

The number one choice, Ernie Davis, the running back from Syracuse, died of cancer before he ever played a game for the Redskins, the team that picked him.

But the San Diego Chargers came up with a fantastic passing combination. John Hadl, the quarterback from Kansas, was picked and lured away from Detroit, which had made him their first round selection.

The Chargers also got Lance Alworth, the wide receiver from Arkansas, away from the 49ers.

Hadl lead the AFL in passing in 1965 with 174 completions of 348 attempts for 2,789 yards. Alworth led the league in receiving in 1968 and 1969.

Over the decade since their selection, the fistfull of dollars that San Diego team owner Conrad Hilton put out for this pair has paid off in good dividends.

In the 1962 draft, the L.A. Rams also picked up two of that team's all-time standouts. Merlin Olsen, a tackle from Utah St., who went on to become one of the Rams "Fearsome Foursome" on the defensive line, and a frequent All-Pro selection.

With another first round choice, the Rams got Roman Gabriel, who reached a peak in 1969 when he was named Most Valuable Player. Jim Bakken, one of the better kickers in the business, was a 7th round Ram choice in 1962.

Junious Buchanan, better known as Buck, was deemed worthy of a 17th round chance by the Packers. The Chiefs signed the big tackle from Grambling and have been happy about it ever since.

One of the other super stars of the class of '62 was end Gary Collins, who came out of Maryland. The Cleveland Browns grabbed the lanky receiver on the first round. In addition to his great talent as a receiver, he was an outstanding punter.

Other outstanding players that started in 1962 were tackle Fred Miller, a Colts selection; Gary Ballman who played tight end for the Steelers; and lineman Irv Goode, the Cardinals' first choice.

The Bears got Ronny Bull, the Baylor back who was rookie of the year in 1962. Other selections like defensive back Benny McRae, of Michigan, guard Jim Cadile, of San Jose State, and defensive end Ed O'Bradovich of Illinois, all helped the Bears to an NFL championship the following year in 1963.

Was '62 a better year than '65? Or are there any other nominations from the floor? You'll have to have a pretty good argument to top the Sayers-Butkus-Namath year, the one we call "the Greatest Draft."

WHAT IT'S LIKE AT A FREE AGENT TRYOUT

GATHER ROUND all you of short wind, of weak calves, of narrow shoulders. Assemble all you who are too fat, too skinny, too small, too slow, too clumsy and otherwise too too. You have missed your chance at fame and fortune.

Don't feel too bad though. When the Chicago Bears held a free agents tryout camp earlier this year everybody who showed up, most of them just like you, (unfortunately for the Bears) blew their chance too.

There were more than 100 of them, truck drivers, gym teachers, pot wallopers, factory hands, salesmen, itinerent musclemen, and even a disc jockey from Omaha. They came all the way from California to Massachusetts and in-between spots like Colorado, South Dakota, Michigan, Connecticut, Oklahoma and Ohio.

"We invited certain guys who wrote or called in asking for a tryout," said Bears vice president Ed McCaskey, "and that was the worst collection of physical specimens I've ever seen.

"There were guys who couldn't chin themselves once. They couldn't run backwards two steps without falling down. If they tried to cross their legs over they tripped themselves.

"We had receivers who couldn't catch, running backs who stumbled over the chalk marks and kickers who didn't know which foot to use.

"There was one guy, a kicker, with a moustache and long black hair, who kept running in circles to stay warm. He was only wearing a pair of shorts, and it was cold and raining. He kept running in circles to stay warm until he got his chance. He never got one through—at any distance, even a normal extra point."

The would-be all-pros were given color-coded arm bands according to position and then put through some preliminary exercises: chin-ups, push-ups, jumping drills, the mile run and some 4-yard sprints. Most of them didn't last through the drills.

Big Abe Gibron, the Bears' gruff head coach walked around surrounded by a hooded parka like a latter-day inquisitor, hollering into his bullhorn, "give 'em the hook. That guy can't even cross his legs without falling down."

It was mostly the honor system, and the reject was supposed to surrender his arm band and depart. "Get rid of them as soon as you can," was Abe's instructions to his staff.

A few of them tried to sneak back in with another group. But they got weeded out no matter where they went.

"Hey man," one would-be linebacker moaned to Dick Butkus, the Bears legitimate All-Pro, who was helping with the prospects, "I played with Cleveland four years."

"Listen, son," the suddenly fatherly Butkus told him, "you can't even turn around without falling over. You better go get your two dollars lunch money from McCaskey.

"They were really something," Butkus said. "They were wearing some of the craziest outfits I ever saw. Bits and pieces they collected from every camp they've ever been to. One guy had on a Detroit jersey, Saints' pants, and a Cowboys' socks. Some guys were just in their street clothes, and honest, did you see that guy who was wearing his karate black belt?

"I had a couple of guys tell me their wives were in the parking lot with the motor running and if they got cut here they were taking right off because they heard the Redskins were holding a camp, too. I never saw anything like it."

The disc jockey from Omaha kept running around yelling, "I can do it, baby! I can do it, baby!"

"Give that guy the hook!" bellowed Gibron.

Within an hour, the light and stardust had gone out of most eyes. All that travel and all that expense had been wasted. A few didn't think they had a fair crack.

"I drove all the way from Connecticut for this," moaned would-be tight end LeVell Hill. "I was going to run a 4.5 forty (40 yards in 4.5 seconds). But they didn't keep me long enough to show them," said the former Langston University (Okla.) flash.

For George Victor, 30, a star high school running back of 12 years past, it was the fulfillment of a dream and the answer to a question. He went back to his job as superintendent of a wrecking company and laid aside his long nourished dream of football glory.

"I never had a chance to go on with football," he said. "I got married young, and I've got four kids. I lied about my age to get out because they didn't want anyone over 28.

"I lost 17 pounds in nine days to get down to 238. This is something I always wanted to do. I didn't make it. But I had my chance. Now I've got no squawks coming.

Or dreams lingering.

Out of that mass of dreams and physical wrecks, the Bears took about eight players, including Booth Lusteg, now 33 and a struggling actor, who once put in NFL time kicking for Buffalo, Miami, Pittsburgh, the New York Jets and Green Bay.

They took an offensive tackle who had to gain 24 pounds before summer camp, a running back who had to lose 15 and an assortment of other guys who probably wouldn't last a week when the hitting started.

For some there's a third chance, although the glory will be diluted. Scouts from the Continental League teams were picking guys up just as fast as Gibron could holler, "Give 'em the hook."

HOW TO BUILD A PRO TEAM

SUPPOSE, JUST SUPPOSE, that by some miraculous combination of vision and lucidity the Supreme Court declared that the owners of the 26 teams of the National Football League were operating in restraint of trade, and dissolved the league, voided all player contracts, declared Pete Roselle superfluous, and confined Howard Cosell.

That would leave a lot of fellows with nothing to do between commercials. So, as an act of common humanity why not start a league of your own with 25 of your friends?

Now through the miracle of imagination we can all become coaches, general manager and club owners. For years we've all known secretly that we could do a better job as we've ranted about stupid trades and lousy drafts picks and raved when they went for three points on fourth and goal from inside the one, or punted on fourth and inches near mid-field.

The chance is yours now to build your own team. Put it together any way you like. If you are partial to pulling guards you can put together a squad of 40 pulling guards, but that's getting a little ahead of ourselves.

Let's assume that each team formerly had control of 60 players, counting veterans, taxi squaders and rookies. Now they're all free agents, but like the old league we don't want to have bidding wars over every player so we will hold a gigantic draft of the 1,560 or so players.

All the names go up on the board and as the founder of the league you, naturally, will get to pick first. Now is the time for your acuteness and acumen to come to the fore. What chance has a Paul Brown, a Don Shula, a George Allen against the likes of you? Against the skills and judgment you've acquired through years of barroom criticism and reading Red Smith?

Out of all those names, many of them great and glorious, which do you take first?

Do you take a quarterback? And if so, which one? There are about 60 of them in various stages of development.

Well, I'll tell you what. I'll make this all a little easier for you. Since it was my idea to begin with I'll tell you what I'd do.

I wouldn't take a quarterback first. A quarterback gives you offensive leadership, but the fact that there are so many of them should tell you something. If nothing else that they aren't too hard to come by. If all 25 teams drafting behind you selected a quarterback, you'd still have another 35 to choose from.

If I had the first pick, as I now seem to have awarded myself, I would want to select the rarest, most difficulty duplicated player in the game. Now the way I break things down by position there are fewer great middle linebackers in the game today than great anything elses—Dick Butkus of the Chicago Bears, Tommy Nobis of the Atlanta Falcons, and Willie Lanier of the Kansas City Chiefs.

And even of that small group, Butkus is in a class by himself. He is more and more being recognized as *the* great player in the game. By taking him as my number one pick I have assured myself a steady, dependable defense. Defense is the more important half of the game. It's what makes you a winner, and week in and week out it is terribly more consistent than offense.

My second pick would be determined by just how many quarterbacks were left and who they were. I wouldn't expect Joe Namath, Daryle Lamonica and Fran Tarkenton to still be up there, but I would expect a lot of class A passers to still be on the board. It is important to remember that as colleges are more and more adopting a pro-style of offense, a number of highly promising passers come into the game every year, at an ever increasing rate.

That means I might still have time. That would mean I'd take a man who'd give me an outstanding pass rush, a Claude Humphrey, a Carl Eller, a Cedrick Hardman, a Bubba Smith or a Rich Jackson. With that kind of rush against the pass and with Butkus in the middle shutting off the run I'd be well on the way to a super defense.

That would mean that the third round is time enough to take a quarterback and still get a good one. I'd expect to still be able to get an outstanding young one; a Greg Landry, a Steve Spurrier, a Greg Cook, a Mike Phipps, a Dan Pastorini, a Jim Plunkett, an Al Woodall, a Terry Bradshaw, or an old timer like John Brodie, Sonny Jurgensen or Len Dawson. I'd gamble that at least one of them would still be left. And that would be a lot of quarterback to start building an offense around.

If all the blue chip young quarterbacks were gone you could take a smart, experienced man like John Unitas, or Earl Morrall and let them help break in their replacement.

After I had my quarterback I'd then take the best cornerback still available to really fill out my defensive team. Here again you're dealing with a position that is not very heavy in outstanding players, there are only about one per every other team. So anybody who can get a Roger Wehrli, a Bruce Taylor, a Willie Brown, a Lem Barney, a Mel Renfro has got a jump on the opposition.

These players are game breakers. They beat you with the interception, with the punt return and with the kick-off return. In some cases, it's like drafting one man and getting three.

After the quarterback the next offensive player I'd take would be the tight end. Here again we are dealing with one of those rare players. As an offensive man he is probably second in importance to the quarterback, and like middle linebackers and cornerbacks he is at a premium.

In all of pro football there are only six or seven men who can block to make the running game go and still have the speed to run the deep pass patterns. Those are the two ways the tight end helps you, and in many respects he is the key to your offense. A tight end who can go deep, and in some instances demand double coverages, really opens things up for the wide receivers and the quarterback.

Whether I'd take the tight end or a cornerback as my fourth or fifth pick would depend on who was available. It would be awfully hard to pass up a Charley Sanders, a Ray Chester, a Jim Mitchell or a Jackie Smith if one of them was still on the board. The chances are I'd take a tight end first because there are roughly twice as many outstanding cornerbacks as tight ends.

After the fifth round I would still try to concentrate more on the defensive team than one of the offensive team. I would try and add another outstanding pass rusher and another outstanding linebacker to play alongside Butkus. Another premier cornerback would be high on my list.

Others may be more offensive oriented and that would work to my advantage. There would be that many more outstanding defensive players still available. And a defense like that not only stops the opposition, but it gives its own offense easy scores and puts points on the board itself.

From the tenth round on I'd start filling out my offensive line, starting with the tackles. Most coaches feel that offensive linemen are the real journeymen of pro football. They think they can load up on flashy pass catchers and dazzling running backs and patch and fill along the line. That's most coaches, but not the consistent winners.

You just notice which coaches draft linemen real high, like number one and two every year, or nearly every year, in the college draft. You'll run across names like Brown, Shula, Hank Stram, Weeb Ewbank Bud Grant, all winners. That's because they're smart enough to think like I do.

With a great defense, a quarterback, a tight end and a good blocking offensive line I'm on my way to a championship. But maybe before the kick-off of the Super Bowl I better explain why I started with offensive tackles.

I take the tackles first because the most consistent pass rush comes from the outside, from the defensive ends, and I first want the men who can shut off the other team's strength.

After putting a line together I can then start looking for wide receivers. There are more outstanding wide receivers in the game than anything else. There are probably about 30 fellows who could be named all-pro every year except that you only need two. Just start naming them: Dick Gordon, Bob Hayes, Lance Alworth, Earl McCullouch, Carroll Dale, both Gene Washingtons, Charley Taylor, Gary Collins, Paul Warfield, Danny Abramowicz, Don Maynard, Fred Biletnikoff, Ron Sellers.

And, there are just as many who are just a shade beneath them. So many in fact that it wouldn't be any trouble at all to find all the wide receivers you'd need even very late in the draft.

The same holds true for running backs. There are so many running backs, outstanding running backs that it is unnecessary to go after them until the end. The list is almost as endless as wide receivers—Gale Sayers, Calvin Hill, Mel Farr, Ron Johnson, Tom Woodeshick, Ken Willard, Norm Bulaich, Larry Csonka, Jim Nance.

To my way of thinking the running back is the most overrated player in football. They are the least helpful, they and the wide receivers, than any other offensive player. No matter how good they are they can't do anything for themselves. Hand them the ball. Knock everybody down and they'll run for a touchdown. A bit of an overstatement perhaps, but think on this.

Great running backs and a great running game are not necessarily the same thing. It wasn't very long ago that a couple of cast-off plodders named Ben Wilson and Chuck Mercein played an important role in getting the Green Bay Packers into Super Bowl II.

In Super Bowl V, it was Tom Nowatzke, a rumbling tank who had been switched to linebacker and then dumped by the Detroit Lions, who was the Baltimore Colts leading rusher and scored one of their two touchdowns. Which just goes to prove that if you don't have the horses up front your running game's in trouble no matter who's doing the ball carrying.

As long as we are going to be opponents I shouldn't try to educate you too much. You might try and outsmart the master some day. But here I am sitting pretty with Dick Butkus and Rich Jackson and Greg Landry and Bruce Taylor, and Merlin Olsen and Jim Mitchell while the rest of you went out and each took four quarterbacks, eight wide receivers and a dozen running backs and one center. Somebody's got to do the blocking.

All we need is for the Supreme Court to hand down that decision and I can start chalking off the field.

The Art of the Passer

THE STORY has been recounted by thousands of bar stool quarterbacks from Bangor, Me. to Bakersfield, Cal., ever since that fateful Super Bowl in 1969. It has become pro football's most cherished legend.

But like any "football fable" that suggests there is a mysterious shortcut to excellence that bypasses discipline and self-denial, it is pure myth.

Most pigskin purists know the story without hearing it again—how the Jets' Joe Willie Namath retired to his room with a bottle of booze and a blonde the night before the big game. How Joe Willie trotted out onto the Orange Bowl turf the next afternoon without

Joe Namath (12)

the slightest signs of hangover or fatigue and passed the Baltimore Colts silly and led the underdog New Yorkers to the first win ever by the upstart American Football League over the "establishment" NFL.

But of course, it never happened that way. Namath's favorite receiver, Don Maynard, tells what really was going on during that famous "night-before."

"My wife and I were in the room next to Joe's and I remember lying awake late, worrying about my hamstring pull," Maynard relates. "And I could hear the projector running in Joe's room."

"Finally, I got up at two o'clock in the morning, and knocked on Joe's door and asked him to turn it off so I could get some sleep."

"He said, 'C'mon in here, I want to show you something.' He'd found the key to beating the Baltimore defense, a certain alignment that we could take advantage of," Maynard concludes.

It hardly sounds like a great night of ribaldry and lust, and it wasn't. When the chips are down in the bump and grind world of pro football, there is no room for such levity, not even for Joe Willie Namath. A quarterback's mind has to be riveted on one thing—beating the defense.

Quarterbacks and coaches have long asserted, and statistics have supported their claims, that the key to "beating the defense" is in the mind and heart of the trigger-man. Physical skills are only of peripheral importance to the great quarterbacks.

"You look at the great quarterbacks in the NFL and they all possess two things—great football minds and guts," says Eddie LeBaron, himself a fine signal-caller for Washington and Dallas. "Of course, having a good arm and mastering all the mechanical skills like setting up quick in the pocket, holding the ball up and quick delivery, is important. But without the great mind and the guts, a quarterback is nothing."

Pro football annals are filled with examples to bolster LeBaron's claim. One immediately recalls the names of "strong-arms" who never won the big game—like Roman Gabriel, Daryle Lamonica, Bobby Douglass, and countless other examples.

Surprisingly, Gabriel himself best describes the "psyching out" process that is probably most responsible for depriving many of the physically gifted types of super-star status.

"The primary emotion I take into a game is fear,"

Gabe confesses. "I fear that the club we are going to play could beat me. If it beats me, I'm in second place. I fear my opponents. When a play breaks down, I'm not able to handle the emotional letdowns. I come back to the huddle thinking: 'Who broke down? What happened?' I get the feeling it is an impossibility—almost an impossibility to get back the yards we've lost."

Gabriel's words are in stark contrast to Joe Namath's "We're going to beat the bleep out of the Colts" claims before the historic Super Bowl of '69. But the contrast underlines the key intangible that all super quarterbacks possess and that all journeymen seek but never find. Maybe the best word for the elusive characteristic is "leadership."

Mystery surrounds the term and explanations sometimes falter when discussing the "haves" and "have nots" among those who are expected and paid to be leaders of men. The great leaders are born and sometimes, as in the case of Green Bay's Bart Starr, they are manufactured. But the key element they all acquire, after years of confidence-building and training, is the positive, "I guarantee you" personality.

Sometimes it borders on arrogance, as with Namath's repeated, "I think I'm the best quarterback in football" assertions. With others, it involves quiet,

John Unitas

Roman Gabriel (18)

but smoldering conviction, as with Johnny Unitas' "I've learned to shut all self-doubts out of my mind."

But whatever the overt manifestations, it is a feeling of supreme self-confidence that teammates sense and are motivated by. All the winners have had it— Bobby Layne at Detroit, Bob Waterfield and Norm Van Brocklin at Los Angeles and Philadelphia, Y. A. Tittle of New York, and Otto Graham at Cleveland. In the modern era, the list includes Unitas, Namath, Starr, Len Dawson at Kansas City, John Brodie of San Francisco and maybe Bob Griese at Miami among the NFL's younger quarterbacks.

The leadership exerted by most of the above has been largely emotional and unspoken, with little face-to-face confrontations of "Get your butts in gear, guys!" Usually, the exhortations are by example, such as Layne taking his licks without a facemask or Namath standing up under the rush with his marshmallow knees.

With many of the great leaders, it becomes a neo-masochistic exercise, as explained by Los Angeles Ram defensive lineman Merlin Olsen in his respectful tribute to Unitas.

"You can't intimidate him," Olsen says of Unitas. "He waits until the last possible second to release the ball, even if it means he's going to take a good lick. When he sees us coming he knows it's going to hurt and we know it's going to hurt, but he just stands there and takes it. No other quarterback has such class.

"I swear that, when he sees you coming out of the corner of his eye, he holds that ball a split second longer than he really needs to—just to let you know he isn't afraid of any man. Then he throws it on the button. I weigh 270 myself, and I don't know if I could stand there, week after week, and say, 'Here I am. Take your best shot.' "

The obvious advantage such raw courage gives a quarterback is the ability to ignore the onrushing front four, stand tall in the pocket and "read" the

Bob Griese

defense. And "reading" the defense naturally is the key to beating it, and the reason Namath spent that long night in January of 1969 watching films of the Baltimore Colts, instead of partying.

Acquiring this ability and putting together a "good football mind" is the second-most important attribute of a winning quarterback and it usually takes years to develop. That is why most of the great winners are veterans who have spent many seasons compiling experience and the knowledge that goes with it.

"An experienced quarterback can tell as soon as the ball is snapped what is happening with the defense," says Namath. "But zones are disguised these days and usually you'll pick up the key by watching the tight safety. But different clubs disguise them differently with exchanges and their own particular wrinkles. That's where playing experience helps. You look at a team for years and you get an instinctive feeling about them. You can look at movies forever, and it's not the same as seeing it in the flesh.

"When you have a pattern called you first have to find out what defense the other team is in, and you do this, say, on your first, second, third, fourth, fifth step going back. Then you judge who to throw to. This is a problem with every quarterback, young and old, missing the coverage, not reading it properly. You have a primary receiver on every play. Of course, if the defense changes you have to go to someone else, the secondary receiver. You throw to your primary receiver, I would say, 75 per cent of the time, otherwise, there's been some bad scouting and some bad reading," Broadway Joe concludes.

The concept of "reading" a defense developed within the last decade as pro defenses became increasingly complex and zones began taking on new looks. And only the great quarterbacks ever perfected the knack of unlocking the keys to an opposing zone and then patiently attacking its weaknesses.

Namath picked apart Baltimore's "strong-side rotation" zone in the '69 Super Bowl by quickly reading that it was designed to stop his flanker, Don Maynard, going deep. He threw instead to split end George Sauer on the other side.

Kansas City's Len Dawson destroyed Minnesota in the Super Bowl the next year by never completing a pass for more than 10 yards. Dawson took what was given him by the zone—the short outs and curl cuts—and nickeled and dimed the Vikings to death.

This patient, methodical approach contrasted favorably with Daryle Lamonica's style in a regular-season game his Oakland Raiders lost to the Cincinnati Bengals during the '69 campaign.

"We zoned Lamonica the whole game," said a Bengal assistant coach. "We took away the long pass, but he still tried to go long. Force, force, force; it was like a personal challenge to him to see if he could drop the bomb on us. I think we intercepted him four times."

The ability to call a "smart" football game rarely has much to do with pure intellect. Marty Domres, a graduate of Ivy League-Columbia and currently quarterbacking for the Colts, often spoke of the "mental exhaustion" he experienced trying to absorb the volumes and volumes of play books and the endless hours of films.

But some of the "smartest" signal-callers are Namath (who once scored 104 on an IQ test) and Unitas (who flunked college entrance exams at Pitt and Louisville).

"Obviously, it's not a matter of brains, really," explains one NFL coach. "It's a matter of how much football smarts the guy was born with and how much he was able to pick up after a few years in the league. Of course, very few ever achieve the perfect blend."

The "perfect blend" of football savvy—that which is learned and that which is instinctive—makes the smartest quarterbacks. Added to the leadership and gutsy attributes, it makes the best quarterbacks, provided they also develop that final, critical asset—hitting the receiver on the break.

"A hundred kids today can throw the ball as well as Sammy Baugh did. In practice. They've got the arm and the strength. And they can fire it on the line, overarm, sidearm, any way you name it. But what makes a passer is this—the ability to hit his man on the break. Some of them never develop it."

Namath always stresses that this knack can never be developed unless the quarterback furiously welds his personality into that of his receivers.

"You have to work together, live together," Namath insists. "I can't stress the point enough about the necessity of playing experience. The relationship between the quarterback and his receivers is awfully vital. You have to be together not one year, two years, but three, four, five years before you really get things meshing together."

San Francisco's John Brodie outlines the same philosophy, perhaps a bit more poetically, when speaking about his relationship with teammate Gene Washington, the 49ers leading pass catcher.

"Gene and I room together and we are good friends," Brodie says. "We've worked out a series of signals that can change even after I've begun my snap count. But most of all, I guess, is that we read each other so well. He knows where I want him to be on a given pass play. Sometimes he will run a set pattern,

but at other times he has to get to a place in the field any way he can."

"The most poetic way to say it is that it's a highly intuitive thing. Sometimes we call a pass for a particular spot on the field, maybe to get a first down. But at other times it's less defined than that and depends upon the communication we have. *Sometimes I let the ball fly before Gene has made his final move, without a pass route being set exactly. That's where intuition and communication come in.*"

All those attributes outlined above blended together create the great passer, along with others—like knowing when to dump the ball out of bounds when all receivers are covered, or taking the sack when there is nowhere to throw.

And there is another—learning to blend the passing attack into the entire offensive system and realizing that a pure passer never got a team anywhere.

Going into the 1973 season, the ten top games for pass completions by a single quarterback were as follows:

Nov. 1, 1964: Houston's George Blanda went 37 for 68 against Buffalo.

Dec. 5, 1948: New York's Charley Conerly went 36 for 53 against Pittsburgh.

Oct. 18, 1970: New York Jet's Joe Namath went 34 for 62 against Baltimore.

Dec. 20, 1964: Denver's Mickey Slaughter went 34 for 56 against Houston.

Dec. 1, 1940: Philadephia's Davey O'Brien went 33 for 60 against Washington.

Sept. 23, 1962: Philadelphia's Sonny Jurgensen went 33 for 57 against New York Giants.

Oct. 25, 1964: Chicago's Billy Wade went 35 for 57 against Washington.

Nov. 26, 1967: Washington's Jurgensen went 32 for 50 against Cleveland.

Nov. 13, 1960: Houston's Blanda went 31 for 55 against Los Angeles.

Nov. 10, 1963: Dallas' Don Meredith went 30 for 48 against San Francicso.

There is a moral that follows the listing of these ten most passingest performances in NFL history: The passer's team lost in every instance.

As Johnny Unitas so wisely pointed out, "throwing is throwing. A lot of people can do that pretty well, but it's only those people who can do everything else a quarterback is supposed to do that win football games."

The Runner's Game

"RUNNING INTO the line, you go into a different world. All around you, guys are scratching, clawing, beating on each other, feeling pain. There are noises from the crowd and from the linemen but during that one moment, I never seem to hear them. Then, going back to the huddle, the sound of the pads slamming together will still be in my ears and I'll listen for the first time. The sensation gives you a real insight into the game. It's too bad more people haven't been in there . . . where football is really played."

—*Larry Csonka, Miami Dolphins*

Few, if any, Sunday-afternoon-experts would accept Csonka's invitation to be "in there . . . where

football is really played." Better to be safely tucked into the lap of an armchair in front of a television than to be "in there," or around end, or behind the line of scrimmage, or anywhere that is part of the runner's world.

It is a punishing, brutal realm of wonder and terror . . . of veers, cuts and collisions, where one step could be into the open road to touchdown-glory, and another might be into the jaws of a career-ending injury.

It is a world in which only the strong survive and at that, even the strong don't survive for long.

"I know my days are numbered . . . they've been numbered pretty good already," reasons Calvin Hill

Calvin Hill (35)

Ray DeAragon

of the Dallas Cowboys, reflecting the fatalism shared by most of his colleagues. "Sometimes I decide to run a little less recklessly and protect myself. But really, you just can't function by trying to think your way along."

That is Calvin's creed and some argue that it is the statement that crystallizes the running experience. There is simply no room for thinking in the "run-to-daylight" realm. As O.J. Simpson once noted, "Thinking is what gets you caught from behind."

"Instinct" and "survival" are the two words thrown around most often to paint word-pictures of the running experience. It is generally accepted that carrying a football is the closest thing to the animal kingdom this side of the jungle. All eyes, ears and noses are wired directly to the medulla and each warrior operates entirely on the level of sensory perception.

"I was never taught to do what I did, and I know I couldn't teach anyone else how to run," comments Red Grange, the man whose strong legs helped George Halas build the NFL.

"Running ability has to be bred into you, you can't learn," adds Donny Anderson, who once was paid the all-time high bonus by Vince Lombardi for his quality breeding.

It is no secret that since the days of Grange, Jim Thorpe and Bronko Nagurski, the split-second, rhythmic sensorium of the runner has been the essence of all football. And it is ironic that in this current age of computerized software that has often threatened to turn the Super Bowl into as complex an operation as the invasion of Normandy, the runner is spearheading a "back to basics" approach that is returning the pro game to the hard-nosed, helmet-popping days of yore.

"People think that when we play this game, we're mechanical," says Miami's Mercury Morris. "But once the ball is snapped, everybody's just human—and you're on your own."

Willie Ellison of the Los Angeles Rams is even more direct, saying that the running game has been rejuvenated lately because, "Coaches are tired of competing against computers."

"As you doubtless know, just about every team in pro football builds its air defense with the help of computers. But when you give the ball to a back and send him into the line, there isn't a computer in the world that can really predict what will happen exactly. It's that human element of unpredictability ... that anything or everything can happen," Ellison concludes.

Of course, there is a misleading element in what Ellison says, and there is a miss-the-mark tone to those "Year of the Runner" headlines that sportswriters have tossed around with such abandon during the last few seasons.

The facts are that runners never really fell out of favor in the NFL, although casual fans may think that way.

Lombardi won the big championships with the big backs (Paul Hornung and Jim Taylor) in the last decade at Green Bay and his hard-nosed approach seemed a dramatic shift in emphasis away from the passing of past champions—say the 1950 Rams of Bob Waterfield and Norm Van Brocklin.

But no team has ever won an NFL title without running more times than it threw the ball. Even Joe Namath's New York Jets of 1969 did not violate this unwritten law—that winners run the ball.

For every Waterfield, there was a Tank Younger. For every Otto Graham, there was a Marion Mottley. For every Namath, there was Matt Snell or Emerson Boozer.

The only thing that really set the last few campaigns apart from previous seasons was that people at last realized how vital the running back had become. And runners replaced quarterbacks as the big stars of the game.

In 1971, five of the top six running teams in the NFL made it into the playoffs and Dallas finally won the Super Bowl with a pair of quarterbacks who will never be Hall of Fame material—Roger Staubach and Craig Morton.

In 1972, Miami ran to the big prize on the legs of Csonka, Morris and Jim Kiick while leaving the quarterbacking to ageless super-sub Earl Morrall during the regular season and then going back to Bob Griese after he recovered from a broken ankle.

The Dolphins' closest competitors were the Washington Redskins, thanks to Larry Brown and his great running season. Coach George Allen handed the signal-calling over to Billy Kilmer, who did just enough passing to keep defenses from piling all over Brown and his running-mate, Charlie Harraway.

"I think it's safe to say that quarterbacking has not been the big factor in the last couple of Super Bowls," offers one NFL general manager.

Adds another, "It's not going to be the year of the runner, it's going to be the decade of the runner. Every Sunday it's going to look like Ohio State playing Texas—13 times."

The most important man leading the runners' domination of the modern era is the Redskins' Brown, who stands unchallenged as the most valuable performer in the NFL currently. In '72, he led the league in rushing for the second-straight year and became only the third runner in history—Cleveland's Jim Brown and everyone's Cookie Gilchrist were the others—to gain 4,000 yards in his first four seasons as a pro.

But Brown was by no means the entire story in '72. Since Beattie Feathers of the Bears became the first NFL back to gain over 1,000 yards in a single season in 1935, only 48 other runners duplicated the

Jim Brown

feat going into the '72 season. No fewer than ten passed the 1,000 mark that season.

Some observers claim there are chalk-and-blackboard reasons for this dramatic statistic. They cite the much-ballyhooed zone pass defense as opening the running lanes and hypnotizing linemen and linebackers into "reading pass first." According to coaches, such split-second mistakes can expose an onrushing lineman to a trap block as he steamrolls after the quarterback, or it can mean that linebackers and deep backs aren't filling holes in the line quickly enough if they drop back to their coverage zones prematurely.

Other theorists reason that the recent rule change, which moved the hashmarks three yards and 21 inches closer to the center of the field has opened up new avenues for the runners. Originally designed to open up the passing game by giving the zone defenses more ground to cover, the hashmarks move has apparently done more to help the runners. With "short side of the field" made wider by the move, defenses can no longer overshift, linebackers must be concerned with a run to either side and the middle is more vulnerable.

Observes the Redskins' George Allen, "Sure, the hashmarks have caused problems for defenses, but don't underestimate the quality of the runners themselves. You can change the rules all you want—you can make the field 20 yards wide—and a Larry Brown will still get yardage. That's the kind of man he is."

Indeed, Brown is that great kind of competitor, as is Csonka, Denver's Floyd Little, Pittsburgh's Franco Harris, Green Bay's John Brockington and many others in the NFL currently. But no matter how great any of them become in their careers, they will probably not eclipse the marks left by the two greatest backs the game has known—Jim Brown of Cleveland and Gale Sayers of the Chicago Bears.

Statistically, no one has ever come close to Jim Brown's accomplishments and it is unlikely anyone ever will, unless Larry Brown can somehow hang on for another five seasons. Big Jim holds almost every major rushing record in the NFL, including most seasons leading the league (8), most consecutive seasons leading the league (5), most yards gained in a season (1,863), most yards gained in a career (12,312) and most touchdowns scored in a career (106).

Big Jim quit the game in the summer of 1966 to take a role in the movie "The Dirty Dozen." But even with at least two good seasons left in him when he hung up his shirt, he still had established himself as the most prolific runner the game will probably ever know. His successor at Cleveland, Leroy Kelly, is the closest active competitor to most of Brown's career marks, but in such categories as career yardage and touchdowns, Kelly is only a little better than halfway toward matching Brown's awesome totals.

The knock on Brown was that he didn't block or carry out fakes . . . that he wasn't the "complete back."

Charged Otto Graham, the ex-Brown quarterback: "If I were the Browns' coach, I would tell the fullback that I would trade him if he didn't block or fake. The Brown's won't do anything as long as Brown is there."

Graham's statement obviously became one of the historic foot-in-the-mouth bloopers of all time and was best answered by Blanton Collier, the man who coached Brown.

Said Blanton simply, "You don't ask a thoroughbred to pull a milk wagon."

As for Sayers, there is no question that he was the greatest break-away threat of all-time. "Mr. Magic" they called him and one of his most-gifted competitors, Paul Hornung, called Gale "the best damned

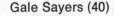
Gale Sayers (40)

ballcarrier I've ever seen."

Before four knee operations abruptly ended his brilliant career, Sayers seemed headed for even greater productivity than Jim Brown. In his first five seasons, he was twice the league's rushing leader and set NFL season records for touchdowns (22), single-game touchdown mark (6) and most touchdowns returning kickoffs (6).

Before the glory ended painfully in 1968 in Wrigley Field, when Kermit Alexander slammed a shoulder into Gale's right knee, new standards had been established for the game-breaker philosophy.

As Sayers explains, "In my book, the first objective is always getting the TD. It's nice to get the first and ten, but I'm looking for the TD and the first downs come second. You can' stop to look for it. It's there and you know it's there. I can't explain it.

"I know that a lot of backs are happy at the end of the season to have a 5.0 average, but a 5.0 average doesn't win ball games for you. Touchdowns win games. This is what I'm looking for—touchdowns. I feel that I can always beat my man one-on-one. And two-on-one I can beat them 75 per cent of the time."

According to one of Sayers' Bear teammates, "The thing that made Gale different was the way he was able to put a move on somebody and not lose a step. He gave a guy a fake while he was going full speed. I give a guy a fake like that and it takes me 15 yards to get back in stride. Watch any runner. They'll all slow down a little when they have a corner to cut or throw a fake—all of them except Gale."

Most contemporary observers agree that nobody currently active in the NFL can match Jim Brown or Sayers, but Larry Brown comes closest of any to combining the skills of both ex-superstars. Without Jim Brown's massive strength, Larry nonetheless is just as durable and maybe a little quicker running inside. Without Sayers uncanny, open-field moves, Larry is perhaps a little more effective at wriggling free once contact is made with the tackler.

To even be compared with neo-immortals like Jim Brown and Sayers is coming a long way for a smallish (5' 11", 195-pound), half-deaf (he wears a hearing aid in his helmet to pick up the quarterback's signals) ghetto-kid from Pittsburgh who was not taken until the eighth round of the NFL draft by Vince Lombardi in 1969.

But Brown will not let himself rest on past achievements. As running-mate Charlie Harraway insists, "Larry is the best because of his determination. When he has the ball, he has it in for the whole world. He has to conquer the world."

Just as awed by Brown's fierce, inner-ragings is a competitor, Larry Wilson of the St. Louis Cardinals. "Larry Brown is the best since Gale Sayers," Wilson offers. "The key to his success is his great desire. What higher tribute to a man than to have teams each week plan their defenses to stop him, and each week see him run with such success."

Of course, the successes could be stopped at any moment. It happened that way for Sayers and Matt Snell and it could happen to Larry Brown.

But still Brown and the other runners keep running, propelled by promises of monetary returns, true, but also by a desire to excel and to experience that feeling that belongs only to the man who carries the football.

As Ron Johnson of the New York Giants explains, "When you have the football, the show is all yours. You're out there alone, matching quick instincts and wits against tacklers. It's a game within a game and you're determining its destiny. Of course, with everybody's eyes on you, you can look like the goat.

"But you also have the chance to be the hero. And chances like that don't come along too often in anybody's life."

Larry Brown (43)

The Receivers—
the Men Who Catch the Home Runs

Garry Garrison

A PRO SCOUT was once asked if he could think of any of the NFL's wide receivers who weren't just a little bit flakey.

The scout pursed his lips, shrugged his shoulders and said, "Off hand, I can't think of any. They're all crazy to a degree."

Just where it all began is anyone's guess, but wide receivers are universally accepted now as "pro football eccentrics." And there is a legion of examples to back up the reputation.

There is Dick Gordon, with his wide-brimmed hats and superfly slacks. There is Warren Wells, with his inability to stay out of jail. And don't forget Lance Rentzel, who can't keep his name out of the newspapers.

Even the so-called "straights" get caught up in the far-out mystique—like Raymond Berry, who allegedly lives alone in a haunted house. Or Don Maynard, who is supposed to do all sorts of hell-raising when he leaves New York and returns to his old stomping grounds in Texas.

"Really, I don't know how this whole thing of me being a wild sort got started," says a puzzled Maynard, who would much rather be remembered as one of the game's best long-ball threats with the Jets.

"I don't smoke and I've never had a drink in my life. I wear cowboy boots but they're not even high-heeled. I guess it's just because most wide receivers seem to get that kind of reputation for doing crazy things and I got caught up with the rest."

Maynard is caught up with the rest of his fellow-pass catchers and pigeon-holed into the "eccentric" class. But most of the reputation he and his colleagues got for "doing crazy things" was built on the football field, rather than in private life.

As one coach said, "Running that post cut, full speed right into the teeth of the free safety, reaching up for the ball and giving him a wide-open shot at your ribs . . . that's got to be about the craziest thing any man can do."

"Catching the ball in a crowd," is the term coaches most often use. It is that ability to go up for the ball, no matter what, to put the sound of the footsteps of a fast-closing defensive back out of one's mind and bring down the football.

It is the one characteristic that most receivers find hardest to acquire and yet, it is the one trait that distinguishes a great receiver from just a good one.

As Chicago Bear flanker George Farmer says, "Anyone can make a catch when he's wide open. But only the supers come down with the ball when there's a defensive man on his back or about to bury a helmet in his ribs."

The key element in developing this single-minded interest in catching a football is absolute concentration. Ted Williams had it when hitting a baseball. And pass receivers like Baltimore's Raymond Berry, Philadelphia's Tommy McDonald, or the New York Jets' George Sauer all were blessed with the same gift.

Sauer, who has since retired to write a book on the evils of pro football, once said that his ability to concentrate was more acquired than innate. He referred back to boyhood days with his father in Waco, Texas.

"We had a backyard with about 13 trees and when my dad would throw the ball to me close to the trees, I'd bounce off 'em after I caught it. I remember my father telling my mother one time, 'With his hands he should be an end.'

"Up here in the NFL, when I catch a pass, sometimes it's like I was still bouncing off those trees in our big ol' backyard in Waco. Except that now those trees are chasing me."

Beyond bouncing off trees in Waco, Texas, other receivers polish and practice the ability to hang onto the football in pretty much the same way. Berry, always known as the foremost scientist of wide receiving in his playing days with the Colts, has incorporated his techniques into his coaching career with the Dallas Cowboys and now the Detroit Lions.

"I tell the guys to take a football with them everywhere . . . to handle it, fondle it, to toss it up and down while they're lying on their beds in their rooms. And when they play catch in practice, I always stress that they tuck it under their arm before they throw it back," Berry says.

Danny Abramowicz, who led the NFL in pass receiving in 1969 with the New Orleans Saints even though like Berry, he does not have great size or speed, outlined the same mental framework.

"I just concentrate on catching the ball, never dropping it, even in practice. If I get my hands on the ball, I should catch it. Oh yes, I rub my hands on a ball before a game. I watch the ball into my hands, watch it all the way. I don't trap it against my chest, like some receivers do . . . I've got great confidence in my hands."

Of course, to be able to use his hands, a wide receiver must be able to run patterns and beat defenders well enough to break clear enough for the quarterback to feel he has a chance for a completion.

Thirty years ago, this was an easy task for Green Bay Packer great Don Hutson, who revolutionized the game with his "I'm going deep, throw the ball as far as you can" patterns. Since Hutson's time however,

pro defenses have become infinitely more sophisticated and have been designed to deny the long-bomb attack. Getting free now involves much more than running fast and throwing far.

Of course, most of the basic patterns used in Hutson's time remain the same. As Hutson himself ex-

Don Hutson

plains, "Pass patterns will never change much, I mean, what more can anybody do?"

There will always be square-outs, square-ins, hooks, curls, posts, flags, slants and fly patterns. The differences will come from the manner in which individual receivers run the patterns and work to get loose in the seams of the defense.

Speed will always have something to do with getting free, but not much. Berry and Sauer were a step away from being downright slow, but they managed to shake loose by running patterns with the precision of a computer, studying defenses like a book and leaving nothing to chance. Outright "burners" like ex-trackmen Don Budd and John Carlos didn't last long enough in the NFL to collect a pension check.

Obviously, combining speed and precise pattern work (along with catching-in-a-crowd concentration) is the ideal composite for a super-receiver. But so few attain anything close to that ideal.

Hutson, McDonald, Cleveland's Bobby Mitchell and Los Angeles' Elroy (Crazylegs) Hirsch were a couple of former greats who came close. Current stars like Don Maynard, Kansas City's Otis Taylor, Dallas' Lance Alworth or San Francisco's Gene Washington have always flashed moments of perfection.

All of them came closest to mastering the ability to work to the open spot and earned the "impossible to cover one-on-one label" that opposing cornerbacks award to only the great receivers in the game. And they did it with great timing with their own quarterbacks, more than pure speed or moves. As Los Angeles' Bernie Casey notes, they all became "receivers who ran with their heads."

"The most important thing for a receiver to get down is that most patterns are predicated on timing," Casey explains. They have so many seconds to get to a certain area—so many tenths of a second—and the quarterback will look for you in that area. Now whatever means you employ to get there in that designated time is up to you. That's where individual talents and abilities come to play.

"It's also important that you get a lot of time with the quarterback so he understands you as a receiver. He must understand your attitude toward receiving, and he must be able to predict what you are going to do in certain situations. In turn, you anticipate what he will do, what kind of passes he will throw. When you're running at a certain angle he may throw one kind of pass. His long passes may have a certain trajectory. Things like that. It's really quite complicated. And then again, it's not complicated at all. Can you understand that?"

Perhaps the man with the clearest understanding of what Casey is saying is the Jets' Maynard. You can rattle off every big game in the book and Maynard has them beat in the statistics book. Fact is, the 36-year-old Texan who was cut in 1959 by the Giants, cut the following year by the Canadian Football League and finally hooked up with old New York Titans of the AFL, will probably hold every major receiving record in pro football when he finally decides to hang up his spikes. And for the time being, that moment isn't in sight.

Maynard's quarterback, Joe Namath, says flatly that "Don is the best long receiver in the game."

Most coaches agree with Namath's assessment (although the Chiefs' Otis Taylor and Miami's Paul Warfield have many advocates) and they also note that the veteran Texan has achieved status as the league's foremost home-run threat without blinding speed.

"He is quick, but not fast. His speed is deceptive," explains one coach. "He is as fast as he has to be and runs full-speed only when he is chasing the ball."

Maynard, himself, attributes most of his success to the intimate on-the-field relationship he has developed with Namath.

"Joe and I know each other inside and out and after a while, we become part of the same machine. He lifts his arm and I move my right foot. He pumps and I turn left," Maynard says.

"At first it's odd, but after a while all the movements become comfortable and we can feel each other's moves, even when we don't see them.

"As a receiver, I count to myself every time I run a pattern and Joe is counting with me. I'll count 'one-thousand-one, one-thousand-two, one-thousand-three,' and I'll make my break off my count and Joe will deliver the ball."

Such completely coordinated thinking between Namath and Maynard is the ultimate achievement in the passing game. And when a passing team has been able to put something like that together, it is always a threat the defense must respect.

The classic example was the 1969 Super Bowl when the Jets upset the Colts and Namath did not complete a single pass to Maynard. However, the mere threat of the Namath-to-Maynard bomb kept the Colt pass defense honest all day long.

"Maynard had a bad leg," recalled one Jet coat, "and Baltimore didn't really know how well he could run. He showed them on one play.

"After probing for weakness, Namath unloaded a bomb for Maynard down the right sideline, a 60-yard shot which missed by inches.

"He showed them on that one play that he could still run. They had to be ready for the rest of the game. I think that one pass put the fear of God into them," the coach concluded.

Perhaps that line, better than any other, crystallizes the true value of the great wide receiver—the flakey-fast eccentric with the ability to "put the fear of God" into an opposing defense.

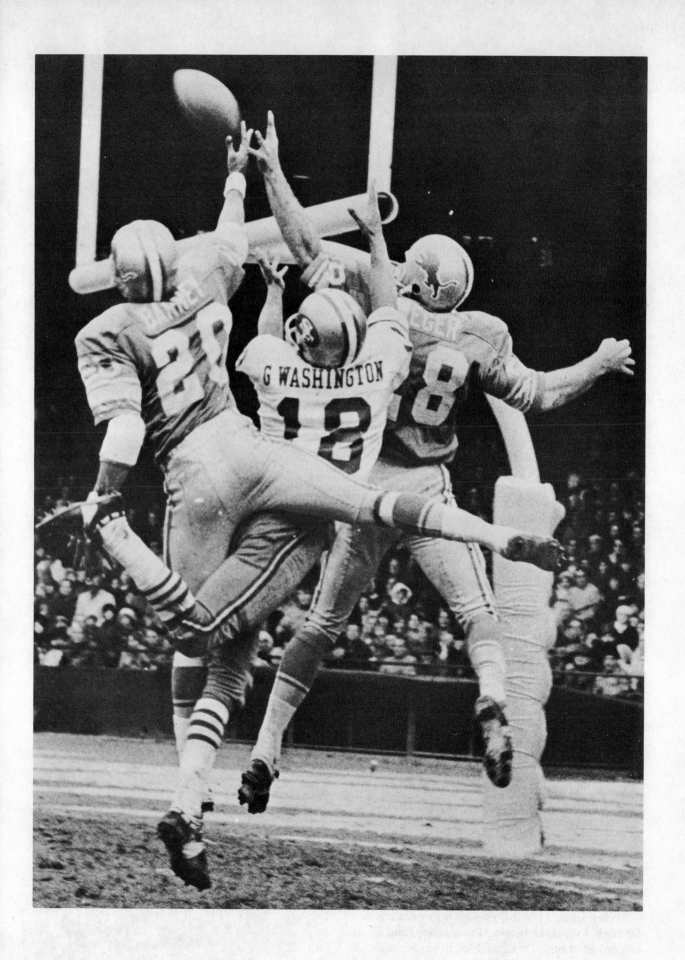

The Tight End—
All Man and a Yard Wide

THERE IS A short period of time, at the beginning of their careers, when the great tight ends relish their meat-grinding roles. They are flattered to be thrust into playing "the most physically demanding position in pro football."

They enjoy being known as the super-blocker, super-receiver—the man around which the entire offense is built. Then they begin to realize what is happening to them, and it is too late.

John Mackey best expressed the early-career euphoria that grips most of his colleagues. Speaking back in 1968 when he was the people's choice as best tight end in history with the Baltimore Colts, Mackey said:

"I think tight end is the best position in football for many reasons. I'll tell you why. I have an opportunity to block like a lineman, to run like a halfback, and also to catch passes like a flanker. It's a combination of all these things that really make it a good position.

"In the past more and more defensive teams were ignoring the tight ends, concentrating more on the outside receivers, leaving a wide-open area in the middle for the tight end to roam. But they are beginning to tighten up more and more now on the tight ends," Mackey concluded, only to discover quickly how prophetic his words would become.

Realizing his importance to the Baltimore attack, defenses did indeed tighten up on Mackey until eventually, the beating took its toll. Big John was injured, lost his starting job and was finally traded in 1972 to San Diego.

The Mackey story was an instant-replay of what happened to both of his predecessors on the throne of best tight end in the business—Mike Ditka and Ron Kramer. Like Mackey, both were ferocious blockers and punishing runners once they caught the football. But their years of peak performance were limited.

Ditka bounced from the Chicago Bears and hung on for years as a journeyman with several clubs, never coming close to re-capturing his glory years in Chicago. Kramer was a key figure in the Lombardi era with Green Bay, but then was traded to Detroit and finally cut ingloriously from the Lion squad.

"When I was 23 or 24, guys used to warn me that I'd begin to feel the beating I was taking, and I just laughed at them," Ditka said in 1968, a couple of years after he had passed his prime. "I never missed

a game in Chicago—84 straight. Now I'm 28 and I defy you to show me another end who's taken the beating I have. Maybe Ron Kramer, and look at him. The Lions just cut him."

Even the younger tight ends, who have supplanted the Ditkas, Kramers and Mackeys as the best at the position, are quickly discovering the physical price they must pay to stay on top. Charley Sanders, who at 26 has been considered the premier tight end in the NFL for the last three seasons, is one of the Young Turks who is beginning to sense trouble ahead.

"Used to be I would flex out and I could look up and know I had a touchdown. This year (1972), I

Charlie Sanders

Clifton Boutelle

look up and see the linebacker over me and the strong safety behind him and the weak safety hanging around nearby. I just wish they'd leave me alone," Sanders said.

When reminded that one of his younger rivals, Jim Mitchell at Atlanta, was having a super season, Sanders scoffed.

"They don't double or triple Jim Mitchell—yet," Sanders said. "When they do, he'll be singing the same tune."

The tune Sanders speaks of is pure blues, a mournful wail inspired by the fearful head-knocking that the best of the tight end bunch absorbs. Sanders played most of the '72 season with awesome array of battle ribbons—a patch over one eye (thanks to some fingers in the face from a linebacker) and bandages over most of the rest of his body. In games against Atlanta and Green Bay, he was knocked goofy and still played, though he scarcely remembered his name when the final whistle sounded.

"It's the price the best ones pay," offers San Francisco's Ted Kwalick, already one of those "best ones" after only two years with the 49ers. "The tight

Ted Kwalick

Ron Mrowiec

end is very important to the offense and he's a marked man right off the bat."

The tight end is to the offense what the middle linebacker is to the defense—a specialist whose specialty is doing everything and doing everything well. He makes the ground game go with his blocking and his receiving is the weapon that can open up an opponent's pass defense. Finding a super-specimen to fulfill all those physical and mental demands is one of the hardest jobs for a pro general manager or coach.

"The good tight end is very, very important to your running game," says one NFL coach. "He must go head-to-head with the strong side linebacker who plays right over him. He must be able to take on the middle linebacker, and at times he must be able to handle the defensive end."

But of course, blocking is only half the tight end story. With increased emphasis on zone defenses in the NFL, tight receivers like Sanders, Mitchell or Jackie Smith of St. Louis are becoming increasingly vital in sustaining the passing attack.

"The tight end runs the control patterns. Because of his position he can operate to any point on the field," the coach continues. "He's the closest receiver to the quarterback and that makes him the easiest man to complete a pass to.

"The split end and flanker, because they are split out so wide from the ball, have a limited area of the field to work in. Even a pass for a short gain involves a long throw. And when you have a tight end with the speed to run the deep patterns, he prevents the defense double-teaming the wide receivers."

Jim Dooley, who thirsted for a good tight end during his five seasons as head coach of the Bears, further described the great value of such a skilled athlete.

"Great tight ends should be your biggest touchdown producers," Dooley said. "Along with the backs, they should give you your highest percentage of completions.

"If you have one with the speed of say a Jerry Smith (Redskins), a Jackie Smith, or a Mackey, you can't cover them with a linebacker and that opens up the entire passing game.

"They are great control receivers and give you added strength in a ball control game with their blocking and receiving. But you eventually win by passing and the winning teams almost always have the tight end who can run the deep pattern," Dooley concluded.

Ditka and Kramer were the first men to win All-Pro at a position designated "tight end." As such, they were the first football players recognized for having the physical skills required for filling the demanding position. And that recognition came in 1962.

But there were a number of predecessors, who perhaps did not measure up to Ditka or Kramer physically, but who played positions that were unlike the tight end slot in name only.

Paul Brown used backs like Ray Renfro and Dub Jones like tight ends by sending them in motion on passing plays. Brown's wrinkle was one of the first deviations from the standard two end-three running back pro look of the late 1940's.

Clark Shaughnessy polished Brown's innovation

Marv Fleming

with Los Angeles about the same time by installing ex-halfback Elroy Hirsch on the flank, a yard off the line of scrimmage. The Detroit Lions of the 1950's accomplished the same thing by using Doak Walker as a combination running back, man-in-motion and set flanker. A few years later, the Bears had the same thing in Bill McCall by putting him in a slot position in the backfield. McCall had the size of a tight end and from his position one-yard deep in the backfield and just outside the tackle, he could block or run the control pass cut.

During most of the early evolution of the tight end position, only one man clearly combined all the physical attributes of a Kramer or a Sanders. That one man was man-mountain, Leon Hart of the Detroit Lions, who stood 6′ 5″ and weighed 265 pounds. He was never known as a "tight end" during his playing days, but he was everything the modern-day product could hope for—a bulldozing blocker and a fearsome pass receiver who put cleat marks up the chest of a defensive back who tried to bring him down in the open field.

But outside of Hart, Mackey, Ditka, Kramer, Sanders, Mitchell, Kwalick and Jackie Smith, the list of truly great tight ends is hardly imposing. Raymond Chester of the Oakland Raiders, Bob Trumpy of Cincinnati and Milt Morin of Cleveland have all had great days but have never sustained the kind of consistency to earn them a "great" label.

Remarked one NFL general manager: "Tight end is a unique position in that you can probably rattle off without much effort the names of anybody who ever came close to playing it well. Maybe it's because it's such a hard position to play, but there just haven't been many 'great' ones over the years. And those who did reach that plateau didn't stay there for long."

One who hovered near the top for as long as anyone without ever reaching superstar status was Marv Fleming, a man lucky enough to play for Super Bowl-winners at Green Bay and Miami. But even as the Dolphins were winning the big prize in 1973, coach Don Shula was giving Fleming's understudy, Jim Mandich, plenty of playing time to prepare for the soon-to-arrive-day when Fleming could no longer get the job done.

"When you come off the football field all beat up, then it's time to quit," Fleming said, looking ahead to that day. "You're going to get bruised up, but when it starts to affect you mentally, that's it.

"I'm not going to be the football player that comes to the dead end road. I'm going to go out shaking everybody's hand and telling them, 'thank you.'"

If Fleming achieves his hope for a graceful good-bye to the NFL, he will be one of the lucky ones. With the exception of maybe Leon Hart, most of the tight ends who faded into oblivion never had a chance to shake any hands on their way to picking up the waiver slip.

The Men in the Pit

IT'S HARDLY HUMAN, the sound that comes from that place in the middle. With each snap of the ball, 2,000 pounds of football flesh cut loose with the accompaniment of grunts, groans and growling as they butt, club and otherwise abuse each other in quest of dominance of the place they call "The Pit."

The low, guttural rumblings of linemen straining against each other is rarely audible to the fat cats in the stands and perhaps that is good, because there might be increasing demands to lock up these vulgar giants after-hours if the sounds came through to ears not in tune to the violent song.

Even Merlin Olsen, the Los Angeles Rams defensive tackle with the reputation for being one of the most pensive and analytical minds in the game, admits that the kicking and clawing in the pit is more animal than human.

"They don't call the middle of the line 'The Pit' for nothing," he says. "We really do get like animals, trying to claw one another apart in there. It is very hard in the Pit. No matter how it seems, no matter what the score is, it's always hard. We get so bruised and battered and tired we sometimes wind up playing in a sort of a coma. By the end of the first half, our instincts have taken over. By the end of the game, we're an animal."

Such is life in the trenches, where football's foot soldiers go about their business. It's a rough business, for sure, but a business nonetheless. And while the approach is far from subtle, all the butting and fighting is done with an objective in mind and each man's work is a part of the same goal of the other ten men on his side.

The action is a complex confrontation of skilled men. But how these men go about their jobs is very different.

They all knock heads with more or less equal fervor, but the offensive and defensive linemen are cut from substantially different cloth. Vince Lombardi, the high-priest of the NFL, once said he could tell whether a big lineman would play offense or defense just by looking at him.

"If he combs his hair and says 'sir' a lot, and 'I'd really like to become an outstanding professional football player,' he'll end up on offense. But if he shows up in a beatup leather jacket and a two-day growth of beard, spits on the floor and demands, 'How much you gonna pay me?' he's got to play defense," quoth Vinnie.

The basic motivation of the defensive lineman is to raise hell. He can forget everything else and just start teeing off on the nearest off-color jersey, if he feels like it. His hands and arms become clubs, good for ringing a quarterback's or a lineman's bell, or dishing out "owies" to other parts of opposing bodies.

"When I come in on a guy, I like to club him," says Buck Buchanan of the Kansas City Chiefs. "If a guy comes at me, I get my shoulder down right away, take his lick with my shoulder, and get my arm out automatically. Bam! The club."

The offensive lineman, however, cannot indulge in such instinctive and emotional responses. He must function as part of a unit, timing every movement and relying on precision and control. It takes a different type of personality.

While the defense can play for the bone-crunching tackle or the splashy quarterback-sack, the faceless offensive lineman takes on an identity only after blowing an assignment or by getting caught holding. People begin to ask, why bother?

"Why did I become an offensive lineman?" says Ron Mix, former San Diego Charger offensive tackle. "For one thing, my size was only ordinary; my skills were mechanical, not instinctive; and emotionally I have the temperment of an offensive lineman. An offensive player is a thinking man. He doesn't get as much mileage out of an emotional state. He might be just as vicious a player as a defensive man, but his viciousness is usually within the rules."

Of course, this does not mean that members of the front four relish being thought of as flesh-eaters. Even an intimidating figure like the late Gene (Big Daddy) Lipscomb, a 6' 7", 275-pound former great for the Baltimore Colts and Pittsburgh Steelers, was not bent on wilfull destruction. Back in the late 50's and early 60's, the sight of Big Daddy, his jersey flapping behind him, chasing enemy quarterbacks or smearing ballcarriers and then helping the little guy to his feet and patting him on the bottom and directing him to his huddle, was quite familiar.

The current Steeler standout at Big Daddy's position—"Mean" Joe Greene, says the mean in his name is not really right-on.

"I'm not out to slaughter anybody," he says. "I just

want to get my hands on a quarterback or a running-back and I try hard. But you'll never see me hurt anybody on purpose."

Instinct is a major part of their game, but a defensive tackle or end cannot hope to merely club his way through the pit.

"I think it takes as many years to develop a top-flight defensive lineman as it does a quarterback," observes Olsen. "Intelligence, determination, concentration, deception, agility and quickness are all my weapons as much as are my size and toughness. But without size and toughness, none of the rest would be of any use."

The basic move among front four defenders is still the straight-ahead rush, especially for the tackle. Olsen says the best approach is to "keep hitting them with your best lick." The one problem is that it becomes quite tiring, so an end and tackle will some-

times work together on stunts. The tackle will charge diagonally to the outside and the end will loop around him to the inside. By switching routes, they can foul up the offensive blocking assignments, which can blow the whole play open.

The defensive end is generally more concerned with the pass rush. He is usually taller and faster, and his greatest responsibility is to teach the quarterback fear—to sack him, to block his pass, or hurry his throw and maybe cause an interception. Fear was the forte of men like the Colts' Gino Marchetti a decade ago, and fear is the strong-suit of Gino's successor in Baltimore, Bubba Smith.

Although brains are becoming more of a factor in line play, with blockers shooting out at different angles, or letting the defender take himself out of the play with his own aggressiveness, the defensive line is still the place where violence is king.

Alex Karras, former All-Pro tackle for the Detroit Lions and current TV funny-man, once said without exaggeration, "You have to be a sadist on the field, no question about it. I'm not talking backs, I'm talking linemen. If I said to you I don't enjoy ripping Bart Starr's head off, I'd be lying. Knocking down an offensive lineman and breaking his head open is something I enjoy."

From an offensive lineman's point of view, Charlie Cowan of the Los Angeles Rams says there are only four things a defender can do to him. "He can take the quick inside or the hard upfield or the slap-and-go-move. Or, he can stunt with another defensive lineman. What I try to do is destroy what he's trying to do. For instance, if it's the slap-and-go, I try to roll with the punch and go with him."

The only problem is that no matter how well Charlie and his offensive colleagues do their job, nobody is likely to notice, except maybe their wives, mothers, or the offensive coaches when they grade the game films. There aren't any statistics to show how good or how bad the offensive lineman is doing. There are few awards and even less recognition.

While the exploits of front foursomes have inspired catchy names— like the Rams' "Fearsome Foursome" of Deacon Jones, Merlin Olsen, Rosy Grier and Lamar Lundy of recent vintage, or the Minnesota Vikings' "Purple People Eaters" which include Carl Eller, Jim Marshall, Alan Page and Gary Larson— offensive linemen are lucky if anybody knows them by name. The standard joke around the NFL is that anyone on the lam from the law could hide out for years in the offensive line.

Although largely unnoticed, the offensive guard will almost always show which way the play is going. If he fires out straight ahead, the play is likely to be a run. If he fires low, it's either a quick pass over the middle, or a run. If he sets to block, look for a pass or a draw. And if he pivots and pulls out, running

"Mean" Joe Greene

Carl Skalak

parallel to the line, look out for football's classic—the end sweep.

Of course, one must be alert for the sucker play, one of the few times a guard will not point to the play. This gamble, a play of pure fakery, has the guard (or even a tackle) pull out as if to lead the blocking for a sweep. But the play is up the middle and the guard is only trying to influence the defensive lineman or linebacker to pursue, taking himself out of the play. If it works, the ballcarrier can break for a long gain. If it doesn't, he can break for the hospital.

The guards are the lucky ones who get to spend most of their Sundays nose-to-nose with a defensive tackle usually 30 or 40 pounds heavier. They are sure to take a physical beating as they absorb all the flailing and butting a tackle can dish out, but if they slow or stop the defensive charge, they are doing their job.

The one chance for an offensive guard to grab some glory is when he is assigned to pull out and lead the sweep. This gets him out of the pit and when he mows down a puny cornerback with an easy, but devastating block, it gets him more recognition than he is likely to get from a whole day of bumping skulls with the front four.

The offensive tackles must be concerned with pass blocking more, since the hulking defensive ends are primarily concerned with doing bodily harm to the quarterback, which in some camps is known as "The Franchise." Consequently, tackles like Winston Hill of the New York Jets take great pride in that department.

"I like pass blocking because you're not just a machine out there," he says. "You're not just punishing people. You're matching the agility of a man 20 to 40 pounds lighter than yourself with your own. I've had pass blocks that were so pretty I wanted to take them and frame them and hang them on the wall. And I've been whipped so bad that I wanted to cry."

As for the center, he is probably the most faceless of a whole line of faceless men-in-the-crowd. After he puts the ball in the quarterback's hands, he sort of disappears. Even football "experts" confess that they can't tell a good center from a bad one. Ron Mix goes so far as to say the position is a racket, "a place to hide a weak brother. All he does on pass blocking is help someone else out. On running plays, he throws cutoff blocks to one side or the other. Big deal. It just means falling down in front of someone."

Still, the cutoff block is an effective gauge of how good a center really is. If he is not quick enough to cut off the defensive charge, the defensive tackle will penetrate and disrupt the entire play. And if it's true that he mainly helps out on pass blocking, the center still must take care of the middle linebacker if he blitzes.

"Take your eye off the middle linebacker," says Jim Ringo, former great for Green Bay and Philadelphia, "and he'll be in on your quarterback before he can even get a grip on the ball."

It is one of pro football ironies that in its history, three of the most famous linemen were centers—Hall of Famers Chuck Bednarik, Mel Hein, and Clyde "Bulldog" Turner. Bednarik, a star with the Philadelphia Eagles from 1949-62, was one of the only players in the two-platoon era to go both ways, making it big both as a center and a middle linebacker. Hein, playing for the New York Giants from 1931-45, revolutionized center play with his mobility. Until he came along, the center remained anchored after the snap. He was also one of the best defensive centers of the time. Turner, with the Chicago Bears, snapped the ball with one hand, greatly increasing his blocking potential.

Today, with two-platoon football firmly established, the durability of a Bednarik or a Hein or a Bulldog is carried on by centers like Jim Otto of the

Bubba Smith (78)

Oakland Raiders, or Mick Tingelhoff of the Vikings.

One thing centers are better at, as a rule, than other linemen is not in the book on how to block. It's called holding, and it's supposed to be illegal. But the flow of bodies around the center is perfect concealment for a little holding, grabbing, and even tackling. All offensive linemen get into the act at some time or another because, faced with the job of pass blocking, they have to choose between a little holding and a broken quarterback.

"If I were an offensive lineman, I'd probably hold because my responsibility would be to keep the guy off the quarterback," says Bob Lilly, defensive great for the Dallas Cowboys. "I wouldn't make it obvious, though, like some people do. But what the hell, it's not called that much anyway."

Not that holding is done all that often. Howard Mudd, who ended his career with the Chicago Bears, once said, "It's not like an insidious little thing, or a diabolical plot to take the man's life, or something like that. It's something you do out of desperation."

It is in that split-second that a lineman realizes he is about to be beaten—badly—that he will be driven to grab on to something for dear life. Consequently, the effects are felt more by the better players, who are more likely to do the beating.

"The better you are, the more you beat your foes, the more they're driven by desperation to illegal tactics," says Merlin Olson. "I've had men hold me on the opening play of the game, before they even tried to stop me fairly. I hate it, but it's difficult to detect and you just have to live with it."

Another thing linemen—both offensive and defensive—must learn to live with is the realization that in a game where scoring is the object, they may play their whole career without once running the ball, let alone score with it. While others take the glory, they must be content to slug it out in the Pit.

"When you watch football on TV, of course everybody watches the ball, the quarterback, the ends, the halfbacks," says Tingelhoff. "But between the five offensive linemen and four defensive linemen, we've got our own little ball game."

Carl Eller (81)

The Linebackers

AFTER SPENDING YEARS in an ill-lit, dreary Menlo Park, New Jersey laboratory, working long hours, watching experiments fail more times than he could remember, Thomas Alva Edison finally invented the light bulb in 1879. It was, quite obviously, an invention that changed the face of the world. At least there wouldn't be any more ill-lit, dreary Menlo Park laboratories.

One sunny Sunday afternoon, 75 years later, in Philadelphia, Pa., after less than 60 minutes ruminating and no time experimenting, young Bill George, a middle guard on the Chicago Bears, changed the face of football. He invented the position of middle linebacker, and consequently, the standard professional 4-3-4 defense that we know today.

"It was back in about '54," George says. "We were playing the Eagles. At that time, I played right on the center's nose. They kept completing little passes right over the middle. George Connor was our captain then and between plays one time, I told him if I stood up they wouldn't be able to complete those passes on us.

"So Connor said, 'Then what the hell are you doing there?' So I stood up and backed away from the center."

Bill George stood up and backed away so well that he made All-Pro at the position he invented eight times and was paid the ultimate compliment of imitation.

Initially of course, the old-line coaches scoffed at the innovation. The 4-3-4 defense was just a fad, they said, like rock 'n roll. It would never last.

But it did. Within two years after Bill George stood up and backed away to keep the Eagles from completing short passes, everyone else was standing up and backing away into the 4-3-4 defense to keep from losing their jobs.

Naturally, it wasn't as simple as a coach walking onto a practice field to tell his players that they were going to use a new defensive formation that included three players called linebackers. The transition was slow and painful and took time mostly to develop the kind of super-athlete necessary to fulfill the demands exacted by the linebacker position.

No one ever argued with Wally Lemm, ex-coach of the St. Louis Cardinals, when he said: "Linebacker is the toughest position to play well."

A linebacker must be as large as a lineman, as fast as a halfback, and as intelligent as a coach. He must be able to chase downfield with a running back on pass coverage, bust through the line to stop the run, pursue down the line to stop the sweep and, at times,

Middle linebacker
Jim Carter of the
Green Bay Packers

Vernon Biever

blitz through the line to tackle the quarterback for a huge loss.

Jake Gaither, the coach at Florida A&M University, has always said that in order to see action on his squad, a player must be "agile, mobile and hostile (all rhyming with Nile)." Ideally, NFL linebackers possess all three of those characteristics, plus great size and football sense.

Ideals, of course, are elusive and rarely found, particularly in football. So, as a smart coach learns to compensate. Walt Michaels, a corner linebacker and captain of two Cleveland Browns championship teams before becoming a defensive coach with the New York Jets among other teams, is such a smart coach.

"First, there's the matter of height," says Michaels of his linebackers. "The book says he's got to be 6-2 or 6-3, certainly no smaller than 6-1. Well, I'll take him an inch smaller if he's got the brains. I want to know what he's thinking when he sees them breaking out of the huddle and lining up in front of him.

"Then, there's his speed. The book says 4.9 for the 40. But the speed comes into it when he's dropping back to cover passes, and what I want to know is how fast is his drop, not how fast he goes straight ahead for 40 yards.

"Next, they say he's got to weigh 225 pounds or more. But I've had 210- or 215-pound people with 235-pound strength. And I've seen some awfully weak 240-pounders," Michaels concludes.

What the coach seems to say then, is that a linebacker must be capable of getting the job done. Which means that he must be a great athlete, often among the best few athletes on a 47-man roster of great athletes.

As a result of this demand for the great athlete, linebackers in the NFL are frequently men who played other positions in college. Sam Huff, who played middle linebacker for the New York Giants and Washington Redskins and who was responsible for bringing glamor to the position when he was the subject of a television documentary entitled "The Violent World of Sam Huff" in 1961, was a two-way tackle at West Virginia.

Mike Curtis, who plays the middle for the Baltimore Colts, was an All-American fullback at Duke. Ralph Baker, an outside linebacker with the New York Jets when they won the 1969 Super Bowl, was an offensive end at Penn State. Marlin McKeever, who plays middle linebacker for the Los Angeles Rams, even played tight end for the Rams and the Minnesota Vikings before he was switched back to defense.

And all three of the starting linebackers and the top sub at the position on Vince Lombardi's championship teams at Green Bay had been offensive players in college. Middle-man Ray Nitschke was a

Bill George

fullback at Illinois, as was right linebacker Lee Roy Caffey at Texas A&M. Left linebacker Dave Robinson starred at end for Penn State, and the top reserve, Tommy Crutcher, was an All-American fullback at Texas Christian.

Beyond great athletic ability, there is this matter of "football sense." A linebacker must seek before he can destroy. He must be able to find an opponents' vulnerable spot on each play before he can attack.

Most often, this means reading the offensive keys. Recognizing the little tips an offensive opponent might give as to which way a play is headed or who will get the ball, is one of the most valuable assets a man-behind-the-defensive line can possess.

For example, Robinson, who played for the Packers during their glory years and their lean years and was still playing when Dan Devine brought them back in 1972, became one of the great ones not only because he was 6'4", 245-pounds with blazing speed, but also because he could read the keys.

"I love hitting," Robinson says. "Blockers as well as ballcarriers. But you have to be selective in who you're hitting, because all the fakes are aimed at linebackers. And that's where your keys come in."

"You can take one key and go all out with it all season, but you're going to be just average, or less. If you have two keys to work from, you'll be better. Three keys, you might be outstanding.

"I have to check the tight end, the near tackle, the near guard, the far guard, the near back and the far

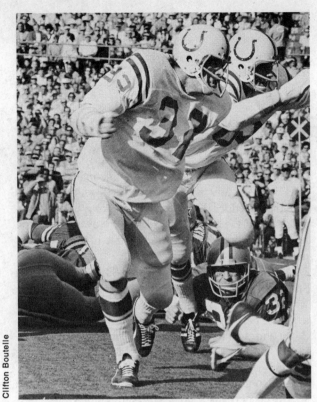

Mike Curtis

back. But I've got less than a second to do it, so I just do the best I can.

"You've got to be careful of the phony key, too. A man blows a play and that might be a phony key, because he isn't going where he should. That's why it's important to have more than one key. They can throw one wrong key at you, one fake, but it's very hard to coordinate two. How do you get a key? One way is to hit that man when he's not trying to block you. The tight end wants to block me on a running play, so he's resigned to getting hit. But if I bust him when he doesn't have to hit me, he's going to learn not to like it.

And he might do something about it—set up a little bit off the line, lean, something like that—to avoid being hit. When he does that, I've got a key. I can tell when he's supposed to block me and when he wants to do something else. Backs can give me a key, too, the way they tilt.

"Oh, I might be off one blocking hole, but I've got the general area pinpointed. Once I do, I'm free to play football.

"That's what the whole idea is, to get me into the area of the play so I can play football."

Larry Grantham, who has played outside linebacker for the New York Jets since they were the old New York Titans of the AFL, agrees that there is more to playing linebacker than muscle (he has to, at 210 pounds), but as he approaches middle age, he finds that it's not an intellectualization of the move-

ment, but rather an intuitive sense of how the play will develop that comes only with years of experience.

"Well, there's something to this being old," says Grantham. "It's not all that bad. I couldn't coach anybody to play linebacker like I do. When you've been around for a while, there are just certain things you pick up. When a back leans forward, he's coming out on a pass or he's getting the hand-off. When he leans back, he's getting himself ready to pass block. The young ones tip most of the time. Sometimes the old ones do, too.

"The screen pass? You just sort of see it opening up. They give you the inside. They invite you in. So I start going wide right away. We've got our keys to play, but if you start figuring them out, you're dead. You've got to look for that first movement, and that's the time to react—not your brain, but your legs. Your brain catches on later. I look at one man, but I'm really seeing about five. And there's absolutely no waiting involved . . . it's instinct, I guess."

Once the linebacker has the play diagnosed and he knows where he should go, there is still that rather large task of busting the play up, using his body to stop the ballcarrier or the blocking convoy, so teammates can make the tackle.

Among all the men who have played the linebacking position, none has played it better than Dick Butkus of the Chicago Bears. Not Bill George. Not Sam Huff, nor Joe Schmidt, nor Nitschke, nor Chuck Bednarik, nor Tommy Nobis, or even Mike Curtis, who insists he is the greatest. All of the above were, or are great. But none as great as Butkus.

George may have invented the position of middle linebacker. And Huff may have glamorized the position, and Schmidt, Nitschke and Bednarik may have popularized and given an identity to the position. But Butkus personifies the position and is the paragon of linebacking virtue. He is big (6'3", 245 pounds), and is quick. But perhaps most of all he is the best in the business because he refuses to be fooled.

Because Butkus combines great size with speed, attitude and a nose for violence, it is said by many that he hits hard. Doug Buffone, who plays alongside Butkus for the Bears, is one who has noticed this propensity.

"There are guys who make tackles and then there's Dick," Buffone says. "He's a mauler. I hit pretty hard, but no matter how hard I hit, I don't hit that hard."

Butkus explains his high quality of play differently. For him, it isn't the violence, the contact, the desire to hit people. It is, instead, the pride and the desire to use his abilities to the fullest. It is the desire to be the best.

"Every time I play a game, I want to play it like it was my last one," he says. "I could get hurt and that would be it for keeps. I wouldn't want my last game to be a lousy one."

Deep Backs

ALL DEFENSIVE BACKS, good ones and bad ones, strive for basically the same thing when they are covering a pass receiver. They try to keep the receiver from getting too close, or too far away and they fight to stay in position to break up the play when the ball is delivered.

Among defensive secondary coaches, this technique is known as "maintaining a good relationship" with the offensive man.

The term is bitterly ironic. If the defensive back maintains that "good relationship" with the receiver, his relationships are good with everyone else—teammates, coaches, management, fans and family. But if he somehow loses touch with the man he is assigned to cover and "gets burned," he can invite all his friends to a party in his locker.

It's common knowledge that defensive backs are the most under-paid, under-praised, over-burdened performers in professional football. All of them, even the very best, live daily with the gnawing fear of making that one, little mistake that will cost their team a touchdown. And when it happens, everyone in the stadium and in the television audience knows who to blame for it.

It happens right out in the open, in plain view of everyone. There is no line to hide behind, no crowd to get lost in. There is only the receiver and the defender, hooked up in a personal duel on a clear field.

If the defender somehow manages to bat down the ball or is enough of a nuisance that the offender can't make the catch, fine. After all, that's only his job and he deserves a polite round of pitty-pat applause for doing it. But if he doesn't do his job and the play is good for long yardage or even a score, the boos ring loud and clear and the coach slams his clipboard to the turf.

When that happens, the defensive back lowers his head and probably thinks to himself what Johnny Sample, the ex-New York Jet bad-boy used to say on such moments of ignominy: "Why do we have to put up with this?"

The most vulnerable of all the deep defenders is the cornerback. Unlike the strong or the free safety who can make a mistake in the middle and hope for help from either side, the corner is all by himself on the fringes of the action. Even in a zone coverage, where there is less emphasis on one-on-one confron-

tations, the cornerback is still the one man a quarterback will "go to work on." The passer will probe and test the defender all afternoon, looking for a weakness. And if the cornerback lets up for even an instant, he can get burned and a whole game of good work is destroyed in one play.

"That's for real," says the San Diego's Ron Smith. "I can do a super job on a receiver for the whole game . . . say shut out my man nine times in a row. Then, on the tenth time, he catches a touchdown and the fans only remember that last time. They blame me for one bad play and forget all the good ones."

"It's something we have to live with, but everyone sees a cornerback's mistake. And I don't care how good a dude is. It could be Lem Barney or Herb Adderley, or anybody. Getting burned happens to the best of us."

Adds John Dockery, who came out of Harvard and semi-pro football to share a piece of the Jets' Super Bowl pie in 1969:

"Do you know how tough this position is—how unbelievably tough? You're standing all by yourself, and you're looking at a guy like Warren Wells who can fly, I mean really fly. One missed step, one stumble and that's it. Curtains."

In the traditional, man-to-man coverage system that was in vogue for many years in the NFL, cornerbacks adopted one of two techniques to keep the "curtains" from falling.

One is best illustrated by Herb Adderley, all-pro for the Lombardi Green Bay Packers and later with the Dallas Cowboys. While conceding immediately that the receiver has the advantage ("because he knows where he's going and you don't"), Adderley has developed a style that was popular for many years before the NFL and AFL merged—covering the receiver one-on-one from five to six yards off the line of scrimmage.

"Very seldom would I hit a guy coming off the line . . . I just tried to stay with him as long as I could and once the ball was in the air, it was as much mine as it was his," Adderley explained.

"I just played the man until the ball was thrown, and then I played the ball. Also, I tried to keep the receiver from getting head up on me. I would work his outside or his inside, forcing him to go only one way. But if he got me head-up, he could go either way and covering him became that much harder."

The other popular style of man-to-man coverage was first developed in the old AFL in the late '60's and was known as "bump-and-run." Using this technique, the cornerback lined up right on the receiver's nose and kept unloading on him all the way down the field, trying to stay inside his jersey.

The Oakland Raiders were one of the early proponents of the bump-and-run style and Kent McCloughan was one of the best in the Raider secondary.

"I played a lot of tight," McCloughan said. "I did a lot of hitting. I wasn't real strong or anything, but I played it close and hit as much as I could get away with. Of course, unloading on a receiver doesn't hurt them much, but it throws their timing off by knocking them off stride or slowing them down."

In recent years, of course, the man-to-man concept has fallen out of favor with pro coaches and the combination zone defense has taken over almost entirely. Even old bump-and-run die-hards like the Jets and the Kansas City Chiefs have switched to the zone look in an effort to cut down on the long bomb and to take some of the pressure off the cornerbacks.

The modern zone had its forerunner when the great coaching innovator, Steve Owen of the New York Giants, devised a defense to stop Otto Graham and the Cleveland Browns.

"In 1950 we developed a defense against the Browns that came to be known as the Umbrella," recalled Emlen Tunnell, a Giant assistant coach who who also one of the greatest defensive backs who ever played the game.

"Our ends, Jim Duncan and Ray Poole, would drift back and cover the flats while tackles Arnie Weinmeister and Al DeRogatis and guards Jon Baker and John Mastrangelo were charged with rushing the passer and containing the run. The lone linebacker, John Canady, was told to follow the Brown fullback wherever he went.

"Tom Landry played the left corner, Harmon Rowe the right, I was the strong safety and Otto Schnellbacher the weak. If you would look at this alignment from high in the stands it looked like an open umbrella. In truth, it was the same 4-3-2-2 used today." Tunnell concluded.

Of course, Owen's innovation has been highly polished and refined over the last 20-plus years. Some coaches brag about having 200 to 300 defenses and a defensive playbook that is too heavy to carry home. But that is stretching it just a bit.

"If a guy talks about running a couple of hundred defenses, he's talking about adjustments, not basic defenses," explains Mike Hudson, once a super strong-safety with the New York Jets. "The Jets play about 24 different defenses per game. We use three basic

Herb Adderley

fronts or formations and have about eight defenses we can call off of each one."

As zone defenses become more sophisticated, many people are crying for it to be outlawed. Especially concerned are television fat cats who worry that viewing audiences will shrink in direct proportion to the number of long touchdown passes the zone takes away from the offense.

Of course, some of the best receivers are worried, too. Paul Warfield of the Miami Dolphins, maybe the greatest one-on-one receiver in the NFL, is one of the plaintiffs against the zone.

"They've taken all the artistry out of pass receiving," Warfield says. "I'd work to beat the man who was covering me. I'd study him thoroughly, how he moved, what he did. I was totally concerned with his reactions to my pass pattern. Now I go out and put three or four moves on a guy and he isn't paying any attention to me," Warfield moans.

"A receiver doesn't need moves any more," he continues. "All he has to do is hit a certain area and find the seams in the zone."

Earlie Thomas, cornerback for the Jets, outlines the situation from the defensive point of view:

"It doesn't take great physical ability to play zone," Thomas says. "But it takes a little more mental ability. In a zone, you've got to work as a unit. You can't

Paul Warfield

Jay Spencer

just be concerned with yourself and what you can do, but with the others. You've got seven people in a zone and you can't have them running into each other.

"There are some backs playing zone right now who could not play man-to-man," Thomas adds.

With increased emphasis on the zone, running backs and tight ends are becoming primary receivers. The zone is strongest against the deep pass cuts and the quick, cheap score is made almost impossible. But there are built-in weaknesses—like swing passes or flares to a back coming out of the backfield, or curls and slants by the tight end breaking into the open areas between the linebackers and the deep backs.

Perhaps the most spectacular thing the zone provides for is "blind-spot interception"—that moment when a free safety or maybe a linebacker who is hovering outside the passer's field of vision, bursts in front of a reciever to pick the ball off when it is delivered.

"I led the league with ten interceptions one year and all of them came out of a zone defense . . . a strong side rotation," says the St. Louis Cardinals' great free safety, Larry Wilson. "The quarterback looked downfield and thought he saw an open man. But he wasn't really open because I was coming just as hard the other way."

Wilson was also the pioneer of another spectacular wrinkle put into the zone by Cardinal assistant coach Chuck Drulis in the '60's. It is known as the "safety blitz," in which the free safety tries to completely surprise the offense and blast between blocking linemen to tackle the quarterback or ball carrier for a big loss.

"It was a real experience at first," Wilson related. "For a couple of years, the other teams just didn't know what I was doing. All I had to do was change to a different hole and they were completely fouled up again. But teams have gotten used to it, and they slide-block and really crunch that safety when he comes in there," he finished.

Wilson's long and prosperous career in the NFL outlined one of the most important prerequisites for playing good pass defense—football smarts. Wilson was neither big (190 lbs.), nor exceptionally fast. But he had a super football mind and in the later years of his career, his experience more than compensated for any loss of speed by helping him anticipate a play and always leading him to where the ball was.

Almost all of the greatest defensive backs survived for a long time in the NFL—Tunnell, Erich Barnes, Dick (Night Train) Lane, Richie Petitbon, to name a few.

As Barnes put it, "Experience is probably the most important thing for a deep back. They say that reactions are 90 per cent of the game back there, but if you already know what's going to happen, that's a lot better than all the reactions in the world."

The Special Teams

THE NFL PUBLICISTS called it "an effort at cultural refinement by Commissioner Pete Rozelle's public relations staff." But as far as most NFL players are concerned, the situation is basically the same. Only the name has been changed to protect the innocent, and not-so-innocent victims.

"Special teams" is the new term that Rozelle and his staff have hung on those courageous souls who hurl their bodies downfield under punts and kickoffs. Rumor had it that the NFL's major domo felt such sobriquets as "suicide squad-member," or one of the "banzai bunch" or just, plain "hey you!" were too demeaning for one of society's model citizens—a pro football player.

Listen to the NFL publicity mills hum now and you might get the impression that receiving an assignment on a kickoff or a punt-return team is one of life's choicer assignments. Forget that most "special team" members have a career expectancy of three-to-four years and maiming injuries and even death can result from their suicidal plunges into walls of human flesh.

"The men who play on the 'special teams' are indeed special," proclaims one hearts-and-flowers writer. "There was a time when pro coaches hand-picked their special team candidates strictly on the basis of size, strength and, in some cases, seniority. Veterans usually didn't want special team duty and younger players and raw rookies had no real choice in the matter (astute observation)."

"Today, however, special teams are elevated to new status and dignity," the writer continues. "The emphasis is not on size and strength alone but also on what pro scouts refer to as 'motor skills'."

That line excites cynical laughter from many of the NFL's "nouveau dignitaries" who have been "elevated" to new status on a special team. One of them is the Chicago Bears' Craig Clemons.

"Motor skills?" he chuckles. " 'No brains' is more like it, or else, 'no choice.' Anyone who tells you he enjoys playing on special teams is crazy. I mean, I don't have it so bad because I can return kicks and things. But those guys who have to break up the wedge. . . ." Clemons concludes with a grimace and a little shudder.

According to most pros, who for reasons of inexperience or lack of first-string talent are relegated to special team status, things haven't changed much from the old, "Suicide Squad" days, edicts from Pete Rozelle's office notwithstanding.

"Coaches are realizing maybe a little more than before the difference a good kick return team or a field goal team can make between winning and losing," says one NFL assistant coach. "But unless there are unusual circumstances, a coach is not going to risk one of his top regulars getting hurt by putting him on a special team.

"The incidence of injury is still incredibly high on kicking teams, and that means you still have to go with rookies and second-line players—ones you can afford to lose," he notes frankly.

Obviously, the most valuable special team members are those who are most willing to play with "reckless abandon." Those who will throw their bodies into a wall of blockers or a tackler running downfield full speed with no thought of injury are the ones the coaches are looking for.

Vince Lombardi used to say gleefully, "Special teams will tell you one thing—who wants to hit and who doesn't. You find that out right away."

Often this will to hit, as Lombardi describes it, is interpreted as Clemons did earlier—no brains. An endless series of one-liners have been unloaded at special team members, even before Howard Cosell's tongue began titillating Monday night TV audiences.

"Everyone is afraid of something. A man without fear belongs in a mental institution—or on special teams, either one," cracked Walt Michaels once upon a time.

In the face of a constant threat of mayhem, special team members devise many ways to keep their spirits up. Many of the younger players remind themselves that there is a chance for promotion to regular status if they continue to shine on the kicking units. As injuries take their toll around mid-season, younger players are usually moved into first-string jobs in direct proportion to how well they perform in a special team situation, or how high their salary is, either one.

Older players doomed to the suicide squad have to be a little more imaginative in keeping spirits high. Alex Hawkins was probably one of the most famous special-teamers in his days with the Baltimore Colts. As captain of the Colts "Doomsday Teams", he kept his teammates loose with his one-liners, wrote a book and parlayed his comic reputation into a job as a TV commentator.

"Sort of makes us feel good that at least one of us Kamikaze pilots made good . . . even if it was that loud-mouthed Hawkins." says another ex-special teamer who left the Cardinals several seasons ago to nurse his wounds.

Other clubs hang nicknames on their special teams.

When the coach calls the squad out on the field by name to practice kickoffs, all eleven men come sprinting forward with a loud "Ar-r-r-r-g-h-h!" that usually cracks up the whole squad.

The Los Angeles Rams' Tommy Prothro used to yell out, "Guillory's Gorillas!" (named after suicide-captain Tony Guillory) and everyone at practice would laugh and clap and whistle and it was a good break in the routine. And after the '72 season, Prothro was fired and suing the Rams for breach of contract.

Of course, super-conscientious special-teamers can get their reward by considering their contributions vital to the squad effort, and they are correct in this assessment. Obviously, the difference between victory and defeat can be a long punt return, or a blocked field goal or a tackle on a kickoff return that nails the opponent inside his own 10-yard line.

But the contribution of the special teams can only be measured in more subtle ways. Mark Smolinski, former captain of the New York Jets' special teams explains how:

"On special teams you've got to hit or be hit. You play with abandon and turn your body completely loose. It's tough and you can get hurt, but it all boils down to pride. If you do it well, the hitting becomes contagious and carries over to the regular offense and defense," Smolinski says.

It is the hitting that carries over and it is hitting that is the entire story of special team activities. The assignments are all but insignificant in any kicking situation. Everyone has a set of basic rules: kickoff coverage must be done in lanes and one must not get blocked. Kickoff return blockers are assigned a man to cut down, or a wedge of four men is formed in front of the ball-carrier to plow a path as close to midfield as possible.

On punt returns, the play call is either to block the kick with an all-out rush, or peel back to set up a return to either sideline. On punt coverage, the assignment is to check one man for two counts, then release downfield and cover the kick, forcing the return man to run to the inside.

And so it goes. Pretty basic stuff, with the key ingredients being raw desire, courage and a lack of fear.

However, even if a special team star has all of the above in abundance, he won't last long unless he finally wins a spot with a regular unit. The emotional stress and high injury risk take a fearsome toll.

A good example was Mike Battle, a 180-pound kick returner for the Jets who lasted two years and then slipped back to California.

"Punchy Mike," as they used to call him, said during his special team days, "Don't ever phone me the days after a game. I'll either be still getting drunk or looking for bail. When you're on a suicide squad like I am, you don't wait until tomorrow to start living."

The Kickers

Garo Yepremian

THESE DAYS when you think of place kickers, you think of soccer style kickers. The little bald guys with the thick accents who face one way and kick another. The guys once described by Alex Karras, who played a little football before becoming a television personality.

"These soccer style guys kill me," Karras said. "Those little 5' 1", 110-pound foreign guys who determine the outcome of games now. They sing their little song, 'I'm goeeng to keeck a tawchdown. I'm goeeng to keeck a tawchdown'. You've got all these 6' 3", 250-pounders killing themselves for 59 minutes and 37 seconds and a little guy kicks a 50-yard field goal and the game is over."

It hasn't always been this way, of course. Alex Karras would have liked the old days, which are as recent as 1963, just fine, even though the kicking product of the pre-1964 days was vastly inferior to the post-1964, or soccer style, days. For in the old days there usually weren't kicking specialists. The kicker was just one of the guys who killed himself for 59 minutes and 37 seconds. And when he was done killing himself, he missed a 50-yard field goal attempt, and the game ended in a tie.

Statistically, with rare exceptions, the part-time kickers and full-time players were an abomination, especially compared to the current crop of kicking specialists. In the 1970 National Football League season, each team average 31 field goal tries, converting 18.4 for a .593 average. Before 1964, when Pete Gogolak joined the Buffalo Bills and became the first soccer style kicker, a .500 average was a rare achievement. From 1951 to 1964, a league 50 per cent field goal accuracy average was accomplished only five times. Before 1951, it was never accomplished. And in 1943, NFL teams average two successful kicks out of 8.5 attempts—for the entire season. Don Hutson of the Packers and Ward Cuff of the Giants tied for the league lead with three apiece.

This isn't to say that there weren't any great kickers during the early and middle days of pro football. There were. There just weren't very many of them.

The greatest kicker of the early years was Jim Thorpe, who is considered by many to be the best athlete ever produced by this country. Thorpe doubled as a punter and place kicker for the Canton Bulldogs. He is said to have kicked a 75-yard field goal for Canton against Indianapolis, a distance which, if true, has yet to be matched, despite technological advance-

George Blanda (16)

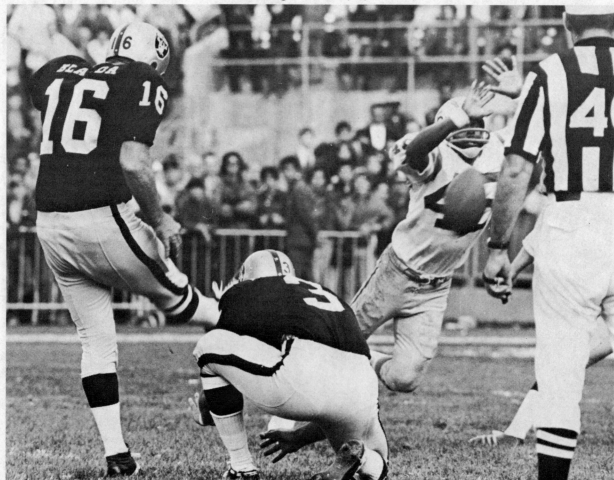

ments that have aided the kicker. It is also said that he lofted high spiraling 70-yard punts with regularity. And between kicks he wasn't a bad man to have carry the ball, either.

After Thorpe, there were several more great kickers. Sammy Baugh, the Washington Redskins' quarterback, averaged 51.3 yards per punt for the 1940 season, which is still a NFL record. (Modern football scholars scoff at that record. They say that much of Baugh's yardage was accumulated by long rolls after quick kicks.) And there were the drop kickers such as Paddy Driscoll and Elbert Bloodgood and "Automatic" Jack Manders. Driscoll once drop kicked four field goals in one game, including a 50-yarder.

But kicking remained a relatively insignificant facet of the game, seldom practiced, seldom crucial, until the late 1940's when a muscular All-Pro offensive tackle started to turn kicking into a specialty, a facet of the game as important as any other. He went by the name of Lou Groza, and frequently he was the reason the Cleveland Browns won a football game, which is something they had a habit of doing.

Groza's success at kicking didn't come easy. As a youngster in Martins Ferry, Pennsylvania, he practiced kicking with a passion. He was a perfectionist, who would practice kicking for hours after his high school team's regular practice had ended.

From Martins Ferry, Lou went to Ohio State. He didn't last long because a war was raging in the Pacific and in Europe, and the military desired his services. But he did last long enough to attract the attention of one Paul Brown, maybe the smartest football mind ever, and in 1946, instead of returning to college he joined the Cleveland Browns.

Groza quickly won the confidence of Brown. Just a few weeks after Groza's arrival, Brown was bragging to reporters about his new star. "Anywhere inside the 50," Brown said, "we never have to punt. We just let Lou go for the field goal." And most of the time he made them.

More and more Brown came to rely on Groza's toe to make the difference in a game. Eleven times Groza kicked three field goals in a single game, with the Browns triumphant in nine of them. And in the two losses, Groza scored all the points.

And in the 1950 NFL championship game against the Los Angeles Rams, Groza kicked a 23-yard field goal with 20 seconds remaining to play to give the Browns a 30-28 victory. The win was especially significant because it ended Cleveland's first season in the NFL after the collapse of the All-America Conference.

Groza's continued success, he lasted from 1946 well into the '60's, and the significant role his foot played in Browns' championships, brought respectability to the kickers of the world. And it was only a matter of time before the NFL discovered that kickers were to be found everywhere in the world.

For a time after the emergence of Groza, the leading kickers continued to be men who also played Alex Karras' murderous 59 minutes and 37 seconds. In Green Bay there were halfback Paul Hornung, who led in the league in scoring by combining his kicking points and his touchdowns, and guard Jerry Kramer. In Detroit there were linebacker Wayne Walker and defensive back Yale Lary, who punted.

But even though the late '50's and early '60's wasn't a time of specialization as we know it now, it was a beginning. In New York, the Giants had Pat Summerrall place kicking, and Don Chandler (who would later do both in Green Bay for Lombardi) punting. In Philadelphia, the Eagles had Sam Baker punting and place kicking.

And then in 1964 came the kicking revolution. It came in the form of a refugee from another revolution—the one in Hungary in 1956. The refugee's name was Pete Gogolak, and he carried with him an Ivy League diploma from Cornell as well as an educated instep.

Not only was the instep educated, but it was Summa Cum Laude. In Gogolak's rookie season with the Buffalo Bills, he finished second in the American Football League in field goals to the Boston Patriots' Gino Cappellitti. In his sophomore AFL season, Gogolak finished second to no one.

And he argued so persuasively with his instep that there were ways other than the straight ahead toe method of place kicking a football that he became the object of a bidding war between the Bills of the AFL, and the Giants of the NFL. He signed with the Giants, and he still is kicking for them. And it is said that his signing caused the negotiations that eventually resulted in the merger of the NFL and the AFL.

Following Pete Gogolak into the NFL has been an irregular but talented army of soccer style kickers, most of them of European origins. They include Pete's brother Charley, who has kicked for the Redskins and the Patriots, and the two glamor boys of the soccer style set, Jan Stenerud of the Kansas City Chiefs and Garo Yepremian of the Miami Dolphins.

Stenerud, a Norwegian, came to the U.S. on a ski jumping scholarship to Montana State. When the basketball coach there discovered his kicking talents, he advised the football coach and a star was born. Although the star can't exactly explain why he is good enough to be a star.

"I don't study myself that closely, and I don't have any set technique," says Stenerud. "I hit it (the ball) with my instep instead of my toe, so maybe that gives me greater surface to hit the ball with. I wear soccer style short cleats, but they are no good on a muddy day, because my left foot, the one that is planted, will slip.

"Kicking is more natural to Europeans, anyway.

Give a European boy a ball and his first instinct is to kick it, not to throw it. If a European starts kicking an American football, he'll probably be better than the American who has never done it before. I can't help but think there must be someone, somewhere, maybe in Asia, who can kick the football even better than me, because I never thought about kicking a football until I tried. The first time I kicked one, I kicked it almost as well as I'm doing now."

There are, however, among the myriad of soccer stylists some very successful straight ahead toe men. Among them are George Blanda of the Raiders, who has been around longer than anyone cares to remember, and Jim Turner, who has kicked for the New York Jets and the Denver Broncos. Turner is one of the many scientists of the trade. To him, a kick is as precise as a mathematical formula. Success not only depends on the kicker but on the snapper and the holder.

"A holder can kill you if he wants to," says Turner. "He can give you the white knuckle—hold the ball down real hard when you get your toe into it—or he can tilt it just a half-inch one way or another. Then the whole equation goes KABLOOM!

"And laces, they can be your worst enemy. They give you a bad surface. The holder's got to spin the ball before you swing your leg, and he has to bring it down all in the same movement—within a second."

At the end of each of his seasons with the Jets, Turner would give the center and the holder a box of expensive cigars. Just to make sure they liked him. Because just as a kicker can be the difference in a game, the center or holder could be the difference in the kick that could be the difference.

And just as the place kicker can be the difference, so can the punter. His job is to kick the ball the farthest with the least return. If he doesn't get the distance, or kicks low enough to permit long returns, the punter is in trouble, because then he is allowing the opposition good field position.

And, as any cardcarrying head football coach will tell you, field position is the name of the game—at least some of the time.

Jim Turner (15)

IT TAKES MORE THAN TALENT
TO SUCCEED IN THE NFL

ODDBALLS, CUT-UPS, and practitioners of various forms of nitwitery have always been part of the sporting scene and pro football has certainly had its share of individuals who have added new dimensions and horizons to the word "colorful."

But at the same time there have been those who have gone beyond the usual hi-jinks, those who from a peculiar quirk or two in their personality, have exhibited a kind of self-destruct tendency, a kind of suicidal urge to throw it all away in one gesture, either magnificent or ridiculous.

It just goes to prove that it takes more than sheer talent to play in the National Football League, and it goes beyond the zanies who scrimmage without a helmet.

Take Joe Kapp as an example. You remember Joe Kapp, the quarterback of Mexican, Indian, Irish and Italian lineage who led the Minnesota Vikings to the NFL championship in 1969, more by running over linebackers than by aerial artistry?

Joe decided he wasn't paying enough income tax so he played out his option to get into a higher bracket. What was then the Boston Patriots decided that Kapp was the solution to their troubles. The financial dealings got so complicated, about $200,000 a year for Joe in various manners, that they couldn't get it worked out before the 1970 season started so Kapp signed a "memorandum of agreement" with the commissioner's office. The next year they wanted Kapp to sign the standard NFL contract.

Kapp refused. He called it, with its option clause binding a player to a club, " a condition of servitude." It became a matter of principle and Joe clung firmly to his principles. Today he's a 34-year-old motel keeper, changing the bedding, but not his principles.

Warren Wells and Dick Gordon were two of the most feared long ball threats in the game, but it's hard to catch the ball if you're not in the stadium. Wells is out of the game now and Gordon, well, he'll bounce around a little longer, maybe.

Wells' troubles were with the law. He was convicted of attempted rape in 1969. He was paroled to his team, the Oakland Raiders, but was stabbed by another 20-year-old girl at a party in a lounge. He spent the 1971 season in jail for parole violation.

Warren tried to make it back in 1972. He was placed on probation and housed 50 miles away from the Raiders training camp at a place called Synanon, a rehabilitation center. He had to return to Synanon every night.

At first the word was that Wells was looking good running down under those Daryle Lamonica bombs. Then he didn't. "Unimpressive and listless" was the way the Raiders staff described him, so at 29 Wells announced his retirement from pro football.

Gordon's troubles involved money. He thinks he's worth more, a lot more, than anyone else thinks he's worth. He led the league in receiving once and made all-pro once. Price, $75,000. No takers.

Those fellows, we know what their problems are. With Duane Thomas nobody knows, not even Duane Thomas. He's been described as, "withdrawn," "intense," "morose," "non-communicative," and other synonyms to describe an offbeat character. He's just a different kind of eccentric.

Thomas, with his speed, moves and power, has been called the perfect back. Except no one can get him to play. The first time the Cowboys got fed up with him they shipped him off to New England. When he got there he refused to get down into a three-point stance, literally, and he was back with the Cowboys in the next mail.

He seemed to straighten out there, except he wouldn't talk to anyone, including his coach, Tom Landry, whom he called, "a plastic man." Hardly the way to endear oneself. But he played well. Until the College All-Star game, he walked instead of ran and generally acted as if it was all just a big bore, far beneath his magnificent talents.

That was enough. The Cowboys traded him to the San Diego Chargers for a couple of willing players. It took weeks for coach Harland Svare to even meet him, and he still wasn't talking. By that time everyone stopped caring.

Joe Don Looney was a sort of Duane Thomas in reverse. Looney lived up to his name instead of his potential.

Just as an aside, nothing hooks a coach like potential. They see a Thomas, a Looney, and an Andy Livingston and they immediately begin fantasizing. In their mind's eye they can see all the wonderful deeds those fellows are capable of performing. It takes years of reality to disturb the dream.

Looney played with four colleges and five pro

teams before it finally came through that he wasn't about to reform or change his ways. There was always trouble with citizens, and team regulations were always for the other 39 guys.

When Harry Gilmer was coaching the Detroit Lions, Looney objected to sharing playing time with Tom Nowatzke. One game he made a dazzling run for a touchdown. On the next series, Nowatzke was at fullback. Gilmer wanted to send Looney in with a play just before the half but he refused because, he didn't want to be anyone's messenger boy. Another suspension.

Just a sequel to the Joe Don Looney story. He was arrested by federal agents for illegal possession of a machine gun.

Just about the first time Livingston ever touched a ball in the NFL he ran back a kick-off for a touchdown against the Minnesota Vikings. He was an 18-year-old high school kid allowed to play as a hardship case.

Old George Halas thought he had a real find for his Bears. For a few games he did, but then came a knee injury and Livingston's problems were just getting started.

His coaches said he was afraid to push himself, afraid to punish his body. He hung around for a few more years. His last season with the Bears, he carried the ball only 17 times from scrimmage. He went to New Orleans and in one glorious year he gained almost 1,400 yards running and receiving. He made the Pro Bowl squad, but then another knee injury, and again his comeback was marred by reluctance for violence, so they said. When last heard from, Andy was unemployed.

Lifestyle, of course, enters into this discussion and fellows like George Sauer, Jr., Chip Oliver and Dave Meggyesy marched to a different drummer than, say, Dick Butkus. They grew to abhor violence and called football a debasing and dehumanizing game.

Sauer, a five time all-league wide receiver with the New York Jets, attacked the gospel of Vince Lombardi. He claimed there could be "excellence without tyranny."

"To be a player is to be treated as a child," he said. Bed check was embarrassing. Coaches' concern with long hair and mustaches he found exceedingly objectionable. He quit at 27 at the peak of his career.

Chip Oliver, the Raiders' linebacker, left the game for a hippie commune and a diet of macro burgers, brewer's yeast, protein powder, and sesame seed butter.

He said football degraded him and caused him to lose his manhood. "They've taken the players and made them into slabs of beef that can charge around and hit each other," he said. He tried a comeback, but 180-pound linebackers have it a little tougher.

Meggyesy was the original pro in the youth-turned-on culture. He wrote an expose type book about the game and called pro football "silly." He gave up a $36,000 a year linebacking job with the St. Louis Cardinals, grew a beard and tied a band around his forehead. His old life represented "the ideology of the death culture," he said. And the game was, "an institution that represents so much that is wrong with our society and dehumanizing to the individual."

Ronnie Knox was another football dropout who sought a higher truth in the world of the mind. He quit to become a poet.

He was first signed by the Chicago Bears out of UCLA. The kid had all kinds of quarterbacking talent, but he also had a step-father who did his agenting and otherwise complicated his life. Finally the Bears suspended him. He drifted into the Canadian League and at 24 quit the game.

"Money isn't everything, and I decided I just couldn't continue," said Knox. "I've been playing football for 13 years and I'm sick to the teeth of it. It's a game for animals and I like to think I'm above that."

Perhaps the saddest case of all is that of Gene "Big Daddy" Lipscomb, the 297 pound, six foot seven inch defensive tackle of the Baltimore Colts in their world championship years of 1958 and 1959 and later with the Pittsburgh Steelers.

At age 31 Big Daddy was dead of what the Baltimore coroner's pathologist said was an overdose of heroin.

Big Daddy was one of those rare pros who never played college football. The Rams scouted him when he was playing for the Camp Pendleton Marines. He sat on the bench there for two years, but then the Colts grabbed him for $100 and he was on his way to glory.

Big Daddy Lipscomb, his jersey tail flapping behind him, chasing the enemy carrier and then helping the little fellow to his feet, patting him on the bottom and directing him to the huddle, was a colorful and familiar sight.

In 1961 the Colts, who must have known something, suddenly traded him to the Steelers. It was after a game and a night on the town that he was found dead in the kitchen of a friend's apartment.

There are a lot of ways to fail in pro football, but the sorriest to player and fan and the game itself, is when they, one way or another, do it to themselves.

The All-Time Greats

PROFESSIONAL FOOTBALL

HALL OF FAME

The All-Pro Teams By Decades

ALL-PRO TWENTIES

These are the men who started it all, the rugged individualists who played five games a week and then looked for more. And always it was the game, the game and the game.

There was Jim Thorpe who organized his own teams and then organized leagues around them. Ernie Nevers who played 29 games a season and threw his helmet to the sideline and played the game bareheaded when the going got rough.

George Halas who brought intellect to the game and turned a small starch factory team into the Monsters of the Midway. There was Paddy Driscoll, a magician with the ball, who may have been the greatest all-around back to ever play the game.

There was Fats Henry and tough-talking George Trafton and Swede Youngstrom and the six Nesser brothers and Fritz Pollard and Ed Healy and Charlie Dresden and Curley Lambeau and Johnny Blood and Jimmy Conzelman.

These are the fellows who played in those funny, misshapen leather helmets, flimsy pads and wool jerseys. These are the fellows who limed the field and passed the hat so there could be another game and another league and a Super Bowl.

These are the men who inspired legends, who have created the lore of the game. And still the arguments go on. What would Thorpe do today? Was Nevers better than Brown? How do you compare Fats Henry to Rayfield Wright?

The arguments are superfluous and irrelevant. These men were the best of their day. No man can be more.

Until 1931 no official All-League teams were selected, but the fans' desire to rate and compare players and to always look for the "best" and "greatest" in any season or era early led to the selection of an All-League team as early as 1920. They here make a rare published appearance.

The Editors of PRO FOOTBALL DIGEST selected the All-Pro team of the Twenties, as they did for each era, an the basis of each player's dominance during that period. Only their performance was taken into account, not, as in the case of someone like George Halas, their overall impact on the game.

The following are the year-by-year All-Pro selections of the 1920's.

1920

ENDS
Bob (Nasty) Nash—Buffalo All Americans
George Halas—Decatur Staleys
TACKLES
Wilbur (Fats) Henry—Canton Bulldogs
Lou Little—Buffalo All Americans

GUARDS

Adolph (Swede) Youngstrom—Buffalo All Americans
Joe Mulbarger—Columbus Panhandles

CENTER

Russell Bailey—Akron Professionals

QUARTERBACK

Earnest (Tommy) Hughitt—Buffalo All Americans

HALFBACKS

John (Paddy) Driscoll—Chicago Cardinals
Jim Thorpe—Canton Bulldogs

FULLBACK

Stanley (Red) Cofall—Massillon Tigers

1921

ENDS

Paul Robeson—Akron Pros
Guy Chamberlan—Chicago Staleys, Canton Bulldogs

TACKLES

Wilbur (Fats) Henry—Canton Bulldogs
Ed Healy—Rock Island Independents

GUARDS

Adolph Youngstrom—Buffalo All Americans
Herman (Dutch) Speck—Canton Bulldogs

CENTER

Russell Bailey—Akron Pros

QUARTERBACK

Earnest Hughitt—Buffalo All Americans

HALFBACKS

Fritz Pollard—Akron Pros
John (Paddy) Driscoll—Chicago Cardinals

FULLBACK

Jim Thorpe—Canton Bulldogs

1922

ENDS

George Halas—Chicago Bears
Al Nesser—Akron Pros

TACKLES

Roy (Link) Lyman—Canton Bulldogs
Wilbur (Fats) Henry—Canton Bulldogs

GUARDS

Herman (Dutch) Speck—Canton Bulldogs
Clarence (Steamer) Horning—Toledo Maroons

CENTER

Herb Stein—Toledo Maroons

QUARTERBACK

Cecil Grigg—Canton Bulldogs

HALFBACKS

John (Paddy) Driscoll—Chicago Cardinals
Henry Gillo—Racine Legions

FULLBACK

Frank Nesser—Columbus Panhandles

1923

ENDS

Guy Chamberlin—Canton Bulldogs
Fred Gillies—Chicago Cardinals

Link Lyman

TACKLES
Wilbur (Fats) Henry—Canton Bulldogs
Ed Healy—Chicago Bears
GUARDS
Alfred Cobb—Akron Pros
Russ Hathaway—Dayton Triangles
CENTER
George Trafton—Chicago Bears
QUARTERBACK
Cecil Grigg—Canton Bulldogs
HALFBACKS
John (Paddy) Driscoll—Chicago Cardinals
Earle Lambeau—Green Bay Packers
FULLBACK
Henry Gillo—Racine Legions

Ed Healy

1924

ENDS
Eddie Anderson—Chicago Cardinals
Guy Chamberlin—Cleveland Bulldogs
TACKLES
Howard (Cub) Buck—Green Bay Packers
Russ Stein—Frankford Yellowjackets
GUARDS
Adolph Youngstrom—Buffalo All Americans
Bill Hoffman—Frankford Yellowjackets
CENTER
George Trafton—Chicago Bears
QUARTERBACK
Jim Conzelman—Milwaukee Badgers
HALFBACKS
Wallace Elliott—Cleveland Bulldogs
Rueben Ursella—Rock Island Independents
FULLBACK
Carl Cramer—Akron Pros

1925

ENDS
Charley Berry—Pottsville Maroons
Lynn Bomar—New York Giants
TACKLES
Steve Owen—Kansas City Cowboys
Ed Sauer—Dayton Triangles
GUARDS
Bull Behman—Frankford Yellowjackets
Bob (Duke) Osborne—Pottsville Maroons
CENTER
George Kinderdine—Dayton Triangles
QUARTERBACK
Jim Conzelman—Detroit Panthers
HALFBACKS
John (Paddy) Driscoll—Chicago Cardinals
Houston Stockton—Frankford Yellowjackets
FULLBACK
Tony Latone—Pottsville Maroons

1926

ENDS
Brick Muller—Los Angeles Buccaneers
Lavern Dilweg—Milwaukee Badgers
TACKLES
Russell (Bull) Behman—Frankford Yellowjackets
Steve Owen—Kansas City Cowboys
GUARDS
Frank Racis—Pottsville Maroons
Bob Osborne—Pottsville Maroons
CENTER
George Trafton—Chicago Bears
QUARTERBACK
Joe Ernst—Pottsville Maroons
HALFBACKS
Jack McBride—New York Giants
Verne Lewellen—Green Bay Packers
FULLBACK
Ernie Nevers—Duluth Eskimos

1927

ENDS
Lavern Dilweg—Green Bay Packers
Lyle Munn—Cleveland Bulldogs

TACKLES
Fred (Duke) Slater—Chicago Cardinals
Steve Owen—New York Giants

GUARDS
Francis (Jugger) Earpe—Green Bay Packers
Al Nesser—New York Giants

CENTER
Clyde Smith—Providence Steamrollers

QUARTERBACK
Henry (Two Bits) Homan—Frankford Yellowjackets

HALFBACKS
John (Paddy) Driscoll—Chicago Bears
Verne Lewellen—Green Bay Packers

FULLBACK
Ernie Nevers—Duluth Eskimos

1928

ENDS
Robert (Cal) Hubbard—New York Giants
Ray Flaherty—New York Yankees

TACKLES
Fred (Duke) Slater—Chicago Cardinals
Russell (Bull) Behman—Frankford Yellowjackets

GUARDS
Gus Sonnenberg—Providence Steamrollers
Alf Graham—Dayton Triangles

CENTER
Clyde Smith—Providence Steamrollers

QUARTERBACK
Henry (Two Bits) Homan—Frankford Yellowjackets

HALFBACKS
George (Wildcat) Wilson—Providence Steamrollers
John (Blood) McNally—Pottsville Maroons

FULLBACK
Tony Latone—Pottsville Maroons

1929

ENDS
Robert (Cal) Hubbard—Green Bay Packers
Lavern Dilweg—Green Bay Packers

TACKLES
Fred (Duke) Slater—Chicago Cardinals
Russell (Bull) Behman—Frankford Yellowjackets

GUARDS
August (Mike) Michalske—Green Bay Packers
Alf Graham—Dayton Triangles

CENTER
George Murtagh—New York Giants

QUARTERBACK
Benny Friedman—New York Giants

HALFBACKS
Harold (Red) Grange—Chicago Bears
John (Blood) McNally—Green Bay Packers

FULLBACK
Ernie Nevers—Chicago Cardinals

John (Blood) McNally

Red Grange (with ball)

ALL-PRO TEAM OF THE DECADE (TWENTIES)

The best of their era. Looking back it was almost a magic time. Certainly it was a different game. And these men, selected as the greatest of their peers, brought to the game a certain dash, a certain color, a sure individuality that will perhaps never be matched.

There can be little argument with the selection. All we can do is acknowledge a certain touch of disappointing in leaving off such fellows as George Halas, Johnny Blood McNally, Jimmy Conzelman, Fred (Duke) Slater, Fritz Pollard, Steve Owens and Ed Healey, the man Halas bought for $100 because he was too tough to play against. But these were the special, the matchless few.

1920-1929

ENDS
Guy Chamberlain—Canton Bulldogs
Lavern Dilweg—Milwaukee Badgers

TACKLES
Wilbur (Fats) Henry—Canton Bulldogs
Russell (Bull) Behman—Frankford Yellowjackets

GUARDS
Adolph (Swede) Youngstrom—Buffalo All Americans
August (Mike) Michalske—Green Bay Packers

CENTER
George Trafton—Chicago Bears

QUARTERBACK
Benny Friedman—New York Giants

HALFBACKS
John (Paddy) Driscoll—Chicago Cardinals
Jim Thorpe—Canton Bulldogs

FULLBACK
Ernie Nevers—Chicago Cardinals

Ernie Nevers

Guy Chamberlin

Jim Thorpe

Mike Michalske

George Trafton

Wilbur (Fats) Henry

Paddy Driscoll

ALL-PRO TEAMS OF THE THIRTIES

THE THIRTIES were a great transition period in pro football. The forward pass began more and more to assert itself as an offense weapon. The great virtuoso performers were giving way to a more disciplined team effort. Occasional practices became daily sessions. New formations put the emphasis on teamwork and execution.

But at the same time it was a period rich with great performers as well as notable eccentrics. Bill Hewitt still played without a helmet. Cliff Battles walked away from the game at the height of his career, as did Dutch Clark and Bronko Nagurski.

For the first time official All-League teams were picked. First by the league and then by the wire services. This is the way they picked them in the Thirties.

1930

ENDS
   Lavern Dilweg—Green Bay Packers
   Morris (Red) Badgro—New York Giants

TACKLES
   Robert (Cal) Hubbard—Green Bay Packers
   Forrest (Jap) Douds—Portsmouth Spartans

GUARDS
   August (Mike) Michalske—Green Bay Packers
   Denver (Butch) Gibson—New York Giants

CENTER
   Nathan Barrager—Frankford Yellowjackets

QUARTERBACK
   Joe (Red) Dunn—Green Bay Packers

HALFBACKS
   John (Blood) McNally—Green Bay Packers
   Ken Strong—Staten Island Stapletons

FULLBACK
   Ernie Nevers—Chicago Cardinals

1931

ENDS
   Lavern Dilweg—Green Bay Packers
   Morris (Red) Badgro—New York Giants

TACKLES
   Robert (Cal) Hubbard—Green Bay Packers
   George Christensen—Portsmouth Spartans

GUARDS
   August (Mike) Michalske—Green Bay Packers
   Denver (Butch) Gibson—New York Giants

CENTER
   Frank McNally—Chicago Cardinals

Arnie Herber

QUARTERBACK
  Earl (Dutch) Clark—Portsmouth Spartans
HALFBACKS
  John (Blood) McNally—Green Bay Packers
  Harold (Red) Grange—Chicago Bears
FULLBACK
  Ernie Nevers—Chicago Cardinals

1932

ENDS
  Ray Flaherty—New York Giants
  Luke Johnsos—Chicago Bears
TACKLES
  Robert (Cal) Hubbard—Green Bay Packers
  Albert (Turk) Edwards—Boston Braves
GUARDS
  Jules Carlson—Chicago Bears
  Walt Kiesling—Chicago Cardinals
CENTER
  Nathan Barrager—Green Bay Packers

QUARTERBACK
  Earl (Dutch) Clark—Portsmouth Spartans
HALFBACKS
  Arnold Herber—Green Bay Packers
  Roy (Father) Lumpkin—Portsmouth Spartans
FULLBACK
  Bronko Nagurski—Chicago Bears

1933

ENDS
  Bill Hewitt—Chicago Bears
  Morris (Red) Badgro—New York Giants
TACKLES
  Robert (Cal) Hubbard—Green Bay Packers
  Albert (Turk) Edwards—Boston Redskins
GUARDS
  Herman Hickman—Brooklyn Dodgers
  Joe Kopcha—Chicago Bears
CENTER
  Mel Hein—New York Giants

Ken Strong

QUARTERBACK

Harry Newman—New York Giants

HALFBACKS

Glenn Presnell—Portsmouth Spartans

Cliff Battles—Boston Redskins

FULLBACK

Bronko Nagurski—Chicago Bears

1934

ENDS

Bill Hewitt—Chicago Bears

Morris (Red) Badgro—New York Giants

TACKLES

George Christensen—Detroit Lions

William Morgan—New York Giants

GUARDS

Denver Gibson—New York Giants

Joe Kopcha—Chicago Bears

CENTER

Mel Hein—New York Giants

QUARTERBACK

Earl (Dutch) Clark—Detroit Lions

HALFBACKS

Beattie Feathers—Chicago Bears

Ken Strong—New York Giants

FULLBACK

Bronko Nagurski—Chicago Bears

1935

ENDS

William Smith—Chicago Cardinals

William Karr—Chicago Bears

TACKLES

William Morgan—New York Giants

George Musso—Chicago Bears

GUARDS

Joe Kopcha—Chicago Bears

August (Mike) Michalske—Green Bay Packers

CENTER

Mel Hein—New York Giants

QUARTERBACK

Earl (Dutch) Clark—Detroit Lions

HALFBACKS

Edward Danowski—New York Giants

Ernie Caddel—Detroit Lions

FULLBACK

Mike Mikulak—Chicago Cardinals

1936

ENDS

Bill Hewitt—Chicago Bears

Don Hutson—Green Bay Packers

TACKLES

Ernest Smith—Green Bay Packers

Albert (Turk) Edwards—Boston Redskins

GUARDS

Lon Evans—Green Bay Packers

Grover (Ox) Emerson—Detroit Lions

CENTER

Mel Hein—New York Giants

QUARTERBACK

Earl (Dutch) Clark—Detroit Lions

HALFBACKS

Cliff Battles—Boston Redskins

Alphonse (Tuffy) Leemans—New York Giants

FULLBACK

Clarke Hinkle—Green Bay Packers

1937

ENDS

Bill Hewitt—Philadelphia Eagles

Gaynell Tinsley—Chicago Cardinals

TACKLES

Joe Stydahar—Chicago Bears

Albert (Turk) Edwards—Washington Redskins

GUARDS

Lon Evans—Green Bay Packers

George Musso—Chicago Bears

CENTER

Mel Hein—New York Giants

QUARTERBACK

Earl (Dutch) Clark—Detroit Lions

HALFBACKS

Cliff Battles—Washington Redskins

Sammy Baugh—Washington Redskins

FULLBACK

Clarke Hinkle—Green Bay Packers

Sammy Baugh

1938

ENDS
Don Hutson—Green Bay Packers
Gaynell Tinsley—Chicago Cardinals
TACKLES
Edwin Widseth—New York Giants
Joe Stydahar—Chicago Bears
GUARDS
Danny Fortmann—Chicago Bears
Russell Letlow—Green Bay Packers
CENTER
Mel Hein—New York Giants
QUARTERBACK
Clarence (Ace) Parker—Brooklyn Dodgers
HALFBACKS
Edward Danowski—New York Giants
Lloyd Cardwell—Detroit Lions
FULLBACK
Clarke Hinkle—Green Bay Packers

1939

ENDS
Don Hutson—Green Bay Packers
James Poole—New York Giants
TACKLES
Joe Stydahar—Chicago Bears
James Barber—Washington Redskins
GUARDS
Danny Fortmann—Chicago Bears
John Dell Isola—New York Giants
CENTER
Mel Hein—New York Giants
QUARTERBACK
Davy O'Brien—Philadelphia Eagles
HALFBACKS
Alphonse (Tuffy) Leemans—New York Giants
Andy Farkas—Washington Redskins
FULLBACK
Bill Osmanski—Chicago Bears

Clarence (Ace) Parker

ALL-PRO TEAM OF THE DECADE (THIRTIES)

1930-1939

ENDS
Bill Hewitt—Chicago Bears, Philadelphia Eagles
Morris (Red) Badgro—New York Giants

TACKLES
Robert (Cal) Hubbard—Green Bay Packers
Albert (Turk) Edwards—Boston Redskins

GUARDS
Joe Kopcha—Chicago Bears
Denver Gibson—New York Giants

CENTER
Mel Hein—New York Giants

QUARTERBACK
Earl (Dutch) Clark—Portsmouth Spartans, Detroit Lions

HALFBACKS
Clark Hinkle—Green Bay Packers
Cliff Battles—Boston Redskins, Washington Redskins

FULLBACK
Bronko Nagurski—Chicago Bears

Cal Hubbard

Turk Edwards

Joe Kopcha

Mel Hein

Earl (Dutch) Clark

Clarke Hinkle

Cliff Battles

Bronko Nagurski

ALL-PRO TEAMS OF THE FORTIES

73 TO 0. The T-Formation with man-in-motion. The war years. A new league to challenge the old. Bright stars fade and new ones arrive. Paul Brown makes football a game of applied science. Franchises merge, split apart and the first merger takes place. Television enters the scene.

Despite science and technology the game will always belong to the artists, those dedicated, brilliant few who by some inner magic stamp an impression of their own on the game and the era.

1940

ENDS
Don Hutson—Green Bay Packers
Perry Schwartz—Brooklyn Dodgers

TACKLES
Joe Stydahar—Chicago Bears
Frank (Bruiser) Kinard—Brooklyn Dodgers

GUARDS
Danny Fortmann—Chicago Bears
John Wiethe—Detroit Lions

CENTER
Mel Hein—New York Giants

QUARTERBACK
Clarence (Ace) Parker—Brooklyn Dodgers

HALFBACKS
Sammy Baugh—Washington Redskins
Byron (Whizzer) White—Detroit Lions

FULLBACK
John Drake—Cleveland Rams

Joe Stydahar

George McAfee

1941

ENDS
Don Hutson—Green Bay Packers
Perry Schwartz—Brooklyn Dodgers
TACKLES
Frank (Bruiser) Kinard—Brooklyn Dodgers
Wilbur Wilkin—Washington Redskins
GUARDS
Danny Fortmann—Chicago Bears
Joe Kuharich—Chicago Cardinals
CENTER
Clyde (Bulldog) Turner—Chicago Bears
QUARTERBACK
Sid Luckman—Chicago Bears
HALFBACKS
Cecil Isbell—Green Bay Packers
George McAfee—Chicago Bears
FULLBACK
Clarke Hinkle—Green Bay Packers

1942

ENDS
Don Hutson—Green Bay Packers
Robert Masterson—Washington Redskins
TACKLES
Wilbur Wilkin—Washington Redskins
Lee Artoe—Chicago Bears
GUARDS
Danny Fortmann—Chicago Bears
William Edwards—New York Giants
CENTER
Clyde (Bulldog) Turner—Chicago Bears
QUARTERBACK
Sid Luckman—Chicago Bears
HALFBACKS
Cecil Isbell—Green Bay Packers
Bill Dudley—Pittsburgh Steelers
FULLBACK
Gary Famiglietti—Chicago Bears

1943

ENDS
Don Hutson—Green Bay Packers
Edward Rucinski—Chicago Cardinals
TACKLES
Frank (Bruiser) Kinard—Brooklyn Dodgers
Al Blozis—New York Giants
GUARDS
Richard Farman—Washington Redskins
Danny Fortmann—Chicago Bears
CENTER
Clyde (Bulldog) Turner—Chicago Bears
QUARTERBACK
Sid Luckman—Chicago Bears
HALFBACKS
Sammy Baugh—Washington Redskins
Harry Clark—Chicago Bears
FULLBACK
Tony Canadeo—Green Bay Packers

Tony Canadeo

1944

ENDS
Don Hutson—Green Bay Packers
Joe Aguirre—Washington Redskins
TACKLES
Al Wistert—Philadelphia Eagles
Frank (Bruiser) Kinard—Brooklyn Tigers
GUARDS
Len Younce—New York Giants
Riley Matheson—Cleveland Rams
CENTER
Clyde (Bulldog) Turner—Chicago Bears
QUARTERBACK
Sid Luckman—Chicago Bears
HALFBACKS
Frank Sinkwich—Detroit Lions
Steve Van Buren—Philadelphia Eagles
FULLBACK
William Paschal—New York Giants

1945

ENDS
Don Hutson—Green Bay Packers
Jim Benton—Cleveland Rams
TACKLES
Al Wistert—Philadelphia Eagles
Frank Cope—New York Giants
GUARDS
Riley Matheson—Cleveland Rams
William Radovich—Detroit Lions

CENTER
Charles Brock—Green Bay Packers
QUARTERBACK
Sammy Baugh—Washington Redskins
HALFBACKS
Steve Van Buren—Philadelphia Eagles
Steve Bagarus—Washington Redskins
FULLBACK
Ted Fritsch—Green Bay Packers

1946

ENDS
Jim Benton—Los Angeles Rams
Ken Kavanaugh—Chicago Bears
TACKLES
Al Wistert—Philadelphia Eagles
Jim White—New York Giants
GUARDS
Augustino Lio—Philadelphia Eagles
Riley Matheson—Los Angeles Rams
CENTER
Clyde (Bulldog) Turner—Chicago Bears
QUARTERBACK
Bob Waterfield—Los Angeles Rams
HALFBACKS
Bill Dudley—Pittsburgh Steelers
Frank Filchock—New York Giants
FULLBACK
Ted Fritsch—Green Bay Packers

Bill Dudley

1947

ENDS
Ken Kavanaugh—Chicago Bears
Mal Kutner—Chicago Cardinals
TACKLES
Al Wistert—Philadelphia Eagles
Fred Davis—Chicago Bears
GUARDS
Len Younce—New York Giants
William Moore—Pittsburgh Steelers
CENTER
Vince Banonis—Chicago Cardinals
QUARTERBACK
Sid Luckman—Chicago Bears
HALFBACKS
Steve Van Buren—Philadelphia Eagles
Sammy Baugh—Washington Redskins
FULLBACK
Pat Harder—Chicago Cardinals

1948

ENDS
Pete Pihos—Philadelphia Eagles
Mal Kutner—Chicago Cardinals
TACKLES
Al Wistert—Philadelphia Eagles
Richard Huffman—Los Angeles Rams
GUARDS
Ray Bray—Chicago Bears
Gerald (Buster) Ramsey—Chicago Cardinals
CENTER
Clyde (Bulldog) Turner—Chicago Bears
QUARTERBACK
Sammy Baugh—Washington Redskins
HALFBACKS
Steve Van Buren—Philadelphia Eagles
Charley Trippi—Chicago Cardinals
FULLBACK
Pat Harder—Chicago Cardinals

1949

ENDS
Pete Pihos—Philadelphia Eagles
Tom Fears—Los Angeles Rams
TACKLES
Vic Sears—Philadelphia Eagles
Richard Huffman—Los Angeles Rams
GUARDS
Ray Bray—Chicago Bears
Gerald (Buster) Ramsey—Chicago Cardinals
CENTER
Fred Naumetz—Los Angeles Rams
QUARTERBACK
Bob Waterfield—Los Angeles Rams
HALFBACKS
Steve Van Buren—Philadelphia Eagles
Tony Canadeo—Green Bay Packers
FULLBACK
Pat Harder—Chicago Cardinals

Charley Trippi

ALL-PRO TEAM OF THE DECADE (FORTIES)

1940-1949

ENDS
  Don Hutson—Green Bay Packers
  Mal Kutner—Chicago Cardinals
TACKLES
  Frank (Bruiser) Kinard—Brooklyn Dodgers, New York Yankees
  Al Wistert—Philadelphia Eagles
GUARDS
  Danny Fortmann—Chicago Bears
  Riley Matheson—Cleveland Rams, Los Angeles Rams
CENTER
  Clyde (Bulldog) Turner—Chicago Bears
QUARTERBACK
  Sid Luckman—Chicago Bears
HALFBACKS
  Steve Van Buren—Philadelphia Eagles
  Sammy Baugh—Washington Redskins
FULLBACK
  Marion Motley—Cleveland Browns

Frank (Bruiser) Kinard

Don Hutson

Danny Fortmann

Clyde (Bulldog) Turner   Sid Luckman   Sammy Baugh

Steve Van Buren   Marion Motley

ALL-PRO TEAMS OF THE FIFTIES

THE AGE OF Specialization begins. The league licenses unlimited free substitution and the days of the two-way player are over. Well, not quite over. Not for a while anyway for tough-as-leather guys like Leo Nomellini, George Connor, Chuck Bednarik, Pete Pihos, Leon Hart, Tank Younger.

These fellows thrive on action and 60 minutes is even too short. They still go both ways. It is a time of some confusion for coaches as well as all-star selectors. Just where do you play a man who can play offense or defense equally well? A fellow like George Connor, for instance, can be named an all-pro seven times in just four years, as an offensive tackle, a defensive tackle, and as a linebacker, being named to the offensive and defensive teams for three straight years. The last man ever to do it.

But they are anacronisms, those fellows, and gradually it all sorts itself out into a now familiar pattern, but it shows that those old days were just yesterday.

Tom Fears

William (Dub) Jones

1950

ENDS
Tom Fears—Los Angeles Rams
Mac Speedie—Cleveland Browns
TACKLES
George Connor—Chicago Bears
Arnie Weinmeister—New York Giants
GUARDS
Dick Barwegan—Chicago Bears
Bill Willis—Cleveland Browns
CENTER
Chuck Bednarik—Philadelphia Eagles
QUARTERBACK
Johnny Lujack—Chicago Bears
HALFBACKS
Doak Walker—Detroit Lions
Joe Geri—Pittsburgh Steelers
FULLBACK
Marion Motley—Cleveland Browns

1951
OFFENSE

ENDS
Elroy Hirsch—Los Angeles Rams
Leon Hart—Detroit Lions
Dante Lavelli—Cleveland Browns

TACKLES
George Connor—Chicago Bears
Lou Groza—Cleveland Browns
Leo Nomellini—San Francisco 49ers
DeWitt (Tex) Coulter—New York Giants

GUARDS
Lou Creekmur—Detroit Lions
Dick Barwegan—Chicago Bears

CENTERS
Vic Lindskog—Philadelphia Eagles
Frank Gatski—Cleveland Browns

QUARTERBACK
Otto Graham—Cleveland Browns

HALFBACKS
Doak Walker—Detroit Lions
William (Dub) Jones—Cleveland Browns

FULLBACKS
Eddie Price—New York Giants
Dan (Deacon) Towler—Los Angeles Rams

DEFENSE

ENDS
Larry Brink—Los Angeles Rams
Leon Hart—Detroit Lions
Len Ford—Cleveland Browns

TACKLES
Arnie Weinmeister—New York Giants
Al DeRogatis—New York Giants
George Connor—Chicago Bears

GUARDS
Bill Willis—Cleveland Browns
Les Bingaman—Detroit Lions
Jon Baker—New York Giants

LINEBACKERS
Chuck Bednarik—Philadelphia Eagles
Paul (Tank) Younger—Los Angeles Rams
Tony Adamle—Cleveland Browns

HALFBACKS
Otto Schnellbacher—New York Giants
Gerald Shipkey—Pittsburgh Steelers
Warren Lahr—Cleveland Browns

SAFETY
Emlen Tunnell—New York Giants

1952
OFFENSE

ENDS
Cloyce Box—Detroit Lions
Mac Speedie—Cleveland Browns
Gordon Soltau—San Francisco 49ers

TACKLES
George Connor—Chicago Bears
Lou Groza—Cleveland Browns
Leo Nomellini—San Francisco 49ers

GUARDS
Lou Creekmur—Detroit Lions
Lou Groza—Cleveland Browns
Bill Fischer—Chicago Cardinals

Paul (Tank) Younger

CENTERS
Frank Gatski—Cleveland Browns
Bill Walsh—Pittsburgh Steelers

QUARTERBACKS
Bobby Layne—Detroit Lions
Otto Graham—Cleveland Browns

HALFBACKS
Hugh McElhenny—San Francisco 49ers
Dan (Deacon) Towler—Los Angeles Rams

FULLBACK
Eddie Price—New York Giants

DEFENSE

ENDS
Larry Brink—Los Angeles Rams
Len Ford—Cleveland Browns
Pete Pihos—Philadelphia Eagles

TACKLES
Arnie Weinmeister—New York Giants
Thurman McGraw—Detroit Lions

GUARDS
Stan West—Los Angeles Rams
Bill Willis—Cleveland Browns
Les Bingaman—Detroit Lions

LINEBACKERS
Chuck Bednarik—Philadelphia Eagles
Gerald Shipkey—Pittsburgh Steelers
George Connor—Chicago Bears

HALFBACKS
Jack Christiansen—Detroit Lions
Ollie Matson—Chicago Cardinals
Jim Smith—Detroit Lions
Herbert Rich—Los Angeles Rams

SAFETY
Emlen Tunnell—New York Giants

1953
OFFENSE

ENDS
Pete Pihos—Philadelphia Eagles
Dante Lavelli—Cleveland Browns
Elroy Hirsch—Los Angeles Rams

TACKLES
George Connor—Chicago Bears
Lou Groza—Cleveland Browns
Lou Creekmur—Detroit Lions

GUARDS
Dick Stanfel—Detroit Lions
Lou Creekmur—Detroit Lions
Bruno Banducci—San Francisco 49ers

CENTER
Frank Gatski—Cleveland Browns

QUARTERBACK
Otto Graham—Cleveland Browns

HALFBACKS
Hugh McElhenny—San Francisco 49ers
Doak Walker—Detroit Lions
Dan (Deacon) Towler—Los Angeles Rams

FULLBACK
Joe Perry—San Francisco 49ers

DEFENSE

ENDS
Len Ford—Cleveland Browns
Andy Robustelli—Los Angeles Rams
Norman Willey—Philadelphia Eagles

TACKLES
Arnie Weinmeister—New York Giants
Leo Nomellini—San Francisco 49ers

GUARDS
Les Bingaman—Detroit Lions
Bill Willis—Cleveland Browns
Dale Dodrill—Pittsburgh Steelers

LINEBACKERS
Chuck Bednarik—Philadelphia Eagles
Don Paul—Los Angeles Rams
George Connor—Chicago Bears
Thomas Thompson—Cleveland Browns

HALFBACKS
Tom Keane—Baltimore Colts
Thomas Thompson—Cleveland Browns
Jack Christiansen—Detroit Lions

SAFETIES
Ken Gorgal—Cleveland Browns
Jack Christiansen—Detroit Lions

Elroy Hirsch

1954
OFFENSE

ENDS
Pete Pihos—Philadelphia Eagles
Robert Boyd—Los Angeles Rams
Harlon Hill—Chicago Bears

TACKLES
Lou Creekmur—Detroit Lions
Lou Groza—Cleveland Browns

GUARDS
Dick Stanfel—Detroit Lions
Bruno Banducci—San Francisco 49ers

CENTER
Bill Walsh—Pittsburgh Steelers

QUARTERBACK
Otto Graham—Cleveland Browns

HALFBACKS
Doak Walker—Detroit Lions
Ollie Matson—Chicago Cardinals

FULLBACK
Joe Perry—San Francisco 49ers

DEFENSE

ENDS
Len Ford—Cleveland Browns
Norman Willey—Philadelphia Eagles

TACKLES
Leo Nomellini—San Francisco 49ers
Art Donovan—Baltimore Colts

GUARDS
Les Bingaman—Detroit Lions
Dale Dodrill—Pittsburgh Steelers
Frank (Bucko) Kilroy—Philadelphia Eagles

LINEBACKERS
Chuck Bednarik—Philadelphia Eagles
Joe Schmidt—Detroit Lions
Roger Zatkoff—Green Bay Packers

Dan (Deacon) Towler

HALFBACKS
Tom Landry—New York Giants
Bobby Dillon—Green Bay Packers
Jim David—Detroit Lions

SAFETY
Jack Christiansen—Detroit Lions

1955
OFFENSE

ENDS
Harlon Hill—Chicago Bears
Billy Wilson—San Francisco 49ers
Pete Pihos—Philadelphia Eagles

TACKLES
Lou Groza—Cleveland Browns
Bill Wightkin—Chicago Bears
Bob St. Clair—San Francisco 49ers

GUARDS
Stan Jones—Chicago Bears
Duane Putnam—Los Angeles Rams
Abe Gibron—Cleveland Browns
Bill Austin—New York Giants

CENTER
Frank Gatski—Cleveland Browns

QUARTERBACK
Otto Graham—Cleveland Browns

HALFBACKS
Ollie Matson—Chicago Cardinals
Frank Gifford—New York Giants
Ron Waller—Los Angeles Rams

FULLBACK
Alan (the Horse) Ameche—Baltimore Colts

DEFENSE

ENDS
Gene Brito—Washington Redskins
Len Ford—Cleveland Browns
Andy Robustelli—Los Angeles Rams

TACKLES
Art Donovan—Baltimore Colts
Bob Toneff—San Francisco 49ers
Don Colo—Cleveland Browns

MIDDLE GUARDS
Bill George—Chicago Bears
Dale Dodrill—Pittsburgh Steelers

LINEBACKERS
Chuck Bednarik—Philadelphia Eagles
George Connor—Chicago Bears
Roger Zatkoff—Green Bay Packers
Joe Schmidt—Detroit Lions

HALFBACKS
Bobby Dillon—Green Bay Packers
Willard Sherman—Los Angeles Rams
Don Paul—Cleveland Browns

SAFETIES
Jack Christiansen—Detroit Lions
Bobby Dillon—Green Bay Packers
Emlen Tunnell—New York Giants

1956
OFFENSE

ENDS
Harlon Hill—Chicago Bears
Billy Howton—Green Bay Packers

TACKLES
Lou Creekmur—Detroit Lions
Roosevelt Brown—New York Giants

GUARDS
Stan Jones—Chicago Bears
Dick Stanfel—Washington Redskins

CENTERS
Larry Strickland—Chicago Bears
Charley Ane—Detroit Lions

QUARTERBACK
Bobby Layne—Detroit Lions

HALFBACKS
Frank Gifford—New York Giants
Ollie Matson—Chicago Cardinals

FULLBACK
Rick Casares—Chicago Bears

DEFENSE

ENDS
Andy Robustelli—New York Giants
Gene Brito—Washington Redskins

TACKLES
Roosevelt Grier—New York Giants
Art Donovan—Baltimore Colts
Ernie Stautner—Pittsburgh Steelers

MIDDLE GUARD
Bill George—Chicago Bears

LINEBACKERS
Joe Schmidt—Detroit Lions
Chuck Bednarik—Philadelphia Eagles
Les Richter—Los Angeles Rams

HALFBACKS
Dick (Night Train) Lane—Chicago Cardinals
Emlen Tunnell—New York Giants
Jack Christiansen—Detroit Lions

SAFETIES
Yale Lary—Detroit Lions
Emlen Tunnell—New York Giants
Jack Christiansen—Detroit Lions
Bobby Dillon—Green Bay Packers

1957
OFFENSE

ENDS
Bill Wilson—San Francisco 49ers
Billy Howton—Green Bay Packers

TACKLES
Roosevelt Brown—New York Giants
Lou Creekmur—Detroit Lions
Lou Groza—Cleveland Browns

GUARDS
Duane Putnam—Los Angeles Rams
Dick Stanfel—Washington Redskins

Ernie Stautner

CENTERS
Jim Ringo—Green Bay Packers
Larry Strickland—Chicago Bears

QUARTERBACK
Y. A. Tittle—San Francisco 49ers

HALFBACKS
Frank Gifford—New York Giants
Ollie Matson—Chicago Cardinals

FULLBACK
Jim Brown—Cleveland Browns

DEFENSE

ENDS
Gino Marchetti—Baltimore Colts
Andy Robustelli—New York Giants
Gene Brito—Washington Redskins

TACKLES
Leo Nomellini—San Francisco 49ers
Art Donovan—Baltimore Colts

LINEBACKERS
Joe Schmidt—Detroit Lions
Marv Matuszak—San Francisco 49ers
Bill George—Chicago Bears

HALFBACKS
Jack Christiansen—Detroit Lions
Bobby Dillon—Green Bay Packers
Jack Butler—Pittsburgh Steelers
Yale Lary—Detroit Lions

Andy Robustelli

SAFETIES
Jack Butler—Pittsburgh Steelers
Milt Davis—Baltimore Colts
Bobby Dillon—Green Bay Packers
Jack Christiansen—Detroit Lions

1958
OFFENSE

ENDS
Ray Berry—Baltimore Colts
Del Shofner—Los Angeles Rams
TACKLES
Roosevelt Brown—New York Giants
Jim Parker—Baltimore Colts
GUARDS
Dick Stanfel—Washington Redskins
Duane Putnam—Los Angeles Rams
CENTER
Ray Wietecha—New York Giants
QUARTERBACK
John Unitas—Baltimore Colts
HALFBACKS
Lenny Moore—Baltimore Colts
Jon Arnett—Los Angeles Rams
FULLBACK
Jim Brown—Cleveland Browns

DEFENSE
ENDS
Gino Marchetti—Baltimore Colts
Andy Robustelli—New York Giants
Gene Brito—Washington Redskins
TACKLES
Paul (Big Daddy) Lipscomb—Baltimore Colts
Ernie Stautner—Pittsburgh Steelers
LINEBACKERS
Joe Schmidt—Detroit Lions
Sam Huff—New York Giants
Bill George—Chicago Bears
HALFBACKS
Jack Butler—Pittsburgh Steelers
Yale Lary—Detroit Lions
SAFETIES
Jim Patton—New York Giants
Bobby Dillon—Green Bay Packers

1959
OFFENSE

ENDS
Ray Berry—Baltimore Colts
Del Shofner—Los Angeles Rams
TACKLES
Roosevelt Brown—New York Giants
Jim Parker—Baltimore Colts
GUARDS
Jim Ray Smith—Cleveland Browns
Stan Jones—Chicago Bears
Art Spinney—Baltimore Colts
CENTER
Jim Ringo—Green Bay Packers
QUARTERBACK
John Unitas—Baltimore Colts
HALFBACKS
Frank Gifford—New York Giants
Lenny Moore—Baltimore Colts
J. D. Smith—San Francisco 49ers
FULLBACK
Jim Brown—Cleveland Browns

DEFENSE
ENDS
Gino Marchetti—Baltimore Colts
Andy Robustelli—New York Giants
TACKLES
Paul (Big Daddy) Lipscomb—Baltimore Colts
Leo Nomellini—San Francisco 49ers
LINEBACKERS
Sam Huff—New York Giants
Bill George—Chicago Bears
Joe Schmidt—Detroit Lions
HALFBACKS
Abe Woodson—San Francisco 49ers
Jack Butler—Pittsburgh Steelers
SAFETIES
Dean Derby—Pittsburgh Steelers
Jim Patton—New York Giants
Andy Nelson—Baltimore Colts

ALL-PRO TEAM OF THE DECADE (FIFTIES)

1950-1959

OFFENSE

ENDS
Pete Pihos—Philadelphia Eagles
Harlon Hill—Chicago Bears

TACKLES
Lou Groza—Cleveland Browns
Roosevelt Brown—New York Giants

GUARDS
Lou Creekmur—Detroit Lions
Dick Stanfel—Detroit Lions, Washington Redskins

CENTER
Frank Gatski—Cleveland Browns

QUARTERBACK
Otto Graham—Cleveland Browns

HALFBACKS
Ollie Matson—Chicago Cardinals
Hugh McElhenny—San Francisco 49ers

FULLBACK
Joe Perry—San Francisco 49ers

DEFENSE

ENDS
Len Ford—Cleveland Browns
Gino Marchetti—Baltimore Colts

TACKLES
Leo Nomellini—San Francisco 49ers
Arthur Donovan—Baltimore Colts

MIDDLE GUARDS
Bill Willis—Cleveland Browns
Les Bingaman—Detroit Lions

LINEBACKERS
Bill George—Chicago Bears
Chuck Bednarik—Philadelphia Eagles
Joe Schmidt—Detroit Lions
George Connor—Chicago Bears

DEEP BACKS
Jack Christiansen—Detroit Lions
Emlen Tunnell—New York Giants
Dick (Night Train) Lane—Chicago Cardinals, Los Angeles Rams, Detroit Lions
Jack Butler—Pittsburgh Steelers

Pete Pihos (35)

Ollie Matson (33)

Hugh McElhenny

Bill George

Otto Graham

Chuck Bednarik

Joe Perry

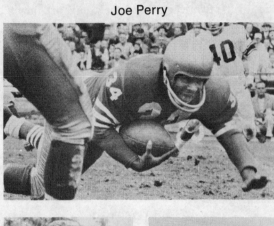

Emlen Tunnell

Jack Christiansen

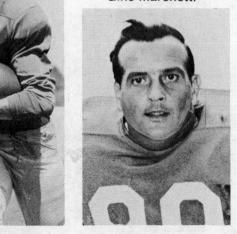

Gino Marchetti

Jack Butler

Art Donovan

George Connor

ALL-PRO TEAMS OF THE SIXTIES

A NEW ERA and a new league. A new galaxy of heroes to rival the old. With the establishment of the American Football League comes a collection of heroes to rival the popularity of the old established stars. Comparisons and disputes over the relative abilities of the two leagues and their stars are inevitable, but it is not until after the merger that a single all-pro team is selected. And that does not stop the arguments. It never does.

The Sixties, with great players like Ray Nitschke, Deacon Jones, Dick Butkus, Larry Wilson, Alex Karras and Herb Adderley, see the final emancipation of the defensive players. They change from anonymous drudges to larger then life heros. The arrival of Dick Butkus forces selectors for the first time to select a Defensive Rookie of the Year, a prize that had always been reserved for a freshman of offensive persuasion.

1960

(National Football League)

OFFENSE

ENDS
Ray Berry—Baltimore Colts
Ulmo (Sonny) Randle—St. Louis Cardinals

TACKLES
Jim Parker—Baltimore Colts
Forrest Gregg—Green Bay Packers

GUARDS
Jim Ray Smith—Cleveland Browns
Stan Jones—Chicago Bears

CENTER
Jim Ringo—Green Bay Packers

QUARTERBACK
Norm Van Brocklin—Philadelphia Eagles

HALFBACKS
Paul Hornung—Green Bay Packers
Lenny Moore—Baltimore Colts

FULLBACK
Jim Brown—Cleveland Browns

DEFENSE

ENDS
Gino Marchetti—Baltimore Colts
Doug Atkins—Chicago Bears

TACKLES
Henry Jordan—Green Bay Packers
Alex Karras—Detroit Lions

LINEBACKERS
Chuck Bednarik—Philadelphia Eagles
Bill George—Chicago Bears
Bill Forester—Green Bay Packers

HALFBACKS
Tom Brookshier—Philadelphia Eagles
Dick (Night Train) Lane—Detroit Lions

SAFETIES
Gerry Norton—St. Louis Cardinals
Jim Patton—New York Giants

Norm Van Brocklin

(American Football League)

OFFENSE

ENDS
Bill Groman—Houston Oilers
Lionel Taylor—Denver Broncos

TACKLES
Richard Michael—Houston Oilers
Ron Mix—Los Angeles Chargers

GUARDS
William Krisher—Dallas Texans
Robert Mischak—New York Titans

CENTER
Jim Otto—Oakland Raiders

QUARTERBACK
Jackie Kemp—Los Angeles Chargers

BACKS
Paul Lowe—Los Angeles Chargers
Abner Haynes—Dallas Texans
David Smith—Houston Oilers

DEFENSE

ENDS
Laverne Torczon—Buffalo Bills
Melvin Branch—Dallas Texans

TACKLES
Bud McFadin—Denver Broncos
Volney Peters—Los Angeles Chargers

LINEBACKERS
Archie Matsos—Buffalo Bills
Sherrill Headrick—Dallas Texans
Thomas Addison—Boston Patriots

BACKS
Richard McCabe—Buffalo Bills
Richard Harris—Los Angeles Chargers
Ross O'Hanley—Boston Patriots
Austin Gonsoulin—Denver Broncos

1961

(National Football League)

OFFENSE

ENDS
Del Shofner—New York Giants
Jim Phillips—Los Angeles Rams

TACKLES
Roosevelt Brown—New York Giants
Forrest Gregg—Green Bay Packers

GUARDS
Fred (Fuzzy) Thurston—Green Bay Packers
Jim Ray Smith—Cleveland Browns

CENTER
Jim Ringo—Green Bay Packers

QUARTERBACK
Christian (Sonny) Jurgensen—Philadelphia Eagles

HALFBACKS
Paul Hornung—Green Bay Packers
Lenny Moore—Baltimore Colts

FULLBACK
Jim Brown—Cleveland Browns

DEFENSE

ENDS
Gino Marchetti—Baltimore Colts
Jim Katcavage—New York Giants

TACKLES
Henry Jordan—Green Bay Packers
Alex Karras—Detroit Lions

LINEBACKERS
Joe Schmidt—Detroit Lions
Bill Forester—Green Bay Packers
Bill George—Chicago Bears

HALFBACKS
Erich E. Barnes—New York Giants
Jess Whittenton—Green Bay Packers

SAFETIES
Jim Patton—New York Giants
Dick (Night Train) Lane—Detroit Lions

Christian (Sonny) Jurgensen

Nate Fine

(American Football League)
OFFENSE
ENDS
Lionel Taylor—Denver Broncos
Charley Hennigan—Houston Oilers
TACKLES
Ron Mix—San Diego Chargers
Alfred Jamison—Houston Oilers
GUARDS
Robert Mischak—New York Titans
Charles Leo—Boston Patriots
CENTER
Jim Otto—Oakland Raiders
QUARTERBACK
George Blanda—Houston Oilers
BACKS
Abner Haynes—Dallas Texans
Bill Mathis—New York Titans
Billy Cannon—Houston Oilers

DEFENSE
ENDS
Earl Faison—San Diego Chargers
Don Floyd—Houston Oilers
TACKLES
Bud McFadin—Denver Broncos
Charles McMurtry—Buffalo Bills
LINEBACKERS
Sherrill Headrick—Dallas Texans
Archie Matsos—Buffalo Bills
Charles Allen—San Diego Chargers
BACKS
James Banfield—Houston Oilers
Richard Harris—San Diego Chargers
David Webster—Dallas Texans
Charles McNeil—San Diego Chargers

1962
(National Football League)
OFFENSE
ENDS
Del Shofner—New York Giants
Mike Ditka—Chicago Bears
TACKLES
Roosevelt Brown—New York Giants
Forrest Gregg—Green Bay Packers
GUARDS
Gerry Kramer—Green Bay Packers
Jim Parker—Baltimore Colts
CENTER
Jim Ringo—Green Bay Packers
QUARTERBACK
Y. A. Tittle—New York Giants
HALFBACKS
Bobby Mitchell—Washington Redskins
Dick Bass—Los Angeles Rams
FULLBACK
Jim Taylor—Green Bay Packers

George Blanda

DEFENSE
ENDS
Gino Marchetti—Baltimore Colts
Willie Davis—Green Bay Packers
TACKLES
Henry Jordan—Green Bay Packers
Alex Karras—Detroit Lions
LINEBACKERS
Joe Schmidt—Detroit Lions
Dan Currie—Green Bay Packers
Bill Forester—Green Bay Packers
HALFBACKS
Dick (Night Train) Lane—Detroit Lions
Herb Adderley—Green Bay Packers
SAFETIES
Jim Patton—New York Giants
Yale Lary—Detroit Lions

(American Football League)
OFFENSE
ENDS
Dave Kocourek—San Diego Chargers
Charley Hennigan—Houston Oilers
FLANKER
Chris Burford—Dallas Texans
TACKLES
Eldon Danenhauer—Denver Broncos
Jim Tyrer—Dallas Texans
GUARDS
Ron Mix—San Diego Chargers
Robert Talamini—Houston Oilers
CENTER
Jim Otto—Oakland Raiders
QUARTERBACK
Len Dawson—Dallas Texans
BACKS
Abner Haynes—Dallas Texans
Charles (Cookie) Gilchrist—Buffalo Bills

Y.A. Tittle

DEFENSE

ENDS
Doug Atkins—Chicago Bears
Jim Katcavage—New York Giants
TACKLES
Henry Jordan—Green Bay Packers
Roger Brown—Detroit Lions
LINEBACKERS
Bill George—Chicago Bears
Joe Fortunato—Chicago Bears
Bill Forester—Green Bay Packers
HALFBACKS
Dick Lynch—New York Giants
Dick (Night Train) Lane—Detroit Lions
SAFETIES
Richie Petitbon—Chicago Bears
Larry Wilson—St. Louis Cardinals

DEFENSE

ENDS
Don Floyd—Houston Oilers
Mel Branch—Dallas Texans
TACKLES
Bud McFadin—Denver Broncos
Gerry Mays—Dallas Texans
LINEBACKERS
Sherrill Headrick—Dallas Texans
Larry Grantham—New York Titans
Emil Holub—Dallas Texans
CORNERBACKS
James Banfield—Houston Oilers
Fred Williamson—Oakland Raiders
SAFETIES
Austin Gonsoulin—Denver Broncos
Bob Zeman—Denver Broncos

1963

(National Football League)
OFFENSE

ENDS
Del Shofner—New York Giants
Mike Ditka—Chicago Bears
TACKLES
Roosevelt Brown—New York Giants
Forrest Gregg—Green Bay Packers
GUARDS
Jerry Kramer—Green Bay Packers
Jim Parker—Baltimore Colts
CENTER
Jim Ringo—Green Bay Packers
QUARTERBACK
Y. A. Tittle—New York Giants
HALFBACKS
Tommy Mason—Minnesota Vikings
Bobby Joe Conrad—St. Louis Cardinals
FULLBACK
Jim Brown—Cleveland Browns

(American Football League)
OFFENSE

ENDS
Fred Arbanas—Kansas City Chiefs
Art Powell—Oakland Raiders
FLANKER
Lance Alworth—San Diego Chargers
TACKLES
Ron Mix—San Diego Chargers
Jim Tyrer—Kansas City Chiefs
GUARDS
William Shaw—Buffalo Bills
Bob Talamini—Houston Oilers
CENTER
Jim Otto—Oakland Raiders
QUARTERBACK
Tobin Rote—San Diego Chargers
BACKS
Clem Daniels—Oakland Raiders
Keith Lincoln—San Diego Chargers

DEFENSE

ENDS
Larry Eisenhauer—Boston Patriots
Earl Faison—San Diego Chargers
TACKLES
Tom Sestak—Buffalo Bills
Houston Antwine—Boston Patriots
LINEBACKERS
Archie Matsos—Oakland Raiders
E. J. Holub—Kansas City Chiefs
Thomas Addison—Boston Patriots
CORNERBACKS
Dave Grayson—Kansas City Chiefs
Fred Williamson—Oakland Raiders
SAFETIES
Fred Glick—Houston Oilers
Austin Gonsoulin—Denver Broncos

1964
(National Football League)
OFFENSE

ENDS
Mike Ditka—Chicago Bears
Bobby Mitchell—Washington Redskins

TACKLES
Forrest Gregg—Green Bay Packers
Dick Schafrath—Cleveland Browns

GUARDS
Jim Parker—Baltimore Colts
Ken Gray—St. Louis Cardinals

CENTER
Mick Tinglehoff—Minnesota Vikings

QUARTERBACK
John Unitas—Baltimore Colts

HALFBACKS
Lenny Moore—Baltimore Colts
Johnny Morris—Chicago Bears

FULLBACK
Jim Brown—Cleveland Browns

DEFENSE

ENDS
Gino Marchetti—Baltimore Colts
Willie Davis—Green Bay Packers

TACKLES
Bob Lilly—Dallas Cowboys
Henry Jordan—Green Bay Packers

LINEBACKERS
Ray Nitschke—Green Bay Packers
Joe Fortunato—Chicago Bears
Maxie Baughan—Philadelphia Eagles

HALFBACKS
Pat Fischer—St. Louis Cardinals
Bobby Boyd—Baltimore Colts

SAFETIES
Paul Krause—Washington Redskins
Willie Wood—Green Bay Packers

(American Football League)
OFFENSE

ENDS
Charley Hennigan—Houston Oilers
Fred Arbanas—Kansas City Chiefs

TACKLES
Ron Mix—San Diego Chargers
Stewart Barber—Buffalo Bills

GUARDS
William Shaw—Buffalo Bills
William Neighbors—Boston Patriots

CENTER
Jim Otto—Oakland Raiders

QUARTERBACK
Vito (Babe) Parilli—Boston Patriots

BACKS
Lance Alworth—San Diego Chargers
Keith Lincoln—San Diego Chargers
Charles (Cookie) Gilchrist—Buffalo Bills

Gale Sayers

DEFENSE

ENDS
Earl Faison—San Diego Chargers
Larry Eisenhauer—Boston Patriots

TACKLES
Tom Sestak—Buffalo Bills
Ernie Ladd—San Diego Chargers

LINEBACKERS
Nick Buoniconti—Boston Patriots
Larry Grantham—New York Jets
Gil Stratton—Buffalo Bills

CORNERBACKS
Dave Grayson—Kansas City Chiefs
Willie Brown—Denver Broncos

SAFETIES
Ronald Hall—Boston Patriots
George Saimes—Buffalo Bills

1965
(National Football League)
OFFENSE

ENDS
Dave Parks—San Francisco 49ers
Pete Retzlaff—Philadelphia Eagles

TACKLES
Dick Schafrath—Cleveland Browns
Forrest Gregg—Green Bay Packers

GUARDS
Jim Parker—Baltimore Colts
Ken Gray—St. Louis Cardinals

CENTER
Mick Tingelhoff—Minnesota Vikings

QUARTERBACK
John Unitas—Baltimore Colts

HALFBACKS
Gale Sayers—Chicago Bears
Gary Collins—Cleveland Browns

FULLBACK

    Jim Brown—Cleveland Browns

DEFENSE

ENDS

    Willie Davis—Green Bay Packers

    David (Deacon) Jones—Los Angeles Rams

TACKLES

    Bob Lilly—Dallas Cowboys

    Alex Karras—Detroit Lions

LINEBACKERS

    Dick Butkus—Chicago Bears

    Joe Fortunato—Chicago Bears

    Ray Nitschke—Green Bay Packers

HALFBACKS

    Herb Adderley—Green Bay Packers

    Bobby Boyd—Baltimore Colts

SAFETIES

    Willie Wood—Green Bay Packers

    Paul Krause—Washington Redskins

Malcolm Emmons

Bob Hayes

1966

(National Football League)
OFFENSE

ENDS

    Bob Hayes—Dallas Cowboys

    John Mackey—Baltimore Colts

TACKLES

    Bob Brown—Philadelphia Eagles

    Forrest Gregg—Green Bay Packers

GUARDS

    Gerry Kramer—Green Bay Packers

    John Gordy—Detroit Lions

CENTER

    Mick Tingelhoff—Minnesota Vikings

QUARTERBACK

    Bart Starr—Green Bay Packers

HALFBACKS

    Gale Sayers—Chicago Bears

    Pat Studstill—Detroit Lions

FULLBACK

    Leroy Kelly—Cleveland Browns

DEFENSE

ENDS

    Willie Davis—Green Bay Packers

    David (Deacon) Jones—Los Angeles Rams

TACKLES

    Bob Lilly—Dallas Cowboys

    Merlin Olsen—Los Angeles Rams

LINEBACKERS

    Chuck Howley—Dallas Cowboys

    Ray Nitschke—Green Bay Packers

    Lee Roy Caffey—Green Bay Packers

HALFBACKS

    Herb Adderley—Green Bay Packers

    Bobby Boyd—Baltimore Colts

SAFETIES

    Willie Wood—Green Bay Packers

    Larry Wilson—St. Louis Cardinals

(American Football League)
OFFENSE

ENDS

    Lionel Taylor—Denver Broncos

    Willie Frazier—Houston Oilers

TACKLES

    Ron Mix—San Diego Chargers

    Jim Tyrer—Kansas City Chiefs

GUARDS

    William Shaw—Buffalo Bills

    Bob Talamini—Houston Oilers

CENTER

    Jim Otto—Oakland Raiders

QUARTERBACK

    Jackie Kemp—Buffalo Bills

BACKS

    Lance Alworth—San Diego Chargers

    Paul Lowe—San Diego Chargers

    Charles (Cookie) Gilchrist—Denver Broncos

DEFENSE

ENDS

    Earl Faison—San Diego Chargers

    Jerry Mays—Kansas City Chiefs

TACKLES

    Ernie Ladd—San Diego Chargers

    Tom Sestak—Buffalo Bills

LINEBACKERS

    Mike Stratton—Buffalo Bills

    Nick Buoniconti—Boston Patriots

    Bobby Bell—Kansas City Chiefs

CORNERBACKS

    Dave Grayson—Oakland Raiders

    George (Butch) Byrd—Buffalo Bills

SAFETIES

    George Saimes—Buffalo Bills

    Dainard Paulson—New York Jets

Len Dawson

Charley Taylor

Leroy Kelly

(American Football League)

OFFENSE

ENDS
Otis Taylor—Kansas City Chiefs
Fred Arbanas—Kansas City Chiefs
TACKLES
Jim Tyrer—Kansas City Chiefs
Ron Mix—San Diego Chargers
GUARDS
Bill Shaw—Buffalo Bills
Wayne Hawkins—Oakland Raiders
CENTER
Jim Otto—Oakland Raiders
QUARTERBACK
Len Dawson—Kansas City Chiefs
BACKS
Lance Alworth—San Diego Chargers
Clem Daniels—Oakland Raiders
Jim Nance—Boston Patriots

DEFENSE

ENDS
Jerry Mays—Kansas City Chiefs
Roland McDole—Buffalo Bills
TACKLES
Junious (Buck) Buchanan—Kansas City Chiefs
Jim Dunaway—Buffalo Bills
LINEBACKERS
Nick Buoniconti—Boston Patriots
Dave Stratton—Buffalo Bills
Bobby Bell—Kansas City Chiefs
CORNERBACKS
George (Butch) Byrd—Buffalo Bills
Kent McCloughan—Oakland Raiders
SAFETIES
Johnny Robinson—Kansas City Chiefs
James (Kenny) Graham—San Diego Chargers

1967

(National Football League)

OFFENSE

ENDS
Charley Taylor—Washington Redskins
Jackie Smith—St. Louis Cardinals
TACKLES
Ralph Neely—Dallas Cowboys
Forrest Gregg—Green Bay Packers
GUARDS
Gerry Kramer—Green Bay Packers
Gene Hickerson—Cleveland Browns
CENTER
Bob DeMarco—St. Louis Cardinals
QUARTERBACK
John Unitas—Baltimore Colts

BACKS
  Leroy Kelly—Cleveland Browns
  Gale Sayers—Chicago Bears
  Willie Richardson—Baltimore Colts
DEFENSE
ENDS
  David (Deacon) Jones—Los Angeles Rams
  Willie Davis—Green Bay Packers
TACKLES
  Merlin Olsen—Los Angeles Rams
  Bob Lilly—Dallas Cowboys
LINEBACKERS
  Dave Robinson—Green Bay Packers
  Dick Butkus—Chicago Bears
  Maxie Baughan—Los Angeles Rams
HALFBACKS
  Bob Jeter—Green Bay Packers
  Cornell Green—Dallas Cowboys
SAFETIES
  Willie Wood—Green Bay Packers
  Larry Wilson—St. Louis Cardinals

(American Football League)
OFFENSE
ENDS
  George Sauer—New York Jets
  Billy Cannon—Oakland Raiders
TACKLES
  Ron Mix—San Diego Chargers
  Jim Tyrer—Kansas City Chiefs
GUARDS
  Walt Sweeney—San Diego Chargers
  Bob Talamini—Houston Oilers
CENTER
  Jim Otto—Oakland Raiders
QUARTERBACK
  Daryle Lamonica—Oakland Raiders
BACKS
  Mike Garrett—Kansas City Chiefs
  Jim Nance—Boston Patriots
  Lance Alworth—San Diego Chargers
DEFENSE
ENDS
  James (Pat) Holmes—Houston Oilers
  Ben Davidson—Oakland Raiders
TACKLES
  Tom Keating—Oakland Raiders
  Junious (Buck) Buchanan—Kansas City Chiefs
LINEBACKERS
  Nick Buoniconti—Boston Patriots
  George Webster—Houston Oilers
  Bobby Bell—Kansas City Chiefs
CORNERBACKS
  Miller Farr—Houston Oilers
  Kent McCloughan—Oakland Raiders
SAFETIES
  George Saimes—Buffalo Bills
  Johnny Robinson—Kansas City Chiefs

1968
(National Football League)
OFFENSE
ENDS
  John Mackey—Baltimore Colts
  Paul Warfield—Cleveland Browns
TACKLES
  Ralph Neely—Dallas Cowboys
  Bob Vogel—Baltimore Colts
GUARDS
  Gene Hickerson—Cleveland Browns
  Howard Mudd—San Francisco 49ers
CENTER
  Mick Tingelhoff—Minnesota Vikings
QUARTERBACK
  Earl Morrall—Baltimore Colts
BACKS
  Leroy Kelly—Cleveland Browns
  Gale Sayers—Chicago Bears
  Clifton McNeil—San Francisco 49ers
DEFENSE
ENDS
  Carl Eller—Minnesota Vikings
  Dave (Deacon) Jones—Los Angeles Rams
TACKLES
  Merlin Olsen—Los Angeles Rams
  Bob Lilly—Dallas Cowboys
LINEBACKERS
  Dick Butkus—Chicago Bears
  Mike Curtis—Baltimore Colts
  Chuck Howley—Dallas Cowboys
HALFBACKS
  Lem Barney—Detroit Lions
  Bobby Boyd—Baltimore Colts
SAFETIES
  Larry Wilson—St. Louis Cardinals
  Ed Meador—Los Angeles Rams

(American Football League)
OFFENSE
ENDS
  George Sauer—New York Jets
  James Whalen—Boston Patriots
TACKLES
  Ron Mix—San Diego Chargers
  Jim Tyrer—Kansas City Chiefs
GUARDS
  Walt Sweeney—San Diego Chargers
  Gene Upshaw—Oakland Raiders
CENTER
  Jim Otto—Oakland Raiders
QUARTERBACK
  Joe Namath—New York Jets
BACKS
  Paul Robinson—Cincinnati Bengals
  Hewritt Dixon—Oakland Raiders
  Lance Alworth—San Diego Chargers

Rich Jackson

Mike Curtis

DEFENSE

ENDS
Gerry Philbin—New York Jets
Rich Jackson—Denver Broncos
TACKLES
Junious (Buck) Buchanan—Kansas City Chiefs
Dan Birdwell—Oakland Raiders
LINEBACKERS
Dan Conners—Oakland Raiders
George Webster—Houston Oilers
Bobby Bell—Kansas City Chiefs
CORNERBACKS
Miller Farr—Houston Oilers
Willie Brown—Oakland Raiders
SAFETIES
Johnny Robinson—Kansas City Chiefs
Dave Grayson—Oakland Raiders

1969
(National Football League)
OFFENSE

ENDS
Roy Jefferson—Pittsburgh Steelers
Gary Collins—Cleveland Browns
Jerry Smith—Washington Redskins

TACKLES
Bob Brown—Los Angeles Rams
Ralph Neely—Dallas Cowboys
GUARDS
Gene Hickerson—Cleveland Browns
John Niland—Dallas Cowboys
CENTER
Mick Tingelhoff—Minnesota Vikings
QUARTERBACK
Roman Gabriel—Los Angeles Rams
BACKS
Gale Sayers—Chicago Bears
Calvin Hill—Dallas Cowboys

DEFENSE

ENDS
Dave (Deacon) Jones—Los Angeles Rams
Carl Eller—Minnesota Vikings
TACKLES
Merlin Olsen—Los Angeles Rams
Bob Lilly—Dallas Cowboys
LINEBACKERS
Dick Butkus—Chicago Bears
Chuck Howley—Dallas Cowboys
Dave Robinson—Green Bay Packers
CORNERBACKS
Lem Barney—Detroit Lions
Herb Adderley—Green Bay Packers
SAFETIES
Larry Wilson—St. Louis Cardinals
Ed Meador—Los Angeles Rams

(American Football League)
OFFENSE

ENDS
Fred Biletnikoff—Oakland Raiders
Lance Alworth—San Diego Chargers
Bob Trumpy—Cincinnati Bengals
TACKLES
Jim Tyrer—Kansas City Chiefs
Harry Schuh—Oakland Raiders
GUARDS
Ed Budde—Kansas City Chiefs
Gene Upshaw—Oakland Raiders
CENTER
Jim Otto—Oakland Raiders
QUARTERBACK
Daryle Lamonica—Oakland Raiders
BACKS
Floyd Little—Denver Broncos
Matt Snell—New York Jets

DEFENSE

ENDS
Rich Jackson—Denver Broncos
Gerry Philbin—New York Jets
TACKLES
John Elliott—New York Jets
Junious (Buck) Buchanan—Kansas City Chiefs

LINEBACKERS
Nick Buoniconti—Miami Dolphins
George Webster—Houston Oilers
Bobby Bell—Kansas City Chiefs
CORNERBACKS
Willie Brown—Oakland Raiders
George Byrd—Buffalo Bills
SAFETIES
Dave Grayson—Oakland Raiders
Johnny Robinson—Kansas City Chiefs

1969 ALL-PRO TEAM*
OFFENSE
WIDE RECEIVER
Lance Alworth—San Diego Chargers (AFL)
Paul Warfield—Cleveland Browns (NFL)
TIGHT END
Bob Trumpy—Cincinnati Bengals (AFL)
TACKLES
Bob Brown—Los Angeles Rams (NFL)
Jim Tyrer—Kansas City Chiefs (AFL)
GUARDS
Tom Mack—Los Angeles Rams (NFL)
Gene Hickerson—Cleveland Browns (NFL)
CENTER
Mick Tingelhoff—Minnesota Vikings (NFL)
QUARTERBACK
Roman Gabriel—Los Angeles Rams (NFL)
RUNNING BACKS
Gale Sayers—Chicago Bears (NFL)
Calvin Hill—Dallas Cowboys (NFL)
PLACEKICKER
Jan Stenerud—Kansas City Chiefs (AFL)
PUNTER
David Lee—Baltimore Colts (NFL)
DEFENSE
ENDS
Dave Jones—Los Angeles Rams (NFL)
Carl Eller—Minnesota Vikings (NFL)
TACKLES
Merlin Olsen—Los Angeles Rams (NFL)
Bob Lilly—Dallas Cowboys (NFL)
OUTSIDE LINEBACKERS
Bobby Bell—Kansas City Chiefs (AFL)
Chuck Howley—Dallas Cowboys (NFL)
MIDDLE LINEBACKER
Dick Butkus—Chicago Bears (NFL)
CORNERBACKS
Lem Barney—Detroit Lions (NFL)
Willie Brown—Oakland Raiders (AFL)
SAFETIES
Larry Wilson—St. Louis Cardinals (NFL)
Johnny Robinson—Kansas City Chiefs (AFL)

*The first combined All-Pro team following the merger of the National Football League and the American Football League.

Daryle Lamonica

Roman Gabriel

Calvin Hill

ALL-PRO TEAM OF THE DECADE (SIXTIES)

1960-1969

OFFENSE

SPLIT END
Ray Berry—Baltimore Colts (NFL)

TIGHT END
Mike Ditka—Chicago Bears, Philadelphia
Eagles, Dallas Cowboys (NFL)

FLANKER
Lance Alworth—San Diego Chargers (AFL)

TACKLES
Forrest Gregg—Green Bay Packers (NFL)
Jim Tyrer—Dallas Texans, Kansas City Chiefs (AFL)

GUARDS
Jim Parker—Baltimore Colts (NFL)
Gerry Kramer—Green Bay Packers (NFL)

CENTER
Jim Otto—Oakland Raiders (AFL)

QUARTERBACK
John Unitas—Baltimore Colts (NFL)

RUNNING BACKS
Jim Brown—Cleveland Browns (NFL)
Jim Taylor—Green Bay Packers (NFL)
Gale Sayers—Chicago Bears (NFL)

DEFENSE

ENDS
David (Deacon) Jones—Los Angeles Rams (NFL)
Willie Davis—Green Bay Packers (NFL)

TACKLES
Bob Lilly—Dallas Cowboys (NFL)
Alex Karras—Detroit Lions (NFL)

LINEBACKERS
Bobby Bell—Kansas City Chiefs (AFL)
Dick Butkus—Chicago Bears (NFL)
Ray Nitschke—Green Bay Packers (NFL)

CORNERBACKS
Herb Adderley—Green Bay Packers (NFL)
Mel Renfro—Dallas Cowboys (NFL)

SAFETIES
Larry Wilson—St. Loius Cardinals (NFL)
Willie Wood—Green Bay Packers (NFL)

Mike Ditka

Gale Sayers

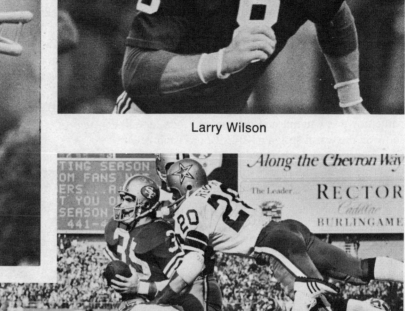

Larry Wilson

Mel Renfro (20)

Jim Taylor

Dick Butkus

ALL-PRO TEAMS OF THE SEVENTIES

THE OLD BREED hangs on, but the new ones are on the way, big, swift and strong like Alan Page, Joe Greene, Ron Yary, Bubba Smith, Mike Reid, Claude Humphrey, Charley Sanders, Ray Chester; tough, punishing runners like Larry Csonka, John Brockington, Steve Owens, Franco Harris; swift receivers like Gene Washington, Harold Jackson.

Some will stand the test of gruelling time. Others will enjoy a few minutes in the sun and then fade like snow on the warm spring hillside. But as each generation has its own heroes and its own idea of heroes these men will endure in memory and in the history of the game as the best of their times.

1970
(American Football Conference)
OFFENSE

ENDS
Paul Warfield—Miami Dolphins
Marlin Briscoe—Buffalo Bills
Bob Trumpy—Cincinnati Bengals

TACKLES
Winston Hill—New York Jets
Jim Tyrer—Kansas City Chiefs

GUARDS
Ed Budde—Kansas City Chiefs
Gene Upshaw—Oakland Raiders

CENTER
Jim Otto—Oakland Raiders

QUARTERBACK
Bob Griese—Miami Dolphins

BACKS
Floyd Little—Denver Broncos
Jess Phillips—Cincinnati Bengals

PLACEKICKER
Jan Stenerud—Kansas City Chiefs

DEFENSE

ENDS
Rich Jackson—Denver Broncos
Bubba Smith—Baltimore Colts

TACKLES
Joe Greene—Pittsburgh Steelers
Tom Keating—Oakland Raiders

LINEBACKERS
Willie Lanier—Kansas City Chiefs
Bobby Bell—Kansas City Chiefs
Andy Russell—Pittsburgh Steelers

CORNERBACKS
Willie Brown—Oakland Raiders
Jim Marsalis—Kansas City Chiefs

SAFETIES
Johnny Robinson—Kansas City Chiefs
Rick Volk—Baltimore Colts

PUNTER
David Lee—Baltimore Colts

Bob Griese

Clifton Boutelle

Joe Greene (75)

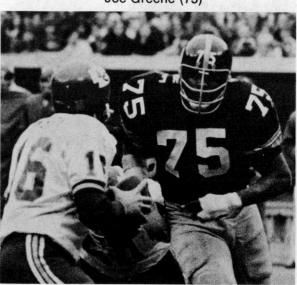

Carl Skalak

Willie Lanier (63)

Fred Cox

Ronald Mrowiec

Charlie Sanders

Clifton Boutelle

(National Football Conference)
OFFENSE

ENDS
Gene Washington—San Francisco 49ers
Dick Gordon—Chicago Bears
Charley Sanders—Detroit Lions

TACKLES
Ernie McMillan—St. Louis Cardinals
Ron Yary—Minnesota Vikings

GUARDS
Tom Mack—Los Angeles Rams
Gale Gillingham—Green Bay Packers

CENTER
Ed Flanagan—Detroit Lions

QUARTERBACK
John Brodie—San Francisco 49ers

BACKS
Larry Brown—Washington Redskins
McArthur Lane—St. Louis Cardinals

PLACEKICKER
Fred Cox—Minnesota Vikings

DEFENSE

ENDS
Carl Eller—Minnesota Vikings
David (Deacon) Jones—Los Angeles Rams

TACKLES
Merlin Olsen—Los Angeles Rams
Alan Page—Minnesota Vikings

LINEBACKERS
Dick Butkus—Chicago Bears
Chris Hanburger—Washington Redskins
Chuck Howley—Dallas Cowboys

CORNERBACKS
Roger Wehrli—St. Louis Cardinals
Jimmy Johnson—San Francisco 49ers

SAFETIES
Larry Wilson—St. Louis Cardinals
Willie Wood—Green Bay Packers

PUNTER
Julian Fagan—New Orleans Saints

1970 ALL-PRO TEAM
OFFENSE

WIDE RECEIVERS
Gene Washington—San Francisco 49ers
Dick Gordon—Chicago Bears

TIGHT END
Charlie Sanders—Detroit Lions

TACKLES
Jim Tyrer—Kansas City Chiefs
Bob Brown—Los Angeles Rams

GUARDS
Gene Upshaw—Oakland Raiders
Gene Hickerson—Cleveland Browns

CENTER
Mick Tingelhoff—Minnesota Vikings

Clifton Boutelle

John Brodie

Mike Reid

QUARTERBACK
John Brodie—San Francisco 49ers
RUNNING BACKS
Larry Brown—Washington Redskins
Ron Johnson—New York Giants
PLACEKICKER
Jan Stenerud—Kansas City Chiefs

DEFENSE
ENDS
Carl Eller—Minnesota Vikings
Rich Jackson—Denver Broncos
TACKLES
Alan Page—Minnesota Vikings
Merlin Olsen—Los Angeles Rams
OUTSIDE LINEBACKERS
Bobby Bell—Kansas City Chiefs
Chuck Howley—Dallas Cowboys
MIDDLE LINEBACKERS
Dick Butkus—Chicago Bears
CORNERBACKS
Willie Brown—Oakland Raiders
Jim Johnson—San Francisco 49ers
SAFETIES
Johnny Robinson—Kansas City Chiefs
Larry Wilson—St. Louis Cardinals
PUNTER
Dave Lewis—Cincinnati Bengals

1971
(American Football Conference)
OFFENSE
ENDS
Otis Taylor—Kansas City Chiefs
Paul Warfield—Miami Dolphins
Milt Morin—Cleveland Browns
TACKLES
Bob Brown—Oakland Raiders
Jim Tyrer—Kansas City Chiefs
GUARDS
Larry Little—Miami Dolphins
Walt Sweeney—San Diego Chargers
CENTER
Jim Otto—Oakland Raiders
QUARTERBACK
Bob Griese—Miami Dolphins
BACKS
Larry Csonka—Miami Dolphins
Floyd Little—Denver Broncos
KICKER
Garo Yepremian—Miami Dolphins

DEFENSE
ENDS
Bubba Smith—Baltimore Colts
Rich Jackson—Denver Broncos
TACKLES
Joe Greene—Pittsburgh Steelers
Mike Reid—Cincinnati Bengals

LINEBACKERS
Bobby Bell—Kansas City Chiefs
Ted Hendricks—Baltimore Colts
Willie Lanier—Kansas City Chiefs

CORNERBACKS
Willie Brown—Oakland Raiders
Emmitt Thomas—Kansas City Chiefs

SAFETIES
Rick Volk—Baltimore Colts
Jake Scott—Miami Dolphins

(National Football Conference)
OFFENSE
ENDS
Gene Washington—San Francisco 49ers
Bob Grim—Minnesota Vikings
Charley Sanders—Detroit Lions

TACKLES
Rayfield Wright—Dallas Cowboys
Ron Yary—Minnesota Vikings

GUARDS
Tom Mack—Los Angeles Rams
John Niland—Dallas Cowboys

CENTER
Forrest Blue—San Francisco 49ers

QUARTERBACK
Roger Staubach—Dallas Cowboys

BACKS
John Brockington—Green Bay Packers
Steve Owens—Detroit Lions

KICKER
Curt Knight—Washington Redskins

DEFENSE
ENDS
Carl Eller—Minnesota Vikings
Claude Humphrey—Atlanta Falcons

TACKLES
Bob Lilly—Dallas Cowboys
Alan Page—Minnesota Vikings

LINEBACKERS
Jack Pardee—Washington Redskins
Dave Wilcox—San Francisco 49ers
Dick Butkus—Chicago Bears

CORNERBACKS
Mel Renfro—Dallas Cowboys
Roger Wehrli—St. Louis Cardinals

SAFETIES
Paul Krause—Minnesota Vikings
Bill Bradley—Philadelphia Eagles

1971 ALL-PRO TEAM
OFFENSE
WIDE RECEIVER
Otis Taylor—Kansas City Chiefs
Paul Warfield—Miami Dolphins

TIGHT END
Charlie Sanders—Detroit Lions

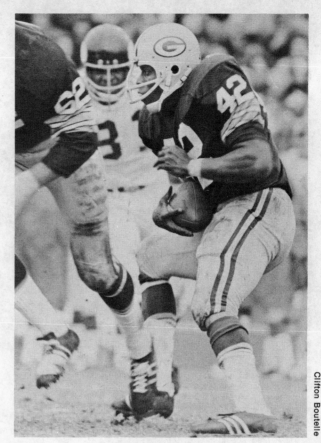

John Brockington

Steve Owens

TACKLES
Ron Yary—Minnesota Vikings
Rayfield Wright—Dallas Cowboys
GUARDS
Larry Little—Miami Dolphins
John Niland—Dallas Cowboys
CENTER
Forrest Blue—San Francisco 49ers
QUARTERBACK
Bob Griese—Miami Dolphins
RUNNING BACKS
John Brockington—Green Bay Packers
Larry Csonka—Miami Dolphins
PLACEKICKER
Garo Yepremian—Miami Dolphins

DEFENSE
ENDS
Carl Eller—Minnesota Vikings
Bubba Smith—Baltimore Colts
TACKLES
Bob Lilly—Dallas Cowboys
Alan Page—Minnesota Vikings
OUTSIDE LINEBACKERS
Ted Hendricks—Baltimore Colts
Dave Wilcox—San Francisco 49ers
MIDDLE LINEBACKER
Willie Lanier—Kansas City Chiefs
CORNERBACKS
Jim Johnson—San Francisco 49ers
Willie Brown—Oakland Raiders
SAFETIES
Rick Volk—Baltimore Colts
Bill Bradley—Philadelphia Eagles
PUNTER
Jerrel Wilson—Kansas City Chiefs

1972
(American Football Conference)
OFFENSE
WIDE RECEIVERS
Fred Biletnikoff—Oakland Raiders
Otis Taylor—Kansas City Chiefs
TIGHT END
Raymond Chester—Oakland Raiders
TACKLES
Bob Brown—Oakland Raiders
Winston Hill—New York Jets
GUARDS
Larry Little—Miami Dolphins
Gene Upshaw—Oakland Raiders
CENTER
Bob Johnson—Cincinnati Bengals
QUARTERBACK
Joe Namath—New York Jets
RUNNING BACKS
Larry Csonka—Miami Dolphins
O.J. Simpson—Buffalo Bills

Larry Csonka

Joe Namath

Ray DeAragon

Gene Washington

Bill Kilmer

Ronald Mrowiec

DEFENSE

ENDS
Bill Stanfill—Miami Dolphins
Dwight White—Pittsburgh Steelers

TACKLES
Joe Greene—Pittsburgh Steelers
Mike Reid—Cincinnati Bengals

LINEBACKERS
Ted Hendricks—Baltimore Colts
Andy Russell—Pittsburgh Steelers

MIDDLE LINEBACKER
Nick Buoniconti—Miami Dolphins

CORNERBACKS
Willie Brown—Oakland Raiders
Robert James—Buffalo Bills

SAFETIES
Dick Anderson—Miami Dolphins
Jake Scott—Miami Dolphins

(National Football Conference)

OFFENSE

WIDE RECEIVER
Harold Jackson—Philadelphia Eagles
Gene Washington—San Francisco 49ers

TIGHT END
Ted Kwalick—San Francisco 49ers

TACKLE
Rayfield Wright—Dallas Cowboys
Ron Yary—Minnesota Vikings

GUARDS
Tom Mack—Los Angeles Rams
John Niland—Dallas Cowboys

CENTER
Forrest Blue—San Francisco 49ers

QUARTERBACK
Bill Kilmer—Washington Redskins

RUNNING BACKS
John Brockington—Green Bay Packers
Larry Brown—Washington Redskins

DEFENSE

ENDS
Jack Gregory—New York Giants
Claude Humphrey—Atlanta Falcons

TACKLES
Bob Lilly—Dallas Cowboys
Alan Page—Minnesota Vikings

LINEBACKERS
Chris Hanburger—Washington Redskins
Dave Wilcox—San Francisco 49ers

MIDDLE LINEBACKER
Dick Butkus—Chicago Bears

CORNERBACKS
Ken Ellis—Green Bay Packers
Jim Johnson—San Francisco 49ers

SAFETIES
Bill Bradley—Philadelphia Eagles
Paul Krause—Minnesota Vikings

1972 ALL-PRO TEAM

OFFENSE

WIDE RECEIVER
Fred Bilenikoff—Oakland Raiders
Otis Taylor—Kansas City Chiefs

TIGHT END
Ted Kwalick—San Francisco 49ers

TACKLES
Rayfield Wright—Dallas Cowboys
Bob Brown—Oakland Raiders

GUARDS
Larry Little—Miami Dolphins
Gene Upshaw—Oakland Raiders

CENTER
Forrest Blue—San Francisco 49ers

QUARTERBACK
Joe Namath—New York Jets

RUNNING BACKS
Larry Brown—Washington Redskins
O. J. Simpson—Buffalo Bills

PLACEKICKER
Chester Marcol—Green Bay Packers

DEFENSE

ENDS
Claude Humphrey—Atlanta Falcons
Jack Gregory—New York Giants

TACKLES
Joe Greene—Pittsburgh Steelers
Mike Reid—Cincinnati Bengals

OUTSIDE LINEBACKERS
Chris Hanburger—Washington Redskins
Dave Wilcox—San Francisco 49ers

MIDDLE LINEBACKER
Dick Butkus—Chicago Bears

CORNERBACKS
Jim Johnson—San Francisco 49ers
Willie Brown—Oakland Raiders

SAFETIES
Dick Anderson—Miami Dolphins
Bill Bradley—Philadelphia Eagles

PUNTER
Jerrel Wilson—Kansas City Chiefs

Larry Brown

O. J. Simpson

The All-Time All-Pro Team

TO BE THE BEST, to be the very best, to be beyond all others who have ever played the game, to belong to that special pantheon of heroes without peer and without contemporaries is an achievement almost without parallel.

But in every endeavor of life there are those few, those specially marked by fate, to be the touchstones, the benchmarks against whom all others before and after will be measured. They are set apart from all others, a special breed within a special breed.

These men possess not only a special talent, but a special fire, a special rage to excell, a desire to stand out above all others. That is what sets them apart and is the true stamp of their greatness.

These men, this special 25, have attained a position in professional football unchallengable. We don't confer an honor. We merely recognize a debt.

SPLIT END
Don Hutson—Green Bay Packers

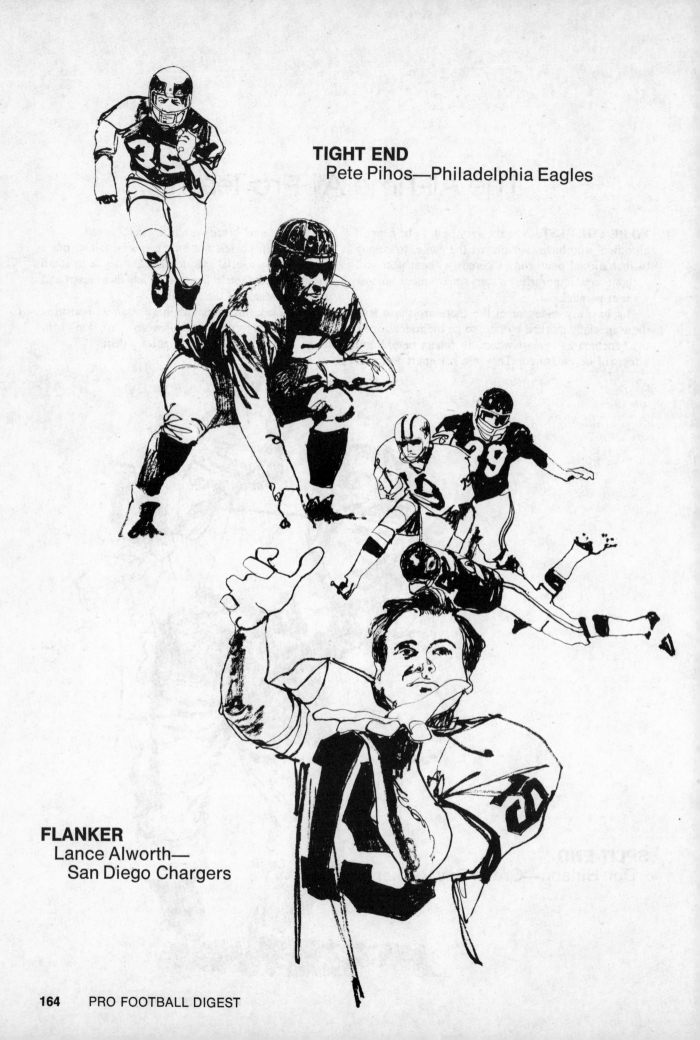

TIGHT END
Pete Pihos—Philadelphia Eagles

FLANKER
Lance Alworth—
San Diego Chargers

TACKLE
Forrest Gregg—Green Bay Packers

TACKLE
Cal Hubbard—Green Bay Packers

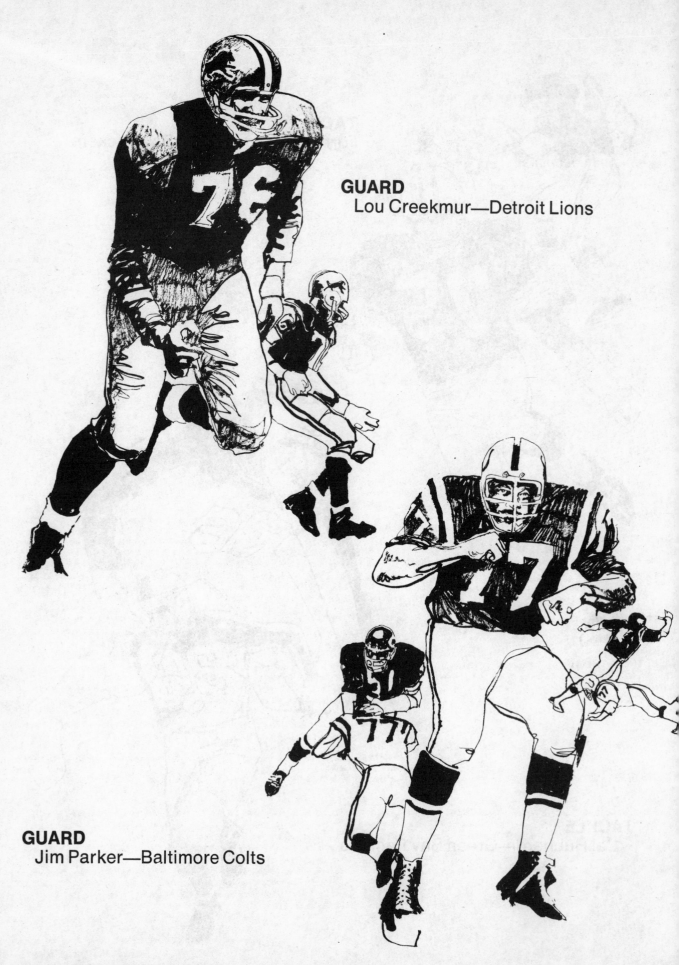

GUARD
Lou Creekmur—Detroit Lions

GUARD
Jim Parker—Baltimore Colts

CENTER
Clyde (Bulldog) Turner—
Chicago Bears

QUARTERBACK
John Unitas—Baltimore Colts

HALFBACK
Gale Sayers—Chicago Bears

HALFBACK
Hugh McElhenny—
San Francisco 49ers

FULLBACK
Jim Brown—Cleveland Browns

PLACEKICKER
George Blanda—Chicago Bears,
Houston Oilers, Oakland Raiders

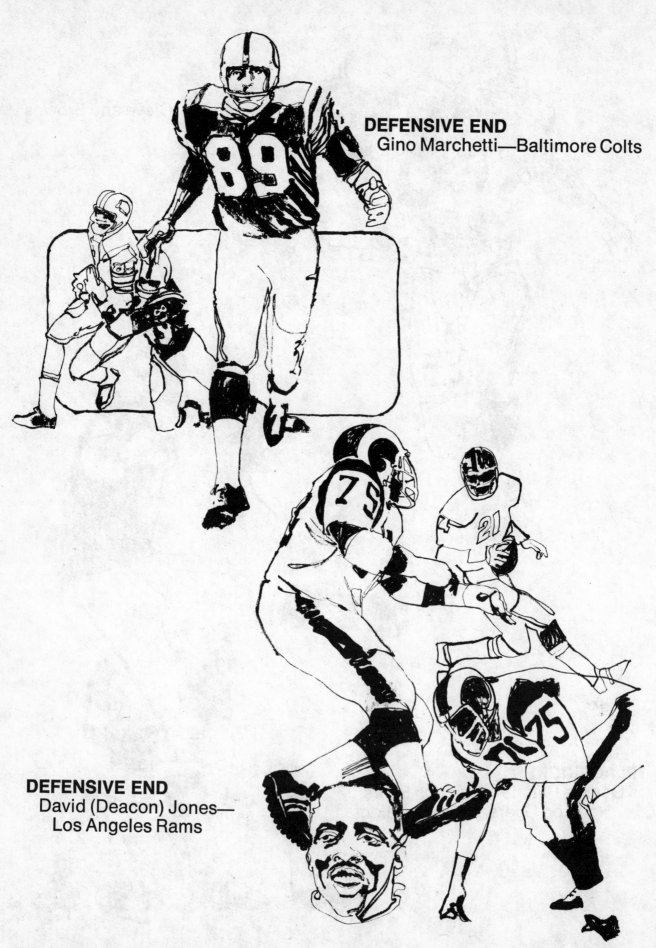

DEFENSIVE END
Gino Marchetti—Baltimore Colts

DEFENSIVE END
David (Deacon) Jones—
Los Angeles Rams

DEFENSIVE TACKLE
Leo Nomellini—
San Francisco 49ers

DEFENSIVE TACKLE
Bob Lilly—Dallas Cowboys

LINEBACKER
Bobby Bell—Kansas City Chiefs

LINEBACKER
Chuck Bednarik—
Philadelphia Eagles

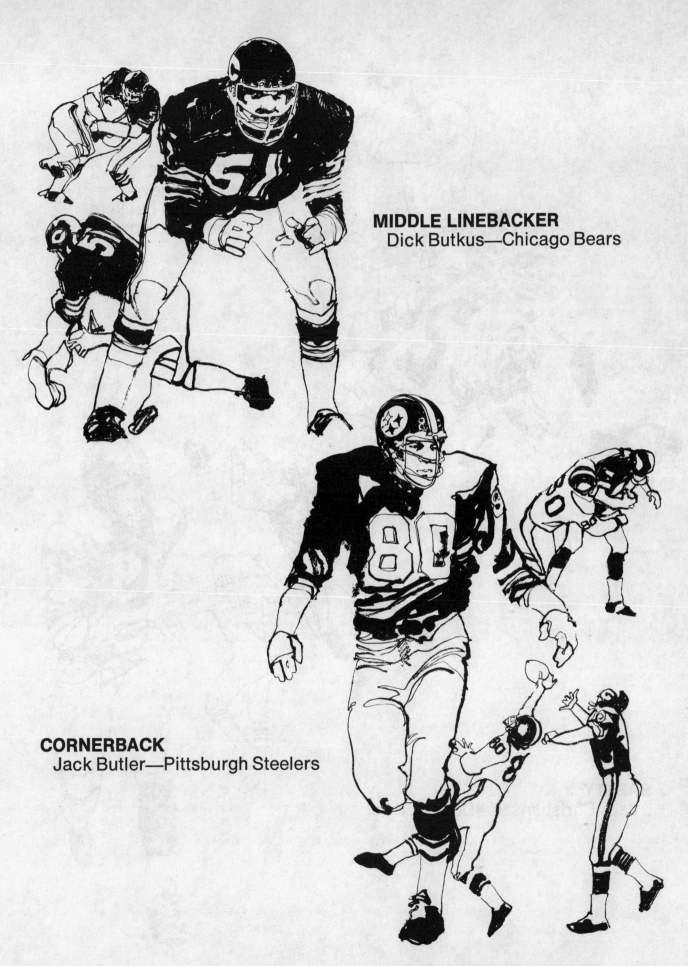

MIDDLE LINEBACKER
Dick Butkus—Chicago Bears

CORNERBACK
Jack Butler—Pittsburgh Steelers

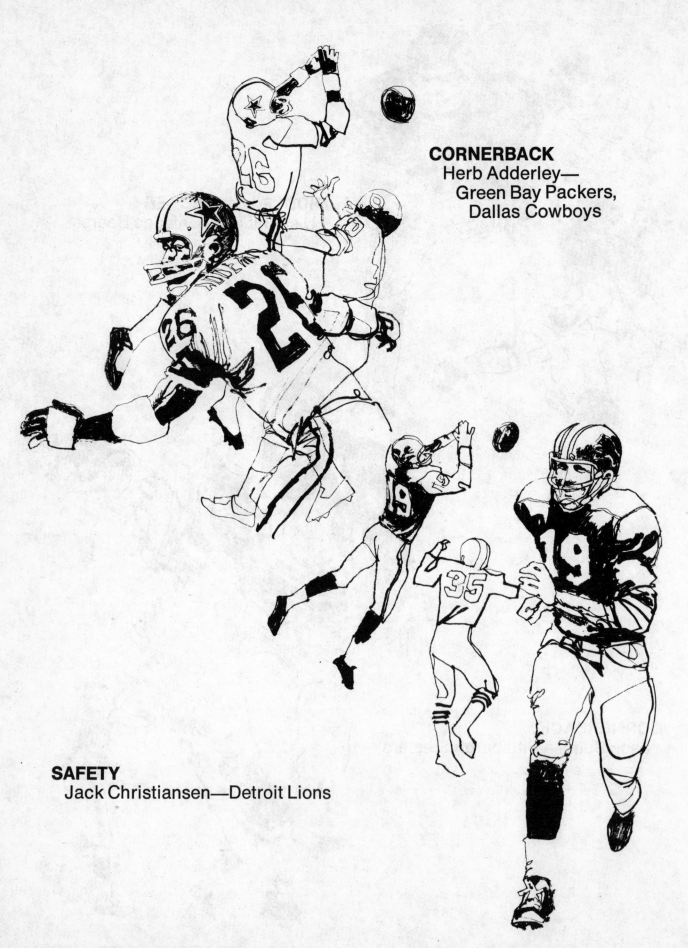

CORNERBACK
Herb Adderley—
Green Bay Packers,
Dallas Cowboys

SAFETY
Jack Christiansen—Detroit Lions

SAFETY
Emlen Tunnell—New York Giants,
Green Bay Packers

PUNTER
Sammy Baugh—
Washington Redskins

The Pro Football Hall of Fame

THE PRO FOOTBALL Hall of Fame was founded in 1962 in Canton, Ohio, the first home of modern pro football. A college quarterback was paid $10 to play a game in Latrobe, Pa., but it was in Canton that the fabled Bulldogs were formed in 1904, and in truth the modern NFL can trace its birth to the formation of the Bulldogs and the American Professional Football Association.

Now housed in a dramatically modern building are the exhibits, the photos, the displays, the equipment and the busts of the 77 men who, of all the 13,000 or more who have played pro football, have made so lasting an impression on the game that they have been enshrined as immortals.

Their story is the story of pro football. They were the giants of the game in thir own times and their star has gained added luster over the years. They are selected by a board of 27 selectors. They must have been retired as active players for at least five years and they must receive the votes of at least 24 of the 27 selectors.

The first group was inducted in ceremonies in 1963 and included 17 charter members: Sammy Baugh, Bert Bell, Joe Carr, Earl (Dutch) Clark, Harold (Red) Grange, George Halas, Mel Hein, Wilbur (Fats) Henry, Robert (Cal) Hubbard, Don Hutson, Earl (Curly) Lambeau, Tim Mara, George P. Marshall, John (Blood) McNally, Bronko Nagurski, Ernie Nevers, and Jim Thorpe.

The final selection is made every year at Super Bowl time and the induction ceremonies take place at the Hall of Fame each summer with a game and the presentation of life size bronze busts of the inductees to be placed in the Hall of Champions.

The Honor Roll:

THE IMMORTAL ROLE

Cliff Battles
(West Virginia Wesleyan)
Halfback, Boston Braves
Boston Redskins
Washington Redskins
Inducted 1968

Sammy Baugh
(Texas Christian)
Quarterback, Washington Redskins
Inducted 1963

Chuck Bednarik
(Pennsylvania)
Center, Linebacker
Philadelphia Eagles
Inducted 1967

Bert Bell
(Pennsylvania)
Founder Philadelphia Eagles
NFL Commissioner
Inducted 1963

Ray Berry
(Southern Methodist)
End, Baltimore Colts
Inducted 1973

Charles Bidwill
(Loyola of Chicago)
Owner Chicago Cardinals
Inducted 1967

Jim Brown
(Syracuse)
Fullback
Cleveland Browns
Inducted 1971

Paul Brown
(Miami, Ohio)
Founder, Coach
Cleveland Browns
Inducted 1967

Earl (Dutch) Clark
(Colorado College)
Quarterback, Portsmouth Spartans
Detroit Lions
Inducted 1963

Jim Conzelman
(Washington, St. Louis)
Halfback, Coach, Owner
Chicago Cardinals
Providence Steamrollers, Others
Inducted 1964

Art Donovan
(Boston College)
Defensive Tackle
Baltimore Colts
New York Yanks, Dallas Texans
Inducted 1968

Joe Carr
Founder Columbus Panhandles
NFL President
Inducted 1963

Guy Chamberlin
(Nebraska)
Coach, End, Canton Bulldogs
Frankford Yellowjackets
Others
Inducted 1965

Jack Christiansen
(Colorado State U.)
Defensive Halfback
Detroit Lions
Inducted 1970

John (Paddy) Driscoll
(Northwestern)
Quarterback, Chicago Cardinals
Chicago Bears
Inducted 1965

Bill Dudley
(Virginia)
Halfback, Pittsburgh Steelers
Detroit Lions
Washington Redskins
Inducted 1966

Turk Edwards
(Washington State)
Tackle, Boston Braves
Boston Redskins
Washington Redskins
Inducted 1969

Tom Fears
(Santa Clara and UCLA)
End
Los Angeles Rams
Inducted 1970

Daniel Fortmann, M.D.
(Colgate)
Guard, Chicago Bears
Inducted 1965

Otto Graham
(Northwestern)
Quarterback, Cleveland Browns
Inducted 1965

Edward Healey
(Dartmouth)
Tackle, Chicago Bears
Rock Island Independents
Inducted 1964

Mel Hein
(Washington State)
Center, New York Giants
Inducted 1963

Wilbur (Pete) Henry
(Washington & Jefferson)
Tackle, Canton Bulldogs
Others
Inducted 1963

Harold (Red) Grange
(Illinois)
Halfback, Chicago Bears
New York Yankees
Inducted 1963

Joe Guyon
(Carlisle, Georgia Tech)
Halfback, Canton Bulldogs
Oorang Indians
Others
Inducted 1966

George Halas
(Illinois)
Founder, Player, Coach
Chicago Bears
Inducted 1963

Arnie Herber
(Regis College)
Quarterback, Green Bay Packers
New York Giants
Inducted 1966

Bill Hewitt
(Michigan)
End, Chicago Bears
Philadelphia Eagles, Phil-Pitt
Inducted 1971

Clarke Hinkle
(Bucknell)
Fullback, Green Bay Packers
Inducted 1964

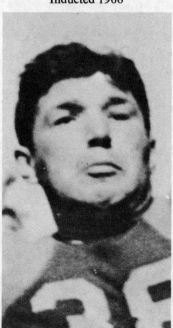

Elroy (Crazylegs) Hirsch
(Wisconsin and Michigan)
Halfback, End
Chicago Rockets
Los Angeles Rams
Inducted 1968

Robert (Cal) Hubbard
(Geneva & Centenary)
Tackle, New York Giants
Green Bay Packers
Pittsburgh Pirates
Inducted 1963

Lamar Hunt
(Southern Methodist)
AFL Founder
Owner, Kansas City Chiefs
Inducted 1972

Earl (Curly) Lambeau
(Notre Dame)
Founder, Player, Coach
Green Bay Packers
Inducted 1963

Bobby Layne
(Texas)
Quarterback, Detroit Lions
Pittsburgh Steelers
Others
Inducted 1967

Vince Lombardi
(Fordham)
Coach
Green Bay Packers
Washington Redskins
Inducted 1971

Don Hutson
(Alabama)
End, Green Bay Packers
Inducted 1963

Walt Kiesling
(St. Thomas, Minn.)
Player, Coach
Chicago Cardinals
Pittsburgh Steelers, Others
Inducted 1966

Frank (Bruiser) Kinard
(Mississippi)
Tackle
Brooklyn Dodgers
New York Yankees (AAFC)
Inducted 1971

Sid Luckman
(Columbia)
Quarterback, Chicago Bears
Inducted 1965

William Roy (Link) Lyman
(Nebraska)
Tackle, Canton Bulldogs
Chicago Bears, Others
Inducted 1964

Tim Mara
Founder, New York Giants
Inducted 1963

George P. Marshall
(Randolph-Macon)
Founder, Boston Braves
President, Washington Redskins
Inducted 1963

George McAfee
(Duke)
Halfback, Chicago Bears
Inducted 1966

Hugh McElhenny
(Washington)
Halfback
San Francisco 49ers
and Others
Inducted 1970

August (Mike) Michalske
(Penn State)
Guard, New York Yankees
Green Bay Packers
Inducted 1964

Wayne Millner
(Notre Dame)
End, Boston Redskins
Washington Redskins
Inducted 1968

Marion Motley
(Nevada)
Fullback, Cleveland Browns
Pittsburgh Steelers
Inducted 1968

John (Blood) McNally
(St. Johns, Minn.)
Halfback, Green Bay Packers
Pittsburgh Pirates
Others
Inducted 1963

Gino Marchetti
(San Francisco)
Defensive End
Dallas Texans
Baltimore Colts
Inducted 1972

Ollie Matson
(San Francisco)
Halfback, Chicago Cardinals
Los Angeles Rams
Detroit Lions, Philadelphia Eagles
Inducted 1972

Bronko Nagurski
(Minnesota)
Fullback, Chicago Bears
Inducted 1963

Earle (Greasy) Neale
(West Virginia Wesleyan)
Coach
Philadelphia Eagles
Inducted 1969

Ernie Nevers
(Stanford)
Fullback, Duluth Eskimos
Chicago Cardinals
Inducted 1963

Leo Nomellini
(Minnesota)
Defensive Tackle
San Francisco 49ers
Inducted 1969

Steve Owen
(Phillips)
Coach, Tackle
Kansas City Cowboys
New York Giants
Inducted 1966

Clarence (Ace) Parker
(Duke)
Quarterback
Brooklyn Dodgers, Boston Yanks
New York Yankees (AAFC)
Inducted 1972

Hugh (Shorty) Ray
(Illinois)
Rules Book Author
Supervisor of Officials
Inducted 1966

Daniel Reeves
(Georgetown)
Founder, Cleveland Rams
President, Los Angeles Rams
Inducted 1967

Andy Robustelli
(Arnold College)
Defensive End
Los Angeles Rams
New York Giants
Inducted 1971

Jim Parker
(Ohio State)
Guard-Tackle
Baltimore Colts
Inducted 1973

Joe Perry
(Compton Junior College)
Fullback
San Francisco 49ers
Baltimore Colts
Inducted 1969

Pete Pihos
(Indiana)
End
Philadelphia Eagles
Inducted 1970

Arthur Rooney
(Georgetown and Duquesne)
Founder,
Pittsburgh Pirates (Steelers)
Inducted 1964

Joe Schmidt
(Pittsburgh)
Linebacker
Detroit Lions
Inducted 1973

Ernie Stautner
(Boston College)
Defensive Tackle
Pittsburgh Steelers
Inducted 1969

Kenneth Strong
(New York University)
Halfback, Staten Island Stapletons
New York Giants
New York Yankees
Inducted 1967

Joe Stydahar
(West Virginia)
Tackle, Chicago Bears
Inducted 1967

Jim Thorpe
(Carlisle)
Halfback, Canton Bulldogs
Others
Inducted 1963

Emlen Tunnell
(Iowa)
Defensive Halfback
New York Giants
Green Bay Packers
Inducted 1967

Clyde (Bulldog) Turner
(Hardin-Simmons)
Center, Chicago Bears
Inducted 1966

Norm Van Brocklin
(Oregon)
Quarterback, Los Angeles Rams
Philadelphia Eagles
Inducted 1971

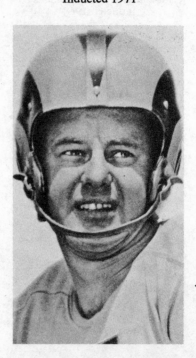

Y. A. Tittle
(Louisiana State)
Quarterback
Baltimore Colts
San Francisco 49ers
New York Giants
Inducted 1971

George Trafton
(Notre Dame)
Center, Chicago Bears
Others
Inducted 1964

Charley Trippi
(Georgia)
Halfback, Quarterback
Chicago Cardinals
Inducted 1968

Steve Van Buren
(Louisiana State)
Halfback, Philadelphia Eagles
Inducted 1965

Bob Waterfield
(U. C. L. A.)
Quarterback, Cleveland Rams
Los Angeles Rams
Inducted 1965

Alex Wojciechowicz
(Fordham)
Center, Linebacker
Detroit Lions, Philadelphia Eagles
Inducted 1968

HEFFELFINGER, NOT BRALLIER, FIRST PRO FOOTBALL PLAYER

CHECK OUT almost any history on professional football and, nine times out of 10, you will find John Brallier listed as the world's first professional football player.

Back in 1895, 16-year-old John Brallier was induced to quarterback the Latrobe, Pa., YMCA team against nearby Jeannette, Pa. For agreeing to play, the erstwhile signal-caller of the Washington and Jefferson college team was to receive the princely sum of $10 and "cakes"—in modern jargon, expenses.

Some say the game was played on September 3, 1895—most report it was on August 31. Some write that Latrobe won, 6-0—others say the score was 12-0. But on Brallier's financial involvement, all historians agree.

Ever since the Pleistocene Age of professional football, this has been the "establishment" version of how it all began. Even the Professional Football Hall of Fame in Canton, Ohio, devotes a large space in its exhibition rotunda to commemorate that historic "first."

Now wipe the slate clean and start anew.

Based on more recent material gathered, ironically, by the Pro Football Hall of Fame and its first director, the late Dick McCann, it now is certain that Brallier, instead of being No. 1, was actually No. 7 or even lower on the list of those who first "tainted" themselves by accepting cash for playing football.

As accurately as can be determined, the list of *known* pro pioneers should read like this:

1. **William (Pudge) Heffelfinger,** Allegheny Athletic Association of Pittsburgh, Pa., $500 for one game, November 12, 1892.
2. **Ben (Sport) Donnelly,** Allegheny Athletic Association, $250 for one game, November 19, 1892.
3-4-5. **Wright, Van Cleve and Rafferty** (first names not available), Allegheny Athletic Association, $50 per game (under contract) for the entire 1893 season.
6. **Lawson Fiscus,** Greensburg, Pa., $20 per game and expenses for the entire 1894 season.
7. **John Brallier,** Latrobe, Pa., YMCA, $10 and expenses for one game, August 31, 1895.

For openers, let's start with a meticulously-prepared, 49-page paper written by researcher Nelson Ross, who describes in minute detail the events leading up to the confrontation of the Allegheny Athletic Associ-ation (AAA) and the Pittsburgh Athletic Club (PAC) football teams in November, 1892.

The AAA team, formed in 1890, and the PAC, started in 1891, were already heated rivals when they struggled to a 6-6 deadlock early in the 1892 season. Adding fuel to the fire was the AAA claim that the PAC's top player and coach, William Kirschner, was a professional because, as a paid instructor for the PAC, his salary went up and his class load down during football season. With controversy raging and interest mounting, both sides began to explore methods of beefing up their squads for the return match.

To fully describe the situation, the story must now shift elsewhere. "Back east" the practice of the time was for many leading AAU grid clubs to reward their stars with expensive trophies (which they could sell) or with expense money (usually far in excess of actual expenses.) The trophy arrangement had been tabooed by the AAU, but the expense money policy was allowed to continue.

"Out west," the Chicago Athletic Association team formed in 1892 adopted the "usual double expense money" practice and, as a result, had trouble scheduling games in the Windy City with college or "pure amateur" clubs.

One of the Chicago stars was Heffelfinger, who had been an all-America guard at Yale in 1889, 1890 and 1891. He was America's biggest football name at the beginning of the Gay Nineties. In 1892, he was a low-salaried railroad office employee in Omaha, Nebraska, but he was granted a leave of absence so that he could join the Chicago team on a six-game tour of the east. According to Chicago newspaper reports, the only consideration to Heffelfinger would be "the usual expense arrangement."

Meanwhile back in Pittsburgh, Kirschner had been sidelined with an injury and the PAC manager, George Barbour, decided to scout the Chicago team in Cleveland in the opening game of its eastern tour. Chicago defeated the Cleveland Athletic Association, 29-0, and Heffelfinger had a great game. Barbour was convinced that Pudge would make an ideal replacement for Kirschner.

The Pittsburgh Press on October 30, 1892, reported:

"A very improbable sort of a story is being circulated at present about the PAC offering Heffelfinger

William (Pudge) Heffelfinger

and Ames of the Chicago football team $250 to play with the East End team on Saturday, November 12, against the AAA."

Thus alerted, the AAA did a little missionary work on its own. On contacting Chicago players in New York after the final game of their tour, AAA representatives found (1) that Ames had decided against risking his amateur status, (2) that Donnelly and another player named Malley would be willing to play for the usual double expense money and (3) that Heffelfinger had decided not to risk his amateur standing for a mere $250.

Thus, in effect, pro football had its first "holdout" even before it had its first pro. For it developed that, for $500, Heffelfinger would play. AAA representatives, eager to outdo their PAC rivals, agreed.

Was it worth it to the AAA? Victory was the goal, so the answer must be "yes." Heffelfinger, who played left guard, scored the game's only touchdown on a 25-yard fumble return following one of his patented bone-jarring tackles of a PAC ball-carrier. Touchdowns were worth four points in 1892 so the AAA won, 4-0. Financially, the AAA netted $621 on the game, in spite of the "bonus" payoff to Heffelfinger and expense payments of $25 each to Heffelfinger, Donnelly and Malley.

The Ross paper goes on report that Donnelly was paid $250 to play the following week and that the AAA had at least three players under regular contract in 1893. Although it names no names, the report says the PAC did the same thing in 1893.

McCann as early as 1963 sought to confirm the findings in Ross' "white paper." Confirmation came in the form of a yellowed and parched expense sheet of the Allegheny Athletic Association, signed by manager O. D. Thompson and detailing expenses of several AAA games in 1892 and 1893. Every detail checks out exactly with the Ross report.

As for Fiscus, the History of Greensburg, Pa., published in 1949, recalls the great town teams of 1892,

1893 and 1894 and innocently states: "Except for one or two players, these organizations were strictly amateur." Fiscus himself admitted that he played for expenses only in 1893 and then for $20 and expenses each game in 1894.

So now we are back to Latrobe and August 31, 1895. There are those who will insist that this was the first pro *game,* implying that everyone was paid to play. Even the National Football League Guide, in its official chronology, makes this notation.

Logic seems to refute this theory. For under those circumstances, there would have been no reason to make such a fuss over Brallier, if he were merely one of 30 or so players in the game who were paid.

The noted football historian, Vernon C. Berry of Latrobe, says his town's first all-pro team came in 1897. He should know for his brother, newspaper publisher David J. Berry, organized the original Latrobe team.

Undoubtedly there were more early-day "pros" whose names may never be known. It also might be argued that those earlier AAU players who received trophies and/or expenses were in reality the first professionals.

But on the basis of what is now known, Heffelfinger must rank as the first person to openly accept payment for playing. And in this first pro venture, he still received his heavy expense allowance.

As for Brallier, it might be said in jest that, through all these years, he simply had a better publicity man. His "publicity" was so good, in fact, that in 1946 the NFL, on the assumption that Latrobe was the true "birthplace of professional football," actually gave preliminary approval to that city as the site for a future Pro Football Hall of Fame.

Now the evidence contradicts all the earlier theories.

And it also looks as though the Pro Football Hall of Fame will have to make a few alterations in its "First Game" display!

The Fans

How to Watch a Game

Behold the fan. Muffled, wrapped, mittened, swaddled, galoshed, blanketed, enveloped in plastic he sits on cold pine buffeted and whipped by the winter wind, roasted and reddened by the summer sun, in rain and snow and mist and sleet he endures, night and day, all for his team.

Behold the fan. Through the bright sweep of glass he entertains friends in his private box high above the artificial greensward. No sudden chill shivers his pleasure. An easy chair provides comfort instead of the jostle of elbows, knees in the back. The chef will prepare his lunch. The sommelier will uncork the wine. Euphoria. All for his team.

Behold the fan. Expectant, cranky, red-eyed, numb-eared, bathed in the glow of 27-inch diagonal living color he lounges, slouches in the family room, the living room, the basement, the den, for another night with Frank and Howard and Dandy, or another afternoon with Ray and Pat or Curt and De Ro, or Frank and Tom who bring him knowledgeability, stop action instant replay, an endless flow of chatter, banter and repartee, and a commercial every time the ball changes hands. Thus he seals himself off from wife, kids, home, job, country and regular meals. All for his team.

But we are not here to study fanhood as a unique specimen of homo sapiens. Rather we are here to observe his actions in his natural habitat, to take note of how he goes about his business of watching a thrilling spectacle unfold before his eyes, taking in all the drama and action without, literally, batting an eye.

Watching a professional football game is a craft, no, it's more than a craft, it's an art, and just as music has many branches to its art so too does football game watching.

There is the art of the season ticket holder. Currently they number about 1½ million throughout the country, residing mostly in the populated urban areas.

Some say they are a diminishing species. They have not yet made the endangered list, but their future is bleak, some say, and will some day vanish from the face of the game.

The season ticket holder sits in the open surrounded by other season ticket holders. His spectating techniques are as old as sport itself, dating back to the Circus Maximus of Rome. They are handed down from father to son, from ticket holder to ticket holder through all the generations of man, tried and true, polished and perfected throughout the ages.

Now much has been written about keeping one's eye on the ball, or watching the quarterback, or "keying" on the middle linebacker. (Keying, by the way, is just another word for watching, but that is a part of the jargon of the game, and a game can be watched clearly and intelligently without any regard to jargon.) Or even keeping the man-in-motion in focus.

That's all nonsense. The most immediate attention of any season ticket holder should be riveted on the back of the head of the season ticket holder sitting

directly in front of him. That's the only way to see the game. Any wandering of attention from the head of the season ticket holder in front of him and our typical season ticket holder will miss the game.

He will miss the exciting action, the long run, the long pass, the blocked punt, because should his attention wander the season ticket holder in front of him will be standing, blocking his view of the field, and all that he will have to describe the following morning at coffee will be the irregularities of the plaid in the fellow's coat.

A good 25 per cent of every game is watched from a standing position, and that's the 25 per cent with all the action. Every regular fan knows this, but if he isn't alert enough to spring to his feet at the same instant, or even before, the season ticket holder in front of him he'll miss it all.

Only a newcomer will yell, "DOWN IN FRONT!" an inept ploy that no experienced season ticket holder would even bother with.

Besides keeping his eye on the head in front of him the season ticket holder must also keep a sharp watch on the scoreboard. The scoreboard clock is the game's official timepiece and it takes precise accuracy, as well as years of experience in the stands, to know, as the clock ticks down the final seconds of the half, the exact moment when it's safe to get up and beat the mob to the washroom at halftime.

This takes an intimate knowledge of the game and, for the season ticket holder, can be the most important play of the game. Some, a few only, can pride themselves on never having stood in a halftime relief line in 20 years of game going. But it takes an expert, one who can compute with certainty the anticipated action depending on which team has the ball, the position on the field, the time-outs remaining, the quarterback's past record in the famous two-minute drill, the chances of a long punt runback, and the tendencies of those season ticket holders sitting around him.

There is, of course, the critical ability to sense the coming time-out at various stages of the game. Most season ticket holders contend that this is something instinctive. It can't be taught. You've either got it or you ain't. And it is this anticipation, the ability to remove the cork at the exact instant the referee begins his signal, that makes for the happiest fan, no matter what the score.

Mobility, lateral movement, rather than sheer speed, is another prime attribute of the season ticket holder. The ability to anticipate the block and with a quick slight shift to see over and around the pennant hawkers, the program peddlers, the hot dog sellers and the beer vendors who tend to pop up at the start of crucial plays. There are case histories of slow-moving season ticket holders who think that the game is strictly a competition between the hot dog and beer salesmen. They think a Unitas is an imported Lithu-anian brew.

As important as imperviousness to the elements, the quick start to the washroom and the head and seat shift, is the dash for the exit.

The experienced season ticket holder must have the capacity to sense when the game is hopelessly lost or completely wrapped up, and then make his quick move for the parking lot to beat the rush home. There are some, a minority to be sure, who think it fashionable to leave the game in the eighth minute of the fourth quarter. This enables them the following morning to report to friends and co-workers, "no, we missed that. It was such a dull game we couldn't bear it any longer." A bit of snobbery that stamps them as experts of high drama.

While the regular season ticket holder is a rare and dedicated breed, and their numbers limited to the number of seats in any given stadium, an even rarer breed, the rarest by far, is the season box holder.

These are the super rich who pay anywhere from $15,000 a season up to $100,000 to sit in glassed-in, thickly carpeted, poshy comfort and sip scotch and martinis, nibble fillets and lamb chops, with ribs and stew thrown in for proletarian laughs, above and away from the vulgar crowd noises.

It is extremely doubtful that as they luxuriate in their little heavens that these season box holders will ever develop the finely tuned game-watching techniques of the season ticket holders. Without distractions and obstructions and with built-in plumbing these muscles and senses will undoubtedly atrophy. But nature always compensates, and as one muscle, sense, or talent diminishes another will enlarge and expand.

The optic nerve, for instance. A new breed of season box holders will surely emerge with ten-power eyes, eyes like binoculars, that can pick up the lip movements of the quarterback as he calls his audibles. This will be the most striking feature of the season box holder of the future. That and an in-bred curvature of the spine from slouching in his easy chair.

There is no telling what viewing techniques will be developed, or what new eating and drinking and other habits either, but these limited, chosen few, now have an unlimited opportunity to improvise new techniques and climb to new heights of viewing virtuosity.

If nothing else they put on some interesting fashion shows in those glass booths, and in a way provide a part of the entertainment for the hoi polloi sitting outside.

Sitting at home by an easy chair near the hearth, alone, or surrounded by other loyal fans and loved ones is really the most difficult way to watch a game.

The true television fan, and they number into the 50 millions, the most numerous of our three species, is beset by a thousand distractions that sorely try his concentrative powers.

There is grass to be cut, hedges to be trimmed, leaves to be raked, a dinner to be eaten, a nagging wife to be ignored, screaming kids to be shouted into submission.

Timing is extremely important. The new television fan will want to set himself before the set a full hour before the kickoff to soak up all the pre-game shows, the experts in their swivel chairs with the film clips of previous games glowing over their left shoulders.

These film clips of exciting old plays showing the common opponents today's teams have met, or uncommon opponents they have played, serves absolutely no useful purpose as far as today's game is concerned. They do, however, adjust the eyes to the blur of action so that once the game starts he will not be caught blinking at the wrong moment.

The pregame shows are also very useful in adjusting the ear to the drone of the announcer's voice, and many dedicated fans use this as an opportunity to take their nap instead of waiting until the third quarter.

The game proper begins with the introduction of the teams. This is to whet the appetite of the fans for violence. The sight of Ray Nitschke without his teeth is a very appetite wheting sight indeed. Most often though, the introduction is interrupted for an automobile or a shaving cream commercial so the home fan must inerpolate most of it in his mind.

The exception to all this though is the Super Bowl pregame show. The Super Bowl pregame show usually starts at least a week before the game and by the time of the introduction of players many fans think that the game has already been played and that the new season is about to begin. This is called viewer shock or the one-eyed syndrome.

Next comes the coin toss, or rather the mock coin toss, because the real coin toss has been held 30 minutes before in a neutral area between the two locker rooms. But the captains and co-captains and tri-captains and quad-captains are trotted out to the middle of the field anyway and the referee, the man in the striped shirt, introduces the players to each other. That's another bit of superfluous nonsense because all the players know each other. They get acquainted on the field, at golf outings, cocktail parties, political rallies, at author's luncheons, on TV talk shows, and they have the same agents.

The experienced home fan will use this time to get things in order. Pop a can, empty the ashtray, fix a sandwich, position the chips and dip and say something to his wife calculated to send her into at least a three hour snit so she won't bother him during the game.

Once the field is cleared of captains the celebrity singer prepares to do the national anthem. The band strikes up, the color guard snaps to, the Goodyear Blimp drifts into position and either the microphone mercifully fails or the horns drown out the off-key wailing.

Previous to this though were the comments and questions. This usually consists of the high-priced announcer in his plaid sports jacket and turtle-neck asking the color man and expert, usually an ex-immortal, in a plaid sports jacket and turtle-neck what he thinks of the day's matchup.

What he should really ask is, "who's gonna win, De Ro?" but instead he asks something ambiguous so that De Ro can spend about ten minutes singlethinking and doubletalking about zones and desire and inside strength versus ball control.

What the fan really wants to hear is that Csonka is going to trample Lanier, or that Butkus is actually going to kill someone today. So, like everything else that happens before the kickoff, the experienced home fan tunes De Ro out.

Now the viewing can begin in earnest. And now begins the time of selective listening and watching. The game comes over best with the sound off. Otherwise every third down becomes the crucial third down of the game and the inexperienced home fan will have his fingers gnawed down to the knuckles before the first two-minute drill, which usually lasts an hour.

Watching the game on the tube the home fan is restricted to what the cameraman and director chose to give him. That's always the ball, except on those plays when the director is faked out, usually not more than ten plays a game. It's silly to try to watch the middle linebacker or the defensive tackle because you'll find yourself spending the afternoon staring at a foot, a couple of knuckles in the upper right hand or lower left hand corner of the screen.

A word of caution. The really experienced home viewer has learned to ignore the instant replays. In the long run it comes out better that way.

One fan, lulled into a stupor by Curt and De Ro, watched six replays of the same touchdown, and then passed out. He went under with the impression that his team had just set a scoring record, six touchdowns in 37 seconds. The next day in discussing the game with his co-workers he couldn't understand their defeatist talk and bet his car and home that his team scored at least 42 points. He lost of course, because his team lost 8 to 7 on four fourth-quarter safeties. So instant replay viewing requires a very alert mind, which few home fans possess.

Albert Droopeyes, one of the game's most famous home fans, a charter member of the Home Fans Hall of Fame, made the discovery one afternoon when the Bills were playing the Eagles, that one actually lost less of the action if one napped through the first half.

By awaking on time he could catch the replay of the first half highlights and be extremely fresh for the critical second half. In the case of the game in which he made his discovery the highlights consisted of two completed snaps from center, one by each team. But not every game can be expected to be as exciting as a Buffalo-Philadelphia encounter.

Waking fresh puts a viewer in the mood for action, and the second half is when the game is won or lost anyway. As the action unfolds the game explains itself. Need we say more?

One note of caution going into the second half, don't eat too much or you'll spoil your dinner. Of course, sometimes the game does that to you anyway. But that is the fate of the fan, to endure.

OFF THE PIGSKIN: PUNTING THE REVOLUTION

By Eric Mann

I'VE BEEN a football fanatic much longer than I've been a communist. No matter what city I'm in I always seek out a newsstand that carries the *New York Post*. The Post has a few front pages of murders and muggings; a few dying liberal columnists like Max Lerner and James Wechsler who are virulent in their attacks on the revolutionary left and meek in their criticisms of genocide; and a mammoth sports section where you can find three different columns in one day analyzing Eddie Bell's amazing catch of the deflection from Joe Namath's last minute desperation heave against the Colts.

Even after I became very active in the Movement and had to place some limits on the amount of sports I could play, read about and discuss I had a friend in Newark I would call from Boston once a week to argue the merits of the Jets versus the Giants, and I always found excuses to avoid Sunday meetings so I could hang a "do not disturb sign" on the door and settle in for the football double header.

I studied the game with energy and passion. I read two or three sports sections a day, and the *Sporting News* and *Pro Football Weekly*—cover to cover. After the annual pro football draft I spent the winter, spring and summer fantasizing how every unheralded player the Jets picked would develop into a superstar. I shut my eyes to the transparent stupidity of Weeb Ewbank and swallowed whole statements like, "Even though Wilbur is only 5 foot 9 and 270 pounds we drafted him because he has good speed and might develop into a fine split end or defensive tackle." I repressed my suspicion that Weeb was really saying, "It was the 16th round and we had no idea who the hell anybody was and we almost died when the kid showed up and looked like a spastic fire hydrant."

I cried, screamed, sat-in, and even occasionally fought over the murders of Cheney, Goodman and Schwerner, Selma and the bombing of North Vietnam, through My Lai and Malcolm X's murder, through tiger cages and black lung disease and lynchings. I came to hate Amerika's army, universities, welfare system, air, water, culture and politics, its vicious treatment of women, children, blacks and browns, reds and whites. But Sunday afternoons I kept pro football locked in a bomb shelter of my own making, protected from the scrutiny and anger I applied to the rest of the system.

On Sunday afternoon I looked the other way when the Star Spangled Banner was played, when Vince Lombardi advocated fascism as the ideal form of human organization, when football players became an entertainment arm of the Defense Department. When Ralph Nader exposed automobiles, when Jessica Mitford exposed funerals, when George Jackson exposed prisons and Seymour Hersh exposed My Lai I yelled, "Pour it on, let's get the truth out to the people." But when Dave Meggysey exposed pro football I mumbled "Right on" and made sure I never went within eye distance of his book.

Football itself is a rough, but potentially humane and exhilarating game. I played tackle football at Concord State Prison in full equipment. I played tackle with and against men convicted of armed robbery, breaking and entering, assault, and murder. We were men deprived of almost all physical enjoyment and personal gratification. Winning was a high priority, both for the opportunity to boast all week in a world of pathetic victories and for the packs of cigarettes bet on the game (which could then be exchanged for a ham sandwich smuggled out of the officers' dining room).

In all the games I played at Concord there was never a serious injury. With all the day-to-day racial tension most white prisoners still could feel at least *some* understanding that the black man on the opposite team was a human being. Then we would watch the "pros." We were out to win; they were out to kill each other. We tackled a runner to knock him down; they tackled to rip off his kneecap. We got satisfaction from hitting the end just before his fingers closed around the ball; they got satisfaction—and bonuses—for spearing a button-hooked end in the spine with their helmets. Defensive players like Ray Nitschke and

Dick Butkus are approvingly dubbed "animals" by their trainers, and earn their money not by just tackling backs and ends, but by putting them "out for the season."

Football is one of my last links to imperialist values, my private reservoir of attachment to the sadistic decadence of American culture, a fantasy island of manageable victories and defeats where I can suspend moral/political judgments and try to escape my unhappiness rather than confront and eliminate it.

When I was in Weatherman and only a few weeks away from the prison term the judge and I both knew he was waiting to give me, I was disintegrating with fear and confusion. I needed the support and advice of my friends, but instead wasted precious hours sneaking off to a pool room to watch the Jets-Kansas City playoff game, and reading *Pro Football Weekly* (guiltily and surreptitiously) on the pot.

When the invasion of Cambodia and the murders at Kent State and Jackson State happened I was four months deep into prison and fuming with anger—at what they were doing to me, my fellow prisoners, the students, and the people of Indochina. I spent hours talking with the brothers about revolution and hours more reading everything I could get my hands on about the day's events.

Shortly before lights-out I took a breather and turned to the *Post* sports section to read an article about Rich Caster, the Jets' second round draft pick who was being touted as an excellent prospect at tight end or wide receiver. I poured over the article in excitement hoping to hear about his skills at running fly patterns or how his college coach said he would be another Otis Taylor. Instead, the article was about Rich Caster's reactions to the murder of two students at Jackson State, the college he attended, not only as a football player, but as a black student. I found myself disappointed that the article was about the murders. I had wanted to know if he preferred the zig-out pattern to the stop-and-go.

A lot of the time I'm a rebel. My deepest happiness has come from military victories of the NLF, the inspiring example of the men at Attica, the rebellions of women against oppressive men, mental patients against their psychiatrists, welfare mothers against their caseworkers and the welfare department, any oppressed person against the institutional bureaucracies suffocating and strangling them.

But when George Sauer quit the Jets because he said the game was dehumanizing him I hoped he would change his mind and keep running those beautiful come-back patterns. When Duane Thomas keeps jerking the chain of the San Diego Chargers I read white sports writers who gloat, "It won't be long before Duane Thomas is forced to give up his hold-out. He's running out of the money and the Texas judge who gave him a five-year probation for possession of mari-

juana will lower his probation if he goes back to playing," and I find myself intellectually revolted but privately a little bit hopeful that Gene Klein, the multimillionaire Charger owner, will put the screws to Duane so I can watch him glide effortlessly through paper-thin holes in the line.

A few weeks ago I had an extremely severe football attack. I could hardly remember my work. It seemed like the whole purpose of the week was to get over as quickly as possible to unite me and the Sunday Redskins-Jets game. Monday I spent worrying that the bumbling, boring Patriots would contaminate my TV screen and block Emerson Boozer and John Riggins and Rich Caster and Steve Tannen and the other 36 Jets plus the taxi squad from staging the impressive victory I fantasized play by play, the score reaching 210 to 0 by half-time, at which point George Allen hung himself.

That anxiety ended Tuesday when I read in the *Globe* that the Patriots were scheduled for the Monday night game. But there was still the tense wait until Saturday to check the week-end listings to make sure that all that anticipation I didn't see — "Sunday at 1, Channel 4, New Orleans at Buffalo; Channel 7, Houston at Philadelphia"—-and stalk furiously around the room like when I was a kid and the baseball game had been rained out.

By Saturday morning the final obstacle was cleared —the CBS executives and I both agreed the Jets-Redskins game was a top attraction.

I woke up Sunday Morning—D Day—after a frightening dream. I was on my deathbed, my life's goals unfulfilled and abandoned. There was a Godlike figure standing over me telling me there *was* a Hell and I was destined for it. My sentence was to be complete separation from the pain and joy of the people's struggle for revolution and—to fill my days—a non-stop diet of football games. I choked down that threatening specter, anesthetized myself by intellectualizing the dream into an "interesting" experience I would tell others about and be thought clever for, and applied myself mechanically to correspondence on the book about George Jackson we're distributing, while my mind kept wandering to, "If the Jets win that'll make them 6 and 2, if Miami loses . . . and even if Miami wins the wild-card slot will look pretty good."

Finally it was pre-game time. Pre-game time is game time for fanatics who just can't bear to wait for the actual game to start and spend an ecstatic hour watching filmed highlights of last week's games, close-up shots of Larry Little's favorite jock strap, and previews of the post-game wrap-up.

The pre-game show featured a film short about Arthur Modell, the owner of the Cleveland Browns. It showed Modell in a trench coat on the practice field with his team, yelling encouragement to "his boys," and patting a 28-year-old black player on the back with his rich white hands and saying, "Fine game, son." The narrator said, "Art Modell is an activist owner. Football is his whole life, his greatest joy . . . Well, almost. It was until four years ago when Art married the beautiful actress Dawn Fawn. Since then, while still maintaining an avid interest in his team, he has also fathered two children." And Dawn added, "Having a family has added a whole new dimension to Art's life."

They flashed to quarterback Mike Phipps throwing a long pass for a winning touchdown to Frank Pitts, and then panned to Modell, whose only relationship to that athletic accomplishment was that he signs the paychecks every week. Yet he was cheering, screaming, slapping his vice-presidents on the back as if he had thrown and caught the pass himself. In his psychotic ugliness, his vicarious, pompous, racist male arrogance, his fanatical fantasy world of ownership and conquest I saw myself, and got sick. What the hell was I doing on a Sunday afternoon sitting riveted into a seat watching this stupid game when there were books to read, woods to walk in, kids to play with, letters to write, music to sing and hear, football to be *played* and a genocidal war still so very much in progress and so much work needing to be done?

For the first time I faced my situation in its fullest truth: I was an addict. I knew exactly what was wrong, but couldn't stop myself from doing it. I'm attracted to football because after working to change the country at a time when Nixon and Kissinger are so unbearably powerful, after living in a decaying society where mistrust and self-hate sometimes form a deadening cloud of psychic pollution, I enjoy a game where I can imagine myself an owner instead of an owned. Like the 60,000 fans at the game, and the millions watching on the TV, like the 50-year-old fat slob who starts panting when he climbs a flight of stairs, I like to strut around the living room when MY TEAM makes a goal line stand, and scream irrationally when one of MY PLAYERS drops a pass. "That damn clumsy fool, we're gonna get rid of him next year, that bum." Like the steelworker and the office worker, like the millions of unhappy powerless people in this country, pro football allows me to be at best a triumphant owner, and at worst, a disappointed owner, until the game is over and the oppressed go back to being oppressed and the real owners go back to counting their gate receipts and TV royalties.

But my revulsion began to subside as Dick Stockton, a blond, Boston-based much-better-than-boring announcer, stood in front of the big board with "Jets" and "Redskins" marked on it. The opening kick-off butterflies were back again; this was a big game for me and I had to be on my toes. Stockton said, in a somber tone, "The game today between the Washington Redskins and the New York Jets will not be broadcast. Striking technicians have resorted to violence and sabotage and have destroyed our broadcasting equipment making it impossible for us to bring you this important game. I repeat, because of violence and sabotage on the part of the striking technicians this game will not be broadcast. Instead, we will bring you the also very exciting and key game. . . ."

When he said "violence" and "sabotage" Stockton's boyish white-bread-and-mayonnaise face curled up into an expression as close as I've ever seen to vomiting. I thought about thousands of oppressed workers pacing furiously in front of their sets, falling for Stockton's pro-management set-up and screaming, "Work all week so a bunch of damn workers can cut off *my* damn game. Sabotage my Sunday fun, just let me get my hands on those damn morons sabotaging other people's property like that."

I felt a little of that too, but this time some better feelings began to fight their way through. I was shocked, disappointed that a whole week's anticipation was shot by the slicing of some cables. But I was also feeling very happy. History is not made by the paralyzed and addicted. It isn't made by those who criticize the system and then participate in it. It's made by those who act, who work to destroy an evil system and help build something better in its place. I was smashed out of my reactionary fantasy by angry workers who were fighting for better working conditions and a cut of the fortune that CBS makes from their labor. Throughout my life I have learned my most valuable lessons from black people, Vietnamese, and women angrier than me who have pushed me to make a choice and helped me to scrape off layers of deadness to discover my own anger and purpose.

I am not in the vanguard of a people's movement against pro football. In fact, I am much more a part of the problem than of the solution. But when George Sauer quits and Duane Thomas torments millionaire owners and technicians sabotage the broadcast equipment I initially resent them, but really respect them for setting an example I'm too weak to set myself. As the liberation of Indochina is being led by the people of Indochina, as the liberation of prisons is being led by prisoners, the liberation of imperialist sports is being led, not by the addicted viewers, but by the most active participants who suffer its exploitation and dehumanization most bitterly.

Eric Mann lives in Boston, and is the author of Comrade George, *a book about George Jackson and the prison movement.*

So You Think You Know Football?

QUESTIONS AND ANSWERS

The Questions

(See Pages 208-213 for the Answers.)

Q. 1. How well do you know NFL rules?

(a) — A pass is complete when a receiver touches the ground with *both* feet inbounds and with the ball in his possession. If a receiver is carried out of bounds by an opponent, while he is in possession inbounds in the air, the pass is complete at the out-of-bounds spot. True or False.

(b) — If a forward pass is deflected by a defensive player and subsequently caught by an offensive player who is not normally an eligible receiver (such as a guard or center), the pass is ruled incomplete. True or False.

Q. 2. Only three players in history have gained 1,400 or more yards in a single season, and all go by the first name of Jim. One is Jim Brown of the Cleveland Browns, and another is Jim Taylor of the Green Bay Packers. If you can, name the third "Jim" to gain 1,400 or more yards in one season.

Jim Taylor

Q. 3. While we're on the subject of 1,000 yard gainers, the Chicago Bears have had three ball carriers to rush for that much in one season. There was Gale Sayers, of course, who gained 1,032 yards in 1969 and 1,231 in 1966. Another Bear to reach that plateau was Beattie Feathers who gained 1,004 yards in 1934. Can you name the third Bear rusher who topped 1,000 yards in one season? A clue: he played college ball at Florida.

Q. 4. During his career with the Cleveland Browns, (1957-1965), Jim Brown scored 126 touchdowns, an NFL record. Who scored the next most lifetime TD's? A hint: He was a great runner for the Baltimore Colts and is now retired.

Q. 5. Willie Ellison, the Ram's powerhouse running back, rushed for 247 yards against the New Orleans Saints in 1971 to set a new NFL single game record. Whose record for most yards gained rushing for a single game did he break?

Q. 6. Can you identify this player? He holds pro football's record for the most yards (4,007) gained passing in one season. He did it in 1967, when his team did not even win a division title. He is neither Johnny Unitas nor Sonny Jurgensen.

Q. 7. What two Hall of Fame members played their college football at Louisiana State University?

Q. 8. Three players hold the NFL record for kicking most points (9) after touchdown. Charlie Gogolak did it for the Washington Redskins vs. the New York Giants on Nov. 27, 1966, and Bob Waterfield did it for the Los Angeles Rams vs. Baltimore on Oct. 22, 1950. The third player to accomplish the feat is a member of Pro Football's Hall of Fame. He did it for the St. Louis Cardinals in 1948. Who is he?

Q. 9. Prior to 1963, what was the name of the New York entry in the American Football League?

Q. 10. Quarterback Bart Starr holds many Green Bay club records. One he doesn't, however, is for the most touchdown passes thrown in a single season. The best Starr has done is 16 TD passes during the 1965

Ronald Mrowiec

Bart Starr

of Alabama to go first in the history of the draft which dates back to 1936. The other Alabama product who was a No. 1 pick was also a quarterback. He was chosen first in 1948 by the Redskins and performed well in pro ball. Who is he? A clue: His first name was Harry.

Q. 15. This defensive lineman is still active, and in 1963 he became the first player from Grambling to be the No. 1 draft pick in the AFL. Who is he?

Q. 16. Notre Dame has had four of its players through the years become the No. 1 pro draft choice. One was quarterback Frank Dancewicz who was drafted No. 1 in 1943 by the old Boston Yanks. Another was Leon Hart, an end, drafted No. 1 in 1950 by the Detroit Lions. Name the other two ND alumni who were No. 1 in the pro draft.

Q. 17. The NFL record for most touchdown passes thrown in one season is 36. It is held jointly by two players, one of whom is Y. A. Tittle (he reached that figure in 1963 with the New York Giants). The other co-holder of the record was still active at the start of the 1973 season. Is he George Blanda, Johnny Unitas, Sonny Jurgensen or John Brodie?

Q. 18. One of pro football's all-time great quarterbacks was more noted for his passing than his kicking, yet he holds the NFL record for the best punting average (51.0 yards) for one season. Who is he?

Q. 19. How many of the following Pro Football Hall of Fame members can you identify:
a. Defensive tackle for the Pittsburgh Steelers, 1950-63.
b. End for the Philadelphia Eagles, 1947-55.
c. Quarterback for the Chicago Bears, 1939-50.
d. Halfback for the New York Giants, Green Bay Packers, 1946-61.
e. Defensive tackle for the San Francisco 49ers, 1950-63.

Q. 20. In 1965, the Dallas Cowboys drafted him on the 11th round, but he has come a long way since then and is one of the better defensive linemen in the NFL today. He attended Elizabeth City State College, stands 6-6, weighs 260, and is neither Bob Lilly, George Andrie or Larry Cole. Who is he?

Q. 21. Which of these infractions does not call for a 15-yard penalty: Clipping, fair catch interference, running into the kicker, ineligible receiver down field.

Q. 22. Don Hutson of the Packers holds the NFL record for most lifetime TD passes caught (100). At

and 1961 seasons. Two other Packer quarterbacks have done better than that. One played in the 1950's and the other in the 1940's.

Q. 11. In the 1971 draft, one AFC team selected quarterbacks on its first two choices. Name the two quarterbacks selected.

Q. 12. In 1962 a great running back from Syracuse was the No. 1 draft pick of the Washington Redskins, but he never got to play in pro ball because of a fatal illness. Who was he?

Q. 13. In that same year, 1962, the Oakland Raiders of the AFL drafted an outstanding quarterback who is still active but with a team in the NFC. Who is he?

Q. 14. When the Jets picked Joe Namath No. 1 in the 1965 AFL draft, he became the second alumnus

the start of the 1973 season, two active receivers were closing in on his career record. One receiver had 88 lifetime TD pass receptions, the other, 85. Who were they?

Q. 23. Which of these players scored the first points of Super Bowl I between the Packers and Chiefs in 1967: Elijah Pitts, Don Chandler, Max McGee or Curtis McClinton?

Q. 24. In Super Bowl V, a Johnny Unitas pass intended for Ed Hinton bounced out of Hinton's grasp, and Dallas defender Mel Renfro grazed the ball with an outstretched hand. That made the ball "alive" again for the offense, and a Baltimore receiver pulled it in and ran for a touchdown. Who was the ultimate receiver?

Q. 25. Only twice in Super Bowl history has a runner rushed for more than 100 yards in one game. That was in 1969 when the Jets defeated the Colts, 16-7. Can you name the two running backs (one from each club) who rushed for more than 100 yards in that game?

Q. 26. What three coaches never lost a Super Bowl game?

Q. 27. The 1970 official All-Pro team (selected by the Professional Football Writers of America) included only one player who appeared in Super Bowl V. He was (and is) a member of the Dallas Cowboys. Who is he?

Q. 28. The famed Jim Thorpe wore No. 3 in his playing days, but there is also one other member of Pro Football's Hall of Fame who wore No. 3 during his career in the NFL. Can you identify him? A clue. He was primarily a fullback.

Q. 29. "When John Brodie is hot," says Merlin Olsen of the Los Angeles Rams, "he's the best quarterback there is." There are many fans who undoubtedly agree with Olsen. However, there was a time earlier in his career when Brodie was not accorded such acclaim, particularly in San Francisco where he inherited the quarterbacking job from a player who was also booed by the local fans. Who was the quarterback for the 49ers preceding Brodie?

Q. 30. In 1960, Pete Rozelle was named commissioner of the National Football League, succeeding the late Bert Bell who died in October, 1959. Who was commissioner before Bell?

(See Pages 208-213 for the Answers.)

Q. 31. In March, 1967, the first combined player selection meeting of the old NFL and AFL was held, and the first player chosen was a former Michigan State defensive lineman. Who was he?

Q. 32. Which of the following place kickers holds the NFL record for the most field goals (7) in one game: Fred Cox, Jim Bakken, Gino Cappelletti, Jim Turner or Gary Yepremian?

Q. 33. The NFL record for most touchdown passes in one game is also seven and has been achieved by no less than five quarterbacks. Who were they?

Q. 34. In 1947, Charlie Trippi joined the Cardinals, then located in Chicago, and rounded out what became known at the time as football's "dream backfield." The Cardinals went on to win the NFL title that year. Can you name the three other members of that original "dream backfield"?

Q. 35. In 1958, the Baltimore Colts defeated the New York Giants in sudden death, 23-17, to win the NFL championship. Who scored the winning touchdown in that game?

Q. 36. The record for most touchdown passes for a quarterback's first two years is held by an active NFL star, who racked up 40 in a pair of 14-game seasons. Can you name him?

Q. 37. In the old All-America Football Conference, coach Paul Brown and the Cleveland Browns had the AAFC's all-time leading rusher and passer as their stars. Can you name them?

Q. 38. Can you name the NFL quarterback who led two different teams—the Los Angeles Rams and Philadephia Eagles—to league championship almost ten years apart—1951 and 1960?

Q. 39. In 1964, the Los Angeles Rams defensive line was known as the "Fearsome Foursome," and included Deacon Jones, Merlin Olsen and two other players now retired. Name the other two members of the Rams' front four.

Q. 40. He was the Detroit Lions' first draft pick in 1962, but joined the American Football League instead and became one of the AFL's best quarterbacks. In fact, a few years ago, he was rated by Joe Namath as "the best passer in the league." He's still active. Who is he?

Q. 41. On a hypothetical play, the innovative Dallas Cowboys come out of their huddle against the San Francisco 49ers and go into a full I-formation, with Walt Garrison, Mike Montgomery and Bob Hayes stacked behind quarterback Craig Morton. Tight end Mike Ditka fools the 49er defense by going in motion to the sideline and Morton connects to him on a long touchdown pass play. Can you tell why the play was called back by penalty?

Q. 42. When New England finished the 1971 season with a 21-7 victory over the Baltimore Colts, rookie quarterback Jim Plunkett wound up with a total of 19 TD passes for the year, second best by a rookie in history. Who was the quarterback who set the record for most TD passes as a rookie? A clue: He did it in 1948 for the New York Giants.

Q. 43. In 1971, the longest game in pro history was played between the Chiefs and Dolphins. Previously, the longest game was played in 1962 when the Dallas Texans won the American Football League championship in the second overtime period—17 minutes and 54 seconds after the end of regulation play. Who were the Texans' losing opponents in that game?

Q. 44 Who is the only rookie head coach ever to win a Super Bowl? He has been called the "Easy Rider," a tribute to the low pressure attitude by him and his staff.

Q. 45 In 1933, for the first time, the NFL divided into a Western and an Eastern Division and played a championship game to decide the title. In that game, the winning touchdown was scored on a flea-flicker pass and lateral. Name the teams in that game.

Q. 46. As a rookie starting quarterback in his first game in 1961 he suffered through a 53-0 defeat including being sacked twice for safeties. He played 11 years in Washington and Philadelphia without being on a winning team. Only Unitas, Brodie, Jurgensen,

Tarkenton, Tittle, Blanda and Layne have thrown for more career passing yards. Who is he?

Q. 47. What do the following men have in common? Lou Saban, Buster Ramsey, Hank Stram, Frank Filchock, Lou Rymkus, Sid Gillman, Sammy Baugh, and Eddie Erdelatz.

Q. 48. Tom Dempsey, now of Philadelphia and then of New Orleans, set the NFL record for the longest field goal with a 63-yard boot to beat the Detroit Lions in 1970. Can you name the kicker who held the record before Dempsey's kick?

Q. 49. Name the last player to lead the NFL in scoring who was not a kicker? Was it: Leroy Kelly of Cleveland, Gale Sayers of Chicago, Jim Brown of Cleveland or Lenny Moore of Baltimore?

Q. 50. Leading the league in scoring is quite an accomplishment. It usually takes around 120 points to win the title. But, one player stands far above all scoring leaders for he holds the one-year scoring record at 176 points. Is it Jim Turner (New York), Paul Hornung (Green Bay) or George Blanda (Oakland)?

Q. 51. Which one of these Hall of Famers played the fewest years in the NFL? Red Grange, Ernie Nevers or Charlies Trippi?

Q. 52. Once, because of a terrible blizzard, an NFL championship game was played indoors on a field only 80 yards long. The contest was a sellout success, but every time one team moved inside the 20-yard line they were moved back 20 yards to make up for the shortened field. Can you name the year of this historic game and the two teams involved?

Q. 53. One of the most remarkable records in NFL history is that set by a team which did not suffer a shutout in 274 consecutive games, a streak stretching from 1950 to 1971. Can you name the team?

Q. 54. In 1970, the San Francisco 49ers had the NFC's Rookie of the Year and the Buffalo Bills had the AFC's winner. Who were they?

Q. 55. Two of the most famous brother combinations in pro football are defensive linemen. Can you name the brothers who play one for Dallas and one for Baltimore, and those who play in the same defensive front for the LA Rams?

Sonny Jurgensen (9)

Nate Fine

(See Pages 208-213 for the Answers.)

Q. 56. Can you remember the all-time NFL record for most points scored by one team in one quarter? Was it: 41 by Green Bay, 38 by Baltimore, 47 by San Diego or 41 by Los Angeles?

Q. 57. Who was the first lineman to be selected No. 1 in the National Football League player draft? Was it: Leon Hart of Notre Dame, Ki Aldrich of Texas Christian or Bob Brown of Nebraska?

Q. 58. In the 1972 player draft what teams drafted the following top five collegians: Defensive end Walt Patulski of Notre Dame, defensive end Sherman White of California, tackle Lionel Antoine of Southern Illinois, running back-wide receiver Bob Moore of Oregon, and tight end Riley Odoms of Houston?

Q. 59. What rookie in 1971 led the Jets in combined yardage gained (769 rushing and 231 pass receiving)?

Q. 60. In 1971, what quarterback threw the most touchdown passes in the NFL? A clue: He played for a non-contender in the AFC, and also racked up the most yardage passing (3,075), most attempts (431) and most completions (233).

Q. 61. The 1952 roster of the San Francisco 49ers included the names of four players who are now members of Pro Football's Hall of Fame. Who are they?

Q. 62. In 1965, what American Football League team drafted both Gale Sayers (No. 1) and Mike Curtis (No. 3), but lost them to NFL teams?

Q. 63. Two of the AFC's best running backs teamed together as collegians in 1964 to help lead Syracuse to a berth in the Sugar Bowl. Who are they?

Q. 64. What two NFL clubs did quarterback Len Dawson play for before joining the Kansas City Chiefs?

Q. 65. What American Football Conference quarterback was traded from Pittsburgh in the NFL to the Detroit Lions in 1958 for quarterback Bobby Layne? Pittsburgh sweetened the pot by also giving up two draft choices to the Lions to get Layne.

Q. 66. Can you match up the schools where these pros played their college football?

RB	Tucker Frederickson, New York Giants	LSU
QB	Bob Berry, Atlanta Falcons	Auburn
DB	Johnny Robinson, Kansas City Chiefs	Ohio State
T	Ron Yary, Minnesota Vikings	Oregon
DB	Dick LeBeau, Detroit Lions	USC

Q. 67. Only seven players, going into the 1971 season, had scored 50 or more touchdowns by rushing in the history of pro football. They included Jim Brown (100), Jim Taylor (87), Steve Van Buren (71), Joe Perry (70), Lenny Moore (63), and Paul Hornung (50). The one player not listed in this group is currently active. Who is he?

Q. 68. Pro fans are familiar with the names of Deacon Jones, defensive end for the Los Angeles Rams; Buck Buchanan, defensive tackle for the Kansas City Chiefs; and Spider Lockhart, defensive back for the New York Giants. What are the real first names of these players?

Q. 69. This former running back for the old New York Yankees in the All-America Football Conference once rushed for the fantastic total of 250 yards in one game, an all-time record. He did it on Oct. 24, 1947 against the Chicago Rockets. His nickname was Spec. Can you identify him?

Q. 70. Can you identify this retired player: He holds the record for scoring the most points (15) in a Super Bowl game. Sorry we can't give you his team or the year, or we'll give it away.

Q. 71. Prior to 1972 it was 27 years since the Washington Redskins appeared in an NFL championship game. In 1945, they lost to the Cleveland Rams, 15-14, in the NFL title game. How many other times in the 1940s did the Redskins play in the NFL championship game: two times, three times, none?

Q. 72. Which of these former players is not in Pro Football's Hall of Fame: Otto Graham, George McAfee, Bill Dudley or George Connor?

Q. 73. Who was the only college linebacker ever to be the No. 1 draft choice in the history of pro football? A clue: He is still active.

Q. 74. For the 1972 season, there were no less than six former members of the Cleveland Browns "family" holding down head coaching jobs in the NFL. They were led, of course, by Paul Brown, head man of the Cincinnati Bengals. Name each of the other five Cleveland Browns "alumni" who were head coaches.

Q. 75. Texas schools have produced three players who are now members of Pro Football's Hall of

(See Pages 208-213 for the Answers.)

Fame. Quarterbacks Bobby Layne (Texas) and Sammy Baugh (TCU) are familiar names. But, there was a third Texas-bred player, a center, who also made it to the Hall of Fame. Who was he?

Q. 76. One of the best defensive tackles in the NFL, he was born in Canton, O., birthplace of pro football. Who is he?

Q. 77. This one-time Green Bay Packers running back has a career total of five TD's on kickoff returns tying him for the NFL record also held by Ollie Matson, Cardinals, and Gale Sayers, Bears. Who is he?

Q. 78. The record for pass interceptions is 14, and was set in 1952 by a rookie back of the Los Angeles Rams. He later played for the Chicago Cardinals and Detroit Lions, and when he retired in 1964 was rated among the game's great defensive backs.

Q. 79. It's quite an achievement for a quarterback to pass for 400 or more yards in one game. Joe Kapp has done it. So has Don Horn, Pete Beathard, Johnny Unitas, Joe Namath, Sonny Jurgensen, Fran Tarkenton and Dandy Don Meredith. But, only two players in history have passed for 500 or more yards in one game. One did it for the LA Rams in 1951 and the other for the NY Giants in 1962. Both are members of the Hall of Fame. Who are they?

Q. 80. Many fans have heard of Roy Riegels' famous wrong-way run in the 1929 Rose Bowl game, but which NFL player went 66 yards the wrong way and crossed his own goal to give the other team a safety? A clue: He is currently active, and completed his wrong-way mission in a game against the 49ers in 1964.

Q. 81. Archie Manning of the Saints was the second player picked in the 1971 college draft. What player was the No. 1 choice?

Q. 82. Fran Tarkenton, once again with the Vikings, was traded in 1967 from Minnesota to the Giants for four blue-chip draft choices. Those four choices helped the Vikings to become winners. Can you name three of the four draft choices the Vikes obtained through that trade?

Q. 83. In 1950, the Los Angeles Rams defeated the Cleveland Browns, 24-17, in the NFL championship game. Seven players in that game later became head coaches in pro football. They included Abe Gibron (Bears), Otto Graham (Redskins), Mac Speedie (Broncos) and Jerry Williams (Eagles). Name two of the other three players who became head

Fran Tarkenton

coaches in the pro ranks.

Q. 84. What do the following players have in common—Jim Plunkett, Blaine Nye, Lionel Alridge, Jim Turner and Randy Vataha?

Q. 85. In the 1972 draft, the Green Bay Packers, for the first time ever, chose a defensive back as their No. 1 draft pick. Who is he?

Q. 86. George Blanda of the Oakland Raiders, at age 46, is the oldest active player in the NFL. How many league championship games has he played in— one, two, four or seven?

Q. 87. Can you match these five players with their original pro team?

Linebacker Myron Pottios	Chicago Bears
Running Back Bill Triplett	Minnesota Vikings
Linebacker Chuck Howley	Pittsburgh Steelers
Quarterback Bob Berry	Cleveland Browns
Defensive Tackle	
Jim Kanicki	St. Louis Cardinals

Q. 88. In 1964, the Cleveland Browns won the NFL title, beating the Colts, 27-0 in the championship game. The Browns' offensive lineup included such standouts as Jim Brown, Gary Collins, Paul Warfield and Gene Hickerson. Who was the quarterback for Cleveland in that game?

(See Pages 208-213 for the Answers.)

QUESTIONS AND ANSWERS

THE ANSWERS

A. 1. The answer to the first question is *true*. In the pros, you must have both feet inbounds with the ball in possession for a legal reception, and you cannot drive an offensive receiver out of bounds before he touches the ground to nullify a reception.

Part two is *false*. Once a forward pass is deflected by a defensive player, all offensive players become eligible receivers.

A. 2. Jim Nance of Boston gained 1,458 yards in 1966. Jim Brown of Cleveland gained 1,400 or more yards in 1965 (1,544), 1964 (1,446), 1963 (1,863), 1961 (1,408), and 1958 (1,527). Jim Taylor gained 1,474 in 1962.

A. 3. Rick Casares is the only other Bear ball carrier who rushed for more than 1,000 yards. He rushed for 1,126 yards in 1956.

A. 4. Next to Jim Brown, Lenny Moore of the Baltimore Colts (1956-1967) has scored the most NFL lifetime touchdowns—113.

A. 5. Willie Ellison in 1971 broke the single game rushing record of 243 yards set by Cookie Gilchrist of Buffalo in a game against the New York Jets in 1963.

A. 6. Joe Namath of the Jets holds the NFL record for most yards gained passing (4,007) in one season.

A. 7. Hall of Fame members from LSU are quarterback Y. A. Tittle, elected in 1971, and halfback Steve Van Buren, elected in 1965.

A. 8. Pat Harder of the St. Louis Cardinals kicked nine points after touchdown in a game against the New York Giants on Oct. 17, 1948. The Cards won the game, 63-45.

A. 9. In 1962, the New York entry in the AFL was known as the Titans. The Titans that year finished dead last in the Eastern Division of the AFL with a 5-9-0 record. They had the worst defensive record in the AFL, allowing 423 points to be scored against them.

A. 10. Cecil Isbell holds the Green Bay Packers' club record for most TD passes in one season—24. He threw that many in 1942. Tobin Rote completed the next most TD passes in Green Bay history—18. He did it in 1956.

A. 11. In 1971, the Houston Oilers chose Dan Pastorini (Santa Clara) and Lynn Dickey (Kansas State) as their No. 1 and 2 draft picks.

Joe Namath

Clifton Boutelle

A. 12. Ernie Davis of Syracuse was selected No. 1 in the 1962 NFL draft, but died of leukemia before being able to use his great running talent.

A. 13. In 1962, the Oakland Raiders made Roman Gabriel of North Carolina State their No. 1 pick. Gabriel, of course, is now with the Los Angeles Rams.

A. 14. The Alabama alumnus who was the No. 1 pick in the 1948 draft was Harry Gilmer, chosen by the Redskins.

A. 15. First player from Grambling selected as a No. 1 draft choice is Buck Buchanan of the Kansas City Chiefs. That same year, 1963, the top NFL draft pick was Terry Baker, Oregon State quarterback.

A. 16. Other Notre Dame players who were No. 1 draft choices were Walt Patulski in 1972, and Paul Hornung in 1957.

A. 17. In 1961, when he was with Houston, George Blanda established the NFL record for most touchdown passes thrown in one season (36), a mark later equalled by Y. A. Tittle.

A. 18. In 1940, Sammy Baugh of the Washington Redskins had a punting average of 51.0 for 35 attempts, a NFL record.

A. 19. (a) Ernie Stautner, (b) Pete Pihos, (c) Sid Luckman, (d) Emlen Tunnell and (e) Leo Nomellini.

A. 20. Jethro Pugh who once complained "every defensive lineman we (the Dallas Cowboys) have (Lilly, Cole and Andrie) has scored a touchdown except me. Each time they score I'm right there waiting for a pitchout, but nobody will throw it to me." Jethro does a great job defensively. He should be worrying about TDs?

A. 21. Running into the kicker calls for a five-yard penalty. The rest of the infractions result in 15-yard assessments.

A. 22. At the start of the 1973 season, Don Maynard of the Jets had 88 lifetime TD pass receptions to his credit. Lance Alworth of the Cowboys had 85.

A. 23. Flanker Max McGee scored the first points in Super Bowl I. He hauled in a pass from Bart Starr for a 37-yard touchdown play in the first quarter against the Chiefs. McGee was filling in for ailing Boyd Dowler in the first Super Bowl game, and although he had caught only three passes during the regular season, he caught seven Starr passes against Kansas City, good for 138 yards and two TD's.

A. 24. Tight end John Mackey scored Baltimore's first touchdown on a deflected pass from Johnny Unitas in Super Bowl V. The play covered 75 yards.

A. 25. In the 1969 Super Bowl, Matt Snell of the Jets gained 121 yards rushing, and Tom Matte of the Colts, 116 yards.

A. 26. In Super Bowl competition, the late Vince Lombardi was 2-0, while Weeb Ewbank of the Jets and Don McCafferty of the Colts, are both 1-0.

A. 27. The only player in Super Bowl V who was selected to the 1970 official All-Pro team was Chuck Howley, outside linebacker for the Cowboys.

A. 28. Bronko Nagurski of the Bears wore No. 3 during most of his NFL career. He also briefly wore No. 16, but No. 3 was his official number.

A. 29. Hall of Famer Y. A. Tittle preceded John Brodie as quarterback with the 49ers. Tittle went to the Giants after leaving San Francisco.

A. 30. Elmer Layden preceded Bert Bell as commissioner of the National Football League. Layden, who had been head coach and athletic director at the University of Notre Dame, was commissioner from 1941 until 1946 when he resigned.

A. 31. In the first combined NFL-AFL draft in 1967, Bubba Smith, former MSU defensive lineman, was the first player chosen. He was picked by the Baltimore Colts.

A. 32. In a game against the Pittsburgh Steelers on Sept. 24, 1967, Jim Bakken of the St. Louis Cardinals kicked seven field goals, a NFL record.

A. 33. The five quarterbacks who have thrown seven touchdown passes in one game include: Sid Luckman (Chicago Bears vs. New York Giants on Nov. 14, 1943); Adrian Burk (Philadelphia vs. Washington, Oct. 17, 1954); George Blanda (Houston vs. New York, Nov. 19, 1961); Y. A. Tittle (New York Giants vs. Washington, Oct. 28, 1962), and Joe Kapp (Minnesota vs. Baltimore, Sept. 28, 1969).

A. 34. In addition to Charlie Trippi, the Cardinals' "dream backfield" of 1947 included Pat Harder, Paul Christman and Elmer Angsman.

Pat Harder

A. 35. In 1958, Alan Ameche crashed over from the one-yard line in 8:15 of overtime as the Baltimore Colts downed the New York Giants for the NFL title.

A. 36. The record for most touchdown passes thrown in a quarterback's first two years in the NFL is held by Fran Tarkenton, who threw 40 (18 and 22) in his first two years with the Minnesota Vikings (1961-62). However, in 11 years Tarkenton has played on teams with winning records only twice and he holds a personal won-loss record of 62-88-4.

A. 37. Marion Motley led the All-America Football Conference in rushing by gaining 3,024 yards and scoring 26 touchdowns in the league's four years (1946-49). Otto Graham quarterbacked those great teams, passing for 10,085 yards for 86 touchdowns and completing 56 percent of his passes over the same period. Both are Hall of Famers.

A. 38. Norm Van Brocklin quarterbacked the 1951 Rams and 1960 Eagles to NFL championships.

A. 39. In addition to Deacon Jones and Merlin Olsen, the Los Angeles Rams front four in 1968 included Rosey Grier (290 pounds) and Lamar Lundy (260). With Jones weighing about 260 and Olsen about 270, opposing lines had to contend with more than a half ton of Ram defenders.

A. 40. John Hadl, now quarterback of the Los Angeles Rams, was the Lions' first draft pick in 1962.

A. 41. In the hypothetical situation, Dallas started the play with seven linemen and four backs. When Ditka went in motion, he left the line of scrimmage and became a back. The penalty for not having seven linemen on the line of scrimmage and an illegal man in motion is five yards from the spot where the play started.

A. 42. The rookie record by a quarterback for the most TD passes thrown in one season is held by Charley Conerly. He threw 22 TD passes for the Giants in 1948.

A. 43. In 1962, the Dallas Texans defeated the Houston Oilers, 20-17, in what, up to that point, was pro football's longest game. Rookie Tommy Brooker kicked a 25-yard field goal for the Texans, ending the Oilers' two-year reign as AFL champions. The game was played in Houston's Jeppessen Stadium.

A. 44. Don McCafferty of the Baltimore Colts won the Super Bowl in 1971, his rookie year as a head coach.

A. 45. The 1933 championship game, first of its kind, was between the New York Giants and Chicago Bears. In Chicago, before 26,000 fans, Bronko Nagurski lobbed a pass over the line to Bill Hewitt (playing without a helmet). Hewitt then lateraled to Bill Karr who went in for the winning touchdown to give the Bears a 23-21 triumph.

A. 46. He is Norm Snead of the New York Giants. It was the Giants who whipped Snead's Redskins in 1961 by the 53-0 humiliation. Snead's coach today, Alex Webster, was a running back for that 1961 New York team and an assistant today, Jim Katcavage, threw Snead for one of the day's two safeties.

A. 47. They are the original coaches of the AFL teams in 1960. Here they are matched with their teams: Lou Saban—Boston Patriots, Buster Ramsey—Buffalo Bills, Hank Stram—Dallas Texans, Frank

Filchock—Denver Broncos, Lou Rymkus—Houston Oilers, Sid Gilman—Los Angeles Chargers, Sammy Baugh—New York Titans, Eddie Erdelatz—Oakland Raiders.

A. 48. The field goal record before Tom Dempsey's record kick of 63 yards was held by Bert Rechichar of the Baltimore Colts with a 56-yarder in 1953 against the Bears.

A. 49. Leroy Kelly of the Cleveland Browns was the last player to lead the NFL in scoring by rushing and pass receiving, not kicking. In 1968, he scored 120 points with 20 touchdowns.

A. 50. Green Bay's versatile running back Paul Hornung set the NFL single season scoring record with 176 points in 1960. He scored 15 touchdowns and kicked 41 extra points and 15 field goals.

A. 51. Harold "Red" Grange played with the Chicago Bears in 1925, 1929-34, with the New York Yankees (AFL) in 1926, and with the Yankees of the NFL in 1927. So, he played in the NFL eight years. Ernie Nevers, inducted with Grange in 1963, played with the Duluth Eskimos (1926-27) and the Chicago Cardinals (1928-31), a total of five years. Charlie Trippi, inducted in 1968, played halfback-quarterback for the Chicago Cardinals from 1947 to 1955, nine years. So, Ernie Nevers played the fewest seasons in the NFL of these three players.

A. 52. The indoor championship was played between the Chicago Bears and Portsmouth (O.) Spartans to decide the 1932 NFL title. The Bears won 9-0 on a touchdown and safety. "I was lying on my back in the endzone when Bronko Nagurski threw one of his famous end-over-end passes to me for the touchdown," recalls Red Grange, now retired in Florida. "They're still arguing whether he was five yards behind the line of scrimmage or not, as you had to be to throw a pass in those days.

"A circus had just played the Chicago Stadium and so when the blizzard struck (Owner George) Halas got the idea to move the game indoors. An important change came from that game. Because of the closeness of the walls, we moved the ball into the center of the field after each play. The next year Halas suggested putting hash marks on the field and the NFL adopted it."

A. 53. The team was the Cleveland Browns, which scored in 274 consecutive games between 1950 and 1971. The Bears shut out the Browns 17 to 0 in 1972, and the Denver Broncos broke the Browns' string with a 27-0 whipping in 1971, the first shutout since the Giants did it in 1950. Green Bay is the runnerup to this consecutive games scoring record with 156 (1958-69).

A. 54. The 1970 NFC Rookie of the Year was San Francisco's Bruce Taylor, older brother of pro basketball player Brian Taylor, and the AFC Rookie of the Year was quarterback Dennis Shaw, who completed 178 of 321 passes in his first season.

A. 55. Two of the most famous NFL brother combinations are Bubba and Tody Smith, playing for Dallas and Baltimore, and the Olsen brothers, Phil and Merlin, of Los Angeles.

A. 56. The most points scored by one team in one quarter is 41, a record held jointly by Green Bay (set in 1945) and Los Angeles (set in 1950).

A. 57. The first lineman ever selected No. 1 in the National Football League draft, which began in 1936, was Ki Aldrich of Texas Christian, picked by the Chicago Cardinals in 1939.

A. 58. Walt Patulski was drafted by Buffalo, Sherman White by Cincinnati, Lionel Antoine by Chicago, Bob Moore by St. Louis, and Riley Odoms by Denver.

A. 59. John Riggins, a rookie from Kansas State, was the first man in the history of the New York Jets to lead the club in combined offense when he gained 1,000 yards during the 1971 season.

A. 60. John Hadl of the San Diego Chargers

John Hadl

threw the most TD passes (21) in the National Football League in 1971. Bob Griese of the Dolphins and Jim Plunkett of the Patriots had the next most TD passes—19.

A. 61. Members of Pro Football's Hall of Fame who were listed on the 1952 San Francisco 49ers roster included quarterback Y. A. Tittle, running backs Joe Perry and Hugh McElhenny, and tackle Leo Nomellini.

Leo Nomellini

A. 62. In 1965, the Kansas City Chiefs drafted Gale Sayers No. 1, lost to the Bears, and Mike Curtis No. 3, lost to the Colts.

A. 63. As collegians, Floyd Little of the Denver Broncos and Jim Nance of the New England Patriots teamed up in the backfield at Syracuse in 1964 to lead the Orangemen to the Sugar Bowl in January, 1965 when they lost to LSU, 13-10.

A. 64. After coming out of Purdue University, Len Dawson played for the Pittsburgh Steelers, 1957-59 and the Cleveland Browns, 1960-61. He spent a year with Dallas in the AFL, 1962, before moving on to the Kansas City Chiefs.

A. 65. Earl Morrall of the Colts was traded from the Steelers to the Lions in 1958 for Bobby Layne.

A. 66. Here is the correct match-up of players and their schools:
RB Tucker Frederickson, Giants (Auburn), QB Bob Berry, Falcons (Oregon), DB Johnny Robinson, Chiefs (LSU), T Ron Yary, Vikings (USC), DB Dick Lebeau, Lions (Ohio State).

A. 67. Leroy Kelly of the Cleveland Browns was the only other player in pro football history to have scored 50 or more career touchdowns rushing.

A. 68. The correct names of the players mentioned are Carl (Spider) Lockhart of the Giants, David (Deacon) Jones of the Rams, and Junious (Buck) Buchanan of the Chiefs.

A. 69. Orban (Spec) Sanders set the all-time one-game rushing record (250 yards) when he was with the old New York Yankees in the AAC.

Orban (Spec) Sanders

A. 70. Kicker Don Chandler of the Green Bay Packers holds the record for scoring the most points in a single Super Bowl game. In 1968, when the Packers downed the Oakland Raiders, 33-14, he scored 15 points on four field goals and three extra points.

A. 71. The Washington Redskins were a powerhouse in the 1940's, appearing in four NFL title games during that decade. In addition to the 1945 game, their appearances in the NFL championship game produced the following results: 1943 — Bears 24, Redskins, 14; 1942 — Redskins, 14, Bears, 6; and 1940—Bears, 73, Redskins, 0.

A. 72. George Connor of the Chicago Bears is not a member of Pro Football's Hall of Fame.

A. 73. Tommy Nobis of the Falcons was the only college linebacker (Texas) to be No. 1 draft choice. Atlanta chose him as No. 1 in 1966.

A. 74. In addition to Paul Brown, members of the Cleveland Browns' "alumni" who are now head coaches in the NFL include Abe Gibron of the Bears, Don Shula of the Dolphins, Chuck Noll, Steelers; Weeb Ewbank, Jets; and Lou Saban, Bills.

A. 75. The other Texas-bred Hall of Famer is Clyde (Bulldog) Turner, the great center of the Chicago Bears who played his college football at Hardin-Simmons.

A. 76. Alan Page of the Vikings, most valuable player in the NFL in the 1971 season, was born in Canton, O.

A. 77. Travis Williams.

A. 78. Dick (Night Train) Lane holds the NFL record for most pass interceptions, 14, in one season, set in 1952 when he was a rookie with the Rams.

A. 79. Hall of Famers Norm Van Brocklin (554 yards vs. NY Yanks in 1951) and Y.A. Tittle (505 yards vs. Washington Redskins in 1962) are the only two NFL quarterbacks ever to pass for more than 500 yards in a single game.

A. 80. Jim Marshall of Minnesota recovered a 49er fumble and ran 66 yards the wrong way to cross the Viking goal, giving San Francisco a safety. Minnesota won the game, nonetheless, 27-22.

A. 81. Jim Plunkett, who led the New England Patriots to a 6-8 season, was the No. 1 draft choice in 1971.

A. 82. The four draft choices obtained by the Vikings in trading Tarkenton to the Giants in 1967 turned out to be: Clinton Jones (Michigan State), Bob Grim (Oregon State), Ron Yary (Southern California) and Ed White (California).

A. 83. Future pro coaches who played in the 1950 NFL championship game also included Tom Fears (New Orleans Saints), Norm Van Brocklin (Minnesota Vikings and Atlanta Falcons) and Bob Waterfield (Los Angeles Rams).

A. 84. All played college football for John Ralston, head coach of the Denver Broncos.

A. 85. He is Willie Buchanon of San Diego State. In his senior year at SDS, only 12 of 46 passes thrown to Willie's man were completed and in his junior year only 11 passes were completed to his man in 11 games!

A. 86. Blanda has played in seven league championship games—with the Chicago Bears (1956), Houston Oilers (1960-61-62) and Oakland Raiders (1967-68-69).

A. 87. Myron Pottios started his pro career with the Steelers. Bill Triplett started with the Cardinals, Chuck Howley with the Bears, Bob Berry with the Vikings and Jim Kanicki with the Browns.

A. 88. The man who directed the Cleveland Browns' offense in 1964 was the thinking man's quarterback, Frank Ryan, who holds a doctorate degree in mathematics.

Jim Plunkett

HOW TO BEAT THE ZONE DEFENSE

It shuts off 'the bomb'
but it also
has built-in weaknesses

THE PROBLEM WITH the zone defense, as Pete Rozelle, commissioner of all the footballs, sees it is that the announcers, advertisers and network vice presidents don't like it.

Their own color men keep talking about how the zone shuts off the long bomb. This cuts down on scoring, and in the viewership-seller equation anything that cuts down on scoring means a dull game, and dull games mean people switching hair sprays.

It's a not unfamiliar argument. Scoring means excitement and what's more exciting than a Bob Hayes or Paul Warfield engaging in a 40-yard footrace with a corner back and a strong safety? Every game should end 89 to 88 with the winning points scored on the last play of the game. That's the old basketball on the grass cliché. Their next move is to outlaw tackling.

These are the same people who said the Super Bowl was a bomb because the Dallas Cowboys ground down the Miami Dolphins in so methodical a fashion, completely ignoring the finesse and execution the Cowboys brought into that game.

The real problem is not with the zone defense. The real problem is that maybe the TV guys really don't like football. To the real fan every game presents its own unique situations and the real enjoyment lies in how the teams rise or fail to rise to the challenges.

The zone defense has been around for a long time. It has brought no real fundamental changes to the game. The change that has come into the game recently that has lowered the scoring—is a return to the running game by all of the winning teams. Besides being less chancy, running the ball eats up the clock, and the longer it takes to score, the fewer chances there are to score.

Do you think the network moguls will want to outlaw the run and the zone as soon as they wise up to this?

After giving the problem, as they think the viewers see it, their deepest consideration, the TV boys, came to the conclusion that they ought to change the field. So, they moved the hash marks in about three yards closer to the middle of the field.

The theory is that the offense will now have a little more room to work with on the short side of the field and will make the defenses perhaps a little more hesitant about revolving to the strong side of the field.

Let's stop here a minute and briefly explain how a zone works, one basic variation anyway. You're on defense and the wide side of the field is to your left and you're in a revolve to the wide side. Here's what happens:

The left cornerback plays bump and run with the wide receiver on that side. The left corner linebacker drops back to the left hash mark, and about 12 yards deep. The middle linebacker drops into a position midway between the two hash marks, and the weak side linebacker drops back to the right hash mark.

The strong safety plays the deep left one-third of the field. The free safety plays the deep middle third and the right cornerback plays the deep right third of the field.

The rule makers think that by moving the hash marks in towards the middle of the field they're going to give the defense all kinds of problems, such as not being able to find the hash marks. Clever.

Makes you wonder if they've stopped to think what this is going to do to the offense. Every team runs the quick out. Three steps up and then into the sideline. What's going to happen to that timing between the quarterback and the receiver, built up over several years of working together, now that the sideline ain't where it used to be?

You also have to wonder what's going to happen to the two-minute drill. Reading the hash marks and field numbers to get out of bounds with the ball was an integral part of the coordination between the receiver and passer. After all, it's the offense that is the highly tuned, finely coordinated part of the game. On defense they go on desire, emotion and instinct.

This brings us to the real argument, which is that the zone defense is an offense problem, not a defensive problem. They're attacking the effects and not the cause when they try, without even realizing what they're doing, to punish the defense because they're doing their job better than the offense is doing theirs.

It's an offensive problem and the real solution, or at least a counter thrust will be provided by some imaginative coach who breaks his mind free of the collective, copyish kind of thinking that is now so com-

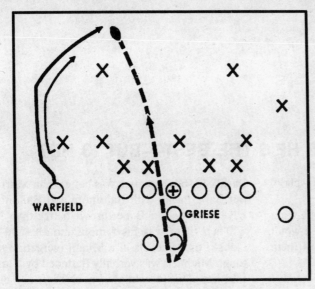

Nixon's Proposed Play

Over-simplified, perhaps, but President Nixon had the right stratagem to beat the zone.

mon in the game.

When it comes down to that, maybe President Nixon should be coaching the Washington Redskins instead of George Allen, but more about that in a minute.

The zone does one thing well. It shuts off the long scoring bomb. Theoretically, that is. There is always the chance that there will be a personnel or communication breakdown somewhere. Didn't the Dolphins hit on one for about 75 yards against the vaunted zone of the Baltimore Colts?

That's what the zone is supposed to do. It cuts down the chances of the quick, cheap score. The cornerback and three linebackers form a wall across the field anywhere from 12 to 20 yards from the line of scrimmage. The deep backs, divide the field into thirds and drop back as deep as 40 yards.

Now that leaves an awful lot of room in front of the linebackers and between the linebackers and the deep backs. That means the zone has certain built-in weaknesses.

It's vulnerable to the short swing pass to a running back. It's vulnerable to a back finding the gap on the short side between the linebacker and the deep back.

A tight end can have a, pardon the expression, field day, running hooks and curls and slants between the linebackers and in the open zone between the linebackers and the deep backs.

It's vulnerable to sweeps being run away from the revolve. On third and medium, five or six yards, a lot of quarterbacks are going to the weak side run because they know the defense will be in an automatic strong side revolve. And they're picking it up. On second and long, when they know the linebackers are going to make a quick deep drop, the quarterbacks are starting to call quick traps and draw plays.

Some teams come out of their zone and go into a straight man-to-man whenever the offense gets down

to their 25-yard line. Other teams wait a few yards longer, but the closer a defense is pushed to its own goal line the more apt it is to be forced out of its zone because there's no longer room on the field to run a deep pass pattern.

If it was a good man you were up against you'd counter him with another good man. You try to beat their strength with your strength. The zone is a formation, not a man, so you counter it with another formation.

There are two easy ways to beat the zone. One is to put both wide receivers to the same side of the field and then go to your tight end. The old Master, Vince Lombardi, always went to his tight end against the zone.

Another, and this will probably be the formation of the next couple of years, is to use a wing formation.

There is nothing in the rules of football that say you have to play with only two wide receivers. Nowhere does it say that one end has to position himself close to a tackle. Why not use three wide receivers? Or four?

Diagram this one. Split a wide receiver and a flanker to one side of the field. Split another wide receiver to the other side. Bring one running back into a semi-wing position behind either tackle.

Now you have what amounts to four wide receivers while still retaining the threat of two running backs. From that formation the offense has a million possibilities. Several anyway.

And President Nixon wasn't far wrong when he told Don Shula that a quick slant to Warfield was the way to beat the Cowboy's zone. It was, and it still is. It's not Warfield's fault, or the fault of the basic idea, that they never got the ball to him.

When it comes right down to it, beating the zone is a football problem and not a network problem. All it takes is a little patience.

JOE NAMATH SAYS HE'S THE BEST—BUT IS HE?

JOE NAMATH still remembers what his high school coach once told him.

"My high school coach said something to the team once. He told us, 'If you don't dream about it, it won't happen.' I've dreamed about things and a lot of them have come true."

Maybe that's the way the sleepy-eyed, mop-headed quarterback of the New York Jets meant it when he said, "I think I'm the best quarterback in football, and those who don't think so, well, we'll wait and see."

The occasion, of course, was the announcement of Joe's signing his new two-year contract. Estimates put his annual salary at $250,000, or about $10,000 a completion. The part-time movie star who—going into the 1972 season—had missed 19 of the Jets last 26 regular season games was defending his right to that kind of money.

"There are a lot of reasons," he said. "New York is the biggest city in the country. The Jets are the only team it has. The Giants are terrible.

"If the Jets are to win they have to hire me, or one just as capable. Or they have to get one out of the washing machine." No one has yet asked Joe Willie to explain that strange allusion to washing machines, unless he's going into the laundry franchise business.

But he still had more to say; "I think I can play better than anyone. They don't have to take a gamble on me. They know what I can do."

Is Joe Willie Namath, *the* Joe Willie Namath from Beaver Falls, Alabama, Miami, Hollywood, the guy they call "Broadway Joe" really the best quarterback in the game?

We have it on his word that he is. Does he really mean it, or is he just dreaming, hoping it'll all come true?

Joe must certainly believe by now that saying it makes it come true. It was his mouth almost as much as his arm that beat the Baltimore Colts on that gray day in the Orange Bowl in Super Bowl III.

Before the teams lined up for picture taking day in Miami, Joe was putting the knock on his rival quarterback, Earl Morrall. He said that Daryle Lamonica of the Oakland Raiders, who he beat for the American Football League championship, was far and away a better quarterback than Morrall, who was Player of the Year in the National Football League.

He went even further and said that Vito "Babe" Parilli, his backup man, was better than Morrall. "You put Babe Parilli with Baltimore and Baltimore might have been better. Babe throws better than Morrall."

Then there was his famous mouth fight with the Colts' Lou Michaels in a Miami recreation spot. The tough Michaels was verbally flattened by Namath who told him, "we're going to knock the . . . . out of you guys." That from a 17-point underdog.

"Haven't you ever heard of the word 'modesty?'" Michaels asked. Anyone who knew Joe could have told him he was asking a silly question.

"We're going to beat you and pick you apart," said Namath, who was just warming to his fun.

It's really not necessary to go any further. The Colts went out there trying to make Namath eat his words. All they did was look silly, because while Namath was waving the cape, the rest of the Jets were stampeding over the Colts.

Is there really a way, though, to measure Namath's self-proclaimed greatness? Well, one way is to look at the records. How have the Jets done since Namath walked into Shea Stadium with his overnight bag stuffed full of Sonny Werblin's money?

The first year, 1965, they were a loser. The next season they were a .500 club. In 1967 he had his finest year, setting an all-time pro record of 4,007 yards through the air with 26 touchdowns. The team won eight games. The next year they won it all, and the year after that they were ten and four but lost to the Kansas City Chiefs in the playoffs. In 1970, Namath played in only the first five games before getting his wrist broken against the Baltimore Colts. The team was one and four at that point. Make your own judgment.

The 1971 season, in which he played only in the last four games, we can just ignore. The Jets were finished before he came back.

Another way would be to compare Joe's first six seasons against those of another quarterback. Take John Unitas. We don't take Unitas because he is Unitas, especially, but because he was thrust into play by the Colts when their regular quarterback, George Shaw, was injured. He started out his rookie year the same as Namath without getting any of that bench and head-set education.

But then again what would be unfair about comparing Joe to John? Joe did say he was the greatest,

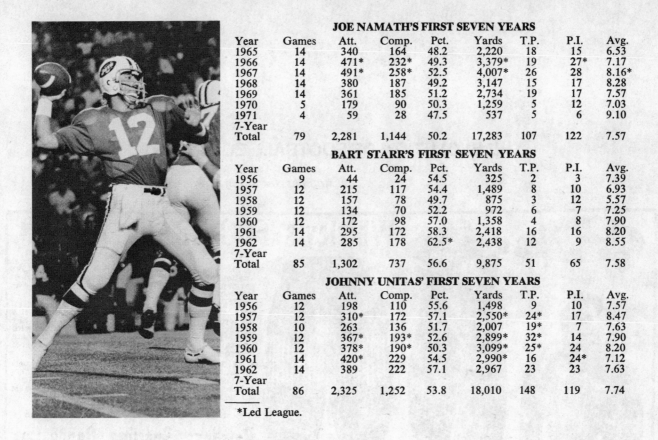

JOE NAMATH'S FIRST SEVEN YEARS

Year	Games	Att.	Comp.	Pct.	Yards	T.P.	P.I.	Avg.
1965	14	340	164	48.2	2,220	18	15	6.53
1966	14	471*	232*	49.3	3,379*	19	27*	7.17
1967	14	491*	258*	52.5	4,007*	26	28	8.16*
1968	14	380	187	49.2	3,147	15	17	8.28
1969	14	361	185	51.2	2,734	19	17	7.57
1970	5	179	90	50.3	1,259	5	12	7.03
1971	4	59	28	47.5	537	5	6	9.10
7-Year Total	79	2,281	1,144	50.2	17,283	107	122	7.57

BART STARR'S FIRST SEVEN YEARS

Year	Games	Att.	Comp.	Pct.	Yards	T.P.	P.I.	Avg.
1956	9	44	24	54.5	325	2	3	7.39
1957	12	215	117	54.4	1,489	8	10	6.93
1958	12	157	78	49.7	875	3	12	5.57
1959	12	134	70	52.2	972	6	7	7.25
1960	12	172	98	57.0	1,358	4	8	7.90
1961	14	295	172	58.3	2,418	16	16	8.20
1962	14	285	178	62.5*	2,438	12	9	8.55
7-Year Total	85	1,302	737	56.6	9,875	51	65	7.58

JOHNNY UNITAS' FIRST SEVEN YEARS

Year	Games	Att.	Comp.	Pct.	Yards	T.P.	P.I.	Avg.
1956	12	198	110	55.6	1,498	9	10	7.57
1957	12	310*	172	57.1	2,550*	24*	17	8.47
1958	10	263	136	51.7	2,007	19*	7	7.63
1959	12	367*	193*	52.6	2,899*	32*	14	7.90
1960	12	378*	190*	50.3	3,099*	25*	24	8.20
1961	14	420*	229	54.5	2,990*	16	24*	7.12
1962	14	389	222	57.1	2,967	23	23	7.63
7-Year Total	86	2,325	1,252	53.8	18,010	148	119	7.74

*Led League.

didn't he? But he didn't specify if he meant for one season, until he's through playing, or for all time. Maybe the comparison would be unfair to John. We'll see.

In his first six years with the Jets, Joe Willie Namath passed for 102 touchdowns, but he had 116 interceptions, and in only three of those years did his completion percentage get above .500. That's a rather low figure, considering his greatness, but Joe had a reason for why it is what it is.

He said it was because he threw most of his passes to his wide receivers who run the longer, deeper, harder-to-complete patterns. "I could have completed 80 per cent if I dropped the ball off to my backs like they do in their (NFL) league," Joe responded to a critic.

As far as his rather high ratio of interceptions to touchdown passes goes Joe has been rather quiet.

In many respects Joe Namath is a perfectionist as well as being an extremely gifted athlete. He has a marvelous arm, takes a great deal of pride in getting back and setting up quickly, and has a hair-trigger release. He is very sharp in reading the defensive coverage as soon as or before the play starts.

He does have one flaw, however, and it is mainly that one flaw that has been responsible for so many of his interceptions. In all his years in football Namath has never overcome the basic fault of throwing off his back foot. He apparently thinks his arm will do all the work. It results in his throwing some sailers that are easy pick-offs by the deep men in the zones.

Unitas started his blitz on the all-time records during the 1956 season. He passed for nine touchdowns, had 10 interceptions, and a completion percentage of 55.6 that first year. By the end of his sixth year he had thrown 125 touchdown passes, had 96 interceptions, and never had a season when his completion percentage was under .500.

Namath took the Jets to the Super Bowl in four years. Well, Unitas had a world's championship in three years, beating the Giants in the sudden-death game in 1958, and repeating the following year as world champions. Not perfect, but then Unitas never said he was the greatest.

All this is not to put Namath down. He's an exciting and a colorful performer and it's a pleasure to have him around. It's just to measure the deeds against the mouth.

All his life Joe Namath has been characterized as, lonely, defiant, cocky. All his life he's been told he's the greatest!

But, when Namath himself said he was No. 1, he established a personal challenge he will be hard-pressed to meet.

And, the verdict won't be in until he peels off his jersey for the last time.

THE EVOLUTION OF FOOTBALL EQUIPMENT

Illustrations courtesy of Rawlings Sporting Goods Company

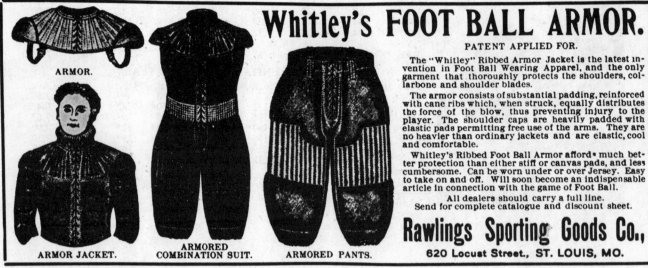

Whitley's FOOT BALL ARMOR.

PATENT APPLIED FOR.

The "Whitley" Ribbed Armor Jacket is the latest invention in Foot Ball Wearing Apparel, and the only garment that thoroughly protects the shoulders, collarbone and shoulder blades.

The armor consists of substantial padding, reinforced with cane ribs which, when struck, equally distributes the force of the blow, thus preventing injury to the player. The shoulder caps are heavily padded with elastic pads permitting free use of the arms. They are no heavier than ordinary jackets and are elastic, cool and comfortable.

Whitley's Ribbed Foot Ball Armor afford● much better protection than either stiff or canvas pads, and less cumbersome. Can be worn under or over Jersey. Easy to take on and off. Will soon become an indispensable article in connection with the game of Foot Ball.

All dealers should carry a full line.
Send for complete catalogue and discount sheet.

Rawlings Sporting Goods Co.,
620 Locust Street., ST. LOUIS, MO.

ARMOR. ARMOR JACKET. ARMORED COMBINATION SUIT. ARMORED PANTS.

Advertisement circa 1902

1895

1919

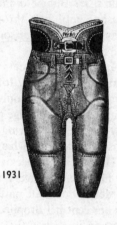

1931

1909

1909

1911

1916

1916

1920

**KIDNEY, HIP AND
SPINE PROTECTOR**

1924

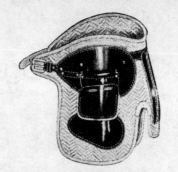

HIP PAD

1933

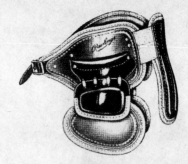

HIP CUSHION

1955

SHOULDER PADS

1898

1909

1916

1920

1919

1919

**SHIN
GUARD**

1898

**THIGH
GUARD**

1934

ZUPPKE SHOULDER PAD

1928

RU SHOULDER PAD

1931

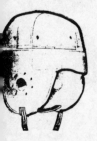

1921

1926

1935

1937

1947

1950

The Official's Signals

Offside, Encroaching Free Kick Violation
Hands on hips

Crawling, Pushing or Helping Runner
Pushing movement of hands to front with arms downward

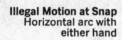 

Illegal Motion at Snap
Horizontal arc with either hand

Illegal Forward Pass
Waving hand behind back
Intentional Grounding of Pass
Same as above followed by raised hand flung downward

First Down
Arm raised then pointed toward defensive team's goal.

Interference With Fair Catch or Forward Pass
Pushing hands forward from shoulder with hands vertical

Holding
Grasping of one wrist
at chest level

**Illegal Use
of Hands**
Grasping wrist, palm
away, pushing
motion

PERSONAL FOUL
Striking of one
wrist above head
**Running into or
Roughing Kicker—**
Followed by a
swinging leg
Running into Passer—
Followed by raised
arm swung forward
Tripping—
Followed by hooking
foot behind
opposite ankle
Clipping—(Below Waist)
Followed by striking
back of calf with hand
Clipping—(Above Waist)
Following by striking
back of thigh with hand

**Delay of Game or
Excess Time-Out**
Folded arms
Illegal Formation
Same signal followed
by over and over
rotation of forearms
in front of body

**Touchdown, Field Goal
or Successful Try**
Both arms extended
above head

Safety
Palms together
over head

Loss of Down
(Follows signal for
foul) Tapping both
shoulders with
finger tips

**Penalty Refused,
Incomplete Pass,
Play Over, or Missed Goal**
Shifting of hands
in horizontal plane

Unsportsmanlike Conduct
Arms outstretched, palms down
(Same signal means continuing
action fouls are disregarded.)

**Dead Ball or Neutral
Zone Established**
One arm aloft open
hand (With fist
closed—Fourth Down)

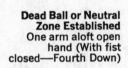

Time-Out
Hands criss-crossed
over head
Referee's Time-Out
Same signal followed
by placing one hand
on top of cap
Touchback
Same signal followed
by arm swung at side

**No Time-Out or
Time-In With Whistle**
Full arm circles to
simulate winding clock

**Ineligible Receiver
Downfield**
Both hands placed on cap

The Records

Super Bowl I

GREEN BAY PACKERS 35   KANSAS CITY CHIEFS 10

AT LOS ANGELES, CALIF., JAN. 15, 1967

In the opening game of the Super Bowl series, a crucial interception by Green Bay safety man Willie Wood in the third period put the skids under the Kansas City Chiefs who had come on the field in the second half trailing the Packers only 14-10.

With three onrushing Packer defenders trying to pounce on him, quarterback Len Dawson of the Chiefs threw the ball into the arms of Wood who ran it all the way back to the Kansas City five-yard line.

"That was the key play," admitted Dawson. "I never should have thrown the ball."

From the five, Elijah Pitts ran in for the score and the conversion by Don Chandler made it, 21-10, and it was downhill the rest of the way for the Packers.

During the second half, the Chiefs failed to get past Green Bay's 45-yard line, and Bart Starr literally picked their defense apart.

Throwing mostly to flanker Max McGee, who was filling in for ailing Boyd Dowler, Starr hit 16 out of 23 attempts for 250 yards.

Two of his passes were pulled in by McGee for touchdown romps of 37 and 13 yards. McGee finished with seven completions good for 138 yards. During the regular season, McGee had caught only three passes.

The Chiefs put their ten points on the board in the second quarter. Dawson hit Curtis McClinton for a seven yard touchdown pass, and Mike Mercer later kicked a 31-yard field goal.

During intermission, Green Bay's defensive strategy for the second half was spelled out by assistant coach Phil Bengston: "We ought to blitz more to neutralize their play action passes and get to the quarterback more," he said.

Early in the second half, Lee Roy Caffey blitzed along with two other Packer defenders and Caffey nicked Dawson's pass intended for Fred Arbanas. The wayward ball was gathered in by Wood who raced 50 yards to set up the subsequent five-yard TD run by Pitts.

Before the game, Chiefs' cornerback Fred Williamson had predicted he would destroy Packer ball carriers with his "hammer blow," a kind of karate chop.

With three minutes left to play in the final period and with the Packers in complete command, Williamson ironically was knocked cold trying to tackle halfback Donny Anderson.

It proved to be a humiliating coup de grace for the outclassed Chiefs.

Green Bay Packers (NFL)	7	7	14	7 —	35
Kansas City Chiefs (AFL)	0	10	0	0 —	10

Tempers flare during Super Bowl I as Max McGee (85) of
Green Bay and Buck Buchanan (86) of Kansas City have words.

Super Bowl II

GREEN BAY PACKERS 33   OAKLAND RAIDERS 14
AT MIAMI, FLA., JAN. 14, 1968

WITH Vince Lombardi on the sidelines for the final time as Packer coach, Green Bay ground down the AFL champion Oakland Raiders, 33-14, in Super Bowl II.

The Packers gave away age (roughly two years per man) and vital speed at some positions, but they had a big edge in experience and their old pros overpowered the Raiders.

In statistics, the Raiders weren't all that bad. They picked up 16 first downs to Green Bay's 19. They ran for 107 yards against the Packers' defense, and they actually outgained Green Bay in the air, 186 yards to 162.

But, the game hinged less on what Oakland did wrong than on what the Packers did exceedingly well.

"Execution," summed up Oakland coach Johnny Rauch, was the key to the Packers' victory.

Quarterback Bart Starr accurately read the stunting Raider defenses, completing 13 out of 24 passes behind strong blocking that crimped Oakland's famed pass rush. Tackle Bob Skoronski, assigned to neutralize Oakland's 6-8, 280 pound defensive end Ben Davidson, did his job so well, Davidson only once got his hands on Starr.

On the other hand, Green Bay's own front four, led by Willie Davis, dumped Raider quarterback Daryl Lamonica three times, and pestered him so much he was constantly forced out of the pocket and had to hurry his passes.

Middle linebacker Ray Nitschke, 31, and in his 10th pro season, typified the Packers' defensive aggressiveness, making five unassisted tackles, helping in four others, and blocking a pass.

"I knew we were going to win," said Nitschke, "the first time we got the ball."

Three field goals by Don Chandler and a 62-yard touchdown pass from Starr to Boyd Dowler gave the Packers a 16-7 lead at halftime.

In the third quarter, Chandler booted another field goal, this one for 31 yards. Earlier, Donny Anderson had punched over from the two-yard line and it was 26-7, Green Bay, going into the final period.

All-Pro cornerback Herb Adderley capped the Green Bay scoring with a 60-yard run with an interception against Lamonica in the fourth quarter.

"We wanted to win for Coach," said Jerry Kramer. "We all thought it would be his last game."

For Lombardi, it was—at least with the Packers. And, fittingly, the Packers won with good execution of the fundamentals Lombardi had drilled into them. They capitalized on Oakland's mistakes, while making practically no mistakes themselves.

Green Bay Packers (NFL)	3	13	10	7 —	33
Oakland Raiders (AFL)	0	7	0	7 —	14

With Vince Lombardi on the sidelines of → Super Bowl II for the final time as Packer coach, the Green Bay players "wanted to win for Coach." Pictured is Lombardi being carried by Jerry Kramer after their 33-14 win over the Oakland Raiders.

Super Bowl III

NEW YORK JETS 16
BALTIMORE COLTS 7
AT MIAMI, FLA., JAN. 12, 1969

BROADWAY Joe Namath predicted victory three days before the game and then went out and led the New York Jets to a surprising 16-7 upset over the Baltimore Colts, giving the American Football League its first triumph in the Super Bowl Series.

A four-yard touchdown run by Matt Snell and three field goals by Jim Turner were all the Jets needed, as the Colts' offense was completely throttled until late in the fourth quarter when Johnny Unitas came off the bench to lead Baltimore to its only score.

At the start of the second quarter with no score on the board, the Colts, defeated only once in 16 games all season, had the ball on New York's six-yard line.

Earl Morrall, filling in for Unitas who had missed

Pass receiver George Sauer is pulled down after good gain by Colt Rick Volk.

most of the season with a sore elbow, spun to his left for a pass, spotting Tom Mitchell free in the end zone. Morrall's pass was grazed by middle linebacker Al Atkinson, and the ball veered higher and went behind Mitchell. The ball bounced off Mitchell's shoulder pads and was caught by the Jets' Randy Beverly in the end zone for a touchback.

That gave the Jets possession on their own 20, and Matt Snell, on four straight running plays aimed at the right side of the Colt defense, moved the ball to their 46.

On that series of plays, New York halfback Emerson Boozer did an effective blocking job on line back Don Shinnick.

"Follow me," Boozer said to Snell in the huddle. "I'm splitting him down the middle."

Namath kept the drive going, hitting end George Sauer with two key passes, the second giving the Jets a first down on the Baltimore 23. On the second pass, Sauer was running a square-out pattern to the left sideline, and the ball was almost intercepted by the Colts' Lenny Lyles.

"I was lucky on that one," admitted Namath. "If Lyles picks it off, he's got a touchdown."

A plunge by Emerson Boozer, a flare pass to Snell, and another run by Snell brought the Jets to the four-yard line. Then Namath handed off to Snell, who was sprung to the outside with the help of a key block by Boozer on safety man Rick Volk, and Snell muscled his way into the end zone.

Turner's kick made it, 7-0, marking the first time in Super Bowl history an AFL team had taken the lead.

In the first half, the Colts had opportunities to score, but Lou Michaels missed two field goal attempts, and Morrall was frisked for three interceptions.

In the third period, Turner booted field goals of 32 and 30 yards, and then with 13.10 left in the game added a third field goal of 9 yards, giving the Jets a commanding 16-0 lead.

Unitas came off the bench, but it wasn't until the final seven minutes of the game he was able to put it together for the Colts who scored their lone touchdown on a one-yard run by Jerry Hill with only three minutes and 19 seconds remaining on the clock.

New York Jets (AFL)	0	7	6	3 —	16
Baltimore Colts (NFL)	0	0	0	7 —	7

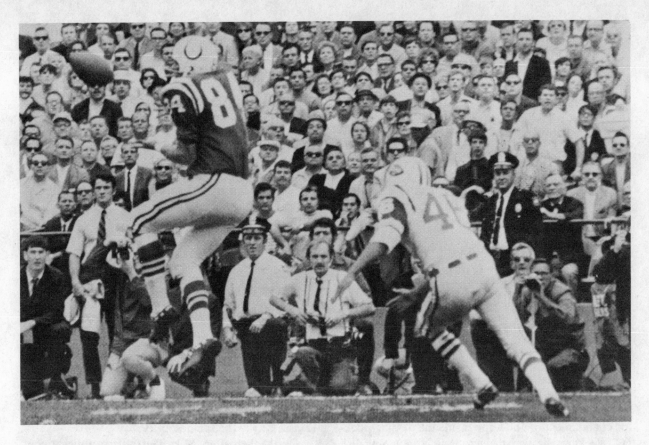

Baltimore's Tom Mitchell (84) takes an Earl Morrall pass and is hit immediately by Jets' Bill Baird.

Jubilant Matt Snell and Dave Herman at the end ➤ of game.

Super Bowl IV

KANSAS CITY CHIEFS 23   MINNESOTA VIKINGS 7
AT NEW ORLEANS, LA., JAN. 11, 1970

LEN DAWSON'S execution was superb as he completed 12 of 17 passes in leading the Kansas City Chiefs to a 23-7 victory over the favored Minnesota Vikings.

One of his passes was a 46-yard touchdown strike in the third quarter to Otis Taylor, who made the play by spinning out of Ersall Mackbee's grasp on the Minnesota 40, and later stiff-arming Paul Krause on the way to the end zone.

"That was the ball game," said the Chief's defensive end Jerry Mays. And, in a way it was because the Vikings had staged a 69-yard scoring drive midway through the quarter and were trailing only 16-7 before the Dawson-to-Taylor caper.

Coach Hank Stram's defensive game plan called for containment of Joe Kapp inside the passing pocket "We knew he was dangerous if he got outside," said Stram.

Mays and Aaron Brown put pressure on Kapp, and kept him from breaking out around the ends. On defense, the Chiefs front four proved the equal of Minnesota's famed "Purple People Eaters," and Kansas City's linebackers were also extremely effective. On one series of plays, Kapp completed three passes in a row and gained a total of only eight yards.

"They took the running game away from us," admittted Kapp who was sacked by Brown late in the game and staggered off with torn ligaments and muscles in his left shoulder.

"We went into the game wanting to run and they were able to take it all away with great defensive play. That Kansas City defensive line looked like a redwood forest."

In addition to Dawson's TD pass to Taylor, one other play helped put the Vikings away.

The Chiefs grabbed a 9-0 lead on three field goals by Jan Stenerud. Then, on the kickoff after Stenerud's third field goal, Minnesota's Charlie West tried a running catch and never gained possession of the football.

The Chiefs had hurried downfield extremely fast on the play and they blocked West from recovering the loose football, with Remi Prudhomme getting it for Kansas City at the Minnesota 19.

Shortly thereafter, Mike Garrett ran a nicely conceived trap play up the middle for five yards and a touchdown to fatten the Chief's lead to 16-0 before halftime. It was a third down play and the Vikings were expecting a pass after two unsuccessful attempts to run it over.

The loss atoned for the Chief's drubbing at the hands of the Packers in the 1967 Super Bowl game.

Kansas City Chiefs (AFL)	3	13	7	0 —	23
Minnesota Vikings (NFL)	0	0	7	0 —	7

← Minnesota's Jim Lindsey is tackled by the Chiefs' Jerry Mays (75) during the first half of Super Bowl IV.

Jan Stenerud, Kansas → City kicker, in the process of making the second of three field goals.

Super Bowl V

BALTIMORE COLTS 16　　　　DALLAS COWBOYS 13
AT MIAMI, FLA., JAN. 17, 1971

THE BIG ONE literally slipped out of the hands of the Dallas Cowboys as the Baltimore Colts emerged a 16-13 winner on a 32-yard field goal by rookie Jim O'Brien with five seconds remaining in the game.

Super Bowl V was sprinkled with lost fumbles (5), interceptions (6), and deflections that set the stage for O'Brien's dramatic boot when the score was tied, 13-13.

"Earl Morrall told me to kick it straight because there was no wind," O'Brien said. "You have to concentrate and can't worry. I just always think of keeping my head down and kicking it through."

The first sudden-death situation in Super Bowl history appeared imminent with little over a minute left in the game when a sudden turnover gave the Colts their opportunity.

Dallas quarterback Craig Morton rolled into the right flat and from his own 27 threw a pass that caromed off the hands of running back Dan Reeves at the 41 and into the arms of Colt linebacker Mike Curtis who returned the ball to the Cowboy's 28.

With Morrall directing the Colts as a replacement for the injured Johnny Unitas, Baltimore used two running plays by Norm Bulaich to eat up time before O'Brien was summoned from the sidelines for his game-winning kick.

With Dallas leading, 6-0, on a pair of field goals by Mike Clark, Baltimore tied it up in the second quarter on a Unitas pass that was deflected by the Cowboys' Mel Renfro and gathered in by tight end John Mackey on a play that covered 75 yards.

Unitas' intended receiver Ed Hinton had reached up and deflected the ball first, and when Renfro grazed it with the tip of his hand, it was enough to make it a "live ball" again for the offense. And when Mackey, who was standing behind all the action as a secondary receiver found the ball floating toward him, he grabbed it and went the distance.

There were nine minutes left in the first half when the Cowboys' Lee Roy Jordan knocked the ball away from Unitas and Jethro Pugh fell on it at the Colts' 28. Three plays later, Morton flipped a screen to Duane Thomas who rolled in for a seven-yard touchdown, giving Dallas a 13-6 lead which held until the final quarter.

The Cowboys had a chance to put the game away in the beginning of the third period when they moved the ball down to the Colts' 2-yard line, but as Thomas tried to twist in for the score, the ball was knocked loose by the Baltimore defense and recovered on the one by Jim Duncan.

"That was undoubtedly the big play of the game," said Dallas coach Tom Landry. "If he scores, they have a lot of catching up to do. We would have been in firm control."

Baltimore pulled even in the fourth quarter after a Morton pass bounced off the hands of Walt Garrison and was intercepted on the run by Rick Volk who returned the ball to the Dallas 3-yard line. On second down, Tom Nowatzke pushed through for the tying touchdown.

And, seven minutes later, the outcome of Super Bowl V was settled by O'Brien's right foot.

Baltimore Colts (AFC)	0	6	0	10	— 16
Dallas Cowboys (NFC)	3	10	0	0	— 13

Earl Morrall

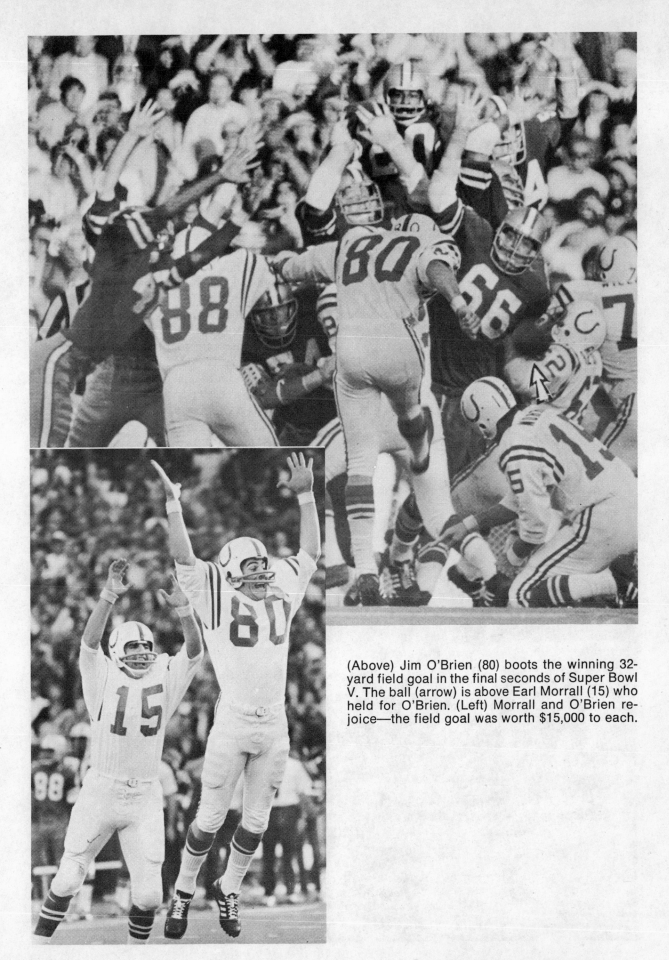

(Above) Jim O'Brien (80) boots the winning 32-yard field goal in the final seconds of Super Bowl V. The ball (arrow) is above Earl Morrall (15) who held for O'Brien. (Left) Morrall and O'Brien rejoice—the field goal was worth $15,000 to each.

Super Bowl VI

DALLAS COWBOYS 24   MIAMI DOLPHINS 3
AT NEW ORLEANS, LA., JAN. 16, 1972

THE DALLAS COWBOYS, who fumbled away Super Bowl V to the Baltimore Colts, came back a year later in New Orleans' Tulane Stadium to steamroller the underdog Miami Dolphins to a 24 to 3 win in the most one-sided Super Bowl game to date.

The Cowboys tough running attack set a game record with 252 yards rushing and controlled the ball for 40 of the game's 60 minutes while the Doomsday Defense was limiting the Dolphins to 185 yards total offense.

Miami fullback Larry Csonka fumbled for the first time all year on his team's second possession in the first quarter and the Cowboys drove down and converted that into a 9-yard field goal by Mike Clark. The Cowboys mounted a second quarter drive culminated by a 7-yard scoring pass from Roger Staubach to Lance Alworth. Just before the half the Dolphins got into the scoring column on a 31-yard field goal by their left-footed Cypriot kicker and off-season tie-maker, Garo Yepremian.

The second half was all Dallas. The Cowboys took the kickoff and marched the ball 71 yards in eight plays with silent man Duane Thomas going the final three for the touchdown. There was little fight and almost no chance left for the Dolphins after that. The final score came in the fourth quarter when Cowboy linebacker Chuck Howley intercepted a Griese pass at the 50 and returned it all the way back to the Miami nine. Three plays later Staubach found Mike Ditka wide open in the end zone.

Dallas Cowboys (NFC)	3	7	7	7	— 24
Miami Dolphins (AFC)	0	3	0	0	— 3

Miami running back Jim Kiick is brought down after a short gain during the first quarter.

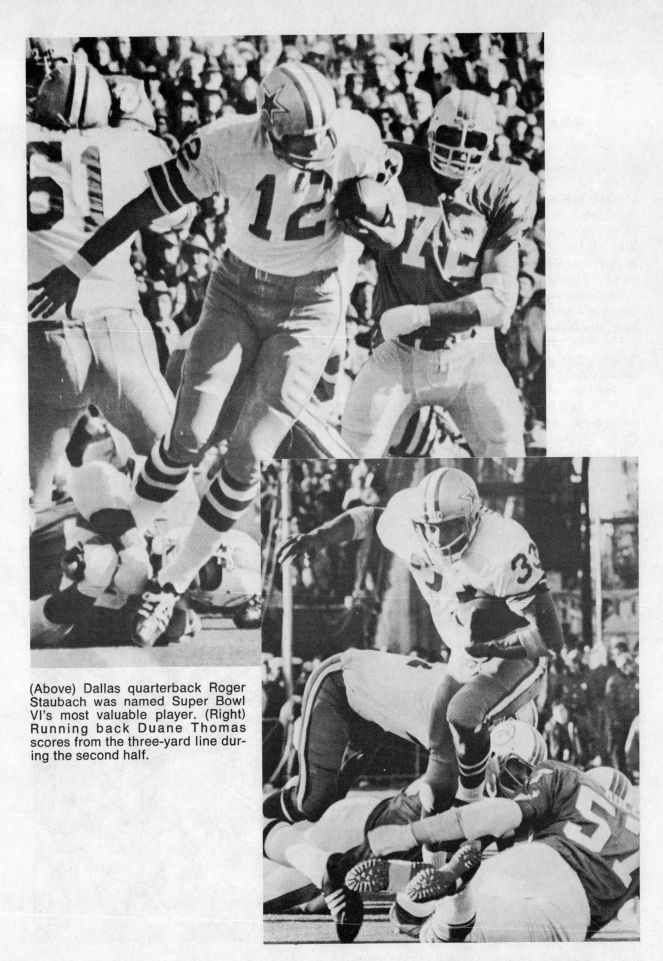

(Above) Dallas quarterback Roger Staubach was named Super Bowl VI's most valuable player. (Right) Running back Duane Thomas scores from the three-yard line during the second half.

Super Bowl VII

MIAMI DOLPHINS 14   WASHINGTON REDSKINS 7
AT LOS ANGELES, CALIF., JAN. 14, 1973

THE MIAMI DOLPHINS as the Chiefs, the Colts and Cowboys before them, continued the tradition of success the second time around in making Super Bowl VII their 17th consecutive victory of the season as they beat the Washington Redskins in an uninspired and sometimes dull game.

The Dolphins, despite their perfect record going in, were slight underdogs to the "Over the Hill" gang from Washington, but the day belonged to youth.

The Skins never could get going, and while their defense played well, except for one big lapse, the offense couldn't even break a sweat.

Miami scored its first touchdown with one second left in the first quarter when flanker Howard Twilley ran a Z-out pattern and got behind cornerback Pat Fischer to take a 28-yard heave from Bob Griese.

They slugged away without effect until in the last two minutes of the half when middle linebacker, Nick Buoniconti picked off a Billy Kilmer pass and ran it back 32 yards to the Redskins 27.

Jim Kiick and Larry Csonka each gained a couple of yards and then tight end Jim Mandich made a div-ing catch at the sidelines to give the Dolphins a first down at the two. Kiick pounded it across in two tries.

The Skins made two long drives in the second half but Curt Knight was wide by at least a dozen yards on a field goal try from the 32 and Jake Scott picked one off in the end zone on Kilmer and ran it out 55 yards to the Skins 48.

It took Garo Yepremian, the Dolphins left-footed Cypriot field goal kicker, to give the Skins new life in the dying minutes. Set to try a long field goal he got a high, lazy pass from center and he squibbed it into the chest of Washington defensive end Bill Brundige. The ball bounced back into Yepremian's hands.

More likely it was the crook of his elbow. He looked around, surprised, bewildered, and danced in place trying to think of something to do with it, and then panic-stricken he launched it, more shove than toss.

It went to Mike Bass, and the Redskins cornerback ran it in 49 yards for their only score of the afternoon.

Miami Dolphins (AFC)	7	7	0	0 — 14
Washington Redskins (NFC)	0	0	0	7 — 7

Larry Csonka of Miami is engulfed by Redskin defenders Mike Bass (41), Chris Hanburger (55) and Roosevelt Taylor (22).

Ray DeAragon

Jim Kiick of Miami scores in the second quarter with Larry Csonka leading the way.

(Below) Miami quarterback Bob Griese uncorks one of his 11 passes during Super Bowl VII. He completed eight.

The Championship Games

To see who is the best. That is the object of every game ever devised by man. Football is no different. However, it wasn't until flamboyant George Preston Marshall bought into the game in Boston that it occured to anyone to divide the 10 existing teams into divisions, Eastern and Western, and have the two winners play for a "world's" championship.

The first playoff took place Dec. 17, 1933 at Wrigley Field in Chicago where a crowd of some 26,000 showed up to watch the Bears play the New York Giants.

The Bears won a hard-fought struggle, and oddly enough it was the passing of Bronko Nagurski, the most feared head-down runner in the game, that turned the tide for the Bears, that and the field goal kicking of "Automatic" Jack Manders.

The Bears first nine points came on Manders' field goals, from 16, 40 and 28 yards, but the Giants led 14 to 9 midway in the third quarter. The Bears fought back with Nagurski battering the line, and then when they massed to stop him he threw a short pass to end Bill Karr for a touchdown.

The Giants retook the lead on a weird lateral and pass play in which fullback Ken Strong lateraled to his quarterback Harry Newman and then raced downfield and caught the touchdown pass from Newman. Back came the Bears to the Giants 36. Nagurski started into the line but stopped, straightened, lobbed an over-the-line pass to end Bill Hewitt. When the Giant defense converged on Hewitt he lateraled to Karr who raced in for the winning touchdown.

Chicago Bears	3	3	10	7 — 23
New York Giants	0	7	7	7 — 21

Bill Hewitt, of the Bears (without helmet) laterals to Bill Karr for winning touchdown.

1934

The two teams met in a rematch a year later at the Polo Grounds in New York on an ice-slicked field. History now knows it as the "Sneaker" game. The Bears came into the game riding a 13-game winning streak, and they were unbeaten in 33 straight games. Their sensational halfback, Beattie Feathers, the first man ever to gain over 1000 yards rushing in a single season (1,004) was out with injuries but the Bears were still heavy favorites.

On the uncertain footing the Bears took a 10 to 3 lead into the locker room at halftime, but Giants coach Steve Owen had his team change their regular cleats for rubber soled basketball shoes.

Jack Manders booted his second field goal, a 24-yarder, to go with his earlier one and Bronko Nagurski's first quarter one-yard plunge, to increase the lead to 13-3 at the end of three quarters. Then it was all New York. Ed Danowski threw a 28-yard scoring pass to Ike Frankian to start the rout. Ken Strong broke off tackle and rambled 42 yards to score. The sure-footed Giants added two more scores on runs by Strong and Danowski, and the Giants had their revenge.

New York Giants	3	0	0	27	— 30
Chicago Bears	0	10	3	0	— 13

1935

The Giants made their third straight appearance in the championship game but were unable to successfully defend their title when they ran into the Detroit Lions steamroller.

The Lions powered to a touchdown right from the opening kickoff with Leroy (Ace) Gutowsky blasting over from the two. The next time they had the ball the Lions scored again with the legendary Earl (Dutch) Clark breaking loose for a 40-yard run. Clark missed the conversion, but the Lions were in command and stayed there.

The Giants only score came in the third period when quarterback Ed Danowski hit fullback Ken Strong on a 42-yard pass and run scoring play. But from there on it was all Detroit. The Lions blocked a Giant punt to set up a four-yard scoring run by Ernie Caddel, and late in the game Raymond (Buddy) Parker, who would later coach the Lions to championships in the Fifties, intercepted a pass and then scored on a nine-yard run.

Detroit Lions	13	0	0	13	— 26
New York Giants	0	7	0	0	— 7

1936

George Preston Marshall refused to hold the championship game in Boston because of poor fan support during the regular season, when his Redskins won the Eastern Division title, and moved the site to the Polo Grounds in New York to meet the Green Bay Packers, champions of the West.

It didn't matter to the Packers where they played. With the game only three minutes old Arnie Herber struck through the air with a 43-yard rifle shot to Don Hutson. The Pack never relinquished the lead.

The Skins lost their great halfback, Cliff Battles, with a leg injury in the first quarter and that just made things that much easier for Green Bay. The Skins scored on a one-yard plunge by Pug Rentner for their only scoring in the second period, but missed the tying point. The Packers struck like lightning with Herber covering 60 yards in two plays on passes to Johnny (Blood) McNally and Milt Gantenbein for one score and, closed it out with a two-yard plunge by Bob Monnett.

Green Bay Packers	7	0	7	7	— 21
Boston Redskins	0	6	0	0	— 6

THE CHAMPIONSHIP GAMES

1937

A tall, gangling rookie named Sammy Baugh brought pro football into a new age with a dazzling passing exhibition that gave the Washington Redskins their first championship on a thriller 28-21 over the Chicago Bears.

Jack Manders of the Bears and Cliff Battles traded ten-yard scoring runs in the first quarter, but the Bears took the lead in the second on a 20-yard pass from Bernie Masterson to Manders.

Slingin' Sam brought the Skins back into a tie in the third period with a 55-yard scoring heave to Wayne Millner, but the Bears came back with a three-yard scoring pass, Masterson to "Eggs" Manske to regain the lead.

It was all Sammy Baugh in the fourth quarter as he opened the game up as it had never been opened before. First came a 78-yard scoring strike to Millner, teams didn't pass that deep in their own territory until Baugh, and for the winner a 35-yard bullet to halfback Ed Justice.

Washington Redskins	7	0	7	14 — 28
Chicago Bears	7	7	7	0 — 21

1938

The largest crowd in championship game history, 48,120, came to the Polo Grounds to watch the New York Giants become the first team ever to win the title for the second time. The player's shares tripled from the previous year, to $900 each for the winning Giants.

The game was no artistic masterpiece but it was thrilling as the Giants built up a 9-0 lead on a Ward Cuff field goal and a "Tuffy" Leemans touchdown smash following two blocked Green Bay Packer punts, and then a 16 to 7 lead on a 20-yard pass from Ed Danowski to Hap Barnard after a five-yard Packer scoring strike from Arnie Herber to Karl Mulleneaux.

Clark Hinkle blasted over from six yards out to cut the Giants lead to 16 to 14 at halftime and the Packers took the lead in the third quarter on a 15-yard Paul Engebretsen field goal. The Giants wrapped it up on a long march capped by a two-yard plunge by Hank Soar. The teams struggled scorelessly in the final period.

New York Giants	9	7	7	0 — 23
Green Bay Packers	0	14	3	0 — 17

1939

The Green Bay Packers were perfection as they rolled over the New York Giants 27-0 in a rematch for the championship in a game played in Milwaukee on a dry day chilled by a 35-mile-an-hour wind.

That didn't stop the Packer passing attack though as Arnie Herber tossed seven yards for a score to Milt Gantenbein in the first period. Cecil Isbell passed 20 yards for a touchdown to Joe Laws in the third period, field goals by Paul Engbertsen and Ernie Smith hiked the score to 20 to 0 and Ed Jankowski finished it off with a plunge from a yard out.

Green Bay Packers	7	0	10	10 — 27
New York Giants	0	0	0	0 — 0

1940

73 to 0!

This game will undoubtedly stand for all time as the symbol of perfection in all of football. Ten different players scored 11 touchdowns as the Chicago Bears put on a brilliant performance of the new T formation's devastating power and finesse, utterly destroying a great Washington Redskin team that had defeated them only a few weeks before.

On the second play from scrimmage the rout was on as Bill Osmanski turned the corner and ran 68 yards for a touchdown. On the next series the Bears marched 80 yards with Sid Luckman going over from the one. Joe Maniaci broke loose for 42 yards, and it was 21 to 0 at the quarter.

Luckman threw a 30-yard scoring strike to Ken Kavanaugh for the only scoring in the second quarter, but in the third the Bears defense utterly demolished the Skins. Hampton Pool ran 19 yards to score with an interception from Sammy Baugh; Ray Nolting bolted 23 yards for a touchdown from scrimmage; George McAfee scored on a 34-yard interception return, and then Bulldog Turner picked off a pass and returned it 21 yards to score. At the end of three periods: Bears 54, Redskins 0.

And still it wasn't over. Harry Clark circled end for 44 yards and a touchdown. Gary Famiglietti plowed over from the two, and Clark became the only Bear to score more than one touchdown by going over from the one to finish it off.

Chicago Bears	21	7	26	19 —	73
Washington Redskins	0	0	0	0 —	0

George McAfee, Bear halfback, making a gain against Washington.

THE CHAMPIONSHIP GAMES

1941

The Monsters of the Midway they were called now, and the Bears proved it again by rolling over the New York Giants to become the first team ever to win two consecutive championships since the inception of the playoff system.

The Giants took an early 6-3 lead on a 31-yard "Tuffy" Leemans to George Frank pass following a Bob Snyder field goal. Snyder kicked two more, from 39 and 37 yards out and Ward Cuff tied it up with a three-pointer from 17 yards away early in the third quarter, but that was it for the Giants.

The Bears got rolling on the power blasts of Norm Stanlee. He smashed over from the two for his first touchdown and followed that up with a seven-yard blast to give the Bears a commanding lead. George McAfee scored from five yards out, and Ken Kavanaugh capped it by running 42 yards with a fumbled lateral.

Chicago Bears	3	6	14	14 —	37
New York Giants	6	0	3	0 —	9

1942

It was a rematch of 1940, but what had been perfection then was now barely functioning as the Washington Redskins held the potent Chicago Bears offense scoreless.

The Bears only touchdown came when tackle Lee Artoe picked up a fumbled pass from center and ran 50 yards to score, but the extra point was missed. The Skins came back on a 25-yard Sammy Baugh to Wilbur Moore scoring pass and wrapped up the scoring on an 80-yard third quarter scoring march with Andy Farkas carring the ball on ten of 12 plays.

Washington Redskins	0	7	7	0 —	14
Chicago Bears	0	6	0	0 —	6

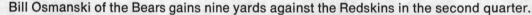

Bill Osmanski of the Bears gains nine yards against the Redskins in the second quarter.

1943

The Chicago Bears and the Washington Redskins hooked up in their third title encounter in four years, the fourth straight for the Bears who once again climbed to the top of the heap.

The game started out like a replay of the '42 game with a scoreless first period, but Andy Farkas bolted over from a yard out in the second to get things started for the Redskins.

Sid Luckman got the Bears on the board with a 31-yard toss to Harry Clark, and the Bears took the lead when Bronko Nagurski, called out of retirement, blasted over from the three just before the half.

Luckman came out winging in the third quarter and hit Dante Magnani with a 36-yarder for a score and then another to Magnani on a play that covered 66 yards. Sammy Baugh closed the gap some with a 17-yard pass to Farkas for the score, but it was Luckman's day. He threw two more touchdown passes, one of 29 yards to end Jim Benton, and a 16-yarder to Harry Clark. Baugh managed one more, a 26-yard toss to Joe Aguirre, but it just wasn't enough. The winning Bears set a new record by taking home $1,146 each, the first time the winner's share had gone over $1,000.

Chicago Bears	0	14	13	14 —	41
Washington Redskins	0	7	7	7 —	21

Andy Farkas, Washington fullback drew first blood with this one-yard touchdown plunge.

1944

For the first time in five years the Chicago Bears failed to win their division title, but the Green Bay Packers upheld the honor of the West by beating the New York Giants 14 to 7.

The Pack did all their scoring in the second period. Fullback Ted Fritsch plunged two yards to cap a drive and put the Pack in front. Minutes later he scored again, on the receiving end of an Irv Comp pass on a play that covered 26 yards.

The Giants got their only score when Ward Cuff went over from the one on the first play of the final quarter.

Green Bay Packers	0	14	0	0 —	14
New York Giants	0	0	0	7 —	7

THE CHAMPIONSHIP GAMES

1945

The icy winds of Municipal Stadium had a hand in the championship as a freak play provided the winning margin as the Cleveland Rams beat the Washington Redskins.

Passing from his own end zone in the first quarter Sammy Baugh hit the goal post when a treacherous gust hit the ball. It resulted in an automatic safety and a one-point Cleveland win. The following year the rule was changed to make all passes hitting the goal posts a dead ball with no penalty.

The Skins took the lead in the second quarter on a pass from Frankie Filchock to Steve Bagarus covering 38 yards. Bob Waterfield then connected on a 37-yard scoring play to end Jim Benton.

Waterfield struck through the air again following the intermission on a play to Jim Gillette that covered 53 yards. The Redskins matched that touchdown with an eight-yard Filchock to Bob Seymour scoring toss, but they couldn't overcome the two points they handed the Rams in the first quarter.

Cleveland Rams	2	7	6	0 —	15
Washington Redskins	0	7	7	0 —	14

1946

Under the cloud of a bribe attempt to fix the game, the Chicago Bears defeated the New York Giants for the NFL championship, but the "world" championship status was challenged by the Cleveland Browns of the newly formed All America conference who whipped the New York Yankees 14 to 9 in their title game.

The Bears great passing combination of Sid Luckman to Ken Kavanaugh struck in the first quarter on a play that covered 21 yards. The Bears added another touchdown on a 19-yard interception return by Dante

Magnani of a Frankie Filchock pass. Filchock was later suspended for failure to report the bribe offer. He played brilliantly though and brought the Giants back with a scoring pass to Frank Liebel covering 38 yards.

Filchock brought his team even in the third period with a five-yard touchdown toss to Steve Filipowicz. The Bears regained the lead when Luckman fooled the Giant defense with a bootleg play, running it in from 19 yards out. Frank Maznicki later added a 26-yard field goal to put the game out of reach.

Chicago Bears	14	0	0	10 —	24
New York Giants	7	0	7	0 —	14

Sid Luckman (42) intercepts New York pass intended for Jack Mead (85) in the fourth quarter.

1947

The "Dream" backfield of the Chicago Cardinals struck with four lightning thrusts to bring the Cardinals their first championship. The Cleveland Browns won again in the AAC defeating the New York Yankees for the second straight year, 14 to 3.

In the NFL title game it was the Cardinal balance versus the bull-like rushes of Steve Van Buren who set a new rushing record, 1,008 yards, the second man ever to rush for over 1,000 in a season, and the eight-man-line defense of the Philadelphia Eagles.

The Cardinals struck first when Charlie Trippi burst through tackle on a quick opener and raced 44 yards to score. On an identical play his running mate at half-

back, Elmer Angsman, broke one for 70 yards in the second quarter. Eagle quarterback "One-eyed" Tommy Thompson brought his team back on a 70-yard scoring play to Pat McHugh.

It was Trippi's turn again in the third quarter, this time on a 75-yard punt return. The Eagles countered by sending Van Buren in from a yard out to cap a 73-yard drive. Angsman iced the game with an exact duplicate of his second quarter run, a 70-yard quick opener for the score. The Eagles marched in for another touchdown with Russ Craft scoring from the one, but it was too late.

Chicago Cardinals	7	7	7	7 — 28
Philadelphia Eagles	0	7	7	7 — 21

Elmer Angsman

THE CHAMPIONSHIP GAMES

1948

In a blinding blizzard, under almost impossible conditions, the Philadelphia Eagles turned a break into a championship against the Chicago Cardinals. In the AAC the Cleveland Browns won their third straight title whalloping Buffalo 49 to 7.

The Eagles avenged the previous year's loss to the Cards when "Bucko" Kilroy recovered Ray Mallouf's fumble on the Card's 17-yard line. Steve Van Buren went the final five to score the game's only points.

| Philadelphia Eagles | 0 | 0 | 0 | 7 — 7 |
| Chicago Cardinals | 0 | 0 | 0 | 0 — 0 |

Steve Van Buren scoring the winning touchdown from the five-yard line.

1949

Bad weather and Eagle power combined to shut out the Los Angeles Rams and give Philadelphia its second consecutive NFL championship. In the AAC the Cleveland Browns made it four straight with a 21 to 7 win over the San Francisco 49ers.

Eagle quarterback Tommy Thompson hit one of his few passes of the game, played in a drenching, driving rain, and connected on a 31-yard second quarter score to end Pete Pihos. The Eagles added another in the third period when Ed Skladany blocked a Bob Waterfield punt and ran it in for a touchdown.

| Philadelphia Eagles | 0 | 7 | 7 | 0 — 14 |
| Los Angeles Rams | 0 | 0 | 0 | 0 — 0 |

1950

On Christmas Eve in frozen Municipal Stadium before only 29,751 fans the Cleveland Browns proved there was nothing flukey about their four straight AAC championships by winning the crown their first year in the NFL in one of the most exciting games ever played.

The Los Angeles Rams scored on the game's first play on a 82-yard bomb from Bob Waterfield to Glenn Davis. The Browns came back on an Otto Graham to "Dub" Jones completion, but the Rams went ahead again when Dick Hoerner blasted five yards for the score.

Graham threw for his second score, this one to Dante Lavelli, but the extra point was missed on a bobbled pass from center. The Browns went ahead for the first time in the game early in the second half on Graham's second TD pass to Lavelli, but the Rams fought back on a long march capped by Hoerner going over from the one. They stretched the lead to eight points when defensive end Larry Brink picked up a Marion Motley fumble and ran it in.

The final period was all Cleveland. Graham passed beautifully, and brought his team to within one point with a touchdown toss to Rex Bumgardner. He engineered a drive in the closing seconds deep into Los Angeles territory, and then with 28 seconds remaining Lou Groza kicked the winning field goal from the 16-yard line.

Cleveland Browns	7	6	7	10	— 30
Los Angeles Rams	14	0	14	0	— 28

Cleveland's Otto Graham picks up 12 yards against the Rams.

THE CHAMPIONSHIP GAMES

1951

The Cleveland Browns and the Los Angeles Rams were in a rematch and before almost 60,000 hometown fans the Rams had their revenge. For the first time the winning players' share exceeded $2,000.

In contrast to the wild opening period of the previous year the two teams battled scorelessly in the first quarter and it was Los Angeles scoring first when Dick Hoerner drove over from the one in the second period.

Cleveland got on the board with a championship game record 52-yard field goal by Lou Groza, and then took the lead with a 17-yard pass from Otto Graham to Dub Jones just before the half.

The Rams regained the lead when Andy Robustelli and Larry Brink combined to smear Graham and recover his fumble. Dan (Deacon) Towler carried it in from the one. Bob Waterfield added a 17-yard field goal to pad the lead early in the fourth quarter, but the Browns drove 70 yards to tie with Ken Carpenter going the final one. Norm Van Brocklin, who alternated with Waterfield, dethroned the Browns with a 73-yard scoring heave to Tom Fears.

Los Angeles Rams	0	7	7	10 —	24
Cleveland Browns	0	10	0	7 —	17

1952

The first of the epic encounters between the Detroit Lions and Cleveland Browns was held in Municipal Stadium three days after Christmas.

Bobby Layne opened the scoring in the second period by sneaking over from the two. It was mostly a defensive battle and the closest the Browns could get was missed field goal attempts of 44 and 47 yards. Doak Walker gave the Lions breathing room with a 67-yard touchdown jaunt in the third quarter, and Cleveland finally got on the board with a seven-yard blast by Chick Jagade. The Lions finished the scoring when Pat Harder kicked a three-pointer from 36 yards out.

Detroit Lions	0	7	7	3 —	17
Cleveland Browns	0	0	7	0 —	7

1953

Bobby Layne marched his team virtually the length of the field in the closing minutes, hitting four of six passes, the last to Jim Doran for 33 yards and a touchdown to make it two straight for the Detroit Lions over the Cleveland Browns in championship play.

Detroit scored first with Doak Walker going over from the one after Les Bingaman recovered an Otto Graham fumble at the Cleveland 13. Lou Groza scored for the Browns on a 13-yard field goal, but Walker matched that with a 23-yarder for the Lions. In the third period Chick Jagade went over from the nine, and Groza added field goals of 15 and 43 yards to put the Browns in the lead and set the stage for Layne's heroics.

Detroit Lions	7	3	0	7 —	17
Cleveland Browns	0	3	7	6 —	16

Bobby Layne

1954

The Cleveland Browns revenged themselves completely in a 56 to 10 pasting of the Detroit Lions. The Lions scored first on Doak Walker's 36-yard field goal, but then the roof fell in as Otto Graham threw first period touchdown passes to Ray Renfro and Pete Brewster, and then ran for two himself and passed to Brewster for another in the second.

Graham scored another himself in the third, to cap one of the great individual performances in a championship game and the Browns rounded out the scoring with touchdown dashes by Fred Morrison and Chet Hanulak.

Cleveland Browns	14	21	14	7 —	56
Detroit Lions	3	7	0	0 —	10

1955

The Cleveland Browns, one of football's all-time great dynasties, made it two-in-a-row by smashing the Los Angeles Rams before a record 85,693 with the winners' share now going over $3,000 for the first time, $3,508 for each winning Brown.

Lou Groza kicked a 26-yard field goal to open the scoring and Don Paul returned an interception from Norm Van Brocklin 65 yards for a score. Van Brocklin threw 67 yards to Bill Quinlan, but Cleveland matched that score with a 50-yard Otto Graham to Dante Lavelli pass.

Cleveland controlled the game with six interceptions as Graham scored two himself and passed to Ray Renfro for another. The final L.A. score came on a four-yard run by Ron Waller.

Cleveland Browns	3	14	14	7 —	38
Los Angeles Rams	0	7	0	7 —	14

Dante Lavelli

THE CHAMPIONSHIP GAMES

1956

In a match-up of two old powers the New York Giants poured across 34 points in the first two periods to bury the Chicago Bears in an eventual 47 to 7 win.

The Giants got on the board early with a 17-yard dash up the middle by Mel Triplett. They converted a fumble by Rick Casares and an interception by Jim Patton of an Eddie Brown pass into a pair of 17-yard field goals by Ben Agajanian. Alex Webster went over from the three and the Bears got their only score when Casares ran nine yards. The Giants scored once more in the second quarter when Ray Beck blocked Brown's punt and Henry Moore fell on it in the end zone. Charlie Conerly threw second half scoring tosses to Kyle Rote and Frank Gifford.

New York Giants	13	21	6	7 — 47
Chicago Bears	0	7	0	0 — 7

Giants' Mel Triplett (33) picks up a block and charges for the game's first touchdown.

1957

The Detroit Lions, scoring two touchdowns in every period, crushed Cleveland 59 to 14 to atone for their trouncing at the hands of the Browns three years earlier.

"Jungle" Jim Martin opened the scoring with a 31-yard field goal and Tobin Rote, playing in place of the injured Bobby Layne, went over from a yard out as did Gene Gedman. Jim Brown ran 17 yards for Cleveland, but Rote threw 26 yards for a score to Steve Junker and Terry Barr picked off a Milt Plum pass and returned it 19 yards for a touchdown.

Lew Carpenter scored for Cleveland on a short plunge following the second half kick-off, but Rote hit Junker for another TD and passed to Jim Doran on a play that covered 78 yards. He threw his fourth TD pass of the game, a 23-yarder to Dave Middleton in the fourth quarter and Gerry Reichow finished it off by throwing a 16-yard scoring strike to "Hop-along" Cassidy. The winning players' share was now over $4,000 ($4,295).

Detroit Lions	17	14	14	14 — 59
Cleveland Browns	0	7	7	0 — 14

1958

It's been called the greatest game ever played, the first sudden death overtime in NFL history. The date Dec. 28, 1958. The place Yankee Stadium, New York. The Baltimore Colts, making their first championship appearance, versus the New York Giants.

The Colts wasted a 60-yard Johnny Unitas to Lennie Moore completion when Sam Huff blocked a 27-yard field goal attempt. The Giants then moved into position of a 38-yard end sweep by Frank Gifford and Pat Summerall kicked a 36-yard field goal. Gifford's fumble on his own 20 was converted to a Colt touchdown in five plays with Alan Ameche going the final two to put Baltimore in the lead. Unitas then moved his team 86 yards after Don Joyce recovered Gifford's fumble at the Colt 14, covering the final 15 yards to Ray Berry.

The Giants made a great goal-line stand in the third quarter and then scored on a fluke play. Charlie Conerly hit Kyle Rote on the fly and Rote fumbled when tackled on the Colt 25, but Alex Webster scooped up the ball and legged it to the one. Mel Triplett banged it over. The Giants took the lead on an 81-yard drive, the big gains coming on passes of 17 and 46 yards to Bob Schnelker and 15 yards to Gifford for the score.

With less than two minutes to go the Colts gained possession on their own 14. Unitas moved his team upfield, hitting Berry with passes good for 25, 15 and 22 yards to the Giants 13, and with seven seconds remaining Steve Myhra tied the game with a field goal.

The Giants won the toss to receive the first sudden-death period kickoff but were inches short of a first down. Baltimore took over on its 20 and with Unitas brilliantly hitting four of five passes moved the length of the field with Alan Ameche scoring from the Giants' one on the 13th play of the drive. There was no try for the extra point.

Baltimore Colts	0	14	0	3	6 —	23
New York Giants	3	0	7	7	0 —	17

Colt's fullback Alan Ameche scores the winning touchdown to end the first NFL sudden death overtime.

1959

The same two teams met in a rematch. The Colts coasted until the fourth period when they exploded for 24 points to swamp the Giants 31-16.

Baltimore struck first on a 59-yard John Unitas-Lennie Moore scoring pass, and then seemed to coast as Pat Summerall kicked field goals of 23, 37 and 22 yards in each of the first three periods to put the Giants on top. But then it was Unitas on a five-yard rollout, and Unitas to Gerry Richardson for 14 yards and a score following Andy Nelson's interception of Charlie Conerly pass. Two more interceptions, by Johnny Sample, the first run back 42 yards for the score, and the second led to Steve Myhra's 25-yard field goal which put the game out of reach. The Giants got a consolation TD on a 32-yard pass from Conerly to Bob Schnelker.

| Baltimore Colts | 7 | 0 | 0 | 24 | — | 31 |
| New York Giants | 3 | 3 | 3 | 7 | — | 16 |

Baltimore's Johnny Unitas scores the Colts second touchdown without an enemy hand touching him.

1960 (NFL)

The Green Bay Packers, revitalized under their new coach, Vince Lombardi, threw away several early scoring chances and then had time run out on them at the end as the Philadelphia Eagles held on in a 17 to 13 thriller.

The two teams traded mistakes deep in Eagle territory in the first quarter but the best the Pack could do was a 20-yard field goal by Paul Hornung. Hornung kicked another early in the second quarter before the Eagles finally got going. Norm Van Brocklin struck quickly with two long passes to Tommy McDonald, the last one of 35 yards to put a touchdown on the board. Bobby Walston kicked a 10-yard field goal to hike the lead and then Hornung missed from the Eagle 13.

The score didn't change until the opening of the final quarter when Bart Starr hit Max McGee with a seven-yard touchdown pass to cap a long drive and put the Pack back on top. But a long kickoff return by Ted Dean to the Packer 39 and a couple of quick traps by Dean and Billy Barnes put the ball on the Green Bay five. Dean swept left end for the touchdown. The Packers fought back with a long march and the game ended with Chuck Bednarik making a game-saving tackle on Jimmy Taylor on the Eagles ten. The winners' share climbed to over $5,000.

Philadelphia Eagles	0	10	0	7 —	17
Green Bay Packers	3	3	0	7 —	13

Green Bay Packer Paul Hornung (5) picks up a couple of yards in first period against Philadelphia.

THE CHAMPIONSHIP GAMES

1960 (AFL)

Once again the NFL wasn't the only show in professional football. The brand new American Football League fielded an eight-team league and their two division winners, the Houston Oilers and the Los Angeles Chargers, played for the title.

The Chargers took a 6-0 lead on first quarter field goals by Ben Agajanian of 38 and 22 yards, and added another of 27-yards in the second quarter, but Houston asserted itself on a 17-yard scoring pass from George Blanda to Dave Smith and Blanda's 18-yard field goal.

Houston widened its lead in the third quarter on Blanda's seven-yard TD pass to Bill Groman, but Los Angeles closed it with a long march with Paul Lowe going over from the two. Blanda iced it in the final quarter with an 88-yard pass to Bill Cannon.

Houston Oilers	0	10	7	7 — 24
Los Angeles Chargers	6	3	7	0 — 16

1961 (NFL)

There was no denying the Green Bay Packers the second time around. On a frozen field in Green Bay, dubbed "Title Town USA," the first time the championship had even been held in that small Wisconsin city, the Pack crushed the New York Giants with a 24-point second quarter explosion.

After a scoreless first period that saw a wide-open Kyle Rote drop Y. A. Tittle's intended TD pass Paul Hornung got the carnage rolling on the first play of the second period when he bolted over from the six. Minutes later middle linebacker Ray Nitschke intercepted a Tittle pass at the Giants 13 and Starr quickly capitalized by throwing 13-yards to Boyd Dowler for the score.

Hank Gremminger picked off another Tittle Pass at the Giant's 33 and this time Starr threw 13 yards to Ron Kramer for the score. A long Giant drive went bust at the Packer six and Starr raced the clock upfield to set up Hornung's 17-yard field goal.

Hornung kicked a third quarter field goal from the Giants' 22 after Joe Morrison fumbled away a punt and later in that quarter Starr threw another TD pass to Kramer, this one also of 13 yards. The final Hornung field goal, from the Giant 19, came after Jess Whittenton intercepted another Tittle pass.

Green Bay Packers	0	24	10	3 — 37
New York Giants	0	0	0	0 — 0

1961 (AFL)

The Houston Oilers were again the dominant force in the AFL beating the now San Diego Chargers, who moved out of Los Angeles after a year, in a hard-fought defensive struggle.

The only score in the first half came on George Blanda's 46-yard field goal, and the game's only touchdown came on Blanda's 35-yard pass to Billy Cannon in the third quarter. San Diego finally got on the board late in the final quarter on a field goal by George Blair.

Houston Oilers	0	3	7	0 — 10
San Diego Chargers	0	0	0	3 — 3

1962 (NFL)

The Green Bay Packers won their second straight championship outslugging the New York Giants on a rock-hard field with bone numbing 40 mile-an-hour winds.

The Packers drove 50 yards the first time they had their hands on the ball but were forced to settle for Jerry Kramer's 26-yard field goal. They upped the lead in the second quarter when Ray Nitschke recovered a Phil King fumble on the Giant 28. Paul Hornung threw 21 yards to Boyd Dowler and then Jimmy Taylor smashed over from the seven.

The Giants were unable to move the ball with success and got their only score of the game when Erich Barnes blocked a Max McGee punt. It was recovered in the end zone by Jim Collier. Green Bay got another field goal by Kramer, this one from the 29, when Sam Horner fumbled a McGee punt. Giant drives were stalled by mistakes and penalties, and Kramer put the game out of reach with a 30-yard field goal in the last two minutes.

Green Bay Packers	3	7	3	3 —	**16**
New York Giants	0	0	7	0 —	**7**

Jim Taylor (31), Green Bay fullback, scores against the New York Giants in the second period.

1962 (AFL)

The Houston Oilers and the Dallas Texans locked in a sudden death struggle that went into the 12th minute of the second overtime period, the longest game ever played, before the Texans finally broke the Oilers grip on the AFL championship.

Dallas jumped off to a 17-0 halftime lead on a 25-yard first quarter field goal by Tom Brooker and two second period touchdowns, a 28-yard pass from Len Dawson to Abner Haynes and a two-yard smash by Haynes.

George Blanda brought his team back in the second half with a third quarter 15-yard TD pass to Willard Dewveall, a one-yard plunge by Charley Tolar to cap a long drive and his own 31-yard field goal to send the game into sudden death.

Dallas put themselves in a bad position at the outset of the suddent death period when team captain Haynes won the toss but elected to kick off. His defense rescued him, however, and the two teams battled scorelessly for the next 27 minutes. Finally Brooker kicked a 25-yard field goal to take the title for the Texans.

Dallas Texans	3	14	0	0	0	3 —	**20**
Houston Oilers	0	0	7	10	0	0 —	**17**

THE CHAMPIONSHIP GAMES

1963 (NFL)

The Chicago Bears broke the Green Bay Packers hold on the Western Division and went on to defeat the New York Giants in the championship playoff, the third straight loss for the Giants in the championship game.

The matchup was a classic between the great Giants offense and the tremendous Bears defense. The Giants scored on a 14-yard pass from Y. A. Tittle to Frank Gifford but the Bears defense equalled that score when linebacker Larry Morris intercepted a Tittle pass and ran it back 61 yards to the Giants five. Bill Wade sneaked in from the one to tie the game.

The Giants moved the ball well but had trouble scoring. They took the lead again when Don Chandler kicked a 13-yard field goal near the end of the half. Another Tittle pass was converted into a Chicago score when Ed O'Bradovich picked off an intended screen pass and ran it to the New York four. Wade took it in again.

Tittle passed his team down the field in the closing seconds, and the game ended with Richie Petitbon making an interception, the fifth by the Bears, in the end zone.

Chicago Bears	7	0	7	0 —	14
New York Giants	7	3	0	0 —	10

New York's Y. A. Tittle has short screen pass intercepted by Bears' defensive end Ed O'Bradovich.

1963 (AFL)

The San Diego Chargers, until now a bridesmaid, scored three touchdowns in the opening period and went on to bomb out the Boston Patriots 51 to 10 in the AFL championship game.

San Diego scored on a two-yard plunge by Tobin Rote and then on runs of 67 and 58 yards by Keith Lincoln and Paul Lowe. Larry Garron scored on a seven-yard run for Boston. George Blair kicked an 11-yard field goal for the Chargers and that was matched by one of 15-yards by Gino Cappelletti, but Rote threw a 14-yard pass to Don Norton to give San Diego a commanding halftime lead.

Rote passed to Lance Alworth for a score in the third period and then John Hadl threw a 25-yard scoring toss to Lincoln and scored himself on a one-yard plunge in the final quarter.

San Diego Chargers	21	10	7	13 —	51
Boston Patriots	7	3	0	0 —	10

1964 (NFL)

The heavily favored Baltimore Colts came to grief in wind-swept Municipal Stadium as the Cleveland Browns pulled off a stunning 27-0 upset. The story of the game is the story of a few men, John Unitas and his inability to master the tricky winds off Lake Erie, Frank Ryan and Gary Collins and their victim, Bobby Boyd, and the tough, resilient Browns' defense. Each winning Brown received over $8,000.

The teams battled scorelessly in the first half, but shortly after the third quarter opened Lou Groza hit on a 43-yard field goal. On their next series the Browns moved into Colt territory with Ryan hitting Collins for an 18-yard TD pass. Again the Colts were stopped. Ryan, now directing a smooth attack, hit Collins again, again over Boyd, for a 42-yard score.

The Browns added 10 more points in the final quarter, a 10-yard field goal by Groza, and Collins' third TD catch of the game, all over Boyd on post patterns, this one for 51 yards.

Cleveland Browns	0	0	17	10 —	27
Baltimore Colts	0	0	0	0 —	0

Gary Collins of the Cleveland Browns goes high for the first score against the Baltimore Colts.

1964 (AFL)

The San Diego Chargers started fast but faded under constant pressure from fine Buffalo defense as the Bills won their first AFL championship.

Tobin Rote opened the scoring with a 26-yard touchdown pass to Dave Kocourek, but the Bills answered that with a 12-yard Pete Gogolak field goal. Wray Carlton put the Bills in front with a four yard smash and Gogolak added a 17-yard field goal. Jackie Kemp put the game away with a one-yard TD plunge in the final quarter.

Buffalo Bills	3	10	0	7 —	20
San Diego Chargers	7	0	0	0 —	7

THE CHAMPIONSHIP GAMES

1965 (NFL)

The Green Bay Packers had to play a sudden death playoff with the Baltimore Colts to make the title game, but when they did they upended the defending champion Cleveland Browns on a great execution of ball control on a snowy, muddy field.

The Packers scored first on a 47-yard pass from Bart Starr to Carroll Dale who was wide open when the Cleveland defender slipped and fell. Cleveland marched the ball in following the kick-off, the last 17 yards coming on a pass from Frank Ryan to Gary Collins. Lou Groza kicked a 24-yard field goal to give the Browns their only lead of the game. Don Chandler kicked two for the Pack, from the 15 and 23, and Groza added one from the 28.

The Pack on the short power runs of Jimmy Taylor and Paul Hornung controlled the ball throughout the second half and held Cleveland scoreless. Hornung went in on a 13-yard run in the third quarter and Chandler kicked a 29-yard field goal in the fourth.

Green Bay Packers	7	6	7	3 —	23
Cleveland Browns	9	3	0	0 —	12

Green Bay flanker Carroll Dale catches a 47-yard Bart Starr pass and goes for the first touchdown.

1965 (AFL)

Buffalo and San Diego met in a rematch and this time Buffalo was even more convincing, shutting out the Chargers 23-0.

The Bills got going after a scoreless first period with an 18-yard scoring pass from Jackie Kemp to Ernie Warlick. Minutes later George Byrd returned a punt 74 yards for a score. The second half scoring was three field goals by Pete Gogolak, of 11, 39 and 32 yards.

Buffalo Bills	0	14	6	3 —	23
San Diego Chargers	0	0	0	0 —	0

Quarterback John Hadl of the San Diego Chargers is trapped during the 1965 AFL Championship game.

Butch Byrd (42) of the Buffalo Bills breaks up a first half Chargers pass.

THE CHAMPIONSHIP GAMES

1966 (NFL)

In a wild game of mistakes and missed opportunities the Green Bay Packers won their second straight championship with a 34-27 win over the Dallas Cowboys.

The Pack jumped off big when Bart Starr hit Elijah Pitts for a 17-yard score, and came right back with another when Jim Grabowski picked up Mel Renfro's fumbled kickoff and ran it in from the 18. Dallas roared back with long marches, the first ending with Dan Reeves going over from the three and the second with Don Perkins bolting up the middle 23 yards. A Carroll Dale pass from Starr, good for 51 yards, put the Pack back on top but Danny Villanueva narrowed it with a 11-yard field goal before the half.

Villanueva added another at the opening of the third quarter but Starr hit Boyd Dowler with a scoring toss from 16 yards out. Starr teamed up with Max McGee in the fourth period for 28-yards and a TD. The kick was blocked. Dallas finally came back on a 68-yarder, Don Meredith to Frank Clarke. Dallas had a first down on the Packer one in the closing minutes but failed to get the tying touchdown.

Green Bay Packers	14	7	7	6 —	34
Dallas Cowboys	14	3	3	7 —	27

Green Bay's quarterback, Bart Starr throws to Boyd Dowler (86) for 16 yards and a touchdown against Dallas in the 1966 NFL championship.

1966 (AFL)

The Kansas City Chiefs took charge in the second quarter and easily dethroned the defending champion Buffalo Bills for the right to represent the AFL in the first Super Bowl.

The Chiefs broke on top when Len Dawson hit tight end Fred Arbanas from 29 yards out. The Bills tied it up on a 69-yard scoring toss from Jackie Kemp to Albert Dubenion, but in the second quarter it was Dawson again, this time to Otis Taylor for 29 yards and the touchdown and the Chiefs added a 43-yard field goal by Mike Mercer.

The teams battled scorelessly throughout the third period but the Chiefs broke it wide open in the fourth on two TD runs by Mike Garrett, the first from a foot away, and the second on an 18-yard dash.

Kansas City Chiefs	7	10	0	14 —	31
Buffalo Bills	7	0	0	0 —	7

1967 (NFL)

Bart Starr drove the Green Bay Packers 68 yards in the closing minutes on a frozen field with the temperature at least 10 below zero and then staked everything on a touchdown bid rather than try for a game-tying field goal.

The Pack looked like they were built for the deep freeze when Starr hit Boyd Dowler on scoring passes of eight and 46 yards in the first two periods. But Starr fumbled one away in the second period when he was smashed down for a 19-yard loss by Willie Townes with George Andrie running it in from the Packer seven. Danny Villaneuva narrowed the lead still further with a 21-yard field goal.

Dallas took the lead when they hit the Pack with their own play, the option pass, good for 50 yards and a touchdown, Dan Reeves to Lance Rentzel. Then Starr marched his team in, going over himself from a yard out with only 13 seconds to play and no time out remaining.

Green Bay Packers	7	7	0	7	— 21
Dallas Cowboys	0	10	0	7	— 17

Bart Starr (arrow) scores the winning touchdown with 13 seconds left and takes another NFL title for Green Bay.

1967 (AFL)

A savage Oakland Raider ground attack that rolled up 263 yards keyed a 40-7 rout of the Houston Oilers while the stout Raider defense kept the Oilers off the board until the fourth quarter.

George Blanda, who led Houston to championships as their quarterback put the Oilers in front early with a 37-yard field goal. In the second quarter Hewritt Dixon broke one all the way for 69 yards and the rout was on minutes later when Daryle Lamonica hit Dave Kocourek for a TD from 17 yards out. A one-yard run by Lamonica and field goals of 40 and 42 yards by Blanda heaped the score to 30 to 0 before the Oilers hit on a five yard scoring toss from Pete Beathard to Willie Frazier. The Raiders finished it off with a 36-yard field goal by Blanda and a 12-yard scoring pass, Lamonica to Bill Miller.

Oakland Raiders	3	14	10	13	— 40
Houston Oilers	0	0	0	7	— 7

THE CHAMPIONSHIP GAMES

1968 (NFL)

The Baltimore Colts completely overwhelmed the Cleveland Browns, gaining revenge for their drubbing of four years earlier and earning a record championship split of $9,265 a man.

The Colts, both offensively and defensively, completely ground down the overmatched Browns. After a scoreless first period Lou Michaels opened up the scoring with a 28-yard field goal, and then the Colts marched for two touchdowns, Tom Matte getting them both on runs of one and 12 yards.

Matte scored again in the third period from two yards away and then the Colts completed the rout in the fourth quarter on Michaels 10-yard field goal and a four-yard TD run by Tim Brown.

Baltimore Colts	0	17	7	10 —	34
Cleveland Browns	0	0	0	0 —	0

1968 (AFL)

The New York Jets won their first AFL championship by pulling out a fourth quarter win over the Oakland Raiders.

The Jets struck first when Joe Namath hit Don Maynard with a 14-yard scoring pass and then padded the lead on Jim Turner's 33-yard field goal. Oakland got on the board in the second quarter when Fred Biletnikoff got free for a 29-yard pass from Daryle Lamonica, and then George Blanda kept pace with Turner's 36-yard field goal.

Namath hit tight end Peter Lammons for a score in the third period and Blanda kicked his second of three field goals to keep the Raiders close. The Raiders took the lead when George Atkinson intercepted a Namath toss on the Jets' 33 and raced it back to five. Pete Banaszak took it across from there. But Namath drove it upfield, with Maynard making a sensational catch for 50 yards, and then catching the winning toss from the five.

New York Jets	10	3	7	7 —	27
Oakland Raiders	0	10	3	10 —	23

Oakland Raiders' Fred Biletnikoff (25) scores with a Daryle Lamonica pass in second quarter.

1969 (NFL)

The Minnesota Vikings made their first appearance in a championship game a successful one by bowling over the pressure-tested Cleveland Browns 27-7 in a game dominated all the way by scrambling quarterback to Joe Kapp and the "Purple Gang" defense.

The Vikings marched the opening kickoff deep into Cleveland territory and Kapp scrambled in for the score from the seven on a broken play. Minutes later he hit Gene Washington with a 75-yard scoring bomb. By halftime the score mounted to 24-0 on a 30-yard Fred Cox field goal and a 20-yard scoring run by Dave Osborn. Cox added another field goal, this one from the 32, in the third quarter to complete the Minnesota scoring. The Browns finally got on the scoreboard with a Bill Nelson to Gary Collins pass in the final quarter.

Minnesota Vikings	14	10	3	0 —	27
Cleveland Browns	0	0	0	7 —	7

Minnesota Vikings' Bill Brown leaps over Cleveland Browns defender Dale Lindsey, but is caught by Browns' Jim Huston after gaining five yards during second quarter of the 1969 NFL championship game.

1969 (AFL)

A determined Kansas City defense dumped Oakland Raider quarterbacks four times for 37 yards and intercepted four passes, three in the crucial fourth quarter, and returned them for 109 yards to play the big role in regaining the league championship.

The Raiders culminated a long first quarter march by sending Charlie Smith over tackle from a yard out. It was to prove their only score of the game.

The Chiefs were not able to tie the score until late in the second quarter when Wendell Hayes went over from a yard out. They took the lead in the third quarter on a five-yard run by Robert Holmes, but the offense gave the Raiders three chances on fumbles in the fourth quarter, but each time the Kansas City defense rose to take the ball away from the Raiders. Emmitt Thomas intercepted a George Blanda pass in the end zone and a Thomas interception set up Jan Stenerud's 22-yard field goal that iced the game.

Kansas City Chiefs	0	7	7	3 —	17
Oakland Raiders	7	0	0	0 —	7

1970 (NFC)

The Dallas Cowboys, for so long dominated by the Green Bay Packers and their own failure to get up for big games, finally won themselves a championship by turning back the San Francisco 49ers in a tough defensive struggle.

The Dallas defense decided the game with key interceptions to set up two third quarter touchdowns and stifled 49er quarterback John Brodie throughout.

The 49ers scored first on Bruce Gossett's 16-yard field goal. That wasn't matched until Mike Clark kicked one through from 21 yards out in the second period. The defensive struggle was broken open in the third quarter when middle linebacker Lee Roy Jordon intercepted a Brodie pass to set up Duane Thomas' 13-yard scoring burst. The next time the 49ers had possession Mel Renfro picked off a pass intended for the fleet Gene Washington. Craig Morton threw five yards for the score to Walt Garrison. Brodie marched his team 73 yards, throwing a 26-yard scoring pass to Dick Witcher, but the Cowboy defense allowed him nothing after that.

Dallas Cowboys	0	3	14	0 —	17
San Francisco 49ers	3	0	7	0 —	10

Dallas Cowboys' linebacker Dave Edwards pounces on San Francisco 49er fullback Ken Willard after a seven-yard gain in the first quarter of the 1970 National Football Conference title game.

1970 (AFC)

Johnny Unitas completed only 11 of 30 passes but they were good for 245 yards as he out-dueled another old pro, George Blanda, and gave the Baltimore Colts the American Conference championship the first year of the newly aligned leagues.

Blanda threw for 271 yards on 17 completions out of 32 attempts after replacing the injured Daryle Lamonica in the second quarter but he suffered three interceptions at the hands of the Colt secondary. Baltimore jumped out on top on a 16-yard field goal by Jim O'Brien and a two-yard run by Norm Bulaich. Blanda got the Raiders going with a 48-yard field goal and tied it up in the third quarter on a 38-yard pass to Fred Biletnikoff.

The Colts came back with another 10-point burst on a 23-yard O'Brien field goal and an 11-yard scoring run by Bulaich off the ancient Statue of Liberty play. Blanda narrowed the gap with a 15-yard scoring toss to Warren Wells, but Unitas put it away with a 68-yard bomb to Ray Perkins.

Baltimore Colts	3	7	10	7 — 27
Oakland Raiders	0	3	7	7 — 17

Baltimore Colts' kicker Jim O'Brien had two field goals during the 1970 American Football Conference championship game.

THE CHAMPIONSHIP GAMES

1971 (NFC)

The Dallas Cowboys and the San Francisco 49ers for the second straight year met in a great defensive struggle for the conference title and the Super Bowl berth.

The great Cowboy defense held the 49ers to a single first down in the first half, and it was the defense that put the first Cowboy points on the scoreboard. Halfway through the second period end George Andrie intercepted a John Brodie screen pass intended for Ken Willard and returned it all the way to the Frisco two. Calvin Hill bolted over from the one a couple of plays later.

San Francisco's only score came on Bruce Gossett's 28-yard field goal in the third quarter. The Cowboys put the game away with a 14-play, 80-yard drive in the fourth quarter with Roger Staubach hitting key passes to Dan Reeves, Billy Truax and Mike Ditka before Duane Thomas carried it the final two yards.

Dallas Cowboys	0	7	0	7 — 14
San Francisco 49ers	0	0	3	0 — 3

Key passes by Dallas Cowboys' Roger Staubach sparked the win over San Francisco.

1971 (AFC)

Bob Griese and Paul Warfield shocked the famed Baltimore Colts' zone defense with a 75-yard second quarter scoring bomb and the Miami Dolphins went on from there to an easy 21-0 win in their first try for a conference championship.

The Dolphins had to play a double overtime against the Kansas City Chiefs in the first round of the play-offs to get into the game against the Colts, but once there the underdog Miamians displayed a surprising superiority.

The teams battled scorelessly following the bomb to Warfield and the Miami defense threw back the Colts on the two when they went for a touchdown instead of settling for a field goal. The Colts were able to move the ball but were unable to score.

Dolphins' safetyman Dick Anderson broke the game wide open with a sensational 62-yard runback, aided by nine open field blocks, of a John Unitas pass. Griese, who completed only four passes all day, hit another bomb to Warfield in the fourth quarter, this one for 50 yards to set up a two-yard scoring plunge by Larry Csonka.

Miami Dolphins	0	7	7	7 —	21
Baltimore Colts	0	0	0	0 —	0

A 75-yard TD pass to Paul Warfield gave the Miami Dolphins their first score.

Ray DeAragon

THE CHAMPIONSHIP GAMES

1972 (NFC)

The Washington Redskins, a team that many experts thought would crumble from old age halfway through the season, demonstrated a convincing superiority over the defending champion Dallas Cowboys in running, passing and kicking their way to an easy 26 to 3 win, the first championship for the Skins in 30 years.

The big drive of the day came midway in the second quarter and put the Redskins in command of the game. Leading 3-0 on Curt Knight's 18-yard field goal they were bogged down, third and ten, on their own 28. They moved into scoring position on one big play as quarterback Billy Kilmer hit split end Charley Taylor with 51-yard bomb.

Larry Brown got six on a tackle trap and it was Kilmer to Taylor again for 15 yards and the touchdown. The Cowboys got their only points on a 35-yard field goal by Toni Fritsch near the end of the quarter.

The teams played scoreless football in the third quarter but then Kilmer and Taylor blew it open. The fleet receiver, who caught seven for 146 yards, got free on a one-on-one situation and Kilmer laid it in his arms from the Cowboys 45 for the score.

Washington completely dominated play from that point on but confined their scoring to some long range bombing by Knight who kicked three-pointers from the 39, the 46 and the 45-yard lines.

Washington Redskins	0	10	0	16 —	26
Dallas Cowboys	0	3	0	0 —	3

Washington Redskins' Curt Knight had four field goals in the 1972 NFC title game.

1972 (AFC)

The Miami Dolphins used trickery and grit to pound out a 21-17 victory over the Cinderella Team of pro football, the Pittsburgh Steelers, the first time in over 40 years in the league the Steelers made it into the big game.

The underdog Steelers moved into an early lead when Terry Bradshaw was hit and fumbled the ball into the Miami end zone where it was recovered by tackle Gerry Mullins. Bradshaw injured his shoulder and had to be taken out.

The Dolphins tied it up in the second quarter when punter Larry Seiple saw the Steelers falling back to set up a return instead of rushing and took off on a 37-yard scamper to a first down on the Pittsburgh 12. Larry Csonka took Earl Morrall's swing pass in for the score from the nine.

Back came the Steelers under the direction of Terry Hanratty, who missed most of the regular season with injuries, but they were forced to settle for a Ray Gerela field goal from the 14.

The Dolphins made a change at quarterback too, replacing Morrall with Bob Griese, who was coming off a broken ankle. On third and six from his 24 Griese pulled out a big play by hitting Paul Warfield on a slant that carried for 52 yards, all the way down to the Steeler 24.

The Dolphins worked it down to fourth and over a yard at about the three, but instead of the field goal Jim Kiick smashed through for the first down. Two plays later Kiick hit pay dirt.

The score stayed that way until the fourth quarter when Miami drove down to a fourth and one at the Steelers five. Again they passed up the easy field goal. They gave it to Csonka and the big fullback crunched through for two yards. Two plays later Kiick took it over.

Bradshaw returned to the game and drove his team 80 yards in four straight completions, the last one covering 12 yards to Al Young. But it wasn't enough and the Dolphins were able to control the ball and the clock.

Miami Dolphins	0	14	0	7	— 21
Pittsburgh Steelers	7	3	0	7	— 17

Pittsburgh Steeler quarterback Terry Bradshaw.

Clifton Boutelle

Individual and Team Records

ALL-TIME INDIVIDUAL AND TEAM RECORDS

(Compiled by Elias Sports Bureau)

Note: The following records reflect all available official information on the National Football League from its formation in 1920 to date. Also included are all applicable records from the American Football League, 1960-69. Official scoresheets are not available from the All-America Conference, 1946-49, nor from other major professional football leagues now defunct.

INDIVIDUAL RECORDS

SERVICE

Most Seasons, Active Player
23   George Blanda, Chi. Bears 1949-58; Balt. 1950; Hou. 1960-66; Oak. 1967-71

Most Games Played, Lifetime
298   George Blanda, Chi. Bears 1949-58; Balt. 1950; Hou. 1960-66; Oak. 1967-71

Most Consecutive Games Played, Lifetime
188   Forrest Gregg, G.B. (187) 1956, 58-70; Dall. (1) 1971

Most Seasons, Head Coach
40   George Halas, Chi. Bears, 1920-29, 33-42, 46-55, 53-67

SCORING

Most Seasons Leading League
5   Don Hutson, G.B. 1940-44
    Gino Cappelletti, Bos. 1961, 63-66

Total Points

Most Points, Lifetime
1742   George Blanda, Chi. Bears 1949-58; Balt. 1950; Hou. 1960-66; Oak. 1967-72 (9-td. 824 pat. 288-fg)

Most Points, Season
176   Paul Hornung, G.B. 1960 (15-td, 41-pat, 15-fg)

Most Points, Game
40   Ernie Nevers, Chi. Cards vs Chi. Bears, Nov. 28, 1929 (6-td, 4-pat)

Most Consecutive Games Scoring
140   Fred Cox, Minn. 1963-72 (current)

Touchdowns

Most Seasons Leading League
8   Don Hutson, G.B. 1935-38, 41-44

Most Touchdowns, Lifetime
126   Jim Brown, Clev. 1957-65 (106-r, 20-p)

Most Touchdowns, Season
22   Gale Sayers, Chi. 1965 (14-r, 6-p, 1-prb, 1-krb)

Most Touchdowns, Game
6   Ernie Nevers, Chi. Cards vs Chi. Bears Nov. 28, 1929 (6-r)
    William (Dub) Jones, Clev. vs Chi. Bears Nov. 25, 1951 (4-r, 2-p)
    Gale Sayers, Chi. vs S.F., Dec. 12, 1965 (4-r, 1-p, 1-prb)

Most Consecutive Games Scoring Touchdowns
18   Lenny Moore, Balt. 1963-65

Points After Touchdown

Most Seasons Leading League
7   George Blanda, Chi. Bears 1956; Hou. 1961-62; Oak. 1967-72

Most Points After Touchdown Attempted, Lifetime
834   George Blanda, Chi. Bears 1949-58; Balt. 1950; Hou. 1960-66; Oak. 1967-72

Most Points After Touchdown Attempted, Season
65   George Blanda, Hou. 1961

Most Points After Touchdown Attempted, Game
10   Charlie Gogolak, Wash. vs N.Y. Giants Nov. 27, 1966

Most Points After Touchdown, Lifetime
824   George Blanda, Chi. Bears 1949-58; Balt. 1950; Hou. 1960-66; Oak. 1967-72

Most Points After Touchdown, Season
64   George Blanda, Hou. 1961

Most Points After Touchdown, Game
9   Marlin (Pat) Harder, Chi. Cards vs N.Y., Oct. 17, 1948
    Bob Waterfield, L.A. vs Balt., Oct. 22, 1950
    Charlie Gogolak, Wash. vs N.Y. Giants, Nov. 27, 1966

Most Consecutive Points After Touchdown
234   Tommy Davis, S.F. 1959-65

Field Goals

Most Seasons Leading League
5   Lou Groza, Clev. 1950, 52-54, 57

Most Field Goals Attempted, Lifetime
567   George Blanda, Chi. Bears 1949-58; Balt. 1950; Hou. 1960-66; Oak. 1967-72

Most Field Goals Attempted, Season
49   Bruce Gossett, L.A. 1966
    Curt Knight, Wash. 1971

Most Field Goals Attempted, Game
9   Jim Bakken, St.L. vs Pitt., Sept. 24, 1967

Most Field Goals, Lifetime
288   George Blanda, Chi. Bears 1949-58; Balt. 1950; Hou. 1960-66; Oak. 1967-72

Most Field Goals, Season
34   Jim Turner, N.Y. Jets 1968

Most Field Goals, Game
7   Jim Bakken, S.L. vs Pitt., Sept. 24, 1967

Most Field Goals, One Quarter
4   Garo Yepremian, Det. vs. Minn., Nov. 13, 1966 (2q)
    Curt Knight, Wash. vs N.Y. Giants, Nov. 15, 1970 (2q)

Most Consecutive Games Kicking Field Goals
31   Fred Cox, Minn. 1968-70

Most Consecutive Field Goals
16   Jan Stenerud, K.C. 1969

Longest Field Goal
63   Tom Dempsey, N.O. vs Det., Nov. 8, 1970

Highest Completion Percentage, Season (14 attempts)
88.5   Lou Groza, Clev. 1953 (26-23)

Highest Completion Percentage, Game (5 attempts)
100.0   Gino Cappelletti, Bos. vs Den., Oct. 4, 1964 (6-6)
        Roger LeClerc, Chi. vs Det., Dec. 3, 1961 (5-5)
        Lou Michaels, Balt. vs S.F., Sept. 25, 1966 (5-5)
        Mac Percival, Chi. vs Phil., Oct. 20, 1968 (5-5)
        Roy Gerela, Hou. vs Mia., Sept. 28, 1969 (5-5)
        Jan Stenerud, K.C. vs Buff., Nov. 2 & Dec. 7, 1969 (5-5)
        Horst Muhlmann, Cin. vs Buff., Nov. 8, 1970 (5-5)

Safeties

Most Safeties, Lifetime
3   Bill McPeak, Pitt. 1954, 56, 57
    Charlie Krueger, S.F. 1959, 60, 61
    Ernie Stautner, Pitt. 1950, 58, 62
    Jim Katcavage, N.Y. Giants 1958, 61, 65
    Roger Brown, Det. 1962 (2), 65
    Bruce Maher, Det. 1960, 63, 67

Most Safeties, Season
2   Tom Nash, G.B. 1932
    Roger Brown, Det. 1962
    Ron McDole, Buff. 1964
    Alan Page, Minn. 1971

Most Safeties, Game
1   By many players

RUSHING

Most Seasons Leading League
8   Jim Brown, Clev. 1957-61, 63-65

Most Consecutive Seasons Leading League
5   Jim Brown, Clev. 1957-61

Rushing Attempts

Most Attempts, Lifetime
2,359   Jim Brown, Clev. 1957-65

Most Attempts, Season
305   Jim Brown, Clev. 1961

Most Attempts, Game
38   Harry Newman, N.Y. vs G.B., Nov. 11, 1934
    Jim Nance, Bos. vs Oak., Oct. 30, 1966

Rushing Yardage

Most Yards Gained, Season
1,863   Jim Brown, Clev. 1963

Most Games, 100 Yds. or More, Rushing, Lifetime
58   Jim Brown, Clev. 1957-65

Most Games, 100 Yds. or More, Rushing, Season
9   Jim Brown, Clev. 1958, 63

Longest Run From Scrimmage
97   Andy Uram, G.B. vs Chi. Cards, Oct. 8, 1939 (td)
    Bob Gage, Pitt. vs Chi. Bears, Dec. 4, 1949 (td)

George Blanda holds a number of records including the most games played and the most points scored, lifetime.

Jim Brown has nine rushing records and has scored the most lifetime touchdowns.

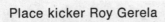

Place kicker Roy Gerela

Ronald Mrowiec

Average Gain Rushing
Highest Average Gain, Lifetime (700 attempts)
   522   Jim Brown, Clev. 1957-65 (2,359-12,312)
Highest Average Gain, Season (Qualifiers)
   9.94   Beattie Feathers, Chi. Bears 1934 (101-1,004)
Highest Average Gain, Game (10 attempts)
   17.09   Marion Motley, Clev. vs Pitt., Oct. 29, 1950 (11-188)

Touchdowns Rushing
Most Touchdowns Rushing, Lifetime
   106   Jim Brown, Clev. 1957-65
Most Touchdowns Rushing, Season
   19   Jim Taylor, G.B. 1962
Most Touchdowns Rushing, Game
   6   Ernie Nevers, Chi. Cards vs. Chi. Bears, Nov. 28, 1929
Most Consecutive Games Rushing For Touchdowns
   11   Lenny Moore, Balt. 1963-64

PASSING
Most Seasons Leading League
   6   Sammy Baugh, Wash. 1937, 40, 43, 45, 47, 49
Most Consecutive Seasons Leading League
   2   Cecil Isbell, G.B. 1941-42
       Milt Plum, Clev. 1960-61

Passing Attempts
Most Passes Attempted, Season
   508   C.A. (Sonny) Jurgensen, Wash. 1967
Most Passes Attempted, Game
   68   George Blanda, Hou. vs. Buff., Nov. 1, 1964

Passing Completions
Most Passes Completed, Season
   288   C.A (Sonny) Jurgensen, Wash. 1967
Most Passes Completed, Game
   37   George Blanda, Hou. vs. Buff., Nov. 1, 1964 (68 att)
Most Consecutive Passes Completed
   15   Len Dawson, K.C. vs Hou., Sept. 9, 1967
        Joe Namath, N.Y. Jets vs. Mia. (12) Oct. 22-vs Bos. (3)
        Oct. 29, 1967

Passing Efficiency
Highest Passing Efficiency, Lifetime (1,500 attempts)
   57.41   Bryan (Bart) Starr, G.B. 1956-71 (3,149-1,808)
Highest Passing Efficiency, Season (Qualifiers)
   70.32   Sammy Baugh, Wash. 1945 (182-128)
Highest Passing Efficiency, Game (20 attempts)
   85.71   Sammy Baugh, Wash. vs Pitt., Oct. 14, 1945 (21-18)

Passing Yardage
Most Yards Gained, Season
   4,007   Joe Namath, N.Y. Jets 1967
Most Yards Gained, Game
   544   Norm Van Brocklin, L.A. vs N.Y. Yanks, Sept. 28, 1951
Most Games, 300 Yds. or More, Passing, Lifetime
   26   John Unitas, Balt. 1956-72
Longest Pass Completion (all TDs)
   99   Frank Filchock (to Farkas) Wash. vs Pitt., Oct. 15, 1939
        George Izo (to Mitchell) Wash. vs Clev., Sept. 15, 1963
        Karl Sweetan (to Studstill) Det. vs Balt., Oct. 16, 1966
        C.A. (Sonny) Jurgensen (to Allen) Wash. vs Chi.,
        Sept. 15, 1968

Touchdown Passes
Most Touchdown Passes, Season
   36   George Blanda, Hou. 1961
        Y.A. Tittle, N.Y. Giants 1963
Most Touchdown Passes, Game
   7   Sid Luckman, Chi. Bears vs N.Y., Nov. 14, 1943
       Adrian Burk, Phil. vs Wash., Oct. 17, 1954
       George Blanda, Hou. vs N.Y. Titans, Nov. 19, 1961
       Y.A. Tittle, N.Y. Giants vs Wash., Oct. 28, 1962
       Joe Kapp, Minn. vs Balt., Sept. 28, 1969
Most Consecutive Games, Touchdown Passes
   47   John Unitas, Balt. 1956-60

Passes Had Intercepted
Fewest Passes Had Intercepted, Lifetime (1,500 attempts)
   92   Tom Flores, Oak. 1960-61, 63-66; Buff. 1967-69; K.C. 1969
Fewest Passes Had Intercepted, Season (Qualifiers)
   3   Gary Wood, N.Y. Giants 1964
       Bryan (Bart) Starr, G.B. 1966
Most Consecutive Passes Attempted, None Intercepted
   294   Bryan (Bart) Starr, G.B. 1964-65
Most Passes Had Intercepted, Lifetime
   276   George Blanda, Chi. Bears 1949-58; Balt. 1950; Hou.
         1960-66; Oak. 1967-72
Most Passes Had Intercepted, Season
   42   George Blanda, Hou. 1962
Most Passes Had Intercepted, Game
   8   Jim Hardy, Chi. Cards vs Phil., Sept. 24, 1950
Lowest Percentage Passes Had Intercepted, Lifetime (1,500 att)
   3.4   Roman Gabriel, L.A. 1962-72 (2,990-97)
Lowest Percentage Passes Had Intercepted, Season (Qualifiers)
   1.19   Bryan (Bart) Starr, G.B. 1966 (251-3)

PASS RECEPTIONS
Most Seasons Leading League
   8   Don Hutson, G.B. 1936-37, 39, 41-45
Most Consecutive Seasons Leading League
   5   Don Hutson, G.B. 1941-45
Most Pass Receptions, Season
   101   Charley Hennigan, Hou. 1964
Most Pass Receptions, Game
   18   Tom Fears, L.A. vs G.B., Dec. 3, 1950
Most Consecutive Games, Pass Receptions
   96   Lance Alworth, S.D. 1962-69

Yardage Receiving
Most Yards Gained, Pass Receiving, Season
   1,746   Charley Hennigan, Hou. 1961
Most Yards Gained, Pass Receiving, Game
   303   Jim Benton, Clev. Rams vs Det., Nov. 22, 1945
Longest Pass Reception (all TDs)
   99   Andy Farkas (from Filchock) Wash. vs Pitt., Oct. 15, 1939
        Bobby Mitchell (from Izo) Wash. vs Cleve., Sept. 15, 1963
        Pat Studstill (from Sweeten) Det. vs Balt., Oct. 16, 1966
        Gerry Allen (from Jurgensen) Wash. vs Chi., Sept. 15, 1968

Touchdowns Receiving
Most Touchdown Passes, Lifetime
   99   Don Hutson, G.B. 1935-45
Most Touchdown Passes, Season
   17   Don Hutson, G.B. 1942
        Elroy Hirsch, L.A. 1951
        Bill Gronan, Hou. 1961
Most Touchdown Passes, Game
   5   Bob Shaw, Chi. Cards vs Balt., Oct. 2, 1950
Most Consecutive Games, Touchdown Passes
   11   Elroy Hirsch, L.A. 1950-51
        Gilbert (Buddy) Dial, Pitt. 1959-60

INTERCEPTIONS BY
Most Seasons Leading League
   2   Bill Bradley, Phil. 1971-72
       Richard (Night Train) Lane, L.A. 1952; Chi. Cards 1954
       Jack Christiansen, Det. 1953, 57
       Milt Davis, Balt. 1957, 59
       Dick Lynch, N.Y. Giants 1961, 63
       Johnny Robinson, K.C. 1966, 70
Most Interceptions By, Lifetime
   79   Emlen Tunnell, N.Y. Giants (74) 1948-58; G.B. (5) 1959-61
Most Interceptions By, Season
   14   Richard (Night Train) Lane, L.A. 1952
Most Interceptions By, Game
   4   Sammy Baugh, Wash. vs Det., Nov. 14, 1943
       Dan Sandfer, Wash. vs Bos. Yanks, Oct. 31, 1948
       Don Doll, Det. vs Chi. Cards, Oct. 23, 1949
       Bob Nussbaumer, Chi. Cards vs N.Y. Bulldogs, Nov.
         13, 1949
       Russ Craft, Phil. vs Chi. Cards, Sept. 24, 1950
       Bob Dillon, G.B. vs Det., Nov. 26, 1953
       Jack Butler, Pitt. vs Wash., Dec. 13, 1953
       Austin Gonsoulin, Den. vs Buff., Sept. 18, 1960
       Jerry Norton, St.L. vs Wash., Nov. 20, 1960; vs Pitt.,
         Nov. 26, 1961
       Dave Baker, S.F. vs L.A. Rams, Dec. 4, 1960
       Bobby Ply, Dall. Texans vs S.D., Dec. 16, 1962
       Bobby Hunt, K.C. vs Hou., Oct. 4, 1964
       Willie Brown, Den. vs N.Y. Jets, Nov. 15, 1964
Most Consecutive Games, Passes Intercepted By
   8   Tom Morrow, Oak. 1962-63

Interception Yardage
Most Yards Returned, Lifetime
   1,282   Emlen Tunnell, N.Y. Giants 1948-58; G.B. 1959-61
Most Yards Returned, Season
   349   Charley McNeil, S.D. 1961
Most Yards Returned, Game
   177   Charley McNeil, S.D. vs Hou., Sept. 24, 1961
Longest Return (all TDs)
   102   Bob Smith, Det. vs Chi. Bears, Nov. 24, 1949
         Erich Barnes, N.Y. Giants vs Dall. Cowboys, Oct. 22, 1961

Touchdowns On Interceptions
Most Touchdowns, Lifetime
   9   Ken Houston, Hou. 1967-71
Most Touchdowns, Season
   4   Ken Houston, Hou. 1971
Most Touchdowns, Game
   2   William Blackburn, Chi. Cards vs Bos., Oct. 24, 1948
       Dan Sandifer, Wash. vs Bos., Oct. 31, 1948
       Bob Franklin, Clev. vs Chi., Dec. 11, 1960
       Bill Stacy, St.L. vs Dall. Cowboys, Nov. 5, 1961
       Jerry Norton, St.L. vs Pitt., Nov. 26, 1961
       Miller Farr, Hou. vs Buff., Dec. 7, 1968
       Ken Houston, Hou. vs S.D., Dec. 19, 1971

PUNTING
Most Seasons Leading League
4 Sammy Baugh, Wash. 1940-43
Most Punts, Lifetime
888 Bobby Joe Green, Pitt. 1960-61; Chi. 1962-72
Most Punts, Season
105 Bob Scarpitto, Den. 1967
Most Punts, Game
14 Sammy Baugh, Wash. vs Phil., Nov. 5, 1939
John Kinscherf, N.Y. vs Det., Nov. 7, 1943
George Taliaferro, N.Y. Yanks vs L.A., Sept. 28, 1951
Longest Punt
98 Steve O'Neal, N.Y. Jets vs Den., Sept. 21, 1969

Average Yards Punting
Highest Average, Punting, Lifetime (300 punts)
45.10 Sammy Baugh, Wash. 1937-52
Highest Average, Punting, Season (Qualifiers)
51.3 Sammy Baugh, Wash. 1940
Highest Average, Punting, Game (4 punts)
59.4 Sammy Baugh, Wash. vs Det., Oct. 27, 1940

PUNT RETURNS
Most Seasons Leading League
3 Les Duncan, S.D. 1965-66; Wash. 1971
Most Punt Returns, Lifetime
258 Emlen Tunnell, N.Y. Giants 1948-58; G.B. 1959-61
Most Punt Returns, Season
53 Alvin Haymond, L.A. 1970
Most Punt Returns, Game
9 Rodger Bird, Oak. vs Den., Sept. 10, 1967

Yards Returning Punts
Most Yards Returned, Lifetime
2,209 Emlen Tunnell, N.Y. Giants 1948-58; G.B. 1959-61
Most Yards Returned, Season
612 Rodger Bird, Oak. 1967
Most Yards Returned, Game
205 George Atkinson, Oak. vs Buff., Sept. 15, 1968
Longest Punt Return (all TDs)
98 Gil LeFebvre, Cin. vs Brk., Dec. 3, 1933
Charlie West, Minn. vs Wash., Nov. 3, 1968

Average Yards Returning Punts
Highest Average, Lifetime (75 returns)
12.78 George McAfee, Chi. Bears 1940-41, 45-50
Highest Average, Season (Qualifiers)
21.47 Jack Christiansen, Det. 1952
Highest Average, Game (3 returns)
47.67 Charles Latourette, St.L. vs N.O., Sept. 29, 1968

Touchdowns Returning Punts
Most Touchdowns, Lifetime
8 Jack Christiansen, Det. 1951 (4), 52 (2), 54, 56
Most Touchdowns, Season
4 Jack Christiansen, Det. 1951
Most Touchdowns, Game
2 Jack Christiansen, Det. vs L.A., Oct. 14 & vs G.B., Nov. 22, 1951
Dick Christy, N.Y. Titans vs Den., Sept. 24, 1961

KICKOFF RETURNS
Most Seasons Leading League
3 Abe Woodson, S.F. 1959, 62-63
Most Kickoff Returns, Lifetime
220 Ron Smith, Chi. 1965, 70-72; Atl. 1966-67; L.A. 1968-69
Most Kickoff Returns, Season
47 Odell Barry, Den. 1964
Most Kickoff Returns, Game
9 Noland Smith, K.C. vs Oak., Nov. 23, 1967

Yards Returning Kickoffs
Most Yards Returned, Lifetime
5,555 Ron Smith, Chi. 1965, 70-72; Atl. 1966-67; L.A. 1968-69
Most Yards Returned, Season
1,317 Bobby Jancik, Hou. 1963
Most Yards Returned, Game
294 Wally Triplett, Det. vs L.A., Oct. 29, 1950
Longest Kickoff Return (all TDs)
106 Al Carmichael, G.B. vs Chi. Bears, Oct. 7, 1956
Noland Smith, K.C. vs Den., Dec. 17, 1967

Average Yards Returning Kickoffs
Highest Average, Lifetime (75 returns)
30.56 Gale Sayers, Chi. 1965-71
Highest Average, Season (Qualifiers)
41.06 Travis Williams, G.B. 1967
Highest Average, Game (3 returns)
73.50 Wally Triplett, Det. vs L.A., Oct. 29, 1950

Sonny Jurgensen

Bobby Joe Green

Ronald Mrowiec

Touchdowns Returning Kickoffs

Most Touchdowns, Lifetime
- 6 Ollie Matson, Chi. Cards 1952 (2), 54, 56, 58 (2)
  Gale Sayers, Chi. 1965, 66 (2), 67 (3)
  Travis Williams, G.B. 1967 (4), 69; L.A. 1971

Most Touchdowns, Season
- 4 Travis Williams, G.B. 1967
  Cecil Turner, Chi. 1970

Most Touchdowns, Game
- 2 Thomas (Tim) Brown, Phil. vs Dall., Nov. 6, 1966
  Travis Williams, G.B. vs Clev., Nov. 12, 1967

COMBINED KICK RETURNS

Most Combined Kick Returns, Lifetime
- 365 Alvin Haymond, Balt. 1964-67; Phil. 1968; L.A. 1969-71
  (p-233, k-132)
- 331 Ron Smith, Chi. 1965, 70-71; Atl. 1966-67; L.A. 1968-69
  (p-141, k-190)

Most Combined Kick Returns, Season
- 88 Alvin Haymond, L.A. 1970 (p-53, k-35)

Most Combined Kick Returns, Game
- 12 Mel Renfro, Dall. vs G.B., Nov. 29, 1964 (p-4, k-8)

Yardage

Most Yards Returned, Lifetime
- 6,505 Ron Smith

Most Yards Returned, Season
- 1,582 Charles Latourette, St.L. 1968

Most Yards Returned, Game
- 294 Wally Triplett, Det. vs L.A., Oct. 29, 1950
  Woody Lewis, L.A. vs Det., Oct. 18, 1953

Touchdowns

Most Touchdowns, Lifetime
- 9 Ollie Matson, Chi. Cards 1952(2), 54(2), 55(2), 56, 58(2)
  (p-3, k-6)

Most Touchdowns, Season
- 4 Emlen Tunnell, N.Y. Giants 1951 (p-3, k-1)
  Gale Sayers, Chi. 1967 (p-1, k-3)

Most Touchdowns, Game
- 2 Jim Patton, N.Y. vs. Wash, Oct. 30, 1955 (p-1, k-1)
  Bobby Mitchell, Clev. vs Phil., Nov. 23, 1958 (p-1, k-1)
  Al Frazier, Den. vs Bos., Dec. 3, 1961 (p-1, k-1)
  Gal Sayers, Chi. vs S.F., Dec. 3, 1967 (p-1, k-1)
  Travis Williams, G.B. vs Pitt., Nov. 2, 1969 (p-1, k-1)

FUMBLES

Most Fumbles, Lifetime
- 92 John Unitas, Balt. 1956-72

Most Fumbles, Season
- 16 Don Meredith, Dall. 1964

Most Fumbles, Game
- 7 Len Dawson, K.C. vs S.D., Nov. 15, 1964

Total Fumbles Recovered

Most Total Fumbles Recovered, Lifetime
- 38 Jack Kemp, Pitt. 1957; L.A./S.D. 1960-62; Buff. 1962-67, 69
  (38-own)

Most Total Fumbles Recovered, Season
- 9 Don Hulz, Minn. 1963 (9-opp)

Most Total Fumbles Recovered, Game
- 4 Otto Graham, Clev. vs. N.Y., Oct. 25, 1953 (4-own)
  Sam Etcheverry, St.L. vs N.Y. Giants, Sept. 17, 1961
  (4-own)
  Roman Gabriel, L.A. vs S.F., Oct. 12, 1969 (4-own)

Own Recovered

Most Own Fumbles Recovered, Season
- 8 Paul Christman, Chi. Cards 1945
  Bill Butler, Minn. 1963

Most Own Fumbles Recovered, Game
- 4 Otto Graham, Clev. vs N.Y., Oct. 25, 1953
  Sam Etcheverry, St.L. vs N.Y. Giants, Sept. 17, 1961
  Roman Gabriel, L.A. vs S.F., Oct. 12, 1969

Opponents' Recovered

Most Opponents' Fumbles Recovered, Lifetime
- 24 Dick Butkus, Chi. Bears 1965-72

Most Opponents' Fumbles Recovered, Season
- 9 Don Hultz, Minn. 1963

Most Opponents' Fumbles Recovered, Game
- 3 Corwin Clatt, Chi. Cards vs Det., Nov. 6, 1949
  Vic Sears, Phil. vs G.B., Nov. 2, 1952
  Ed Beatty, S.F. vs L.A., Oct. 7, 1956

Yards Returning Fumbles

Longest Fumble Run (all TDs)
- 104 Jack Tatum, Oak. vs G.B., Sept. 24 (td)

Touchdowns

Most Touchdowns, Lifetime (Total)
- 3 Ralph Heywood, Bos. 1948 (2); N.Y. Bulldogs 1949
  Leo Sugar, Chi. Cards 1954, 57(2)
  Lewis (Bud) McFadin, L.A. 1956; Den. 1962, 63
  Charles Cline, Hou. 1961(2), 66

Most Touchdowns, Season (Total)
- 2 Frank Maznicki, Bos. 1947
  Fred Evans, Chi. Bears 1948
  Ralph Heywood, Bos. 1948
  Arthur Tait, N.Y. Yanks 1951
  John Dwyer, L.A. 1952
  Leo Sugar, Chi. Cards 1957
  Charles Cline, Hou. 1961
  Jim Bradshaw, Pitt. 1964
  Royce Berry, Cin. 1970

Most Touchdowns, Lifetime (Own Recovered)
- 2 Ken Kavanaugh, Chi. Bears 1948, 50
  Mike Ditka, Chi. 1962, 64
  Gail Cogdill, Det. 1962, 64

Most Touchdowns, Lifetime (Opponents' Recovered)
- 3 Leo Sugar, Chi. Cards 1954, 57(2)
  Lewis (Bud) McFadin, L.A. 1956; Den. 1962, 63
  Charles Cline, Hou. 1961(2), 66

Most Touchdowns, Game (Opponents' Recovered)
- 2 Fred Evans, Chi. Bears vs Wash., Nov. 28, 1948

COMBINED NET YARDS GAINED

(Includes Rushes, Pass Receptions, Runback of Pass
Interceptions, Punts, Kickoffs and Fumbles)

Attempts

Most Attempts, Lifetime
- 2,658 Jim Brown, Clev. 1957-65

Most Attempts, Season
- 354 Jim Brown, Clev. 1961

Most Attempts, Game
- 41 Ron Johnson, N.Y. Giants

Yards

Most Yards Gained, Lifetime
- 15,459 Jim Brown, Clev. 1957-65

Most Yards Gained, Season
- 2,440 Gale Sayers, Chi. 1966

Most Yards Gained, Game (two or more categories)
- 373 Billy Cannon, Hou. vs N.Y. Titans, Dec. 10, 1961

Average Gain

Highest Average Gain, Lifetime (750 attempts)
- 11.62 Bobby Mitchell, Clev. 1958-61; Wash. 1962-68
  (1,212-14,078)

Highest Average Gain, Season (150 attempts)
- 11.92 Bill Grimes, G.B. 1950 (159-1,896)

Highest Average Gain, Game (two or more categories—15 att.)
- 19.76 Gale Sayers, Chi. vs S.F., Dec. 12, 1965 (17-336)

MISCELLANEOUS

Scoring

Most Drop Kick Field Goals, Game
- 4 John (Paddy) Driscoll, Chi. Cards vs Columbus,
  Oct. 11, 1925
  (23, 18, 50 & 35 yards)
  Elbert Bloodgood, K.C. vs Duluth, Dec. 12, 1926
  (35, 32, 20 & 25 yards)

Longest Drop Kick Field Goal
- 50 John (Paddy) Driscoll, Chi. Cards vs Milwaukee, Sept. 28,
  1924; vs Columbus, Oct. 11, 1925
  Wilbur Henry, Canton vs Toledo, Nov. 13, 1922

Longest Return of Missed Field Goal (all TDs)
- 101 Al Nelson, Phil. vs Dall., Sept. 26, 1971

Dick Butkus has recovered 24 opponents' fumbles during his football career.

Gary Settle

Royce Berry (82)

Clifton Boutelle

TEAM RECORDS

OFFENSE
CHAMPIONSHIPS

Most Seasons League Champion
11   Green Bay 1929-31; 36, 39, 44, 61-62, 65-67
Most Consecutive Seasons League Champion
3   Green Bay 1929-31; 1965-67
Most Seasons Leading Conference (Since 1933)
14   New York Giants 1933-35, 38-39, 41, 44, 46, 56, 58-59, 61-63
Most Consecutive Seasons Leading Conference
6   Cleveland 1950-55

GAMES

Most Consecutive Victories (All Games)
18   Chicago Bears 1933-34; 1941-42
Most Consecutive Victories (Regular Season)
17   Chicago Bears 1933-34
Most Consecutive Games Without Defeat (Regular Season)
24   Canton 1922-23 (won-21, tied-3)
     Chicago Bears 1941-43 (won-23, tied-1)
Most Victories, Season (Since 1933)
13   Chicago Bears 1934
     Green Bay 1962
     Oakland 1967
     Baltimore 1968
Most Consecutive Losses (Regular Season)
29   Chicago Cards 1942-45
Most Losses, Season (Since 1933)
13   Oakland 1962
     Chicago Bears 1969
     Pittsburgh 1969
     Buffalo 1971
Most Tie Games, Season
6   Chicago Bears 1932
Most Consecutive Tie Games
3   Chicago Bears 1932
Scoreless Tie Games
16   Scoreless tie games. Last by:
     New York at Detroit, Nov. 7, 1943
Most Consecutive Shutout Victories (Regular Season)
7   Detroit 1934
Most Consecutive Shutout Losses (Regular Season)
6   Brooklyn 1942-43

SCORING

Most Seasons Leading League
9   Chicago Bears 1934-35, 39, 41-43, 46-47, 56

Total Points

Most Points, Season
513   Houston 1961
Most Points, Game
72   Washington vs N.Y. Giants, Nov. 27, 1966
Most Points, Both Teams, Game
113   Washington (72) vs N.Y. Giants (41), Nov. 27, 1966
Most Points, One Quarter
41   Green Bay vs Det., Oct. 7, 1945 (2nd Q)
     Los Angeles vs. Det., Oct. 29, 1950 (3rd Q)
Most Points, Both Teams, One Quarter
49   Oakland (28) vs Hou. (21), Dec. 22, 1963 (2nd Q)
Most Points, Each Quarter
1st: 35   Green Bay vs Clev., Nov. 12, 1967
2nd: 41   Green Bay vs Det., Oct. 7, 1945
3rd: 41   Los Angeles vs Det., Oct. 29, 1950
4th: 31   Oakland vs Den., Dec. 17, 1960
          Oakland vs S.D., Dec. 8, 1963
Most Points, Both Teams, Each Quarter
1st: 42   Green Bay (35) vs Clev. (7), Nov. 12, 1967
2nd: 49   Oakland (28) vs Hou. (21), Dec. 22, 1963
3rd: 48   Los Angeles (41) vs Det. (7), Oct. 29, 1950
4th: 42   Chicago Cards (28) vs. Phil. (14), Dec. 7, 1947
          Green Bay (28) vs Chi. Bears (14), Nov. 6, 1955
          New York Jets (28) vs Bos. (14), Oct. 27, 1968
          Pittsburgh (21) vs Cleve. (21), Oct 18, 1969

Games

Most Consecutive Games Scoring
274   Cleveland 1950-71

Touchdowns

Most Touchdowns, Season
66   Houston 1961
Most Touchdowns, Game
10   Philadelphia vs Cin., Nov. 6, 1934
     Los Angeles vs Balt., Oct. 22, 1950
     Washington vs N.Y. Giants, Nov. 27, 1966

Points After Touchdowns

Most Touchdowns, Both Teams, Game
16   Washington (10) vs N.Y. Giants (6), Nov. 27, 1966

Field Goals

Most Field Goals Attempted, Both Teams, Game
11   St. Louis (6) vs Pitt. (5), Nov. 13, 1966
     Washington (6) vs Chi. (5), Nov. 14, 1971
Most Field Goals, Both Teams, Game
8   Cleveland (4) vs St.L. (4), Sept. 20, 1964
    Chicago Bears (5) vs Phil. (3), Oct. 20, 1968
    Washington (5) vs Chi. (3), Nov. 14, 1971
    Kansas City (5) vs Buff. (3), Dec. 19, 1971
Most Consecutive Games Scoring Field Goals
31   Minnesota 1968-70

Safeties

Most Safeties, Season
4   Detroit 1962
Most Safeties, Game
2   Cincinnati vs Chi. Cards, Nov. 19, 1933
    Detroit vs. Brk., Dec. 1, 1935
    New York Giants vs Pitt., Sept. 17, 1950
    New York Giants vs Wash., Nov. 5, 1961
    Chicago Bears vs Pitt., Nov. 9, 1969

FIRST DOWNS

Most Seasons Leading League
8   Chicago Bears 1935, 41, 43, 45, 47-49, 55
Most First Downs, Season
297   Dallas 1968
Fewest First Downs, Season
51   Cincinnati 1933
Most First Downs, Game
38   Los Angeles vs N.Y. Giants, Nov. 13, 1966
Fewest First Downs, Game
0   Hammond vs. Canton, Sept. 30, 1923
    Racine vs Chi. Cards, Oct. 3, 1926
    New York Giants vs. G.B., Oct. 1, 1933
    Pittsburgh vs Bos. Redskins, Oct. 29, 1933
    Philadelphia vs Det., Sept. 20, 1935
    New York Giants vs Wash, Sept. 27, 1942
    Denver vs Hou., Sept. 3, 1966
Most First Downs, Both Teams, Game
58   Los Angeles (30) vs Chi. Bears (28), Oct. 24, 1954
Fewest First Downs, Both Teams, Game
5   New York Giants (0) vs G.B. (5), Oct. 1, 1933
Most First Downs, Rushing, Season
145   Green Bay 1962
Fewest First Downs, Rushing, Season
36   Cleveland Rams 1942
     Boston Redskins 1944
Most First Downs, Rushing, Game
25   Philadelphia vs Wash., Dec. 2, 1951
Fewest First Downs, Rushing, Game
0   By many teams
Most First Downs, Passing, Season
186   Houston 1964
      Oakland 1964
Fewest First Downs, Passing, Season
18   Pittsburgh 1941
Most First Downs, Passing, Game
24   Houston vs Buff., Nov. 1, 1964
     Minnesota vs Balt., Sept. 28, 1969
Fewest First Downs, Passing, Game
0   By many teams
Most First Downs, Penalty, Season
34   Detroit 1971
Fewest First Downs, Penalty, Season
4   New York Giants 1942, 44
    Washington 1944
    Cleveland 1952
    Kansas City 1969
Most First Downs, Penalty, Game
9   Chicago Bears vs Cleve., Nov. 25, 1951
Fewest First Downs, Penalty, Game
0   By many teams

NET YARDS GAINED
(Rushing and Passing)

Most Seasons Leading League
12   Chicago Bears 1932, 34-35, 39, 41-44, 47, 49, 55-56
Most Yards Gained, Season
6,288   Houston 1961
Fewest Yards Gained, Season
1,113   Cincinnati 1933
Most Yards Gained, Game
735   Los Angeles vs N.Y. Yanks, Sept. 28, 1951
Fewest Yards Gained, Game
-5   Denver vs Oak., Sept. 10, 1967
14   Chicago Cards vs Det., Sept. 15, 1940
16   Detroit vs Chi. Cards, Sept. 15, 1940
Most Yards Gained, Both Teams, Game
1,133   Los Angeles (636) vs N.Y. Yanks (497), Nov. 19, 1950
Fewest Yards Gained, Both Teams, Game
30   Chicago Cards (14) vs Det. (16), Sept. 15, 1940

The New York Giants starting lineup for the 1946 NFL championship game: Left to right (rear) are George Franck, Frank Filchock, Steve Filipowicz and Merle Hapes. (Front) Jim Lee Howell, Jim White, Len Younce, Chet Gladchuk, Bob Dobelstein, Tex Coulter and Jim Poole.

Chicago Bears George Seals (67) and Gale Sayers (40).

RUSHING

Most Seasons Leading League
11   Chicago Bears 1932, 34-35, 39-42, 51, 55-56, 68
Most Rushing Attempts, Season
632   Detroit 1934
        Philadelphia 1949
Fewest Rushing Attempts, Season
274   Detroit 1946
Most Rushing Attempts, Game
72   Chicago Bears vs Brk., Oct. 20, 1935
Fewest Rushing Attempts, Game
6   Chicago Cards vs Bos. Redskins, Oct. 29, 1933
Most Rushing Attempts, Both Teams, Game
108   Chicago Cards (70) vs G.B. (38), Dec. 5, 1948
Fewest Rushing Attempts, Both Teams, Game
34   Cincinnati (16) vs Chi. Bears (18), Sept. 30, 1934
Most Yards Gained Rushing, Season
2,885   Detroit 1936
2,847   Chicago Bears 1934
Fewest Yards Gained Rushing, Season
298   Philadelphia 1940
Most Yards Gained Rushing, Game
426   Detroit vs Pitt., Nov. 4, 1934
Fewest Yards Gained Rushing, Game
-36   Philadelphia vs Chi. Bears, Nov. 19, 1939
Most Yards Gained Rushing, Both Teams, Game
595   Los Angeles (371) vs N.Y. Yanks (224), Nov. 18, 1951
Fewest Yards Gained Rushing, Both Teams, Game
4   Detroit (-10) vs Chi. Cards (14), Sept. 15, 1940
Most Touchdowns, Rushing, Season
36   Green Bay 1962
Most Touchdowns, Rushing Game
6   By many teams. Last:
      New York Jets vs Bos., Oct. 27, 1968
Most Touchdowns, Rushing, Both Teams, Game
8   Los Angeles (6) vs N.Y. Yanks (2), Nov. 18, 1951
      Cleveland (6) vs L.A. (2), Nov. 24, 1957

PASSING

Most Seasons Leading League
9   Washington 1927, 39-40, 42-45, 47, 67

Passing Attempts

Most Passes Attempted, Season
592   Houston 1964
Fewest Passes Attempted, Season
102   Cincinnati 1933
Most Passes Attempted, Game
68   Houston vs Buff., Nov. 1, 1964
Fewest Passes Attempted, Game
0   Green Bay vs Portsmouth, Oct. 8, 1933; vs Chi. Bears,
      Sept. 25, 1949
      Detroit vs Cleve. Rams, Sept. 10, 1937
      Pittsburgh vs Brk., Nov. 16, 1941; vs L.A., Nov. 13, 1949
      Cleveland vs Phil., Dec. 3, 1950
Most Passes Attempted, Both Teams, Game
98   Minnesota (56) vs Balt. (42), Sept. 28, 1969
Fewest Passes Attempted, Both Teams, Game
4   Chicago Cards (1) vs Det. (3), Nov. 3, 1935
      Detroit (0) vs Clev. Rams (4), Sept. 10, 1937

Passing Completions

Most Passes Completed, Season
301   Washington 1967
Fewest Passes Completed, Season
25   Cincinnati 1933
Most Passes Completed, Game
37   Houston vs Buff., Nov. 1, 1964
Most Passes Completed, Both Teams, Game
56   Minnesota (36) vs Balt. (20), Sept. 28, 1969
Fewest Passes Completed, Both Teams, Game
1   Chicago Cards (0) vs Phil. (1), Nov. 8, 1936
      Detroit (0) vs Clev. Rams (1), Sept. 10, 1937
      Chicago Cards (0) vs Det. (1), Sept. 15, 1940

Passing Yardage

Most Seasons Leading League, Passing Yardage
8   Chicago Bears 1932, 39, 41, 43, 45, 49, 54, 64
Most Yards Gained Passing, Season
4,392   Houston 1961
Fewest Yards Gained, Passing, Season
302   Chicago Cards 1934
Most Yards Gained, Passing, Game
554   Los Angeles vs N.Y. Yanks, Sept. 28, 1951
Fewest Yards Gained, Passing, Game
-53   Denver vs Oak., Sept. 10, 1967
Most Yards Gained, Passing, Both Teams, Game
851   New York Giants (505) vs Wash. (346), Oct. 28, 1962
Fewest Yards Gained, Passing, Both Teams, Game
-11   Green Bay (-10) vs Dall. (-1), Oct. 24, 1965

Tackled, Attempting Passes

Most Times Tackled, Attempting Passes, Season
70   Atlanta 1968
Fewest Times Tackled, Attempting Passes, Season
8   San Francisco 1970

Most Times Tackled, Attempting Passes, Game
12   Pittsburgh vs Dall., Nov. 20, 1966
Most Times Tackled, Attempting Passes, Both Teams, Game
17   Buffalo (10) vs N.Y. Titans (7), Nov. 23, 1961
      Pittsburgh (12) vs Dall. (5), Nov. 20, 1966

Passing Completion Percentage

Most Seasons Leading League, Completion Percentage
11   Washington 1937, 39-40, 42-45, 47-48, 69-70

Touchdowns

Most Touchdowns, Passing, Season
48   Houston 1961
Fewest Touchdowns, Passing, Season
0   Pittsburgh 1945
Most Touchdowns, Passing, Game
7   Chicago Bears vs N.Y. Giants, Nov. 14, 1943
      Philadelphia vs Wash., Oct. 17, 1954
      Houston vs N.Y. Titans, Nov. 19, 1961 & Oct. 14, 1962
      New York Giants vs Wash., Oct. 28, 1962
      Minnesota vs Balt., Sept. 28, 1969
Most Touchdowns, Passing, Both Teams, Game
12   New Orleans (6) vs St.L. (6), Nov. 2, 1969

Passes Had Intercepted

Most Passes Had Intercepted, Season
48   Houston 1962
Fewest Passes Had Intercepted, Season
5   Cleveland 1960
      Green Bay 1966
Most Passes Had Intercepted, Game
9   Detroit vs G.B., Oct. 24, 1943
      Pittsburgh vs Phil., Dec. 12, 1965
Most Passes Had Intercepted, Both Teams, Game
13   Denver (8) vs Hou. (5), Dec. 2, 1962

PUNTING

Most Punts, Season
113   Boston 1934
        Brooklyn 1934
Fewest Punts, Season
32   Chicago Bears 1941
Most Punts, Game
17   Chicago Bears vs G.B., Oct. 22, 1933
      Cincinnati vs Pitt., Oct. 22, 1933
Fewest Punts, Game
0   By many teams. Last:
      Detroit vs K.C., Nov. 25, 1971
Most Punts, Both Teams, Game
31   Cincinnati (17) vs Pitt. (14), Oct. 22, 1933
      Chicago Bears (17) vs G.B. (14), Oct. 22, 1933
Highest Average Distance, Punting, Season
47.6   Detroit 1961

PUNT RETURNS

Most Punt Returns, Season
63   Denver 1970
Fewest Punt Returns, Season
14   Los Angeles 1961
      Philadelphia 1962
Most Punt Returns, Game
12   Philadelphia vs Clev., Dec. 3, 1950
Most Punt Returns, Both Teams, Game
17   Philadelphia (12) vs Clev. (5), Dec. 3, 1950

Yards Returning Punts

Most Yards, Punt Returns, Season
781   Chicago Bears 1948
Most Yards, Punt Returns, Game
231   Detroit vs S.F., Oct. 6, 1963
Most Yards, Punt Returns, Both Teams, Game
245   Detroit (231) vs S.F. (14), Oct. 6, 1963

Average Yards Returning Punts

Highest Average, Punt Returns, Season
20.2   Chicago Bears 1941

Touchdowns Returning Punts

Most Touchdowns, Punt Returns, Season
5   Chicago Cards 1959
Most Touchdowns, Punt Returns, Game
2   Detroit vs L.A., Oct. 14 & vs G.B., Nov. 22, 1951
      Chicago Cards vs Pitt., Nov. 1 & vs N.Y. Giants, Nov. 22,
      1959
      New York Titans vs Denver, Sept. 24, 1961

Yards Returning Kickoffs

Most Yards, Kickoff Returns, Season
1,824   Houston 1963
Most Yards, Kickoff Returns, Game
362   Detroit vs L.A., Oct. 29, 1950
Most Yards, Kickoff Returns, Both Teams, Game
560   Detroit (362) vs L.A. (198), Oct. 29, 1950

Average Yards Returning Kickoff
Highest Average, Kickoff Returns, Season
28.9 Pittsburgh 1952

Touchdowns Returning Kickoffs
Most Touchdowns, Kickoff Returns, Season
4 Green Bay 1967
Chicago Bears 1970
Most Touchdowns, Kickoff Returns, Game
2 Chicago Bears vs G.B., Nov. 9, 1952
Philadelphia vs Dall., Nov. 6, 1966
Green Bay vs Clev., Nov. 12, 1967

FUMBLES
Most Fumbles, Season
56 Chicago Bears 1938
Fewest Fumbles, Season
8 Cleveland 1959
Most Fumbles, Game
10 Phil/Pitt vs N.Y. Giants, Oct. 9, 1943
Detroit vs Minn., Nov. 12, 1967
Kansas City vs Hou., Oct. 12, 1969
Most Fumbles, Both Teams, Game
14 Chicago Bears (7) vs Clev. Rams (7), Nov. 24, 1940
St. Louis (8) vs N.Y. Giants (6), Sept. 17, 1961
Kansas City (10) vs Hous. (4), Oct. 12, 1969

Fumbles Recovered
Most Fumbles Recovered, Season (Own and Opponents')
58 Minnesota 1963
Fewest Fumbles Recovered, Season (Own and Opponents')
13 Kansas City 1966
Baltimore 1967
New York Jets 1967
Philadelphia 1968
Most Fumbles Recovered, Game (Own and Opponents')
10 Denver vs Buff., Dec. 13, 1964
Most Own Fumbles Recovered, Season
27 Philadelphia 1946
Minnesota 1963
Fewest Own Fumbles Recovered, Season
2 Washington 1958
Most Opponents' Fumbles Recovered, Season
31 Minnesota 1963
Fewest Opponents' Fumbles Recovered, Season
4 Philadelphia 1944
Most Opponents' Fumbles Recovered, Game
7 Buffalo vs Cin., Nov. 30, 1969

Most Touchdowns, Fumbles Recovered, Season (Own and Opponents')
5 Los Angeles 1952 (1-own, 4-opp)
San Francisco 1965 (1-own, 4-opp)
Most Touchdowns, Own Fumbles Recovered, Season
2 Chicago Bears 1953
Most Touchdowns, Opponents' Fumbles Recovered, Season
4 Boston Yanks 1948
Los Angeles 1952
San Francisco 1965

PENALTIES
Most Seasons Leading League, Fewest Penalties
9 Pittsburgh 1946-47, 50-52, 54, 63, 65, 68
Most Seasons Leading League, Most Penalties
15 Chicago Bears 1941-44, 46-49, 51, 59-61, 63, 65, 68
Fewest Penalties, Season
19 Detroit 1937
Most Penalties, Season
122 Washington 1948
Chicago Bears 1948
Fewest Penalties, Game
0 By many teams
Most Penalties, Game
22 Brooklyn vs G.B., Sept. 17, 1944
Chicago Bears vs Phil., Nov. 26, 1944
Fewest Penalties, Both Teams, Game
0 Brooklyn vs Pitt., Oct. 28, 1934
Brooklyn vs Bos. Redskins, Sept. 28, 1936
Cleveland Rams vs Chi. Bears, Oct. 9, 1938
Pittsburgh vs Phil., Nov. 10, 1940
Most Penalties, Both Teams, Game
37 Cleveland (21) vs Chi. Bears (16), Nov. 25, 1951
Most Seasons Leading League, Fewest Yards Penalized
7 Pittsburgh 1946-47, 50, 52, 62, 65, 68
Bos./Wash. 1935, 53-54, 56-58, 70
Fewest Yards Penalized, Season
139 Detroit 1937
Most Yards Penalized, Season
1,274 Oakland 1969
Fewest Yards Penalized, Game
0 By many teams
Most Yards Penalized, Game
209 Cleveland vs Chi. Bears, Nov. 25, 1951
Fewest Yards Penalized, Both Teams, Game
0 Brooklyn vs Pitt., Oct. 28, 1934
Brooklyn vs Bos. Redskins, Sept. 28, 1936
Cleveland vs Chi. Bears, Oct. 9, 1938
Pittsburgh vs Phil., Nov. 10, 1940
Most Yards Penalized, Both Teams, Game
374 Cleveland (209) vs Chi. Bears (165), Nov. 25, 1951

The Washington Redskins have led the NFL in passing during nine seasons.

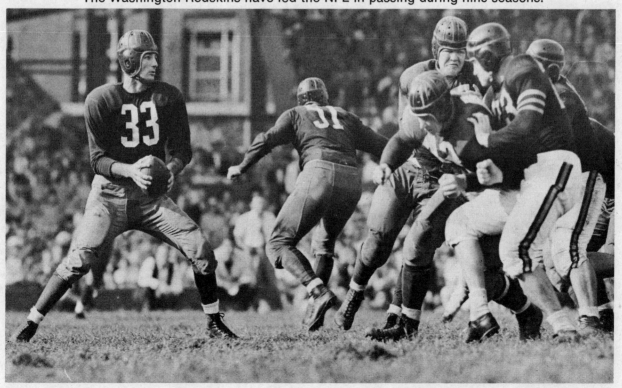

DEFENSE
SCORING
Fewest Points Allowed, Season
15   Canton 1922
Since 1932
44   Chicago Bears 1932
Most Points Allowed, Season
501   New York Giants 1966
Fewest Touchdowns Allowed, Season
1   Canton 1923
Since 1932
7   Detroit 1934
Most Touchdowns Allowed, Season
66   New York Giants 1966

FIRST DOWNS
Fewest First Downs Allowed, Season
86   Philadelphia 1944
Most First Downs Allowed, Season
304   San Francisco 1963
Fewest First Downs Allowed, Rushing, Season
35   Chicago Bears 1942
Most First Downs Allowed, Rushing, Season
150   Baltimore 1950
Fewest First Downs Allowed, Passing, Season
33   Chicago Bears 1943
Most First Downs Allowed, Passing, Season
185   St. Louis 1969
Fewest First Downs Allowed, Penalty, Season
1   Boston Yanks 1944
Most First Downs Allowed, Penalty, Season
36   Washington 1965
Chicago Bears 1968

NET YARDS ALLOWED
Rushing and Passing
Fewest Yards Allowed, Season
1,578   Chicago Cards 1934
Most Yards Allowed, Season
5,593   Minnesota 1961
RUSHING
Fewest Yards Allowed, Rushing, Season
519   Chicago Bears 1942

Most Yards Allowed, Rushing, Season
2,857   Baltimore 1950
Fewest Touchdowns Allowed, Rushing, Season
1   New York Giants 1927
Most Touchdowns Allowed, Rushing, Season
36   Oakland 1961

PASSING
Fewest Yards Allowed, Passing, Season
625   Chicago Cards 1934
Most Yards Allowed, Passing, Season
3,674   Dallas Cowboys 1962
Most Opponents Tackled Attempting Passes, Season
67   Oakland 1967
Fewest Touchdowns Allowed, Passing Season
2   New York 1927
Most Touchdowns Allowed, Passing, Season
40   Denver 1963

INTERCEPTIONS BY
Most Passes Intercepted By, Season
49   San Diego 1961
Fewest Passes Intercepted By, Season
7   Los Angeles 1959
Most Consecutive Games, One or More Interceptions By
46   L.A./S.D. 1960-63
Most Yards Returning Interceptions, Season
929   San Diego 1961
Most Yards Returning Interceptions, Game
314   Los Angeles vs S.F., Oct. 18, 1964
Most Touchdowns, Returning Interceptions, Season
9   San Diego 1961
Most Touchdowns, Returning Interceptions, Game
3   Baltimore vs G.B., Nov. 5, 1950
Cleveland vs Chi. Bears, Dec. 11, 1960
Philadelphia vs Pitt., Dec. 12, 1965
Baltimore vs Pitt., Sept. 29, 1968
Buffalo vs N.Y. Jets, Sept. 29, 1968
Houston vs S.D., Dec. 19, 1971
Most Touchdowns, Returning Interceptions, Both Teams, Game
4   Philadelphia (3) vs Pitt. (1), Dec. 12, 1965

PAST POST SEASON RESULTS

MIAMI PLAYOFF BOWL
(Western Conference won 8, Eastern Conference won 2)
1970—Los Angeles Rams 31; Dallas Cowboys 0
1969—Dallas Cowboys 17; Minnesota Vikings 13
1968—Los Angeles Rams 30; Cleveland Browns 6
1967—Baltimore Colts 20; Philadelphia Eagles 14
1966—Baltimore Colts 35; Dallas Cowboys 3
1965—St. Louis Cardinals 24; Green Bay Packers 17
1964—Green Bay Packers 40; Cleveland Browns 23
1963—Detroit Lions 17; Pittsburgh Steelers 10
1962—Detroit Lions 28; Philadelphia Eagles 10
1961—Detroit Lions 17; Cleveland Browns 16

NFL PRO BOWL AT LOS ANGELES
(Western Conference won 13, Eastern Conference won 7)
1970—West 16, East 13	1960—West 38, East 21
1969—West 10, East 7	1959—East 28, West 21
1968—West 38, East 20	1958—West 26, East 7
1967—East 20, West 10	1957—West 19, East 10
1966—East 36, West 7	1956—East 31, West 30
1965—West 34, East 14	1955—West 26, East 19
1964—West 31, East 17	1954—East 20, West 9
1963—East 30, West 20	1953—West 27, East 7
1962—West 31, East 30	1952—West 30, East 13
1961—West 35, East 31	1951—East 28, West 27

AFL ALL-STAR GAME
1970—West 26, East 3	1965—West 38, East 14
1969—West 38, East 25	1964—West 27, East 24
1968—East 25, West 24	1963—West 21, East 21
1967—East 30, West 23	1962—West 47, East 27
1966—All-Stars 30, Buffalo 19	

NFC-AFC PRO BOWL
1972—AFC 33, NFC 28   1970—NFC 27, AFC 6
1971—AFC 26, NFC 13

CHICAGO ALL-STAR GAME RESULTS
(Pro teams won 28, lost 9, tied 2)
1972—Dallas 20, All-Stars 7	1952—Los Ang. 10, All-Stars 7
1971—Balt. 24, All-Stars 17	1951—Cleve. 33, All-Stars 0
1970—Kans. City 24, All-Stars 3	1950—All-Stars 17, Phila. 7
1969—N.Y. Jets 26, All-Stars 24	1949—Phila. 38, All-Stars 0
1968—Gr'n Bay 34, All-Stars 17	1948—Chi. Card. 28, All-Stars 0
1967—Gr'n Bay 27, All-Stars 0	1947—All-Stars 16, Chi. Bears 0
1966—Gr'n Bay 38, All-Stars 0	1946—All-Stars 16, Los Ang. 0
1965—Cleve. 24, All-Stars 16	1945—Gr'n Bay 19, All-Stars 7
1964—Chicago 28, All-Stars 17	1944—Chi. B'rs 24, All-Stars 21
1963—All-Stars 20, Gr'n Bay 17	1943—All-Stars 27, Wash. 7
1962—Gr'n Bay 42, All-Stars 20	1942—Chi. B'rs 21, All-Stars 0
1961—Phila. 28, All-Stars 14	1941—Chi. B'rs 37, All-Stars 13
1960—Balt. 32, All-Stars 7	1940—Gr'n Bay 45, All-Stars 28
1959—Balt. 29, All-Stars 0	1939—New York 9, All-Stars 0
1958—All-Stars 35, Detroit 19	1938—All-Stars 28, Wash. 16
1957—N. York 22, All-Stars 12	1937—All-Stars 6, Gr'n Bay 0
1956—Cleve. 26, All-Stars 0	1936—Detroit 7, All-Stars 7, tie
1955—All-Stars 30, Cleve. 27	1935—Chi. B'rs 5, All-Stars 0
1954—Detroit 31, All-Stars 6	1934—Chi. B'rs 0, All-Stars 0, tie
1953—Detroit 24, All-Stars 10	

1957 Chicago All-Star Game—coach Curly Lambeau with College All-Stars (l. to r.) John Brodie, Otto Graham (quarterback coach), Len Dawson, and Paul Hornung.

1961 NFL Pro Bowl action with John Unitas (19), Jon Arnett (26) and Andy Robustelli (80).

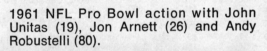

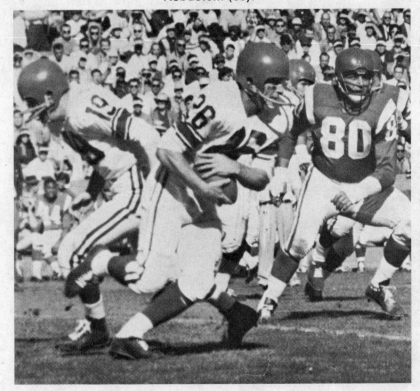

1964 NFL Pro Bowl Game—coach George Halas (right) with Phil Handler.

INDIVIDUAL HONORS

JIM THORPE TROPHY (Most Valuable Player)

1972—Larry Brown
1971—Bob Griese
1970—John Brodie
1969—Roman Gabriel
1968—Earl Morrall
1967—John Unitas
1966—Bryan Starr
1965—Jim Brown
1964—Leonard Moore

1963—Jim Brown and Y. A. Tittle
1962—Jim Taylor
1961—Y. A. Tittle
1960—Norman Van Brocklin
1959—Charles Conerly
1958—James Brown
1957—John Unitas
1956—Frank Gifford
1955—Harlon Hill

ROOKIE OF YEAR (NFL/NFC/AFL/AFC)

1972—Franco Harris, Pitts. (AFC) offense
    Tommy Casanova, Cincy. (AFC) defense
1971—John Brockington, G.B. (NFC), offense
    Isiah Robertson, L.A. (NFC), defense
1970—Bruce Taylor, S.F. (NFC), defense
    Dennis Shaw, Buff. (AFC), offense

1969—Calvin Hill, Dal.
    Carl Garrett, Bos. (AFL)
1968—Earl McCullouch, Det.
    Paul Robinson, Cin. (AFL)
1967—Mel Farr, Det.
    George Webster, Hou. (AFL)
1966—John Roland, St. L.
    Bobby Burnett, Buff. (AFL)
1965—Gale Sayers, Chi.
    Joe Namath, N.Y. (AFL)
1964—Charlie Taylor, Wash.
    Matt Snell, N.Y. (AFL)
1963—Paul Flatley, Minn.
    Billy Joe, Den. (AFL)
1962—Ronnie Bull, Chi.
    Curtis McClinton, K.C. (AFL)
1961—Mike Ditka, Chi.
    Earl Faison, S.D. (AFL)
1960—Gail Cogdill, Det.
    Abner Haynes, Dal. (AFL)
1959—Nick Pietrosante, Det.
1958—Bobby Mitchell, Clev.

STATISTICAL LEADERS YEAR BY YEAR

SCORING — INDIVIDUAL

		TDs	XP	FG	Points
1972	— Chester Marcol, G.B. (NFC)	0	29	33	128
	— Bobby Howfield, N.Y. (AFC)	0	40	27	121
1971	— Garo Yepremian, Miami (AFC)	0	33	28	117
	— Curt Knight, Washington (NFC)	0	27	29	114
1970	— Fred Cox, Minnesota (NFC)	0	35	30	125
	— Jan Stenerud, Kansas City (AFC)	0	26	30	116
1969	— Jim Turner, New York (AFL)	0	33	32	129
	— Fred Cox, Minnesota (NFL)	0	43	26	121
1968	— Jim Turner, New York (AFL)	0	43	34	145
	— Leroy Kelly, Cleveland (NFL)	20	0	0	120
1967	— Jim Bakken, St. Louis (NFL)	0	36	27	117
	— George Blanda, Oakland (AFL)	0	56	20	116
1966	— Gino Cappelletti, Boston (AFL)	6	35	16	119
	— Bruce Gossett, Los Angeles (NFL)	0	29	28	113
1965	— Gale Sayers, Chicago (NFL)	22	0	0	132
	— Gino Cappelletti, Boston (AFL)	9	27	17	132
1964	— Gino Cappelletti, Boston (AFL)	7	36	25	155
	— Lenny Moore, Baltimore (NFL)	20	0	0	120
1963	— Gino Cappelletti, Boston (AFL)	2	35	22	113
	— Don Chandler, New York (NFL)	0	52	18	106
1962	— Gene Mingo, Denver (AFL)	4	32	27	137
	— Jim Taylor, Green Bay (NFL)	19	0	0	114
1961	— Gino Cappelletti, Boston (AFL)	8	48	17	147
	— Paul Hornung, Green Bay (NFL)	10	41	15	146
1960	— Paul Hornung, Green Bay (NFL)	15	41	15	176
	— Gene Mingo, Denver (AFL)	6	33	18	123
1959	— Paul Hornung, Green Bay	7	31	7	94
1958	— Jim Brown, Cleveland Browns	18	0	0	108
1957	— Sam Baker, Washington	1	29	14	77
	— Lou Groza, Cleveland Browns	0	32	15	77
1956	— Bobby Layne, Detroit	5	33	12	99
1955	— Doak Walker, Detroit	7	27	9	96
1954	— Robert Walston, Philadelphia	11	36	4	114
1953	— Gordon Soltau, San Francisco	6	48	10	114
1952	— Gordon Soltau, San Francisco	7	34	6	94
1951	— Elroy Hirsch, Los Angeles	17	0	0	102
1950	— Doak Walker, Detroit*	11	38	8	128
1949	— Pat Harder, Chicago Cardinals	8	45	3	102
	— Gene Roberts, New York Giants	17	0	0	102
1948	— Pat Harder, Chicago Cardinals	6	53	7	110
1947	— Pat Harder, Chicago Cardinals	7	39	7	102
1946	— Ted Fritsch, Green Bay	10	13	9	100
1945	— Steve Van Buren, Philadelphia	18	2	0	110
1944	— Don Hutson, Green Bay	9	31	0	85
1943	— Don Hutson, Green Bay	12	36	3	117
1942	— Don Hutson, Green Bay	17	33	1	136
1941	— Don Hutson, Green Bay	12	20	1	95
1940	— Don Hutson, Green Bay	7	15	0	57
1939	— Andy Farkas, Washington	11	2	0	68
1938	— Clarke Hinkle, Green Bay	7	7	3	58
1937	— Jack Manders, Chicago Bears	5	15	8	69
1936	— Earl (Dutch) Clark, Detroit	7	19	4	73
1935	— Earl (Dutch) Clark, Detroit	6	16	1	55
1934	— Jack Manders, Chicago Bears	3	28	10	76
1933	— Ken Strong, New York Giants	6	13	5	64
	— Glenn Presnell, Portsmouth	6	10	6	64
1932	— Earl (Dutch) Clark, Portsmouth	6	10	3	55

*First year in league

RUSHING — INDIVIDUAL

		Yards	Ats	TDs
1972	— O. J. Simpson, Buffalo (AFC)	1,251	292	6
	— Larry Brown, Washington (NFC)	1,216	285	8
1971	— Floyd Little, Denver (AFC)	1,133	284	6
	— John Brockington, Green Bay (NFC)	1,105	216	4
1970	— Larry Brown, Washington (NFC)	1,125	237	5
	— Floyd Little, Denver (AFC)	901	209	3
1969	— Gale Sayers, Chicago (NFL)	1,032	236	8
	— Dick Post, San Diego (AFL)	873	182	6
1968	— Leroy Kelly, Cleveland (NFL)	1,239	248	16
	— Paul Robinson, Cincinnati (AFL)*	1,023	238	8
1967	— Jim Nance, Boston (AFL)	1,216	269	7
	— Leroy Kelly, Cleveland (NFL)	1,205	235	11
1966	— Jim Nance, Boston (AFL)	1,458	299	11
	— Gale Sayers, Chicago (NFL)	1,231	229	8
1965	— Jim Brown, Cleveland (NFL)	1,544	289	17
	— Paul Lowe, San Diego (AFL)	1,121	222	7
1964	— Jim Brown, Cleveland (NFL)	1,446	280	7
	— Cookie Gilchrist, Buffalo (AFL)	981	230	6
1963	— Jim Brown, Cleveland (NFL)	1,863	291	12
	— Clem Daniels, Oakland (AFL)	1,099	215	3
1962	— Jim Taylor, Green Bay (NFL)	1,474	272	19
	— Cookie Gilchrist, Buffalo (AFL)	1,096	214	13
1961	— Jim Brown, Cleveland (NFL)	1,408	305	8
	— Billy Cannon, Houston (AFL)	948	200	6
1960	— Jim Brown, Cleveland (NFL)	1,257	215	9
	— Abner Haynes, Dallas (AFL)	875	156	9
1959	— Jim Brown, Cleveland	1,329	290	14
1958	— Jim Brown, Cleveland	1,527	257	17
1957	— Jim Brown, Cleveland*	942	202	9
1956	— Rick Casares, Chicago Bears	1,126	234	12
1955	— Alan Ameche, Baltimore*	961	213	9
1954	— Joe Perry, San Francisco	1,049	173	8
1953	— Joe Perry, San Francisco	1,018	192	10
1952	— Dan Towler, Los Angeles	894	156	10
1951	— Eddie Price, New York Giants	971	271	7
1950	— Marion Motley, Cleveland*	810	140	3
1949	— Steve Van Buren, Philadelphia	1,146	263	11
1948	— Steve Van Buren, Philadelphia	945	201	10
1947	— Steve Van Buren, Philadelphia	1,008	217	13
1946	— Bill Dudley, Pittsburgh	604	146	3
1945	— Steve Van Buren, Philadelphia	832	143	15
1944	— Bill Paschal, New York	737	196	9
1943	— Bill Paschal, New York*	572	147	10
1942	— Bill Dudley, Pittsburgh*	696	162	5
1941	— Clarence Manders, Brooklyn	486	111	6
1940	— Byron White, Detroit	514	146	5
1939	— Bill Osmanski, Chicago Bears*	699	121	7
1938	— Byron White, Pittsburgh*	567	152	4
1937	— Cliff Battles, Washington	874	216	6
1936	— Alphonse Leemans, New York*	830	206	2
1935	— Doug Russell, Chicago Cardinals	499	140	0
1934	— Beattie Feathers, Chicago Bears*	1,004	101	8
1933	— Jim Musick, Boston	809	173	5
1932	— Cliff Battles, Boston	576	148	0

*First year in League

Larry Brown, 1972's Most Valuable Player.

Franco Harris, 1972 Rookie of the Year (offense).

Clifton Boutelle

Floyd Little, the AFC's Leading Rusher for 1971.

Gale Sayers, 1966 NFL rushing leader, 1965 NFL scoring leader and 1965 NFL Rookie of the Year.

PASSING — INDIVIDUAL

Year	Player	Passes	Comp	Yards	Tds	Inter.
1972	Norm Snead, N.Y. (NFC)	325	196	2,307	17	12
	Earl Morrall, Miami (AFC)	150	83	1,360	11	7
1971	Roger Staubach, Dallas (NFC)	211	126	1,882	15	4
	Bob Griese, Miami (AFC)	263	145	2,089	19	9
1970	John Brodie, San Fran. (NFC)	378	223	2,941	24	10
	Daryl Lamonica, Oakland (AFC)	356	179	2,516	22	15
1969	(Sonny) Jurgensen, Wa. (NFL)	442	274	3,102	22	15
	Greg Cook, Cincinnati (AFL)*	197	106	1,854	15	11
1968	Len Dawson, Kan. City (AFL)	224	131	2,109	17	9
	Earl Morrall, Baltimore (NFL)	317	182	2,909	26	17
1967	(Sonny) Jurgensen, Wa. (NFL)	508	288	3,747	31	16
	Daryl Lamonica, Oakland (AFL)	425	220	3,228	30	20
1966	Bart Starr, Green Bay (NFL)	251	156	2,257	14	3
	Len Dawson, Kan. City (AFL)	284	159	2,527	26	10
1965	Rudy Bukich, Chicago (NFL)	312	176	2,641	20	9
	John Hadl, San Diego (AFL)	348	174	2,798	20	21
1964	Len Dawson, Kan. City (AFL)	354	199	2,879	30	18
	Bart Starr, Green Bay (NFL)	272	163	2,144	15	4
1963	Y. A. Tittle, New York (NFL)	367	221	3,145	36	14
	Tobin Rote, San Diego (AFL)	286	170	2,510	20	17
1962	Len Dawson, Dallas (AFL)	310	189	2,759	29	17
	Bart Starr, Green Bay (NFL)	285	178	2,438	12	9
1961	George Blanda, Houston (AFL)	362	187	3,330	36	22
	Milt Plum, Cleveland (NFL)	302	177	2,416	18	10
1960	Milt Plum, Cleveland (NFL)	250	151	2,297	21	5
	Jack Kemp, Los Angeles (AFL)	406	211	3,018	20	25
1959	Charles Conerly, New York	194	113	1,706	14	4
1958	Eddie LeBaron, Washington	145	79	1,365	11	10
1957	Tommy O'Connell, Cleveland	110	63	1,229	9	8
1956	Eddie Brown, Chicago Bears	168	96	1,667	11	12
1955	Otto Graham, Cleveland	185	98	1,721	15	8
1954	Norman Van Brocklin, L.A.	260	139	2,637	13	21
1953	Otto Graham, Cleveland	258	167	2,722	11	9
1952	Norman Van Brocklin, L.A.	205	113	1,736	14	17
1951	Bob Waterfield, L.A.	176	88	1,566	13	10
1950	Norman Van Brocklin, L.A.	233	127	2,061	18	14
1949	Sammy Baugh, Washington	255	145	1,903	18	14
1948	Tommy Thompson, Phila.	246	141	1,965	25	11
1947	Sammy Baugh, Washington	354	210	2,938	25	15
1946	Bob Waterfield, L.A.	251	127	1,747	18	17
1945	Sammy Baugh, Washington	182	128	1,669	11	4
	Sid Luckman, Chicago Bears	217	117	1,725	14	10
1944	Frank Filchock, Washington	147	84	1,139	13	9
1943	Sammy Baugh, Washington	239	133	1,754	23	19
1942	Cecil Isbell, Green Bay	268	146	2,021	24	14
1941	Cecil Isbell, Green Bay	206	117	1,479	15	11
1940	Sammy Baugh, Washington	177	111	1,367	12	10
1939	Parker Hall, Cleveland Rams*	208	106	1,227	9	13
1938	Ed Danowski, N.Y. Giants	129	70	848	8	8
1937	Sammy Baugh, Washington*	171	81	1,127	7	14
1936	Arnie Herber, Green Bay	173	77	1,239	9	13
1935	Ed Danowski, N.Y. Giants	113	57	794	9	9
1934	Arnie Herber, Green Bay	115	42	790	8	12
1933	Harry Newman, New York*	136	53	973	8	17
1932	Arnie Herber, Green Bay	101	37	639	9	9

*First year in League

PASS RECEIVING — INDIVIDUAL

Year	Player	No.	Yards	TDs
1972	Harold Jackson, Philly (NFL)	62	1,048	4
	Fred Biletnikoff, Oakland (AFC)	58	804	7
1971	Fred Biletnikoff, Oakland (AFC)	61	929	9
	Bob Tucker, New York Giants (NFC)	59	791	4
1970	Dick Gordon, Chicago (NFC)	71	1,026	13
	Marlin Briscoe, Buffalo (AFC)	57	1,036	8
1969	Dan Abramowicz, New Orleans (NFL)	73	1,015	7
	Lance Alworth, San Diego (AFL)	64	1,003	4
1968	Clifton McNeil, San Francisco (NFL)	71	994	7
	Lance Alworth, San Diego (AFL)	68	1,312	10
1967	George Sauer, New York (AFL)	75	1,189	6
	Charley Taylor, Washington (NFL)	70	990	9
1966	Lance Alworth, San Diego (AFL)	73	1,383	13
	Charley Taylor, Washington (NFL)	72	1,119	12
1965	Lionel Taylor, Denver (AFL)	85	1,131	6
	Dave Parks, San Francisco (NFL)	80	1,344	12
1964	Charley Hennigan, Houston (AFL)	101	1,546	8
	Johnny Morris, Chicago (NFL)	93	1,200	10
1963	Lionel Taylor, Denver (AFL)	78	1,101	10
	Bobby Joe Conrad, St. Louis (NFL)	73	967	10
1962	Lionel Taylor, Denver (AFL)	77	908	4
	Bobby Mitchell, Washington (NFL)	72	1,384	11
1961	Lionel Taylor, Denver (AFL)	100	1,176	4
	Jim Phillips, Los Angeles (NFL)	78	1,092	5
1960	Lionel Taylor, Denver (AFL)	92	1,235	12
	Raymond Berry, Baltimore (NFL)	74	1,298	10
1959	Raymond Berry, Baltimore	66	959	14
1958	Raymond Berry, Baltimore &	56	794	9
	Pete Retzlaff, Philadelphia	56	766	2
1957	Billy Wilson, San Francisco	52	757	6
1956	Billy Wilson, San Francisco	60	889	5
1955	Pete Pihos, Philadelphia	62	864	7
1954	Pete Pihos, Philadelphia &	60	872	10
	Billy Watson, San Francisco	60	830	5

1953	Pete Pihos, Philadelphia	63	1,049	10
1952	Mac Speedie, Cleveland	62	911	5
1951	Elroy Hirsch, Los Angeles	66	1,495	17
1950	Tom Fears, Los Angeles	84	1,116	7
1949	Tom Fears, Los Angeles	77	1,013	9
1948	Tom Fears, Los Angeles*	51	698	4
1947	Jim Keane, Chicago Bears	64	910	10
1946	Jim Benton, Los Angeles	63	981	6
1945	Don Hutson, Green Bay	47	834	9
1944	Don Hutson, Green Bay	58	866	9
1943	Don Hutson, Green Bay	47	776	11
1942	Don Hutson, Green Bay	74	1,211	17
1941	Don Hutson, Green Bay	58	738	10
1940	Don Looney, Philadelphia*	58	707	4
1939	Don Hutson, Green Bay	34	846	6
1938	Gaynell Tinsley, Chi. Cards	41	516	1
1937	Don Hutson, Green Bay	41	552	7
1936	Don Hutson, Green Bay	34	536	8
1935	Tod Goodwin, New York*	26	432	4
1934	Joe Carter, Philadelphia	16	238	4
	Morris Badgro, New York Giants	16	206	0
1933	John Kelly, Brooklyn	22	246	3
1932	Ray Flaherty, New York Giants	21	350	3

*First year in League

MOST FIELD GOALS — INDIVIDUALS

1972	Chester Marcol, Green Bay (NFC)	33
	Roy Gerela, Pittsburgh (AFC)	28
1971	Curt Knight, Washington (NFC)	29
	Garo Yepremian, Miami (AFC)	28
1970	Fred Cox, Minnesota (NFC)	30
	Jan Stenerud, Kansas City (AFC)	30
1969	Jim Turner, New York (AFL)	32
	Fred Cox, Minnesota (NFL)	26
1968	Jim Turner, New York (AFL)	34
	Mac Percival, Chicago (NFL)	25
1967	Jim Bakken, St. Louis (NFL)	27
	Jan Stenerud, Kansas City (AFL)	21
1966	Bruce Gossett, Los Angeles (NFL)	28
	Mike Mercer, Oakland-Kansas City (AFL)	21
1965	Pete Gogolak, Buffalo (AFL)	28
	Fred Cox, Minnesota (NFL)	23
1964	Jim Bakken, St. Louis (NFL)	25
	G. Cappelletti, Boston (AFL)	25
1963	Jim Martin, Baltimore (NFL)	24
	G. Cappelletti, Boston (AFL)	22
1962	Gene Mingo, Denver (AFL)	27
	Lou Michaels, Pittsburgh (NFL)	26
1961	Steve Myhra, Baltimore (NFL)	21
	G. Cappelletti, Boston (AFL)	17
1960	Tommy Davis, San Francisco (NFL)	19
	Gene Mingo, Denver (AFL)	18
1959	Pat Summerall, New York	20
1958	Paige Cothren, Los Angeles & Tom Miner, Pittsburgh*	14
1957	Lou Groza, Cleveland	15
1956	Sam Baker, Washington	17
1955	Fred Cone, Green Bay	16
1954	Lou Groza, Cleveland	16
1953	Lou Groza, Cleveland	23
1952	Lou Groza, Cleveland	19
1951	Bob Waterfield, Los Angeles	13
1950	Lou Groza, Cleveland*	13
1949	Cliff Patton, Philadelphia & Bob Waterfield, Los Angeles	9
1948	Cliff Patton, Philadelphia	8
1947	Ward Cuff, Green Bay, Pat Harder, Chicago Cards & Bob Waterfield, Los Angeles	7
1946	Ted Fritsch, Green Bay	9
1945	Joe Aguirre, Washington	7
1944	Ken Strong, New York	6
1943	Ward Cuff, New York & Don Hutson, Green Bay	3
1942	Bill Daddio, Chicago Cards	5
1941	Clark Hinkle, Green Bay	6
1940	Clark Hinkle, Green Bay	9
1939	Ward Cuff, New York	7
1938	Ward Cuff, New York & Ralph Kercheval, Brooklyn	5
1937	Jack Manders, Chicago Bears	8
1936	Jack Manders, Chicago Bears & Armand Niccolai, Pittsburgh	7
1935	Armand Niccolai, Pittsburgh & Bill Smith, Chicago Cards	6
1934	Jack Manders, Chicago Bears	10
1933	Jack Manders, Chicago Bears* & Glenn Presnell, Portsmouth	6
1932	Earl Clark, Portsmouth	3

*First year in League

INTERCEPTIONS — INDIVIDUAL

Year	Player	No.	Yards
1972	Bill Bradley, Philadelphia (NFC)	9	73
	Mike Sensibaugh, Kansas City (AFC)	8	65
1971	Bill Bradley, Philadelphia (NFC)	11	248
	Ken Houston, Houston (AFC)	9	220
1970	Johnny Robinson, Kansas City (AFC)	10	155
	Dick LeBeau, Detroit (NFC)	9	96
1969	Mel Renfro, Dallas (NFL)	10	118
	Emmitt Thomas, Kansas City (AFL)	9	146

(Above) Bob Griese, 1971 AFC passing champ. (Right) Bob Tucker (38), the NFC's leading pass receiver in 1971. (Below) Fred Cox, field goal leader of the NFC in 1970.

Ronald Mrowiec

Clifton Boutelle

1968 — Dave Grayson, Oakland (AFL) ... 10 ... 195
— Willie Williams, New York (NFL) ... 10 ... 103
1967 — Miller Farr, Houston (AFL) ... 10 ... 264
— Lem Barney, Detroit (NFL) ... 10 ... 232
— Tom Janik, Buffalo (AFL) ... 10 ... 222
— Dave Whitsell, New Orleans (NFL) ... 10 ... 178
— Dick Westmoreland, Miami (AFL) ... 10 ... 127
1966 — Larry Wilson, St. Louis (NFL) ... 10 ... 180
— Johnny Robinson, Kansas City (AFL) ... 10 ... 136
— Bobby Hunt, Kansas City (AFL) ... 10 ... 113
1965 — W. K. Hicks, Houston (AFL) ... 9 ... 156
— Bobby Boyd, Baltimore (NFL) ... 9 ... 78
1964 — Dainard Paulson, New York (AFL) ... 12 ... 157
— Paul Krause, Washington (NFL)* ... 12 ... 140
1963 — Fred Glick, Houston (AFL) ... 12 ... 180
— Dick Lynch, New York (NFL) ... 9 ... 251
— Rosie Taylor, Chicago (NFL) ... 9 ... 172
1962 — Lee Riley, New York (AFL) ... 11 ... 122
— Willie Wood, Green Bay (NFL) ... 9 ... 132
1961 — Billy Atkins, Buffalo (AFL) ... 10 ... 158
— Dick Lynch, New York (NFL) ... 9 ... 60
1960 — Austin Gonsoulin, Denver (AFL)* ... 11 ... 98
— Dave Baker, San Francisco (NFL) ... 10 ... 96
— Jerry Norton, St. Louis (NFL) ... 10 ... 96
1959 — Dean Derby, Pittsburgh and ... 7 ... 127
Milt Davis, Baltimore and ... 7 ... 119
Don Shinnick, Baltimore ... 7 ... 70
1958 — Jim Patton, New York ... 11 ... 183
1957 — Milt Davis, Baltimore* ... 10 ... 219
Jack Christiansen, Detroit ... 10 ... 137
Jack Butler, Pittsburgh ... 10 ... 85
1956 — Lindon Crow, Chicago Cardinals ... 11 ... 170
1955 — Will Sherman, Los Angeles ... 11 ... 101
1954 — Dick (Night Train) Lane, Chicago Cardinals ... 10 ... 181
1953 — Jack Christiansen, Detroit ... 12 ... 238
1952 — Dick (Night Train) Lane, Los Angeles* ... 14 ... 298
1951 — Otto Schnellbacher, New York Giants ... 11 ... 194
1950 — Orban (Spec) Sanders, New York Yanks* ... 13 ... 199
1949 — Bob Nussbaumer, Chicago Cardinals ... 12 ... 157
1948 — Dan Sandifer, Washington* ... 13 ... 258
1947 — Frank Reagan, New York Giants and ... 10 ... 203
Frank Seno, Boston Yanks ... 10 ... 100
1946 — Bill Dudley, Pittsburgh ... 10 ... 242
1945 — Roy Zimmerman, Philadelphia ... 7 ... 90
1944 — Howard Livingston, New York Giants* ... 9 ... 172
1943 — Sammy Baugh, Washington ... 11 ... 112
1942 — Clyde (Bulldog) Turner, Chicago Bears ... 8 ... 96
1941 — Marshall Goldberg, Chicago Cardinals and ... 7 ... 54
Arthur Jones, Pittsburgh* ... 7 ... 35
1940 — Clarence (Ace) Parker, Brooklyn ... 6 ... 146
— Kent Ryan, Detroit ... 6 ... 65
— Don Hutson, Green Bay ... 6 ... 24

*First year in League

PUNTING — INDIVIDUAL

	Att.	Avg.
1972 — Jerrel Wilson, Kansas City (AFC)	66	44.8
— Dave Chapple, Los Angeles (NFC)	53	44.2
1971 — Dave Lewis, Cincinnati (AFC)	72	44.8
— Tom McNeill, Philadelphia (NFC)	73	42.0
1970 — Dave Lewis, Cincinnati (AFC)*	79	46.2
— Julian Fagan, New Orleans (NFC)*	77	42.5
1969 — David Lee, Baltimore (NFL)	57	45.3
— Dennis Partee, San Diego (AFL)	71	44.6
1968 — Jerrel Wilson, Kansas City (AFL)	63	45.1
— Billy Lothridge, Atlanta (NFL)	75	44.3
1967 — Bob Scarpitto, Denver (AFL)	105	44.9
— Billy Lothridge, Atlanta (NFL)	87	43.7
1966 — Bob Scarpitto, Denver (AFL)	76	45.8
— David Lee, Baltimore (NFL)	49	45.6
1965 — Gary Collins, Cleveland (NFL)	65	46.7
— Jerrel Wilson, Kansas City (AFL)	69	45.4
1964 — Bobby Walden, Minnesota (NFL)	72	46.4
— Jim Fraser, Denver (AFL)	73	44.2
1963 — Yale Lary, Detroit (NFL)	35	48.9
— Jim Fraser, Denver (AFL)	81	44.4
1962 — Tommy Davis, San Francisco (NFL)	48	45.6
— Jim Fraser, Denver (AFL)	55	43.6
1961 — Yale Lary, Detroit (NFL)	52	48.4
— Billy Atkins, Buffalo (AFL)	85	44.5
1960 — Jerry Norton, St. Louis (NFL)	39	45.6
— Paul Maguire, Los Angeles (AFL)*	43	40.5
1959 — Yale Lary, Detroit	45	47.1
1958 — Sam Baker, Washington	48	45.4
1957 — Don Chandler, New York	60	44.6
1956 — Norm Van Brocklin, Los Angeles	48	43.1
1955 — Norm Van Brocklin, Los Angeles	60	44.6
1954 — Pat Brady, Pittsburgh	66	43.2
1953 — Pat Brady, Pittsburgh	80	46.8
1952 — Horace Gillom, Cleveland Browns	61	45.7
1951 — Horace Gillom, Cleveland Browns	73	45.5
1950 — Fred Morrison, Chicago Bears*	57	43.3
1949 — Mike Boyda, N.Y. Bulldogs*	56	44.2
1948 — Joe Muha, Philadelphia	57	47.3
1947 — Jack Jacobs, Green Bay	57	43.5

1946 — Roy McKay, Green Bay	64	42.7
1945 — Roy McKay, Green Bay	44	41.2
1944 — Frank Sinkwich, Detroit	45	41.0
1943 — Sammy Baugh, Washington	50	45.9
1942 — Sammy Baugh, Washington	37	43.2
1941 — Sammy Baugh, Washington	30	48.7
1940 — Sammy Baugh, Washington	35	51.4
1939 — Parker Hall, Cleveland Rams*	58	40.8

*First year in League.

PUNT RETURNS — INDIVIDUAL

	No.	Yds.	Avg.
1972 — Ken Ellis, Green Bay (NFC)	14	215	15.4
— Chris Farasopoulos, New York (AFC)	17	179	10.5
1971 — Les (Speedy) Duncan, Washington (NFC)	22	233	10.6
— Leroy Kelly, Cleveland (AFC)	30	292	9.7
1970 — Ed Podolak, Kansas City (AFC)	23	311	13.5
— Bruce Taylor, San Francisco (NFC)*	43	516	12.0
1969 — Alvin Haymond, Los Angeles (NFL)	33	435	13.2
— Bill Thompson, Denver (AFL)*	25	288	11.5
1968 — Bob Hayes, Dallas (NFL)	15	312	20.8
— Noland Smith, Kansas City (AFL)	18	270	15.0
1967 — Floyd Little, Denver (AFL)*	16	270	16.9
— Ben Davis, Cleveland (NFL)	18	229	12.7
1966 — Les (Speedy) Duncan, San Diego (AFL)	18	238	13.2
— John Roland, St. Louis (NFL)*	20	221	11.1
1965 — Leroy Kelly, Cleveland (NFL)	17	265	15.6
— Les (Speedy) Duncan, San Diego (AFL)	30	464	15.5
1964 — Bobby Jancik, Houston (AFL)	12	220	18.3
— Tommy Watkins, Detroit (NFL)	16	238	14.9
1963 — Dick James, Washington (NFL)	16	214	13.4
— Claude (Hoot) Gibson, Oakland (AFL)	26	307	11.8
1962 — Dick Christy, New York (AFL)	15	250	16.7
— Pat Studstill, Detroit (NFL)	29	457	15.8
1961 — Dick Christy, New York (AFL)	18	383	21.3
— Willie Wood, Green Bay (NFL)	14	225	16.1
1960 — Abner Haynes, Dallas (AFL)	14	215	15.4
— Abe Woodson, San Francisco (NFL)	13	174	13.4
1959 — Johnny Morris, Chicago Bears	14	171	12.2
1958 — Jon Arnett, Los Angeles	13	223	12.4
1957 — Bert Zagers, Washington	14	217	15.5
1956 — Ken Konz, Cleveland Browns	13	187	14.4
1955 — Ollie Matson, Chicago Cardinals	13	245	18.8
1954 — Veryl Switzer, Green Bay*	24	306	12.8
1953 — Charley Trippi, Chicago Cardinals	21	239	11.4
1952 — Jack Christiansen Detroit	15	322	21.5
1951 — Buddy Young, N.Y. Yanks	12	231	19.3
1950 — Herb Rich, Baltimore*	12	276	23.0
1949 — Vitamin Smith, Los Angeles*	27	427	15.8
1948 — George McAfee, Chicago Bears	30	417	13.9
1947 — Walt Slater, Pittsburgh*	28	435	15.5
1946 — Bill Dudley, Pittsburgh	27	385	14.2
1945 — Dave Ryan, Detroit*	15	220	14.7
1944 — Steve Van Buren, Philadelphia*	15	230	15.3
1943 — Andy Farkas, Washington	15	168	11.2
1942 — Merlyn Condit, Brooklyn	21	210	10.0
1941 — Byron (Whizzer) White, Detroit	19	262	13.8

*First year in league.

KICKOFF RETURNS — INDIVIDUAL

	No.	Yds.	Avg.
1972 — Ron Smith, Chicago (NFC)	30	924	30.8
— Bruce Laird, Baltimore (AFC)	29	843	29.1
1971 — Travis Williams, Los Angeles (NFC)	25	743	29.7
— Eugene (Mercury) Morris, Miami (AFC)	15	423	28.2
1970 — Jim Duncan, Baltimore (AFC)	20	707	35.4
— Cecil Turner, Chicago (NFC)	23	752	32.7
1969 — Bobby Williams, Detroit (NFL)	17	563	33.1
— Bill Thompson, Denver (AFL)*	18	513	28.5
1968 — Preston Pearson, Baltimore (NFL)	15	527	35.1
— George Atkinson, Oakland (AFL)*	32	802	25.1
1967 — Travis Williams, Green Bay (NFL)*	18	739	41.1
— Zeke Moore, Houston (AFL)*	14	405	28.9
1966 — Gale Sayers, Chicago (NFL)	23	718	31.2
— Goldie Sellers, Denver (AFL)*	19	541	28.5
1965 — Tommy Watkins, Detroit (NFL)	17	584	34.4
— Abner Haynes, Denver (AFL)	34	901	26.5
1964 — Clarence Childs, New York (NFL)*	34	987	29.0
— Bo Roberson, Oakland (AFL)	36	975	27.1
1963 — Abe Woodson, San Francisco (NFL)	29	935	32.3
— Bobby Jancik, Houston (AFL)*	45	1,317	29.3
1962 — Abe Woodson, San Francisco (NFL)	37	1,157	31.3
— Bobby Jancik, Houston (AFL)*	24	726	30.3
1961 — Dick Bass, Los Angeles (NFL)	23	698	30.3
— Dave Grayson, Dallas (AFL)*	16	453	28.3
1960 — Tom Moore, Green Bay (NFL)	12	397	33.1
— Ken Hall, Houston (AFL)	19	594	31.3
1959 — Abe Woodson, San Francisco	13	382	29.4
1958 — Ollie Matson, Chicago Cardinals	14	497	35.5
1957 — Jon Arnett, Los Angeles*	18	504	28.0
1956 — Tom Wilson, Los Angeles*	15	477	31.8
1955 — Al Carmichael, Green Bay	14	418	29.9
1954 — Billy Reynolds, Cleveland Browns	14	413	29.5

(Right) Bobby Walden, the NFL's leading punter in 1964. (Below left) Ed Podolak, punt return leader of the AFC in 1970. (Below right) Leroy Kelly, leading punt returner for the AFC in 1971.

1953 — Joe Arenas, San Francisco	16	551	34.4
1952 — Lynn Chandnois, Pittsburgh	17	599	35.2
1951 — Lynn Chandnois, Pittsburgh	12	390	32.5
1950 — Vitamin Smith, Los Angeles	22	724	33.7
1949 — Don Doll, Detroit*	21	536	25.5
1948 — Joe Scott, N.Y. Giants*	20	569	28.5
1947 — Ed Saenz, Washington	29	797	27.4
1946 — Abe Karnofsky, Boston Yanks	21	599	28.5
1945 — Steve Van Buren, Philadelphia	13	373	28.7
1944 — Bob Thurbon, Card/Pitt.	12	291	24.3
1943 — Ken Heineman, Brooklyn	16	444	27.8
1942 — Marshall Goldberg, Chicago Cardinals	15	393	26.2
1941 — Marshall Goldberg, Chicago Cardinals	12	290	24.2

*First year in league.

ALL-TIME TOP PERFORMERS

TOP TEN RUSHERS — LIFETIME

Player	Seasons	Yards	Attempts
Jim Brown	9	12,312	2,359
Jim Taylor	10	8,597	1,941
Joe Perry	14	8,378	1,737
Leroy Kelly	9	6,885	1,595
John Henry Johnson	13	6,803	1,571
Don Perkins	8	6,217	1,500
Steve Van Buren	8	5,860	1,320
Rick Casares	12	5,797	1,431
Bill Brown	12	5,591	1,583
Dick Bass	10	5,417	1,218

TOP TEN PASS RECEIVERS — LIFETIME

Player	Seasons	No.	Yards
Don Maynard	14	632	11,816
Raymond Berry	13	631	9,275
Lionel Taylor	9	567	7,195
Lance Alworth	11	542	10,266
Bobby Mitchell	11	521	7,954
Billy Howton	12	503	8,459
Tommy McDonald	12	495	8,410
Don Hutson	11	488	7,991
Art Powell	10	479	8,046
Boyd Dowler	12	474	7,270

TOP TEN INTERCEPTORS — LIFETIME

Player	Seasons	No.	Yards
Emlen Tunnell	14	79	1,282
Dick (Night Train) Lane	14	68	1,207
Dick Le Beau	13	62	762
Paul Krause	9	58	808
Bob Boyd	9	57	994
Johnny Robinson	12	57	741
Bob Dillon	8	52	976
Jack Butler	9	52	826
Jim Patton	12	52	712
Yale Lary	11	50	787
Don Burroughs	10	50	564

TOP TEN SCORERS — LIFETIME

Player	Seasons	TDs	XP	FG	Points
George Blanda	23	9	924	288	1,742
Lou Groza	17	1	641	234	1,349
Gino Cappelletti	11	42	350**	176	1,130
Fred Cox	10	0	351	209	978
Sam Baker	15	2	428	179	977
Lou Michaels	13	1	386	189	955*
Jim Bakken	11	0	338	189	905
Bobby Walston	12	46	365	80	881
Jim Turner	9	0	293	198	887
Don Hutson	11	105	172	7	823

* Includes Safety.
** Includes 2 two-point plays.

MOST TOUCHDOWNS, GAME

6 Ernie Nevers, Chi. Cards vs Chi. Bears, Nov. 28, 1929 (6-r)
  William (Dub) Jones, Clev. vs Chi. Bears, Nov. 25, 1951 (4-r, 2p)
  Gale Sayers, Chi. vs S.F., Dec. 12, 1965 (4-r, 1-p, 1-prb)
5 Bob Shaw, Chi. Cards vs Balt., Oct. 2, 1950 (5-p)
  Jim Brown, Clev. vs Balt., Nov. 1, 1959 (5-r)
  Paul Hornung, G.B. vs Balt., Dec. 12, 1965 (3-r, 2-p)
  Abner Haynes, Dall. Texans vs Oak., Nov. 26, 1961 (4-r, 1-p)
  Billy Cannon, Hou. vs N.Y. Titans, Dec. 10, 1961 (3-r, 2-p)
  Cookie Gilchrist, Buff. vs N.Y. Jets, Dec. 8, 1963 (5-r)
4 By many players

LONGEST RUN FROM SCRIMMAGE

97 Andy Uram, G.B. vs Chi. Cards, Oct. 8, 1939 (td)
  Bob Gage, Pitt. vs Chi. Bears, Dec. 4, 1949 (td)
96 Jim Spivital, Balt. vs G.B., Nov. 5, 1950 (td)
  Bob Hoernschemeyer, Det. vs N.Y. Yanks, Nov. 23, 1950 (td)
92 Kenny Washington, L.A. vs Chi. Cards, Nov. 2, 1947 (td)

LONGEST PASS COMPLETION (all TDs)

99 Frank Filchock (to Farkas) Wash. vs Pitt., Oct. 15, 1939
  George Izo (to Mitchell) Wash. vs Clev., Sept. 15, 1963
  Karl Sweetan (to Studstill) Det. vs Balt., Oct. 16, 1966
  C. A. (Sonny) Jurgensen (to Allen) Wash. vs Chi., Sept. 15, 1968
98 Doug Russell (to Tinsley) Chi. Cards vs Clev. Rams, Nov. 27, 1938
  Ogden Compton (to Lane) Chi. Cards vs G.B., Nov. 13, 1955
  Bill Wade (to Farrington) Chi. Bears vs Det., Oct. 8, 1961
  Jacky Lee (to Dewveall) Hou. vs S.D., Nov. 25, 1962
  Earl Morrall (to Jones) N.Y. Giants vs Pitt., Sept. 11, 1966
97 Pat Coffee (to Tinsley) Chi. Cards vs Chi. Bears, Dec. 5, 1937
  Bobby Lane (to Box) Det. vs G.B., Nov. 26, 1953
  George Shaw (to Tarr) Den. vs Bos., Sept. 21, 1962

LONGEST INTERCEPTION RETURN (all TDs)

102 Bob Smith, Det. vs Chi. Bears, Nov. 24, 1949
  Erich Barnes, N.Y. Giants vs Dall. Cowboys, Oct. 22, 1961
101 Richie Petitbon, Chi. vs L.A., Dec. 9, 1962
  Henry Carr, N.Y. Giants vs L.A., Nov. 13, 1966
100 Vern Huffman, Det. vs Brk., Oct. 17, 1937
  Mike Gaechter, Dall. Cowboys vs Phil., Oct. 14, 1962
  Les Duncan, S.D. vs K.C., Oct. 15, 1967
  Tom Janik, Buff. vs N.Y. Jets, Sept. 29, 1968

LONGEST PUNT RETURN (all TDs)

98 Gil LeFebvre, Cin. vs Brk., Dec. 3, 1933
  Charlie West, Minn. vs Wash., Nov. 3, 1968
96 Bill Dudley, Wash. vs Pitt., Dec. 3, 1950
95 Frank Bernardi, Chi. Cards vs Wash., Oct. 14, 1956
  Les Duncan, S.D. vs N.Y. Jets, Nov. 24, 1968

LONGEST KICKOFF RETURN (all TDs)

106 Al Carmichael, G.B. vs Chi. Bears, Oct. 7, 1956
  Noland Smith, K.C. vs Den., Dec. 17, 1967
105 Frank Seno, Chi. Cards vs N.Y. Giants, Oct. 20, 1946
  Ollie Matson, Chi. Cards vs Wash., Oct. 14, 1956
  Abe Woodson, S.F. vs L.A., Nov. 8, 1959
  Thomas (Tim) Brown, Phil. vs Clev., Sept. 17, 1961
  Jon Arnett, L.A. vs Det., Oct. 29, 1961
  Eugene Morris, Mia. vs Cin., Sept. 14, 1969
  Travis Williams, L.A. vs N.O., Dec. 5, 1971
104 By many players

YARDS RETURNING FUMBLES
LONGEST FUMBLE RUN (all TDs)

104 Jack Tatum, Oakland vs G.B., Sept. 24, 1972
98 George Halas, Chi. Bears vs Marion, Nov. 4, 1923
97 Chuck Howley, Dall. vs Atl., Oct 2, 1966
92 Joe Carter, Phil. vs N.Y., Sept. 25, 1938

TOP TEN LEADING PASSERS — LIFETIME
1,500 or more attempts

Player	Yrs.	Atts.	Comp.	Pct.	Yards	TDs	Had Int.	Pct. Int.	Avg. Gain	Pts.
Sonny Jurgensen	16	3,891	2,200	56.5	29,502	236	175	4.5	7.58	17
Len Dawson	16	2,960	1,664	56.2	23,483	212	149	5.0	7.93	21½
John Unitas	17	4,953	2,708	54.7	38,657	283	240	4.8	7.80	22
Bart Starr	16	3,149	1,808	57.4	24,688	152	138	4.4	7.84	24
Fran Tarkenton	12	3,797	2,075	54.6	28,484	216	167	4.4	7.50	28
John Brodie	16	4,187	2,301	55.0	29,517	202	204	4.9	7.05	48
Y. A. Tittle	15	3,817	2,118	55.5	28,339	212	221	5.8	7.42	48½
Frank Ryan	13	2,133	1,090	51.1	16,042	149	111	5.2	7.52	52
Norm Van Brocklin	12	2,895	1,553	53.6	23,611	173	178	6.1	8.16	52½
Earl Morrall	17	2,555	1,309	51.0	18,474	144	131	5.4	7.68	59

Rating points adwarded in inverse order, in following categories: Comp. Pct.; TDs; Pct. Int.; Avg. Gain.